How
To Survive Your
Adolescent's
Adolescence

How To Survive Your Adolescent's Adolescence

Robert C. Kolodny, M.D.

Nancy J. Kolodny, M.A., M.S.W.

Thomas E. Bratter, Ed.D.

Cheryl A. Deep, M.A.

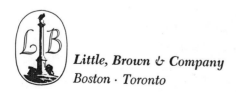

Little, Brown & Company
Boston · Toronto

First Edition

The authors are grateful for permission to use the following:
Excerpt from *The Journals of Sylvia Plath*, edited by Ted Hughes. Copyright © 1982 by Ted Hughes, as Executor of the Estate of Sylvia Plath. A Dial Press book, reprinted by permission of Doubleday & Company, Inc.
Excerpt from *The New York Times Book Review*, Copyright © 1982 by The New York Times Company. Reprinted by permission.

Library of Congress Cataloging in Publication Data
Main entry under title

How to survive your adolescent's adolescence.

Bibliography: p.
1. Youth—United States.   2. Parenting—United States.
3. Adolescence.   I. Kolodny, Robert C.
HQ796.H7   1984   649'.125   84-9702
ISBN 0-316-50158-1

BP

Designed by Patricia Girvin Dunbar

*Published simultaneously in Canada
by Little, Brown & Company (Canada) Limited*

PRINTED IN THE UNITED STATES OF AMERICA

Contents

How To Survive Your Adolescent's Adolescence

Introduction

America's infatuation with adolescence is a longstanding affair of the heart. Ricky Nelson's television appearances, Holden Caulfield's literary presence, and Dick Clark's menagerie on the original American Bandstand have given way to "Saturday Night Fever," New Wave rock, and television shows ranging from "The Facts of Life" to "One Day at a Time," but our cultural fascination with adolescence continues. Perhaps this is simply because adolescence, like death and taxes, is unavoidable. More likely, though, the complexity of our fascination is grounded in the nature of adolescence itself: its transitional role between the playful creativity of childhood and the firmer realities of adulthood; its potential for tumultuous rebellion and seemingly irrational, impulsive acts; its bittersweet moments of discovery and growing up; and last, but not least, its promise of unmitigated freedom and fun.

While glamorizing adolescence in many ways, we also tend to trivialize it — to regard the teenage years as a situation comedy that runs for a few seasons and then exists only in the reruns of our memories. Few parents spend any time meaningfully preparing themselves for the challenges that will confront them in raising a teenager, perhaps believing that having successfully maneuvered through their own adolescences, they are immune to the vagaries and catastrophies of adolescent life and will pass this immunity to their children. Other parents view adolescence with indifference because they have the sense — as they read about teenage junkies, runaways, and pregnancies — that "these things can't happen to my teen." As a result, the parents of adolescents today frequently feel secure in their authoritative admonitions to their kids, realizing only too late, after serious problems arise, that there may have been more effective means of parenting.

At the opposite extreme are the many parents who view the task of raising a teenager as a frightening, incomprehensible process. These parents are sometimes terrified of their teens, whom they don't understand, and are typically alarmed by the kinds of trouble adolescents may encounter in today's complicated world. These parents unwittingly seem to be saying that because the terrain is slippery and treacherous, the safest thing to do is stay inside and wait it out. They tend towards overprotectiveness and rigidity in their parenting styles and are apt to panic or overreact in crisis situations.

Fortunately, there is a more realistic and satisfying way for parents to guide their teenagers through adolescence. The approach is one we call *positive parenting*, which has three primary parts: first, continuing attention to nurturing, growth-enhancing parental attitudes and behaviors; second, awareness of preventive strategies that can help teens avoid major problems in their lives; and third, developing crisis-solving skills for dealing effectively with disasters if they occur. Although this entire book is about positive parenting, we will briefly outline some of its key features here as a preview of what's ahead.

Positive parenting begins with self-awareness — understanding both who you are as a parent and what you expect from your teen. It also requires a deliberate effort to understand who your child is and to strive for an empathic awareness of his or her world. Given these foundations, the nurturing side of positive parenting involves not simply loving your teen, but also taking specific steps to foster his or her self-esteem. Generally, this means encouraging adolescents to be risk-takers when the potential payoffs are high and the probable costs or consequences are low. It also means avoiding toxic, ego-deflating criticism in favor of a more supportive type of constructive criticism when you're impatient with your teen. Finally, it requires that parents encourage progressive independence in their teens in a manner commensurate with their willingness to assume self-responsibility. This means that disciplinary patterns must change in emphasis so that parent-directed discipline becomes self-directed discipline.

The preventive component of positive parenting is a vitally important one because even the well-loved teen with strong self-esteem can fall victim to numerous calamities. While there are no guarantees that prevention is always possible, we are firmly convinced that informed, concerned, action-oriented parents are in a better position to influence their teens' behaviors in a beneficial way, reducing the risk of self-destructive tailspins. Even when complete prevention isn't possible — as with the adolescent who can't resist "experimenting" with drugs — having the right information at hand and being concerned enough to use it will frequently allow a problem to be nipped in the bud before it grows into an explosive, difficult-to-manage situation. The preventive approach is a tricky one, however, requiring astute judgment, patience, and a certain element of luck. Because it doesn't always work, there's always a chance a crisis will occur.

Suppose you discover that your son's dealing drugs . or your daughter's pregnant . . . or your teen has swallowed a bottle of sleeping pills. What do you do? Where can you go for help? What are the things you should consider before making final, irrevocable decisions? The crises that can occur during adolescence are so numerous that it's impossible to be fully prepared for each one. But it is possible to develop a sense of crisis management that will allow you to take a levelheaded, thoughtful approach to even the most serious catastrophes and then know where to turn and what to ask about before deciding what to do next. Perhaps equally important is the skillfulness a parent uses in going beyond the immediate crisis period to a phase of rebuilding trust and mutual empathy.

How to Survive Your Adolescent's Adolescence is a handbook that is organized to emphasize the power and effectiveness of positive parenting. The first section of the book emphasizes self-awareness and awareness of your teen by beginning with a discussion of how you look back on your own adolescence and how it may have differed from that facing teenagers today. It then examines three important aspects of parenting: parents as role models, the role of parents in family relations, and the fundamental principles of parent-teen communications.

The second section of the book provides a detailed look at the most ubiquitous problems in the lives of teenagers — sex, drugs, social skills, school, and a number of miscellaneous topics like curfews, driving, personal grooming, and so forth. These are the areas we are most often asked about by parents, and the specific information we present is geared throughout to familiarize parents with the necessary facts and to provide key strategies for practicing the preventive component of positive parenting.

The third part of the book is about crises. It begins with an overview of the general principles of crises resolution and goes on to address a number of sobering situations: divorce, eating disorders, teenage pregnancy, runaways, cults, and suicide. The last two chapters in this section tell you how to find competent professional help and when and why to call the police. While it may seem tempting at first to skip this entire section, hoping that you won't ever need to know about these issues, we strongly urge that you read this material in its entirety, since it is packed with information on recognizing the warning signs of impending trouble.

The last portion of the book is, in a sense, an advanced course in positive parenting. It begins by explaining how and when to be an advocate or agent for your teen — covering topics ranging from helping your teen find a job to your role in the college admissions process. Next, it looks at the joys (and risks) of sharing with your adolescent, the intricacies of parent-teen togetherness, and the myriad ways in which caring about your child are expressed in your attitudes and behavior. The concluding chapter of the book focuses on one of the most surprisingly difficult parts of raising an adolescent: letting go.

Supplementing these detailed, practically oriented chapters, we've provided a list of suggested readings and an extensive appendix listing organizations, treatment facilities, and other groups providing a wide range of resources for dealing with the problems of the adolescent years.

We believe that we have brought a unique blend of expertise to the preparation of this book. Dr. Kolodny is a widely-known physician and sex researcher who has studied and written extensively about puberty, teenage sexual behavior, and alcohol and drug abuse. He has testified before U.S. Senate subcommittee hearings on the health effects of marihuana, served as Associate Director and Director of Training at the prestigious Masters & Johnson Institute, and received the 1983 National Award from the Society for the Scientific Study of Sex in recognition of his work. Nancy Kolodny, M.A., M.S.W., has two different perspectives on adolescence. She has extensive experience as an educator, both as a high school teacher and an advocate for gifted students, as well as special expertise in dealing with eating disorders in adolescents — particularly anorexia nervosa, the "self-starvation" disease, and bulimia, the binge-purge eating addiction that is now rampant among teens. She is currently Executive Director of the Behavioral Medicine Institute and Director of its Eating Disorders Section. Dr. Bratter is a psychologist in private practice who has specialized for over twenty years in treating the entire range of adolescent problems, with a special emphasis on teenage drug addiction and abuse. He has published over one hundred articles in professional journals and has edited several books; in addition, he is on the editorial boards of several drug abuse journals. Cheryl Deep, M.A., is both an astute observer of teenage cultural trends and a polished writer. Previously Special Projects Coordinator at the Masters & Johnson Institute, she is now working for Bulimia-Anorexia Self-Help, Inc., in St. Louis.

Our professional credentials aside, we also have the personal perspective of being parents ourselves: Dr. Bratter and his wife, Carole, have a nineteen-year-old son and sixteen-year-old daughter, while the Kolodnys have three girls, ages twelve, ten, and six. Our empathy with parents of teens is forged by personal experience, not distant sympathy or theory alone.

There are no instant solutions to the problems of raising an adolescent. And unquestionably there is a good deal of frustration and anguish that each of you — parent and teen alike — will experience during these somewhat trying years. But the basic contention of this book is that by preparing yourself to think through the many problems and issues you may face and applying the techniques of positive parenting, you can increase the chances that both you and your teenager emerge from the adolescent years not only none the worse for wear but enjoying a positive relationship together as adults.

PART ONE

General Issues

1

Revisiting Your Own Adolescence

It is hard for Americans to give up the idea that adolescence is a simple-minded stage somewhere between "Leave It To Beaver" and "Grease."
—M. A. O'Roarke, 1982

By a not so strange quirk of fate, every parent of a teenager has already lived through the adolescent experience from a very personal vantage point — his or her own teenage years. How we remember this phase of our lives is likely to influence our objectivity, expectations, and performance as parents, yet we have little to help put our own adolescent memories into useful perspective. The premise of this chapter, and the logical starting point for this book, is that an introspective glimpse back at our own days as adolescents — and the way we remember those times today — can be of value in raising our own children when they reach their teenage years.

Down Memory Lane

For many of us, high school yearbooks are the museums of teenage memories — repositories of images, thoughts, and even artifacts of by-gone days. Like museums, yearbooks freeze selected experiences in time, making them eternally accessible to us and our children. The reality the yearbooks represent is evoked each time we leaf through the pages, read

11

the dedications, look at pictures of our friends, and even feel twinges of emotions we once experienced as adolescents. But that reality is very much like a hologram — a projected image that seems three-dimensional and lifelike but is in fact illusion with no substance. To try to grasp or embrace a hologram is futile — the very process can block the projected image and cause it to disintegrate. So, too, when we try to recapture our own adolescent years by remembering, what we get can be illusion, although the images may seem just as real as holograms.

In truth, it's almost impossible for memories of our adolescent experiences to survive intact. We are generally left with a selective set of memories — some good, some bad — with much of the detail obscured or long-forgotten. As a result, when we look back into our own days as adolescents, our partial recollections are not usually the best vehicle for dealing with our own teenage children because they distort, omit, or oversimplify the way it was back then.

As a case in point, try to remember why you broke up with your first boyfriend or girlfriend. Chances are you'll be unable to shake loose the details of what triggered this calamitous occurrence, who instigated it, or who became the next object of your romantic inclinations. Yet when it happened, these were newsworthy events that usurped great portions of your energies and emotions. Adults often remember the ceremonial aspects of adolescence — going to the Senior Prom, taking their first driving test, having a Sweet Sixteen party — with much clearer vision than we remember the day-to-day meanderings of our teenage lives. This is apt to give us a distorted or superficial vision of what adolescence was really like and explains why movies like *American Graffiti* strike an emotional chord: they fill in the once familiar, minute details of everyday teenage existence.

Adults also tend to skew their memories of adolescence so it winds up sounding either like an unmitigated disaster or an almost unending series of glorious, happy days. For those whose teenage years were marked by popularity, achievement, and fun, it is likely that the undercurrents of anxiety and unavoidable family and school hassles will be omitted in the retelling, especially to their own children. Similarly, for those whose adolescence was a particularly painful time, the positive moments and small victories tend to be overlooked.

Whatever your current assessment and memories of your adolescence, it is helpful to recognize that they are probably only partially true. Memories tend to exaggerate and shape things as we need them to be, or as we fear they might have been, but they don't possess much factual objectivity. After all, we didn't live through the experiences objectively, so it is unlikely that we could store or recall them with any greater objectivity today.

This selective memory can create problems for parents who try to remember how they felt as teenagers in a particular situation, or try to recall how they solved a problem in their lives, or even how they attained a particular success. While wanting to empathize with one's own teenager is both natural and laudable, parents usually have only a limited capacity to put themselves in their adolescent's shoes.

We need to remember what being a teenager was like, not so much for ourselves but for our adolescents. The emotional insights of an honest glimpse back into our teens are difficult, if not impossible, to obtain in any other way. We need to recall the gut-wrenching worries of social ostracism . . . the sweaty palms of our first kiss . . . the shameful pain of athletic failure . . . the sense of worthlessness that swept over us with any display of ineptness or uncertainty. We need to recall the soaring elation of being in love and the warm camaraderie of friendships not so much for their own sake but for knowledge of the opposite sensations — being rejected, breaking up, riding the roller coaster of emotions and uncertainties that once jangled our nerves and that now affects our teenagers. We need to remember these agonies so that we can place the unique vulnerabilities of our adolescent children in reasonable perspective. And we need to remember so that we can keep ourselves from always imposing our adult perspective, with its different brand of logic and priorities, on our teenagers' lives. In other words, through remembering we may help ourselves to see that our perceptions as parents may lead us to erroneous assumptions or incorrect analyses that just don't fit our teenagers' needs. Remembering how it was for us may be just what we need to give us the courage to watch our teenagers risk making mistakes in order to learn and grow.

Triumphs and Tragedies

It is almost unavoidable for us as parents to live vicariously through our adolescents' lives, seeing something of ourselves in our children's personalities and identifying with the process of growth and discovery that is so much a part of the teenage years. This vicarious identification gives us a chance to be young again (at least as observers), to relive our own most meaningful adolescent passages (this time with the benefit of hard-earned wisdom we selflessly pass on in the form of parental advice), and to guide our teenager towards opportunities we missed or paths we found were most successful. This sense of the adolescent as an extension of ourselves is an important part of the parent-child bond that certainly contributes to our commitment to our offspring and our understanding of their problems.

There is, however, another side to this phenomenon. Consider the father who was the starting quarterback of his high school football team and who has spent countless hours tossing a football with his son preparing Junior for a varsity career. If Junior develops a stronger interest in playing the guitar than performing on the gridiron, Dad may feel let down, disappointed, and even angry. The source of his consternation really lies within himself, which would be apparent to him if he could just see for a moment how much he had projected himself and his fantasies into the sports career he had carefully planned for his son. But parents often fail to see how emphatically they attempt to mold their children into reincarnations of themselves and how often this process creates pressures and conflicts for the adolescent.

Even children who show real similarities to their parents in talents and capabilities can be smothered, rather than helped, by being pushed into living a replica of a parent's life. More destructive still, in the sense that it leads to a feeling of failure in the child, is the parent who pushes a child towards a path for which that child displays no special skill or interest.

There's nothing wrong about urging your teenagers to try an activity or sport that is meaningful to you, but if it turns out that they prefer playing with a computer to playing the violin, don't persistently bemoan their lack of dedication or belittle their appreciation for what's "really" important.

Beyond this, recognize that the achievements of your own adolescence that were most important and gratifying to you may not have quite the same meanings to your child. It's much too easy to try to relive our personal triumphs — perhaps even magnifying their glory — through our teenagers, with the result being unnecessary pressures and unrealistic expectations. The flip side of the coin is also worth examining. If we try to guard and protect our children against the setbacks and disappointments we ran into — the "tragedies" of our teenage years — we can block them from making their own accomplishments or at least having the experience of pursuing an independent, unprogrammed course of action.

Perhaps even more to the point, we must realize the danger in portraying our own teenage years in a glorified, idealized way. If our kids think that we never failed or experienced the harsh letdown of rejection or never were confused or conflicted in our lives, how can they believe we have the capacity to understand and help them when they are down? They will simply assume that our experiences are not relevant to theirs.

By recalling our own failings and mistakes, we increase our own credibility as people. We show our teens that there is no sin in failing or being rejected because these are integral parts of life. We also show them that post-adolescent happiness and success is possible even if we made mistakes in our teens. More important, by sharing our adolescent disappointments and tragedies with our children rather than just recounting our triumphs, we humanize ourselves as parents and give our teens a chance to feel that maybe — just maybe — we might be able to talk together and begin to understand.

Then and Now

We have already mentioned some of the ways in which adolescence today is no different from what it's always been. There are several other notable similarities that we should examine before we go on to look at how being a teenager today is different from the way it was for us. A good example can be found in the almost universal adolescent quest for autonomy and independence. To achieve this autonomy, it is necessary to break away from parental authority to a certain degree; in this process, most teenagers turn to friends and classmates for support and guidance and quickly become subjected to what is formally known as "peer-group pressures." Intriguingly, in trying to become free the adolescent actually risks becoming a captive of another set of behavior-controlling standards. Indeed, the tyranny of the peer group, which seems to boast, "You can only find yourself by joining us," which intimidates by implicit threats of ridicule or rejection if its rules are not followed, is a major source of conflict and stress in teenagers' lives today just as it has been for decades.

In much the same way, the intergenerational clash is a long-standing tradition that will undoubtedly be with us for ages to come. Parents and teens often don't see eye-to-eye on values, with differences more apt to show up in key areas of everyday living rather than global philosophies — that is, parents and teens are more likely to differ in views on how to wear their hair than on views about nuclear disarmament or censorship of the press.

Clearly, the adolescent's search for independence, the struggle with the peer group, and the often-found clash with parental values are nearly universal themes of adolescence in our society. There are other points of similarity that we could discuss, but there are also many areas of differences between then and now. Let's look at just a few of the more obvious ones.

Back in the days when we were teenagers, our difficult decisions were primarily as follows:

— To smoke or not to smoke (without benefit of the *Surgeon General's Report on Smoking and Health*).
— To use alcohol at parties or not.
— For females: whether to wear "falsies," how to decide if "making out" was permissible on the third or fourth date, and how to apply mascara and eye shadow without looking like a floozie.
— For males: how to fake it when you didn't have a car of your own,

finding a hiding place for your copies of *Playboy*, and plotting a way to become sexually experienced.

If these concerns that once occupied so much of our attention seem rather simple and straightforward in retrospect, it's because the problems confronting teenagers today are far more complex and troubling.

To understand properly the contemporary world of adolescence, parents need to see just how different things are now from how they used to be. Can we really understand how peer pressure leads teenagers to try drugs? Do we grasp what it means for kids today to be able to buy marihuana or cocaine or heroin at school or in their neighborhood hangouts just as easily as we purchase a loaf of bread at the store? Can we relate to the nonchalance of the thirteen-year-old who knows his best friend overdosed on PCP? Is the ubiquity of drugs for today's teenager really equivalent to our use of alcohol at parties when we were teens? Anyone who thinks these dynamics are the same is incredibly poorly informed.

Even if we look at an area that is not so foreign to our own adolescent experience — sexuality — we must readily admit that the rules of the game have changed considerably. Teenagers today have a drastically different set of sexual values and a greater amount of sexual knowledge than we did when we were teens. The widespread availability of contraception and abortion, changing social norms, greater societal openness about sex, the advent of feminism, and a number of other factors have led to marked changes in patterns of teenage sexual behavior. These changes involve not only the "should-I-guard-my-virginity?" type of question: today, the question is somewhat more likely to be "How do I know if I'm straight or gay?"

One of the most startling differences for teenagers today compared to adolescents two or more decades ago is the high rate of separation, divorce, and remarriage in their families. Not only do these marital problems seem to catch teenagers in the middle, uncertain of what to do and whom to side with; marital dissolution and its aftermath — including remarriage — seems to leave many of today's teens convinced that getting married is more a matter of convenience and hope than commitment or promise. In fact, one of the more alarming things that teenagers of divorced parents say — and we are speaking here of an estimated five million adolescents — is "I doubt if I'll really want to get married . . . it just doesn't look like much fun." In addition, many of the teenagers who come from homes broken by divorce voice a concern that they won't be competent enough or wise enough to find and keep a mate — so, they say, maybe they shouldn't try.

Of course, divorce is not the sole cause of a general disparagement of marriage that today affects teenagers perhaps more strongly than anyone else. Nontraditional families are flourishing in a number of different guises, whether they're two lesbians raising a child together; single, never-married women having children; divorced women living with, but not marrying, men; marriages that are arranged by cult leaders like the Reverend Sun Myung Moon of the Unification Church; marriages with househusbands and career wives; voluntarily childless marriages, and a host of other varieties not mentioned here. Not only are many of these options seen by teens as diluting the marriage bond in its more traditional sense; these numerous permutations on the marital theme make infinitely complex the decisions that teens must face about their futures.

Today, teenage females are freed from many of the old constraints. They are no longer looked down on if they are good students. It's no longer considered unfeminine to run for long distances, have a good jump shot, or lift weights. A girl who is not a virgin probably doesn't have to worry about developing a "reputation" unless she's brought up in a most conservative community. And girls can now attend Harvard, Yale, Columbia, and Princeton just as teenage boys can. But these changes are illusory in some ways, for it's safe to say that in many locales the old double standard still lingers on, girls are still considered members of the weaker sex, and outstanding educational attainment by a female is simply a ticket to the same job a comparably trained male will get, but at lower pay.

One other monumental difference has developed between teenagers today and their recent predecessors: many adolescents are afraid there won't be any adulthood for them because we're on the verge of destroying our planet in a nuclear holocaust. A national survey of more than 40,000 teenagers in 1982 ranked this as the number one concern of teenage boys and the number two concern of teenage girls, overshadowed among girls only by fear of the death of a parent. This nuclear holocaust anxiety is not so difficult to understand in a generation of adolescents who watched news clips of the Vietnam war and listened to body count statistics and bombing reports presented in the same manner as the weather forecast. Fear of destruction alters the way many teenagers think about the future and changes the constraints they feel about present behavior. If you're going to die prematurely in a nuclear war, what's so risky about doing drugs? If you may not live to get married, why not try sex now, while you can? The impact of this type of pressure on today's adolescents can be particularly hard for adults to comprehend fully.

The world of today's adolescents is complicated in ways we, as adults, rarely stop to consider. There was no such thing as an ecology movement when many of us were in our teens; we did not grow up with any facility with the world of computers; we had little awareness of rape as a political issue; we had never heard of transsexual surgery. This is not to say that we were blind to the world around us, because we too were sensitive and bright and caring as only teenagers can be, but the world in which we grew up seemed far simpler — no, it actually *was* far simpler — and so we must admit that we can't quite grasp what's making it so much more complicated today. Today's teenager faces many problems and potential catastrophes that we didn't need to think about when we were teenagers ourselves. To misread the impact these developments have on adolescents today is like driving at night without your headlights on.

You Can't Go Home Again

Thomas Wolfe's observation astutely identified a basic premise with which we'd like to conclude this chapter. No matter how much we'd like to go back to our own adolescent days — whether to relive old pleasures or to undo old pains — we simply aren't able to "go home again" through our teenagers' lives.

This is not to say we should try to ignore the autobiographical memories that being parents of a teenager can awaken for us. Instead, it is a plea for sensibility in maintaining some perspective on these points:

(1) Our children are not the same people we are, despite how much we might like them to be.

(2) No matter how smart we are, teenagers will come up with new wrinkles in their lives that we're unprepared to deal with because we didn't face these issues ourselves.

(3) Trying to pretend you're a teenager again will only cause resentment and discomfort in your child instead of producing the camaraderie you'd like it to.

Your teenagers need the benefit of your adulthood to see them through those trying adolescent times. You're worth much more to them as a parent than as an aspiring peer.

2

Parents as Responsible Role Models

Providing love and sustenance to our children as they grow is undoubtedly the most important element of positive parenting. Yet clearly, love is not enough — being a good parent requires much more. Ranking high on the list of crucial parental functions, but all too often virtually ignored in discussions of adolescence, is how we serve as role models in our children's lives.

To be a role model ordinarily means that someone observing you is impressed enough by your actions (or your status) to want to act like you or think like you or handle problems the way you do. While this isn't a simple matter of mimicry, the person utilizing a role model typically tries out the role gradually, bit by bit, to determine if the style of behavior is pleasing either because it feels inherently good or because it leads to some external reward. Thus, a four-year-old boy may swagger about the living room with a bottle of beer in his hand and loudly proclaim, "I don't want any noise now while I watch my football game," precisely replicating his father's Sunday afternoon behavior but getting completely different rewards from the situation. He feels grown up, he observes the effect of giving an order, and he enjoys (but doesn't really comprehend) the smiles he gets from his mother, who thinks what he's doing is cute even though it isn't Sunday and there isn't any football game to watch. This four-year-old has just learned, however, that acting like his father can make him feel important and happy, and chances are that he'll try again to act like his dad. Psychologists call the mother's behavior "positive reinforcement," recognizing that a pleasant result leads to repeating the same type of behavior. (If the mother in this example had responded to her son by taking away the beer bottle and telling him he couldn't watch T.V., he probably wouldn't try this particular approach again.)

People generally recognize the importance of parental role models during the formative years of early and middle childhood as they see the sometimes subtle and sometimes obvious ways in which characteristics of the parents become part of the child's personality. "She's got her mother's patience," and "He's got his father's temper" are common examples of this recognition. Less widely realized is that the parents' function as role models continues, and in some ways even expands, during the teenage years. There are three basic reasons for this:

(1) teenagers are better than children are at observing and analyzing their parents' behavior;

(2) teenagers are more skilled at integrating into their lives behavior which is presented to them by role models;

(3) teenagers are more critical of the role models they choose to follow, as well as those they choose to reject — in part, because they typically have a broader range of role models to choose from than do younger children.

"All right," you may say, "I'll agree with what you have told me about role models, but MY child is a teenager and it doesn't seem as though any of this applies to our relationship. Teenagers REJECT their parents, and that's a normal part of growing up." Other parents point to the ways in which parent-child relations usually change during the teenage years — communications become strained, simple household rules may be constantly challenged, arguments replace conversation, and the parental function seems to boil down to providing room, board, and telephone answering service — and say, "Role modeling? Out the window!" As we shall see, these are incorrect assumptions that need to be replaced with a more accurate (and realistic) view of providing role models for your teenager.

The Power of Modeling

THREE FACTS EVERY PARENT SHOULD KNOW ABOUT BEING A ROLE MODEL FOR A TEENAGER:

(1) Teens are quick to recognize the difference between a "performance" put on for their sake and an adult's genuine, spontaneous behavior. They won't pay much attention to "performances."

(2) Inconsistency undermines credibility.

(3) A parent can't start being a role model when the child hits puberty.

Let's look at two specific examples to see how these principles apply to everyday situations. First, consider the case of the father who's coaching his teen's soccer team. For the last three weeks the team has been soundly trounced, and his ego has been bruised in the process. Having spent the last half hour pacing the sidelines muttering angrily at the opponents, the officials, and his own players, at the conclusion of the game he's the first to say "Let's all be good sports about losing," as he makes a point of ceremoniously crossing the field to congratulate the other team. This performance fools no one; the role model the coach has provided is hardly apt to foster good sportsmanship at all.

The second example illustrates how inconsistency undermines credibility:

> Margaret had always taught her children that honesty is the best policy, going out of her way to emphasize her belief that truthfulness is a cornerstone of human relations. Yet in her own dealings with her teenage son and daughter, she was apt to stretch the truth or sometimes tell an outright lie. When her son applied for college, she was horrified to discover that he had lied about earning a varsity letter in tennis, but he angrily told her, "Look Mom, if you can stretch the truth, so can I."

While it *is* true that as children evolve into teenagers parental influence as role models may seem to wane in favor of input from peer groups and school sources, the fact is that adolescents tend to measure themselves against an imaginary yardstick composed in large part of the role models provided over the years by their parents. This yardstick — a composite of perceived values, beliefs, and behavioral skills — serves as both an evaluative device, allowing the teenager to see how he or she "measures up" in the quest for independence and maturity, and as a familiar point of reference to which teenagers can return, again and again, for a sense of direction and guidance.

In some cases, this imaginary yardstick functions in a negative sense rather than a positive one: teenagers can and do strive to be just the opposite of what they see that they don't like, and parents aren't exempt from this practice. So, for example, the teenager who perceives Mom and Dad as preoccupied with material things may make it a point to dress in shabby clothes and show no interest in money; and the adolescent who feels that his or her parents are hypocritical or deceptive may pursue absolute honesty like a Holy Grail. Conversely, many teenagers will follow in the footsteps of their parents so faithfully that they will acquire all of the role-modeled persona, right down to the last blemish and imperfection. Thus, negative role models don't always result in the opposite behavior but instead may predispose the child to the very same problems later in life. A startling example of this unfortunate fact is that many parents who physically abuse their children were themselves abused as children.

The real source of power for parental role models derives from three separate but related conditions: (1) the teenager is exposed to parental role models at close range rather than at a distance; (2) this exposure continues over a lengthy period of time; and (3) parents are the principal authority figures in the adolescent's world. Each of these conditions ensures that teenagers will carefully observe what their parents are doing and saying, even when it appears that exactly the opposite is true. Teenagers who pretend to be deaf, dumb, and blind when it comes to interacting with parents are still monitoring every heartbeat of the parental pulse and checking for any discernible rise in the collective parental blood pressure. Consider this apparent rejection to be a kind of Parenting Stress Test — the teenager uses it to check on the resiliency of parental role models, just as the cardiologist puts a patient on an exercise treadmill to test the resiliency of his or her heart.

Despite many frustrating moments when all parents wonder about their effectiveness — "Am I really getting through?" — the reward of seeing that their usefulness as role models has paid off can be uplifting beyond belief. Imagine how the parents of the teens described below felt.

> Seventeen-year-old Dan, after a heated argument with his father, storms up to his room and slams the door. Dad says, "If you don't leave now, you'll miss the start of the movie." Dan answers, "I'm too mad to see straight right now, and you've always said that was no time to drive a car."

> Thirteen-year-old Lisa, coming home after a party, tells her parents: "Some kids were smoking pot tonight and tried to get me to try it. But I told them that my family doesn't need drugs to feel good; we can feel good from just being ourselves."

> Fifteen-year-old Ellen has been dating one boy for eight months. He has been pressuring her to have intercourse with him since "all the kids are doing it." She has decided to tell him they can't go out so seriously any more since she thinks she is more than just "one of the crowd" and will make up her own mind when she's good and ready. She asks if her mother thinks this is the right approach to take with the boy.

These teenagers are neither fictitious nor too good to be true; in fact, similar examples of the lasting impact of parental role models can be found over and over again if you'll just look for them. But as with Norman Vincent Peale's admonition about "the power of positive thinking," remember that the power of positive parental role models is apt to be more persuasive and compelling than negative ones.

A brief word of caution about the ultimate power of parental role models is in order. Your worth as a parent is *not* measured by whether your teen blindly accepts what you believe and mimics how you behave to the point of becoming a parental clone. When teenagers modify or even reject the role models provided by their parents, it shows that they are paying attention and are trying to apply them to their own identities and needs. Successful parents allow the give-and-take that will help their teenagers integrate the role models into their own lives rather than wearing them as cloaks, for the sake of appearance, as actors and actresses do when they "become" the characters in a script, hoping to please or entertain an audience.

"Do What I Say, not What I Do"

The way in which parents most frequently undermine the credibility and power of their role models is the "Do what I say, not what I do" syndrome. Here, one or both parents repeatedly displays a marked inconsistency between the advice or admonitions given to their teenager and the way in which the parent acts. For example, parents who advocate absolute honesty but frequently use "little white lies" in their own lives are victims of this malady. Consider also the mixed message given by the parent who tells a teen that alcohol is dangerous but has a couple of martinis before dinner every night in order to relax. While all of us probably fall into this self-contradictory trap once in a while, it's important to realize that if this becomes a persistent pattern it seriously erodes our impact as role models.

Teenagers, of course, are no fools — and when there is an unbridgeable gap between what their parents say and what they do, the teenager recognizes HYPOCRISY just as surely as if it were displayed in giant flashing neon lights. Because teenagers demand authenticity and despise phoniness, especially from their parents, the effect of the "Do what I say, not what I do" syndrome is likely to be highly problematical. Here are a few of the ways teenagers may react:

(1) *Accept hypocrisy as a viable way of behaving and being "grown up."* The teenager begins to say one thing to parents but acts in ways that are inconsistent with what is said. In effect, the teen has absorbed the role model all too well, right down to flaws and imperfections.

(2) *Reject the value of parental role models.* In many ways this is tantamount to rejecting the parents. Lines of communication between the adolescent and parent are apt to be short-circuited; the teenager may seek other useful role models (such as a friend's parent, a favorite teacher, a coach) who replace the function of the now-ignored parents;

or, in extreme cases, the teenager may run away in order to cope with the disillusion or even hatred that can occur.

(3) *Rebel against all "authority figures."* Adolescents may extend their distrust of parental role models to a distrust of all adults. If adults are all viewed as "playing by their own rules," which can be changed as the game goes along, the teenager may give up any attempt at self-control and give in to temporary (and rule-breaking) behavior with drugs, sex, truancy, or breaking the law. Such teens may have problems at school or work because they can't believe that teachers or employers are consistent in their limit-setting and actually mean what they say.

There is no reliable antidote to the "Do what I say, not what I do" dilemma once it has affected parent-teen relations. To be sure, the parent caught in a bluff or in a point of philosophical inconsistency with the reality of his or her behavior may be able to rescue the situation by being honest about it and openly admitting the facts. Yet it is also true that such openness will carry parental credibility only to a point: the more the teen perceives parental hypocrisy in action, the more all parental role models are tarnished and diminished. This is certainly a case where an ounce of prevention is worth far more than a pound of cure — by avoiding the trap of "Do what I say, not what I do," parents can maximize their effectiveness as role models and give their teenagers a firm reference point for learning how to deal with the adult world.

Of Mirrors and Magnifying Glasses

We parents have a tendency to evaluate our success or failure as role models by examining how closely our teens mirror our own values, attitudes, talents, and behaviors. While we may not want them to be carbon copies, we wouldn't mind if our teens could turn into new, improved versions of ourselves by retaining our strengths and modifying our imperfections.

When we look at our teenagers, we are in one sense looking at a mirror of ourselves; however, because we scrutinize our adolescents' lives so intently (an understandable and justifiable prerogative of exercising parental responsibility), we must also realize that we are looking through a magnifying glass that distorts what we see and always presents our teenagers' actions in larger-than-life proportions.

Both ways of looking at our teenagers — in a mirror or through a parental magnifying glass — can result in problems. In the "look-in-the-mirror" viewpoint we see our children as extensions of ourselves, and there is the obvious danger of not recognizing the teenagers' individuality. It's easy to confuse physical appearance and other superficial resemblances with personal identity. At the same time, it's also very easy to judge a teenager too harshly when we measure him or her against ourselves. We should not expect an adolescent to be in command of a full repertoire of adult skills and insights, yet it is tempting to react with disdain or anger when our "mirror image" doesn't handle a situation with aplomb or finesse. The mirror can be beneficial if we can use it to recognize our shortcomings and maintain a better tolerance for the teen's imperfections.

The magnifying glass viewpoint is linked to a similar set of difficulties. By definition, the magnifying glass will enlarge an image so that all the blemishes and flaws of the teenager become vividly apparent, tempting us to become hypercritical of what we see. It can just as easily lead to an exaggerated view of a teenager's positive features, distorting parental perception in almost as destructive a fashion. This rose-colored magnifying glass may lead the parents of a dean's list student on athletic scholarship to believe that she *can't* get pregnant or get involved with drugs — after all, "She's so good." In contrast, the "black and white" magnifying glass may blind parents to their teenager's talents because they are so intently aware of his or her deficiencies.

While it's unlikely we'll completely abandon our mirrors and magnifying glasses, awareness of their potential distortions can lead us to a more realistic view of our teenagers. This quest for a reality-based view of our kids can be fostered by the following strategies:

(1) *Take some time each week to distance yourself physically and emotionally from your teenager.* Try to neutralize your reactions to your child's behavior and allow your *logical* self to decide how accurate your *emotional* self has been that week.

(2) *If you've been hypercritical, stop and do something about it.* No one, especially during their teenage years, likes to be criticized incessantly. Sit down and talk with your adolescents, explaining how you feel and giving them the chance to voice feelings too. Don't be too proud to apologize — in addition to providing a useful role model for learning how to admit to a mistake, this may help ease some of the pressure. Don't be afraid to use praise and encouragement even when your relationship has been severely strained.

(3) *Think before you speak.* A five-point checklist can be useful:
— Are you being overly judgmental?
— Are you being a nag?
— Are you talking in anger?
— Are you allowing for your teen's feelings?
— Are you being fair?

After necessary adjustments, proceed with the conversation or remark if needed.

The Expectation Exchange

No discussion of parental role models would be complete without some consideration of why parents try to provide examples for their children to follow. In a nutshell, it is because of the expectations parents have for their children: a combination of hopes, fears, and standards that define how parents feel about their teenager's place under the sun. These expectations, which can play a central role in determining how parents react to their adolescents, do not exist in a vacuum — they are paralleled by expectations that teenagers have regarding their parents. Understanding the sometimes subtle, sometimes clamorous interaction between these two sets of expectations is an important part of positive parenting.

The expectation exchange can be viewed as a paraphrased version of a fundamental law of physics: for every parental expectation, there is an opposite (and usually equal or nearly equal) expectation on the part of the teenager. Sometimes this seems to take on a "tit for tat" style: "If you'll let me drive the car more often, I promise I'll get my grades up," or "I'll practice the piano every day if you'll let me stay out until midnight on weekends." Other times, though, the bargaining is far more complex and much less trivial since the life of a teenager is likely to be indelibly influenced by parental expectations, with major impact on the adolescent's self-esteem and behavior.

Parents who demand perfection or, conversely, have inordinately low expectations for their teens, and parents who have rigid, even predetermined expectations can trigger major problems for their adolescents. Continual parental expectations for perfection can turn teens into highstrung individuals who react to the constant pressure by becoming burned out, by giving up, or by rebelling against their parents. Even if these teens live up to high expectations, they may pay a later price by lack of resilience in the face of frustration or temporary setbacks, or by feeling like failures when they don't always come out on top. Many examples can be found in the ranks of teenage athletic stars who never make it on to college stardom or to an Olympic medal, just as among their academic counterparts those who were pushed towards the pinnacle of law school or medical school don't always succeed and may suffer gnawing disappointment.

At the opposite end of the spectrum are those parents who give up on their kids and have only the most paltry, deflated expectations about what the teens can achieve. Parents who give up on their teens frequently have teens who give up on themselves, who are satisfied just to get by, setting very low goals, developing a complacent attitude towards life that can be difficult to overcome in adulthood. They may never try to develop, or even identify, their talents and may perpetually consider themselves as dull-average people with little ingenuity, creativity, or drive.

Parental expectations that are marked by inflexible or unrealistic thinking usually require teens to adhere to their parents' priorities with little or no consideration for the teen's needs or capabilities. A father who expects his 135-pound, 5'5" teenage son to become a football star may become furious if the son shows more interest in computer programming than gridiron action. Even if the boy tries to accommodate his father's wishes, the chances are that he's doomed to failure by the unrealistic nature of the expectation. A somewhat different version of the difficulty with parental inflexibility is exemplified by doctors who expect their children to follow their advice as explicitly as their patients would, or by ministers who expect their teenagers to live morally unblemished lives with not so much as a single profane syllable crossing their lips. The teenager who feels trapped by such rigidity may overreact in the process of breaking away from authority and may be unable to distinguish between minor transgressions of parental rules and acts with far more serious consequences.

Teenagers can also have difficulties with expectations regarding their parents. They may be unrealistic because they don't know very much about what their parents can and can't do for them, they may sell their parents short by deciding that they're uninterested in their lives or insensitive about their feelings, or they can set up such perfectionistic expectations of their parents that it becomes impossible for the flesh-and-blood person to live up to this idealistic and unrealistic identity. In such cases, when a crisis comes along in the parents' lives such as a divorce, getting fired, or some other personal hardship, the teenager sees the parents as failures and there is no hope for a balanced perspective.

There is no precise formula for developing a healthy expectation exchange between parents and teens, but the following practical pointers may be useful:

(1) Anchor your expectations firmly in reality.

(2) Don't expect perfection, since doing this preordains disappointment.

(3) Be flexible about your expectations, as circumstances and needs may change faster than you think.

(4) Periodically reassess your expectations and discuss them with your teenagers (after all, you can't expect them to read your mind and their feedback can give you valuable insights).

(5) Don't hold on to your expectations forever. By recognizing just how powerfully our expectations can affect our teens, we can hope to learn to keep our expectations open-ended and encouraging rather than rigid and stultifying.

3

Family Relations

A good deal of attention has been paid lately to the demise of the modern American family. Divorce rates have been escalating, violence between spouses and child abuse are alarmingly common, extramarital sex is on the rise, illegitimate births are almost epidemic, and young adults are postponing marriage — or choosing to remain single — in increasing numbers. Concerned by such recent trends, the sociologist Amitai Etzioni of Columbia University suggested, "At the present accelerating rate of depletion, the United States will run out of families not long after it runs out of oil."

Despite such rhetoric, holding funeral services for the American family as a social institution may be quite premature. While families in America are certainly in a state of flux, they are far from extinct. Definitions of family vary so widely in the 1980s because family configurations have become diverse. Today, in addition to the traditional nuclear family of Mom, Dad and kids, we find single-parent families; cohabiting, unmarried couples raising children; homosexual and lesbian couples who are as much "parents" to their kids as heterosexual couples could be; communal families in which several sets of parents share in raising one another's children; reconstituted families that are the result of previously divorced parents' marrying and bringing two (or more) sets of children to the new alliance; and other versions of family configurations we have probably overlooked. In fact, the arrival of a new pluralism in American family styles is neither inherently bad nor a sign of declining social stability; instead, it may mark an evolution in family forms and functions that may possess a unique adaptability and survival value of its own.

The Family System: An Overview

What is the purpose of the American family? How can it most effectively function? When your children are young, answering these questions seems easy. The family provides a stable, nurturing, protective environment for children who could not be expected to survive on their own. Mother and father supply food, clothing, shelter, love, and discipline, and educate and socialize the young child towards the independence necessary to survive outside the boundaries of the family. Clearcut, isn't it? Anything children are unable to do for themselves, parents do for them.

But what happens when the child is suddenly sixteen, drives a car, earns money outside the home, and is generally capable of an independent existence? Do parents become relegated to the role of spectators, enthusiastically rooting their child on to success but no longer a participant in the process? Does the family unit lose its meaning and function, or, even worse, does the family serve only as a last hurdle to be overcome on the track to true independence? The answer is a complicated one that puzzles many families.

Although every family has a unique personality and style, having a teenager as a family member is apt to produce strains and pressures that didn't exist at an earlier time. They occur not only because adolescents are hard to understand and difficult to get along with — especially if the parents expect them to act rationally, like adults, or obediently, like children — but also because adolescents arrive on the scene at the same time in parents' lives that other changes are going on that themselves create problems and uncertainties. For instance, many parents face the uncertainties and problems of middle age just as their children reach adolescence. Teenage sexuality may be perceived as threatening in families where the spark may be fading from the parents' own sexual relationship. And some parents experience anxiety as they watch their adolescent children choosing careers and charting future life courses because it provides them with a stark reminder of the ambitions they haven't fulfilled for themselves — a reminder that is all the more distressing because they have a sense that time is passing them by and lost opportunities aren't recoverable. Furthermore, parents are apt to have an unrealistic view of what raising a teenager should be like and are painfully shocked to find in their home displays of moodiness, disobedience, and outright rebellion that were never shown on *Father Knows Best* or *Happy Days*.

How the parents and the family cope with such a situation — and how the teenager, in turn, copes with the rest of the family — is largely a matter of family dynamics. Family dynamics can be defined as the way in which family members interact with each other and the way in which the family, both as a whole and via its subsystems, deals with new issues and conflicts as they arise. In some families, the prevailing dynamic may be pretty much like marine boot camp: the parents command the family autocratically, discipline and order become the primary objectives, and feelings and needs that don't match up with the "system" are camouflaged or hidden completely. In other families, parents try to be the teenager's best friends, refusing to set limits and leaving almost all decisions to the adolescent's judgment in an ultraliberal abdication of parental authority. In still other families, the disruptiveness of the teenager is dealt with by making someone the family scapegoat or sacrificial lamb — blaming everything that goes wrong on this person, with all the other family members aligned together in an accusatory manner saying, "Look what you did," or "Look what you made me do."

Families may also develop ways of interacting that are manipulative rather than straightforward. Sometimes these styles are not a conscious response to a teenager but are, instead, extensions of patterns that have been going on for years. A common example is found in families whose members find it convenient to slip into the roles of Persecutor, Victim, and Rescuer in response to various situations. Typically, adolescents love to play the victim and try to make one parent into the persecutor, which prompts another family member to jump in as the mediator, savior, or rescuer. Here's how it might proceed:

TEEN: I need $10 for my date tonight.
MOM: You're overdrawn on your allowance and you're just being selfish. Don't you think the rest of us need things, too? (*Persecutor*)
TEEN: Mom, why do you hate me? You wouldn't lecture at the other kids like this if one of them needed an advance. (*Victim*)
DAD (*to Mom*): Why are you making such a big deal out of a simple request? You know he'll pay us back. Besides, we're not in the poorhouse yet and the kid deserves a good time. (*Rescuer*)
MOM: You always take his side against mine. (*Now she has become the victim. The dialogue may continue with new roles defined for each of the participants.*)

Even in the most functional families, the tensions created by adolescents are bound to test their parents' mettle sorely, not to mention the patience of other family members. You, as parents, need to understand that these tensions are a necessary catalyst for adolescent maturation and so should not be ignored or erased but allowed to play out. For example, it is vitally important for teenagers to come to see their parents as real human beings, with shortcomings and imperfections, rather than as the omniscient parent figures seen by younger children. During this process, teenagers may criticize their parents or reject many of their values, not out of disrespect as much as a signal of growth and maturation. Similarly, teenagers and their parents seem to be perpetually having arguments, but this is also a necessary part of the maturation process. In order to gain independence, the teenager must make increasing demands for privileges; parents, on the other hand, tend to be conservative and restrictive, not wanting to give privileges too fast. Maneuvering about these issues often becomes heated, yet it helps the adolescent gain practice in learning how to negotiate with adults and how generally to end in a compromise that permits a gradual exposure to independence rather than a precipitous nosedive into uncharted waters.

Despite the complexity of issues facing all families with adolescent children and despite the temptation to yell and scream to make oneself understood in this family maze, it is possible to help the family not only survive but even flourish. Contrary to popular thought, parents may find themselves feeling closer to their teenagers now than when they were infants as the parents begin to see the adolescents as persons rather than as dependents.

Sibling Rivalry and Other Sibling Matters

All parents of more than one child are veteran observers of sibling rivalry in action. In early childhood, the rivalry expresses itself in pure, sometimes picturesque ways, as in the case of the three-year-old son of an army family who asked his mother a week after the arrival of a new baby sister, "When do we take her back to the P.X., Mom?" Pushing, fighting, tattling, and stealing food or toys are other ways in which young brothers and sisters act out their jealousies and anger and compete for their parents' affections. Even pets can demonstrate sibling rivalries! By adolescence, however, such sibling rivalries have obviously been left behind, right? Not quite.

The basic premises of adolescent sibling rivalry are somewhat different than they were at earlier ages. Teenagers seem to be less preoccupied with being rivals for their parents' love than involved in either competitive skirmishes or attempts to mete out familial justice. Incessant comparisons of who gets to do what, and at what age, are frequently the focus of such "fairness" appeals. Here, the teenager attempts to gain status by having more privileges (e.g., staying out later, having a personal telephone, getting the car) either by virtue of a direct award *or* by getting brother or sister's privileges curtailed. The search for equity in setting and applying parental rules for behavior is sometimes devious in its own right.

JOHN: "Can I have the car tonight, Mom?"
JUDY (*14 years old, unable to drive*): "Ma, he didn't mow the lawn like you told him to."
JOHN (*looking fiercely at Judy*): "Aw, I'll mow the lawn tomorrow."

The best preparation for the inevitable "unfairness" call is having well-considered reasons for your decisions and a thorough knowledge of all the factors affecting them. If this is done, when a teenager says, "Meg got to go out three nights last week and I only got to go out once," you can calmly answer, "But Meg did all her homework and also cleaned out the garage; you haven't finished your term paper and haven't managed to clean up your room." This type of approach explains, in reasonable, unemotional terms, the rationale behind your decision. Meg's privileges aren't random nor are they given because you "like Meg better." Meg simply lived up to her responsibilities, thus providing a good lesson for all adolescents if they wish to grasp the workings of the adult world.

Sibling rivalry between teens is apt to be more virulent than between a teenager and a younger child. Similarly, rivalry between brothers or between sisters is likely to be more intense than the rivalry between brother and sister. Jeff isn't likely to "borrow" Lisa's best sweater, and Lisa probably won't appropriate Jeff's centerfold collection for her own use. Yet, there are many opposite-sex sibling rivalries that parents should recognize. For instance, Lisa may flirt with Jeff's friends who come over to shoot baskets; Jeff may start dating Lisa's best friend and compete for her time and attention. Brother and sister may quarrel over telephone time, use of the hairdryer, what to watch on television, and a host of other issues. In most of these instances, parents will do well to simply stand back and give their kids room to work out the situation. There is much to be learned here by the teenagers that can help prepare them for getting along with others in the future.

However, parents sometimes need to step in as referees when they see real trouble brewing. This is particularly true when "innocent" barbs of sibling rivalry approach the stage of cruelty and hurtfulness, which teenagers tend to see as a perverse form of justice. Another situation that calls for parental intervention is when one sibling constantly bullies another into acquiescence. On the other hand, trying to force your teenage children *always* to be polite to each other can lead to a stilted set of family relations in which everyone begins to act out a charade that barely masks the anger lurking beneath the surface. It's OK to tell fourteen-year-old Tony, "I think you're being a bully and intimidating. Your sister doesn't say those things to you. You'll have to learn how to disagree with her without name-calling and threats." Usually, it's healthier for all concerned to get feelings out into the open, where they can be dealt with as part of a realistic search for a reasonable solution.

Parents should also avoid comparative statements that pit sibling against sibling, setting up an unwanted, artificial rivalry that is often destructive to family unity. Do *not* tell your teenage son, "When your brother was your age, he got straight A's *and* played football, so I don't see why you can't do better than you are." Comparisons of this sort are bound to create jealousy and resentment and often lead to a "good boy/bad boy" (or "good girl/bad girl") attitude that may backfire as the labeling process leads the teen to give up trying since everyone is already convinced he or she is no good.

Adolescents in families with more than a few years' gap between siblings face and create different problems than near-age brothers and sisters. The most pervasive difficulty is the "tag along" phenomenon where the younger child always wants to accompany the teenager and his or her friends. For the long-term welfare of all concerned, tagging along should be discouraged. The younger child needs to form friendships among age-mates and, of course, the adolescent needs and deserves a certain privacy in activities with peers and freedom from being a convenient, inexpensive babysitter.

Fortunately, rivalry between siblings is not the only dimension of the sibling relationship. Siblings also provide each other with intense emotional support that can be an important buffer when parents are annoyed or angry or preoccupied with other issues. Add to this the respect and loyalty that siblings usually feel for one another, and it's no surprise that these aspects of sibling relations serve to mutually reinforce self-esteem. Even in competitive situations, losing to a sibling is not without honor, and in many cases an older brother or sister presents a role model to be emulated or surpassed. Finally, siblings tend to pull together and present a united front if they think their parents are being unfair, providing a moderating influence on unilaterally made decisions.

If, no matter what you do, your teenagers seem to continually go for each others' throats or divide themselves from each other with an iron curtain of silence, take heart. Several studies have shown that a majority of siblings who did not get along during their adolescence grew extremely close to each other after about age twenty-five, with many describing their brothers or sisters as "best friends." Despite the tribulations of adolescent sibling relations, good things may come to those who wait.

The Only-Child Family

Sibling rivalry won't surface as the problem here, but "parent rivalry" might become an issue. The only child grows up in a totally center-stage position in most families, accustomed to being in the spotlight at all times. As this child reaches early adolescence, however, it is quite common for parents to divert at least some of their attention from their child back towards each other — for companionship, comfort, support, and other reasons. As a result, the only child is apt to feel neglected, rejected, or even jealous, as though left standing center-stage in the dark. To turn the spotlight back on himself or herself in the starring role, the only child may resort to a number of theatrical ploys and manipulative performances including dramatic mood swings, experiencing exaggerated crises in life outside the home, or showing just enough rebelliousness to get Mom and Dad's attention without thoroughly angering them.

Parents should not try to solve this problem by swinging their focus back to the adolescent exclusively, but should instead encourage their child to seek other people who can provide attention and comfort when necessary. Whether the teenager can or can't develop an extrafamilial support network from friends, teachers, neighbors, other relatives, teammates, or other sources, the simple fact is that sooner or later, for the adolescent's well-being as much as the parents, the only child must be weaned from home. If this growing away doesn't occur, growing up won't occur either, and the child may never leave the psychological nest of parental devotion.

The flip side of this problem is the only child who affiliates with a peer group with astounding abandon, almost relinquishing any individual identity in the process. Having had little or no prior experience with "group feeling," the only child teenager may have the need to prove that he or she can be just like the other teenagers, accepted as a brother or sister. Parents can do little when their child falls into this "peer trap" except confirm the importance of individuality to the teen and be patient. Most teens outgrow this peer dominance in a few years. In the meantime, group membership offers adolescents a chance to learn cooperation and the subtle techniques of social interaction. On the positive side of raising an only child, the pressure to compete with siblings does not exist. A few parents become adept at substituting relative or neighbor pressure for this, saying "Your cousin Al won a scholarship to Rutgers when he was a senior. Why don't you try for a scholarship to Yale?" In fairness, though, this type of competitive egging on — as insidious as it is — rarely approaches the intensity of sibling runoffs.

Throughout the more traumatic times of adolescence with their moments of self-doubt, depression, and fears of inferiority, the only child may feel a great sense of isolation. He or she has not had the benefit of seeing an older sibling experience similar emotions and will probably feel (more than would an adolescent from a larger family) like the only kid in history to hurt so badly. Heart-to-heart talks between parents and teen where Mom and Dad discuss their own rough times as teenagers rarely help because of the perceived gap between the generations. Again, an extended support group of family and friends can cushion these pains, which will pass with time and maturity.

Beyond the Nuclear Family

Most of us have an assortment of relatives lurking in the wings who constitute our extended family system. In some cases, whether due to geographic separation or personal choice, we interact with these relatives in only the most sporadic fashion, and our teenage children see or talk with them only on special occasions like reunions, weddings, or funerals. In other families, interactions with relatives occur on a regular, ongoing basis. It is this latter category that we will discuss briefly here.

It's common to find that one or more of your relatives not only feels love for your family but also believes their relationship lets them speak with a special voice of authority to your children. Determining how much authority and in which areas requires finely tuned judgment, an almost psychic ability to predict responses, stoic patience, and unfaltering faith in the overall goodness of human nature. Aunts, uncles, cousins, and grandparents all have their own individual notions of how to manage your teenager's life. "Be stricter with him," your father may tell you. Your mother-in-law may suggest you loosen the rules you set for your daughter — "Times are changing, you know." Uncle Harry writes, "If you'd just send the twins to spend a summer with me, I'd make *men* out of them." But you may not want your fourteen-year-old sons drinking beer in the bleachers of the baseball stadium all summer or playing in Uncle Harry's marathon weekend poker games. Just how do you proceed?

First recognize that the functioning of your family is ultimately your responsibility, and any attempt by an outside authority to usurp that responsibility must be firmly turned away. This doesn't mean you won't stop to consider advice proffered by a helpful and (usually) well-meaning relative, but it *does* mean you're perfectly free to ignore that advice if it doesn't seem to fit. Otherwise, you're relinquishing your control and respect — and doing that may have dire consequences. On the other hand, don't be ashamed to ask relatives for advice — you might be pleasantly surprised by their wisdom, especially if it comes from professional knowledge or from more experience in dealing with teenagers than you've had.

A different type of family problem can arise if your adolescent takes a strong dislike to a relative and repeatedly declines social invitations in order to avoid that person. No law states that one must enjoy the company of one's relatives, but teens need to learn respect, politeness, and tolerance. This may seem a lot to ask from a fifteen-year-old know-it-all more than willing to express his or her negative feelings verbally, but a primary function of the family is to socialize its children, teaching them how to deal effectively with the complexities of our society. Tolerating others when personalities tend to clash is a skill needed in many avenues of adult life. One teaches this skill by providing a good role model for that kind of behavior and by insisting that a teenager not drop out of family activities because of a dislike for one member. However, you must make allowances for the teenager's perspective, too. If Friday night dinner at Aunt Emma's clashes with the varsity basketball game, you can't expect your teen to sacrifice basketball to preserve family unity. Besides, Aunt Emma will probably understand.

The importance of the extended family usually increases if the adolescent's parents are separated or divorced or if one parent has died. Family members can provide role models of appropriate same- or opposite-sex behavior as well as make themselves available as listeners to teens who feel uncomfortable talking about certain things to their parents. The relative who is one step removed from the tight circle of the nuclear family can be viewed as a safer harbor for self-disclosure, a comfortable friend whose interest in the teen is not so vested that it sometimes interferes with listening and understanding. Parents may feel some jealousy over this type of relationship, but this feeling usually lessens when they see they are being augmented rather than replaced and can recognize the benefits of the teen communicating with a trustworthy, loving adult.

The Single-Parent Family

Once a relative rarity in the United States, the single-parent family has now become something of a social fixture. According to the Census Bureau, 12.6 million children under eighteen years of age live with only one parent; stated another way, 20 percent of all American children are being reared in single-parent homes. While divorce accounts for the largest proportion of these families, separation, desertion, births to unwed mothers, and death of a spouse are also contributing factors. Many of the stresses and strains of being a single parent relate to being constantly on the spot and having no one with whom to share decision-making responsibilities, but several other problems emerge as relatively unique issues.

To begin with, when a teenager has trouble getting along with one parent, a good relationship with the other parent is usually able to rescue the situation and preserve both a sense of family equilibrium and the teenager's self-esteem. In single-parent families, this balance is missing, so the adolescent is much more apt to feel rejected, persecuted, or ignored. At the same time, because a single parent has no ready means of regularly deflecting an adolescent's anger or contempt onto another parental figure, single parenthood can quickly begin to feel like perpetual combat with all the artillery aimed in your direction.

The single parent also faces a problem in dealing with personal loneliness and the need for new relationships. Forming such relationships generally requires being away from the children, which often leads to feelings of guilt. Staying home and trying to be Supermom or Superdad without respite from the kids, though, lead to resentment, short tempers, and guilt for a different reason. As one thirty-six-year-old mother of a young teenage son put it, "If I don't get out to meet some men, I'll never be able to marry again and give my boy a father. But when I try to date, I find myself constantly worrying about where my son is and whether he resents what I'm doing." Compounding the intricacies of this issue is a remarkable role reversal from the usual parent-teen pattern: many single parents are anxious about what their teenagers will think about their sexual behavior, real or imagined.

One other difficulty confronting the single parent is the temptation when trouble is encountered to give up in order to try to win the teen's friendship and acceptance. Giving up can also occur because the single parent has a built-in excuse for failure: "If only she'd had her mother around ..." In part, this "my-kid-will-never-turn-out-right-no-matter-what-I-do" attitude grew out of popular psychology theories of the 1950s and 1960s that stressed the importance of having both a mother and father at home. According to these notions, boys without fathers were likely to become homosexual, girls without fathers often became promiscuous, boys without mothers were destined to be unfeeling, impulsive adults, and so on. Social scientists now know that most of this theorizing was faulty. For every boy from a single-parent family who becomes homosexual, there are several from two-parent families who turn out the same way. Despite these statistics, some single parents continue to feel helpless and inadequate and may inadvertently program their adolescents to think they are disadvantaged and preordained to calamity.

In light of such pressures, what steps can a single parent take to deal effectively with teenagers? The following pointers may be of some assistance:

(1) *Get your attitude in gear.* If you begin with a defeatist outlook, chances are that it will rub off on your kids. If you believe in yourself, your kids will, too, making your job easier. Some single parents find that the support provided by organizations such as Parents Without Partners can help them get on the right track; if this doesn't work, find a counselor who can help.

(2) *Don't expect the impossible.* Single parents often set unrealistic expectations for what they should be able to do and then castigate themselves when they prove to be less than perfect. Don't set yourself up for this no-win situation; instead, set realistic goals for yourself. As a result, you'll be more relaxed, and this will have a beneficial effect on your style of parenting. Instead of trying to be Supermom or Superdad — holding down a full-time job, preparing gourmet meals, cleaning the house, and

being with your kids — draw up a practical budget for your time and energy that gives you a chance to be yourself. While you may have to give up Tuesday night veal cordon bleu in favor of a Big Mac or a tuna-fish casserole, you might well decide that the priorities of your life, including your family's needs, will be the ultimate winners. In deciding what's realistic and what's not, the critical variable is being able to set aside your guilt over not being perfect — but then, few of us really are.

(3) *Develop allies and resources and use them.* Single parents often talk about feeling outnumbered when dealing with their kids. Having another adult ally can help you regain a sense of control. Likely candidates include relatives, friends, neighbors, teachers, coaches, counselors, members of the clergy, or anyone else the teenager knows and respects. You can seek out such people to discuss problems you're having (this gives you a second opinion if you're unsure of yourself), or turn to them to provide role models or advice directly for your child. In many instances, a teenager will be receptive to developing such a surrogate-parent relationship.

(4) *Spend prime-quality time with your teen on a regular basis.* Being available to your adolescent is a little different from watching T.V. together. Recognizing that work pressures and financial considerations may create some difficulties in getting a lot of leisure time as a single parent, it is still possible to devise time where you and your teenager can interact in an uninterrupted way. Try to have at least one meal together each day. Share chores around the house — surprisingly, this may prove to be a great catalyst to communication. Block out at least two hours each weekend where you can share an activity or catch up on family news or simply philosophize with each other. Pay particular attention to events that are important to your teen: find some way to get to the school play or the big track meet or the concert if your teen is involved.

(5) *Give your teen an active role in family responsibilities.* Single-parent families can easily become tyrannical unless the children have a voice of sorts in family decision-making. Actively solicit their opinions and, when feasible, try out what they have to say. At the same time, assign specific responsibilities to them and then stand back to let them carry them out.

(6) *Be yourself.* Sacrificing your own identity to be a better parent almost always results in just the opposite result. Just as adolescents seek a degree of independence, you too need some independence. A little breathing space is likely to create a better atmosphere for both you and your teen.

Single-parent families have some distinct strengths that are often overlooked. For one thing, they provide a decidedly better atmosphere than a bad marriage does for raising a family, and they often foster a particularly strong bond betweeen parent and teen. In addition, they often lead to an improved sense of self-esteem on the parent's part. Single mothers are often surprised by their capacity for self-reliance, while many single fathers report an improved awareness of their ability to nurture. Add to these benefits the fact that teenagers often feel a greater sense of responsibility for family cohesiveness in single-parent families, thus taking a giant step towards maturity, and you can see that despite the rigorous challenges of this situation, it is possible to find rewards and pleasures there as well.

Stepparents and Second Marriages

According to current estimates, thirty-five million people now live in stepfamilies, including seven million children under eighteen years of age. While all members of stepfamilies are somewhat handicapped at the outset by the trauma of the breakup of their former families, therapists and researchers agree that young children have the easiest time adjusting to the remarriage of a parent. In contrast, teenagers tend to have great difficulty adapting to their new family arrangements.

A parent's remarriage can be threatening to the adolescent for a number of reasons. Kay Colvin, a researcher at Florida State University who recently studied two thousand teens in stepfamilies, points out, "Adolescents are going through so many changes of their own that they have a special need for stability at home, and a parent's remarriage always upsets that at first." She goes on to note that the issue of parental sexuality in remarried families is particularly distressing to some adolescents. "Teens in intact families tend to think of their parents as nonsexual beings, but they can't do that in a home where mom and stepdad are kissing and holding hands the way newlyweds do." Adolescents are also apt to be troubled by a strong loyalty to their absent biological parent, difficulty adjusting to the presence of new stepbrothers or stepsisters, and ambiguity about what to expect from their stepparent in day-to-day relations.

Despite these troubles, adolescents often sound surprisingly indifferent when asked how they feel about a parent's second marriage. "If it's what Mom wants, it's okay with me," said thirteen-year-old Karen, who brought up her deep resentment and worry only after several hours with a counselor. "It didn't matter one way or the other to me," eighteen-year-old Sam casually remarked. "I was going away to college in a few months anyway." The adolescent mind, fond of absolutes, tends to forget that even going away to school will not eternally orphan him from his family. Teens want so desperately to be on their own they often dismiss the family as unimportant to their future, sometimes convincing themselves the family situation is worse than it really is so breaking away will be easier. Whatever the reason, the pretense of disinterest is seldom an accurate portrayal of the teenager's real feelings, but rather more of a counteroffensive move. Teens fear their real parent won't care as deeply for them after the remarriage, so they retaliate by being the first to claim emotional apathy.

Some of this reaction can be curbed with a simple family discussion explaining that although membership has been opened to an outsider, charter members of the family will continue to maintain their closeness. A straightforward discussion like this, though, needs to be followed up with actions that reinforce the philosophy. Any family routines, activities, or patterns of interaction that fostered warmth and caring between the teenager and the natural parent should be continued as much as possible. The reconstituted family must *show* the adolescent — not just tell him or her — that the love and sense of belonging he or she felt before the second marriage will continue to be available after it.

From the stepparent's perspective, even the simplest interaction may seem strained and uncomfortable. One such parent complained of innocently asking his fifteen-year-old stepson how school was going, only to be glared at angrily and told: "I suppose you're talking about my F on yesterday's English test. I wish you'd just come out and say it instead of trying to be polite." The stepfather, who hadn't known about the test or its dire outcome, was caught in a trap. While he could try to explain his intent, his explanation might not be believed or might lead to a shouting match. Thus, backing off rather than pressing ahead may be the wisest thing to do. In fact, the problem here is often that the stepparent is trying too hard. He or she will never exactly replace the original parent. The family will always be "reconstituted," seldom as comfortable to all its members as the original family had been. If the stepparent stops straining for the impossible, stops expecting changes that will probably never occur, the tension often dissipates. This does not diminish the stepparent's role in raising an adolescent, but puts it in a realistic perspective. In fact, because an adolescent is usually given enough nurturance by the biological parent in a stepfamily situation, the best stepparents try to be friends — and they don't try too hard at that, either. Acceptance takes time.

Some of the distance between stepparent and child will never go away if remarriage occurred in the child's teenage years. One is, after all, asking two grown persons with little more than a passing acquaintanceship to live together and share a loved one. Personality clashes ensue and instead of the love, cooperation, and overflowing respect of the Brady Bunch, you strive for mere politeness and restraint. A family that allows its members their distance may eventually move closer, but teenagers forced to "love" a new stepparent often react with full-scale rebellion.

The passive acceptance the teen was prepared to feel for the stepparent soon turns to active dislike.

These and similar problems are now being actively addressed by the Stepfamily Association of America, a rapidly growing national organization designed to help families adjust to the challenges of remarriages involving children. The founder, psychologist Emily Visher, explains, "These families were running up against all sorts of hurdles. Their expectations were way out of line. They anticipated instant love and a smooth-running household, but it doesn't happen that way. It takes time to work out different roles and rules." Fighting to reduce the social stigma still attached to stepfamilies as a legacy of fairy tales featuring wicked stepmothers and victimized stepchildren, Dr. Visher and others agree that hard work lies ahead. If all parties concerned realize from the beginning that problems will occur and have patience in working them out, the chances of developing a happy, stable family unit increase considerably.

4

Games Adolescents Play

The psychiatrist Eric Berne's insightful bestseller called *Games People Play* described common behavior patterns adults employ in interpersonal relations. Teenagers, however, are unsurpassed as the true masters of gamesmanship in everyday life. The games adolescents play — and here we're not talking about PacMan, Space Invaders, or contract bridge — are an integral part of the developmental transition from childhood to adulthood. Drawing on various degrees of ritual, imitation, and inventiveness, teenagers use games to serve two principal goals: manipulation and defense. In the process, they seek to discover two key facts of life — how to assert their own feelings and needs according to acceptable adult "rules," and how to recognize when their own goals must be shifted or abandoned with some degree of face-saving.

The word *game* generally implies both recreation and a form of contest with a specific set of rules. The behavioral games of the adolescent typically incorporate both of these components, although the recreational aspect is likely to be hidden beneath a facade of utter seriousness. The fourteen-year-old girl who insists she won't waste her Saturday by accompanying her parents on a visit to Aunt Harriet is apt to be simply engaging in sport, asserting her will in a minicontest over a trivial event, mostly unconcerned about the outcome but happy to test herself against her parents as preparation for a more important contest in the future. In a sense, then, the recreational side of adolescent gamesmanship is practice for the real thing, just as shooting baskets or hitting a tennis ball against a wall can both amuse and prepare.

The behavioral games adolescents play are usually marked by an intently serious side too. The process of the "game" is a form of skill-testing, the objective typically being to find a solution to a problem or a way to cope. At other times, the aim is primarily to make things difficult, to stir things up — in other words, to be an expression of rebellion or contempt. The cumulative effect of the adolescent gamesmanship experience is the development of a broad repertoire of familiar (thus comfortable) ways of handling a variety of situations. The adolescent permitted to deal with life by habitually slipping into the "game time" approach is in danger of becoming a shallow, manipulative adult. On the other hand, the adolescent repeatedly denied the chance to "practice" his or her social skills via game-playing is likely to be at a definite disadvantage in the real world where we're all called on to play certain roles in order to adjust.

By virtue of their convenient proximity and their usual (unwitting) willingness to play, a teenager's parents are the most likely targets (or opponents) of adolescent games. In the following pages, we will offer some practical guidelines for recognizing the game format, understanding the rules and motivations of various game ploys, and helping parents decide when and how to play or call "time out."

Strategy, Strategy

Just as the football strategist must decide when to run, pass, or kick (or to react defensively to these offensive moves), the players in adolescent gamesmanship must also make a series of strategic decisions. While in many cases the choice of a particular strategy may seem an arbitrary, spur-of-the-moment thing, the more important the matter at hand to your teenager, the more likely it is that he or she has planned an approach with great care, including at times the design of alternate ploys if the first stratagem fails. The advanced adolescent strategist may even enter the fray with a "decoy" strategy meant as camouflage to distract or confuse, with the true plan held in reserve for delivering the anticipated coup de grace triumphantly at exactly the right moment.

> *A seventeen-year-old boy:* I wanted to use my parents' car for the junior prom, but I knew they didn't want me driving at night. So I told them first that Janet and I wanted to go with Bob and his date to the beach for an all-nighter after the prom, and when they argued about that — I knew they would — it was easy to say, "Well, if I have to be home by one, then I'll need to have the car." They thought they'd won, but I got what I wanted, didn't I?

This adolescent strategic planning was just a simple version of bait-and-switch. In more complex variations, the adolescent may disguise the real request by a preceding string of irritating or "impossible" requests so when the actual question is popped, parents are likely to acquiesce resignedly. Chalk up another victory for the compleat adolescent strategist.

Parents are apt to be at an initial disadvantage when teenagers switch into their game-playing mode. They may not recognize it's game time, they may misunderstand which game is being played (or what the stakes are for winning or losing), or they may be preoccupied with other matters and thus give an answer that is regretted later. Teenagers quickly realize the edge this initial element of surprise can give them and are likely to develop a high degree of proficiency at seizing their opportunities at just the "wrong" moment for parents. The only consistently effective defense parents have here is to refuse to play if they are at a sizeable handicap. Postpone things ("I'll have to think about that and get back to you") or set a specific time for playing ("Let's discuss that right after dinner tonight") so everyone is on an equal *undistracted* footing.

Parents should also recognize the rules that apply to adolescent games. While there are certainly stylistic differences from one teenager to another, and you must know your own child's personal philosophy in setting the rules that apply between you, here are several key aspects to keep in mind:

(1) *Exaggeration is a characteristic part of most adolescent game-playing, but lying is not.* The urgency, necessity, or desirability of a particular issue is described to you with fervor — your teenager is, after all, trying to sell you an idea. Most adolescents, however, realize that flagrant lying (as distinguished from the "mild" form of stretching the truth that exaggeration encompasses) is likely to lead to serious repercussions if discovered — so lies are avoided except in the most dire of circumstances. (*Note: Frequent lying signals a serious problem that probably requires professional help. Allowing this situation to continue does no one any good.*)

(2) *The emotional fervor behind an appeal is not always (or usually) proportional to the importance of the outcome.* An issue that seems "critical" today is often quickly forgotten in the crush of other "important" issues tomorrow. Parents who are easily misled by histrionics, tantrums, and insistent circular reasoning aren't likely to fare well in the gamesmanship process; too often, they can't see the forest because they've become lost in the trees.

(3) *Teens are expert at identifying the chinks in your armor.* If they find a particular means of getting their own way, they'll return to it again and again as long as it keeps working. One mother we know gave in to her daughter's wishes whenever she was confronted with being too "uptight" because this was exactly the term her psychiatrist used to describe her and she wanted to be more flexible and relaxed. The daughter had no

inkling of what the psychiatrist had said, but she knew when she'd struck gold. Other examples of Achille's heels that parents might not realize they have include the inability to withstand an onslaught of their adolescent's tears, or difficulty in saying no when a request is couched in terms that foster competitiveness with friends or neighbors — "Well, if you don't want me to get those special hockey skates I won't, but Johnny's parents got them for him." Parents who allow themselves to be easy marks may be incessantly victimized until they assert a responsible authority. The real victim of this situation, of course, is the teenager — and the consequences may be considerable.

(4) *Initiating a game may actually be a request for an in-depth discussion.* Don't take all requests from your teen at face value, because the glib, smooth banter may be just an exploratory thrust. If you just "play" without seeing what's behind the request, you'll sometimes miss a cry for help or a genuine desire for your advice.

Divide and Conquer

One time-honored strategy used almost universally by teenagers to manipulate situations to their own purposes is based on military logic. Teenagers, like generals, know a unified front is more difficult to attack than split forces, so whenever possible, teens try to negotiate by approaching one parent privately. Even if unsuccessful, they'll have another chance to coax, convince, or cajole the other parent into agreement.

Typically, the adolescent first sidles up to whichever parent is seen as more likely to be sympathetic. For example, Sally may try to get Dad to endorse her new dress purchase before Mom hears about it, knowing her mother has already bemoaned the size and expense of Sally's wardrobe.

In some cases, teenagers have previously established fairly accurate perceptions of which parent is more permissive in certain situations (e.g., socially, economically) and try to capitalize profitably on this knowledge. At other times, the teenager knows that a particular parent is less likely to object to something if prior approval has been obtained from the other parent. This is particularly true in families where parents make a concerted effort not to overrule or dispute their partner's decisions (a laudable style of parenting, to be sure, but one that can sometimes be taken to extremes simply to preserve the sanctity of parental agreement).

The advanced teenage strategist can even use the "divide and conquer" concept to create a positive response in the face of overwhelming adversity, as when both parents are opposed to whatever option is being discussed. Here's how it's done by an expert:

TEEN: I'm invited to go on a terrific ski trip next weekend with Larry and Peter. I'll just be gone overnight and the whole thing only costs $45.

FATHER: Well, I'm not sure about that. . . .

TEEN (*quickly and emphatically*): I know it's OK with Mom. Whaddya say, Dad? Please?

FATHER (*skeptically*): Oh, I suppose, if it's okay with your mother . . .

[*A little later in a private discussion with Mother.*]

TEEN: I've got a chance to go skiing next weekend with Larry and Peter, and Dad says I can go. Is there anything you want me to do before then to help you out?

MOM (*hesitantly*): Well, if your father says OK, it's all right with me, too.

Here, by neatly *implying* the approval of the opposite parent, the teenager has successfully convinced both parents to say yes. Sleight-of-hand at its finest, this prime example of adolescent gamesmanship shows why parents need to communicate clearly with one another to establish just who said what to whom. (A slightly different version of this strategy is for one teen's parents to be told that a friend's parents have given their approval for something. After this convinces the second set of parents to acquiesce to the desired plan, this news is used to extract an endorsement from the friend's parents.)

The divide-and-conquer strategy is occasionally used by teenagers to precipitate a parental argument if other approaches have failed. The aim is to get the parents so annoyed with each other that one eventually tries to control the situation by siding with the adolescent to gang up on the spouse. While this game is generally restricted to issues of some emotional volatility where the parents are known to have markedly divergent viewpoints, it can also be used when parental tempers are flaring over some other matter.

"Everyone Else Gets to . . ."

The hands down perennial favorite of the American teenager's repertoire for manipulating parental permission is a simple appeal to conformity. "Why can't I go barefoot, Ma? Everyone else gets to do it." "How will it look if I don't have a gold class ring? Everyone else is going to have one." "I need my own phone . . . everyone else has one." The not-so-subtle pressure tactics of this strategic approach seem to emphasize three components: (1) I'll look foolish compared to my friends if I don't have what I want; (2) You're being unfair if you deprive me of this (*object, article, opportunity*), since the consensus of everyone else's parents is obviously fair; and (3) Why do you mistreat me so? The adolescent's aim is to inculcate a glimmer of guilt in his or her parents in the hopes it will lead them to instantaneous agreement. At the same time, the teenager cannily plays on the widespread parental wish to keep up with the Joneses.

The inelegant simplicity of the "everyone else gets to" argument is generally overshadowed by the numerous ways in which this plea can be presented: indignantly, quietly, passionately, matter-of-factly, and — in the finest tradition of adolescent anguish — in a shrill, whining appeal of incessant irritation. Whichever style is chosen, teenagers are convinced they're presenting an irrefutable fact with its own compelling internal logic. "Everyone else gets to" implies "so I should, too" and that is understood by all concerned.

You can easily and effectively counter this game if you keep your wits about you. First, be certain you understand the real issue at hand. In advanced versions, there may be several requests commingled in one "package," so you must sort out the importance of each issue before you respond. Second, whatever your answer, make it clear you are not basing your response on what "everyone else" does, but on what's right for your son or daughter. Third, don't hesitate to negotiate terms if you feel negotiation is warranted. For instance, "I'm happy to let you get your own phone if you pull your average up to a B," or "Sure you can get a set of golf clubs — but you'll have to pay for half."

At times, a different type of strategy can be used by parents to deflate quickly the "everyone else" ploy. You can turn the game to your own advantage by offering to check on what everyone else actually gets or does before reaching your decision. This is likely to strike panic in your teen, whose reaction may indicate a hasty reappraisal of reality: everyone else may *not*, in fact, get to do or have what your teen is requesting. You'll know you're on the right track if your teen responds with a far more modest counterproposal. Be careful, though, in using this variation — there's always the chance your teenager's argument is firmly based in fact.

"Who, Me?"

The "Who, me?" game is actually a defensive maneuver, a plea of innocence or noninvolvement that serves multiple purposes for the adolescent. At one level, "Who, me?" is a disclaimer — a protestation that the wrong person has been fingered ("Johnny, did you take $5 from my bureau?" "Who, me?"). At another level, it is a challenging response, throwing down the gauntlet to say silently, "Maybe I did, but you can't prove it." At still another level, the "Who, me?" reply is an expression of hurt or pain — "How could you ever think I did that?" However, because "Who, me?" is almost a basic reflex of adolescence, it can be tricky to interpret the exact nuance of its use in any given situation. In fact, it may pop out so automatically that it serves as a rhetorical question, a preamble to an answer rather than the answer itself (e.g., "Susan, did you use all the gas in the car?" "Who, me? [pause] Oh yeah, I guess I did").

The teenager using the "Who, me?" reply frequently blurs the distinction between evasiveness as a defense and outright lying. While "Who, me?" doesn't come right out and say "I didn't do it," as an adolescent will huffily point out if trapped, it initially implies innocence or at least lack of awareness. As a result, this strategy is often chosen in situations where the teenager has failed to perform a requested task (e.g., "I *asked* you to take out the garbage!" "Who, me?"), also serving as a delay tactic. The follow-up response is likely to be "I heard you, I heard you," although there may still be no movement towards fulfilling the request.

When addressing a teenager, you should also realize that the "Who, me?" reply can be an indication of preoccupation with other thoughts, in which case "Who, me?" serves as a sort of busy signal to lines of communication.

"I Know What I'm Doing"

As adolescents grope for a sense of identity and autonomy, they are typically confronted with an incredible array of situations in which they must decide whether to go it alone or to ask for advice or assistance. When parents try to intervene in this process by offering help or questioning a teenager's capability, the result is often an automatic decision to choose the independence route. The rallying cry — a combination of annoyance, optimism, and bravado — is likely to be "I know what I'm doing." Regrettably, these glib words are not always an indication of the teenager's knowledge or capabilities, so they all too frequently foreshadow some sort of disaster.

"I know what I'm doing" is a transitional announcement, an expression of self-confidence and determination as well as a declaration that "I'm more grown up than you think." In this latter sense, "I know what I'm doing" is a form of defiance, preliminary notice that a teenager is acquiring—or hopes to acquire—the skills to get by independently. Unfortunately, it may indicate wishful thinking more than maturity, and parents are advised to proceed cautiously any time this game is introduced.

Parental judgment must be used in deciding if the risk of undermining an adolescent's burgeoning self-confidence overpowers the potential consequences if the teenager is allowed to proceed independently. It's one thing to let your daughter botch up a batch of brownies because she's adding too much sugar and quite another to let her hitchhike to visit a friend four hundred miles away because it's not fashionable to take the Greyhound bus. Many times it will be beneficial to let teenagers try things on their own, even if they fail, because their failure can be a valuable learning experience. But if the price to pay for learning is too high or the risk of catastrophe too steep, parents must act swiftly and responsibly to control the situation by setting appropriate limits. Although this can sometimes be done with grace and diplomacy to allow the teenager to save face, at other times it requires a no-nonsense approach that may be temporarily embarrassing or frustrating — but necessary.

"Up Yours"

Although the notion of adolescent rebelliousness has probably been overworked, its reality is readily apparent to most parents experienced in raising teenagers. Even the most cooperative, parent-pleasing teen has occasional outbursts of the ornery and argumentative, and some adolescents seem to acquire a perpetual chip on their shoulders. This leads to a troubling form of gamesmanship in which the teenager closes disagreements or discussions with such phrases as "Bug off," "Leave me alone," or "I don't give a damn." Collectively, these responses all translate into a more emphatic, if less eloquent, expression: "Up yours!"

There's certainly nothing wrong with having a teenager vociferously disagree with your thinking or advice, nor must they like the rules you set down for them. In fact, the totally unrebellious teenager may be in an unhealthy situation, masking an inner turmoil that will explode unexpectedly and uncontrollably at some future time. But there's a big difference between an occasional "Up yours" as an unceremonious sign of unhappiness, and a persistent pattern of disagreement, blame, and anger. The frequent use of "Up yours" as a rejoinder by your adolescent is a strong symptom of faulty parent-child communications and may also be an indicator of psychological problems. In either case, the logical starting point is a thoughtful discussion in which your teenager can air his or her gripes and you get to speak your mind, too. If this proves impossible or nonproductive, a visit to a family therapist or other source of professional help is in order. In effect, an objective referee may be required to help you both find a viable solution.

One word of warning about dealing with the "Up yours" response. While parents aren't saints and can't be expected to always keep their tempers, avoid the temptation to react in kind. Getting into a shouting match, no matter what the issue, is no way to solve the impasse between you. A more effective strategy that can also serve as a useful model for your teenager's behavior is to say something like "Right now I'm very upset with your reply to me. More discussion now isn't likely to help, so let's both cool off and return to this subject later." In following up on this, don't try to force an apology, though, because doing that is more likely to be inflammatory than productive.

Winning and Losing

It would be naive to think that the discussion thus far has provided an exhaustive catalogue of all games adolescents play with their parents. We haven't mentioned the line that goes, "If you loved me, you'd . . ." nor have we discussed the "I don't care" syndrome, where the appearance of sullen indifference is used to mask strongly held preferences in the hope parents will consider the matter unimportant and default on making a decision. These and other forms of adolescent gamesmanship will be considered in later chapters, where they will be discussed in the context of particular teenage problems and crises.

At this juncture, though, it is helpful to look at the intricacies of adolescent gamesmanship from a different angle — winning and losing, or how to keep score. Teenagers almost universally view these interactions in black and white terms: "I win, you lose," or "You win, I lose." This viewpoint is based on the adolescent's usual reason for playing a game: to provide a contest between parental authority and their own ingenuity and independence. Teenagers may actually be disappointed if they get their own way too easily, without parental opposition, because it deprives them of the chance to test their skills. The thrill of victory and the agony of defeat can exist only within true competition — no one likes to win because the other team won't take the field.

Some parents also regard their interactions with their teenage children in terms of winning and losing, anxiously bolstering their sense of being "good" parents by their ability to assert authority and make their adolescent toe the line. A few parents even gain some psychic satisfaction from beating their teenager at his or her own game, taking pleasure from their child's hurt or frustration as much as from their own victory.

The fact is that there usually is *not* one winner and one loser in this process. The outcome of adolescent games affects parents and teens together — either they both win or they both lose. While this may not be immediately apparent in some of the mundane skirmishes that arise in day-to-day living ("Which T.V. show should we watch at nine?" or "You can't have dessert unless you clear the table"), the entire process of adolescent maturation is strongly influenced by the learning that occurs from game-playing. Even more importantly, the welfare of the teenager is largely dependent on successfully negotiating the gamut of decisions, large and small, that are often subject to the game process.

5

The Art and Science of Communicating with a Teenager

One of the most common complaints parents have about teenagers is that they seem to go through their adolescence tuned in to a different wavelength from the one on which parents broadcast. "I can't get through to him at all," one parent will say. Another parent ruefully notes, "We don't seem to be speaking the same language." Curiously, teenagers voice exactly the same complaints about their parents — "I can't get through to them," "They never seem to understand what I mean." Why this dilemma occurs, and how it can be corrected, is the topic for this chapter.

The Communications Quandary

When we talk about communications, we are really talking about a process of transmitting information. On the face of it, that sounds like a simple enough thing. Why, then, do parents and teenagers have such difficulty communicating with each other?

The answer lies in three separate aspects of parent-teen interactions that can be succinctly identified as motivation, style, and meaning. Parents and teens each tend to be suspicious of the motivations underlying the other's communications with them. Parents, for example, are often afraid that the teenager is hiding something, or being manipulative, or isn't telling them the truth. Teenagers, on the other hand, regard many of the questions asked by parents as attempts to invade their privacy and view other parental messages as propaganda or commands. It's no wonder that communicating clearly is difficult when this sort of interference is present even before the dialogue begins.

This is hardly the end of the story, however. The style in which parents and adolescents communicate also is apt to create problems. When parents talk with their teenage children, they often use a tone of condescension that says, in effect, "I'm the parent and you're the child and don't you forget that." This attitude carries over into other stylistic matters: for instance, by considering what they, the parents, have to say as more important than the teenager's thoughts or feelings (another example of the condescension phenomenon), parents often interrupt their teenagers without being aware of doing so. A few other examples of stylistic obstacles to communications unwittingly common among parents are:

(1) Initiating communications when *the parents* are ready for it, without thinking about their teen's receptivity at the time (and being unreceptive themselves when the teenager wishes to talk — "Can't you see I'm busy now?").

(2) Beginning communications with a statement of blame or criticism — "Young lady, I think we need to talk about your grades" — which prematurely cuts off the potential for an honest interchange by putting the teenager immediately into a defensive posture.

(3) Delivering lectures or monologues that don't permit the teenager to interact and respond.

(4) Being obstinate and one-sided in their ways; refusing to look at a situation from the teenager's perspective.

(5) Yelling in order to get a point across.

Teenagers, too, are guilty of erecting stylistic obstacles to communications. Perhaps the most common, and certainly the most annoying, is the "nonresponse" to a query from a parent. "How was school today?" "OK, I guess." "Where are you going tonight?" "Out with the guys." "Did you finish your homework?" "Sort of." Other examples of teenage obfuscations in communications include acting bored, exaggerating, being silly or flip or coy, deliberately distorting what the parent is saying, and the classic teenage maneuver of not listening.

Finally, the content or meaning of communications between parent and adolescent can also be a major source of problems. Teenagers resent being put down by their parents, which happens any time a parent speaks in an accusatory or judgmental fashion. Similarly, teenagers don't enjoy being ordered around or being diagnosed or psychoanalyzed. ("*I* know why you're doing that. You're doing that just to get your mother's attention.") Likewise, teenagers (just like everyone else) dislike rejection, yet parents often try to get their teen's attention by using rejecting or disparaging statements rather than by using statements that validate the teen as a person. On the other side of the parent-teen communications coin, parents resent it when teenagers tell them, "You just don't understand," both because the parents usually *want* to understand and because they are offended by the implicit notion that they're too old or too insensitive to comprehend the issue. Parents are also annoyed by the circuitous logic teenagers use in analyzing a problem — "Everybody's doing it," for example, is usually not a good reason to support a particular course of action or behavior. Parents also may be alarmed at the teenager's seeming inability to look at long-range consequences of behavior or the teenager's unwillingness to be cooperative on family issues rather than taking a self-centered view.

In short, despite the fact that parents and teens both say that they'd like to communicate more effectively with each other, consistently effective communications are only rarely achieved. Nevertheless, a meeting of the minds is more than possible if parents will simply prepare themselves to be adept at the two principal parts of communication: sending clear messages and learning how to listen.

Sending Signals Clearly

To say that effective communication begins with the clarity of the message sent from one person to another is simply to state the obvious. If a garbled or ambiguous message goes out, even the most attentive listener is apt to be confused and forced to guess at the meaning unless further clarification can be obtained. Unfortunately, parents send garbled or hard-to-understand messages to their adolescents more often than they generally imagine, and teenagers tend to be attentive listeners only when it suits them.

Let's look at some of the sources of ambiguity in sending messages. First, there is the obvious problem of the parent who doesn't say what he or she really means. This can occur because the parent probably hasn't thought in advance about what to say or because the parent is afraid to say something, fearing the consequences. For example, when fourteen-year-old Karen asked her mother whether birth control pills were dangerous or not, her mother *wanted* to say, "They're not as dangerous as getting pregnant at your age," but found herself saying instead, "You're too young to think about that." Karen's mother was caught in a dilemma: since she was opposed to teenage sexual activity, she didn't want her daughter to think she was endorsing such behavior by saying it was OK to use the pill. Although she certainly didn't want her daughter to get pregnant, her answer — while clear enough in itself — didn't accurately say what she meant.

A second source of murkiness in parent-teen communications comes from the mixed messages parents sometimes send. These contradictory missives lack logical consistency, with one part of the message negating the other. Here are two examples: "I don't expect you to be perfect, Jim, but I can't understand why you just got a B on your chemistry test — you know how important that exam was." "Come on, Lisa, you know you're too young to wear lipstick and eye shadow. . . . [three minutes later in the same conversation] Can't you act more grown-up, Lisa? You're not a kid anymore, you know."

Mixed messages also occur inadvertently when there is an obvious discrepancy between the words that are spoken and the nonverbal message a parent conveys simultaneously. When your seventeen-year-old daughter, just home from a date, asks what you thought of her new boyfriend, you may answer, "He seems really nice." But your tone of voice, the hesitancy of your delivery, or the frown on your face may convey a different message, leaving your teen wondering what your opinion *really* is. When you tell your adolescent through gritted teeth, "I'm *not* mad at you," slowly enunciating each word, your nonverbal cues give away the fact that you're not exactly ecstatic — you're trying hard to keep control.

A third contribution to lack of clarity in parent-teen communications comes when parents fail to be specific in what they say. You tell your son not to make any more phone calls this evening, and fifteen minutes later he's back on the phone. When you demand to know what's going on, he says, "*I* didn't make the call — Kevin called *me.*" Another example: you tell the family that the yard needs to be cleaned this weekend. Saturday morning, as your daughter heads out of the house to go to the beach with some friends, you protest. "Gee, Mom," she says innocently, "you didn't say it had to be done *today.*"

Fortunately, there are a number of ways to increase the clarity of your communications with your teens. This list provides a good foundation for the positive parenting approach:

(1) *Use "I" messages to state your feelings and expectations.* Messages that describe what you're feeling or what you need provide teens with precise facts, making it unnecessary for them to guess what's on your mind. In contrast, sentences that start with the pronoun *you* tend to be heard as accusatory or demanding. Instead of saying, "You're always leaving a mess in the bathroom," try saying, "I get very annoyed when the bathroom's messy. I'd really like it if you could help out by keeping it neat."

(2) *Think through what you want to say and how you'll say it before tackling something important.* This can provide some organizational clarity to your words and help prevent your saying something you don't really mean. Especially with emotionally charged issues, prior rehearsal can be a big help. If you practice this in ordinary, mundane situations, it will be infinitely easier to communicate clearly in more complicated times.

(3) *Make your priorities clear.* Many conversations touch on a number of different issues. Be certain to specify what's most important to you (and what isn't) so you don't leave your teen guessing.

(4) *Don't leave loopholes in your messages.* If you want your teen to do something, specify what it is, when it's to be done, and how you want it handled. If there's no rush, say so, but be clear in what you say.

(5) *Be concise whenever possible.* Long-winded discussions lose your teen's attention and may obfuscate your meaning.

(6) *Tell your teen, "I love you," and mean it — then go on to make your point.* Sometimes it's hard to love your teenager. He or she may look like an alien life form, may behave in ways that horrify you, or may cling to ideas that are completely antithetical to your own personal beliefs. But your comments or requests will be heard as a form of rejection if you never verbalize your love. The parent who can genuinely say, "I love you," and then say what's on his or her mind is more likely to be heard. Remember, you can love your teen but still retain the right to disapprove of something he or she is doing.

(7) *Ask for feedback from your teen.* Feedback provides you with a way of double-checking what your teen has heard. If you've been misunderstood, you have a chance to correct the misconception. If your teen has gotten your point precisely, some feedback gives you a sense of his or her immediate reaction. In either case, you both benefit.

(8) *Be aware of your teen's attentiveness.* If your son or daughter is preoccupied with getting ready for a date, it isn't a good time for a heart-to-heart talk. Likewise, if your teen's mind seems to be wandering, wrap up the talk for another time.

(9) *If verbal discussion is too painful, emotional, or frustrating, try putting your thoughts in a letter to your teen.* By writing, you give yourself a chance to consider your exact message carefully and to communicate without being interrupted. Your teen may be impressed that you cared enough to commit your thoughts to paper; he or she also has the chance to reread your words, to think them over carefully. Letters can also be used to express pride, praise, and congratulations — not just problems.

Learning to Listen

While many people assume that being a good listener requires nothing more than closing your mouth and sitting back in your chair, the process of effective listening is actually quite complex. Since learning to listen to your adolescent is both a critical component of parent-teen communications and one of the key elements of preventive parenting, it pays to give some thought to your own listening style and how it can be improved. The following pointers may be of some help.

(1) *Effective listening requires your undivided attention.* Listening with half an ear — e.g., while you're watching T.V. or reading the newspaper — tells your teen that you don't consider what he or she has to say as very important. In addition, it increases the likelihood that you'll miss hearing a detail or two of your teenager's request or statement, leaving you poorly informed or in the dark.

(2) *Listening is usually most effective in unhurried circumstances.* If you're in a rush to get somewhere or do something, the chances are you will be impatient in your listening — and your teenager will quickly recognize this. Not only will your effectiveness as a listener be reduced, in many instances your teens will be forced into an incomplete, hurried version of saying what they want or what they feel. In fact, hurrying may sometimes lead to your teens' withdrawal from the discussion prematurely, before they've said what they really wanted to, because they are put off by your impatience.

(3) *Ask questions as you listen, but do so in a way that doesn't interrupt or put your teen on the defensive.* Listening is not enough when you don't understand just what your adolescent means. Instead of guessing at the meaning, or trying to interpret the message on the basis of your own assumptions and perceptions, don't be afraid to ask for specific clarification when and where you need it. Recognize, though, that too many questions can turn the discussion into an interrogation rather than a conversation or can interrupt your teenager's train of thought in a way that limits, rather than improves, communication opportunities.

(4) *Be patient in your listening style.* Teenagers often feel nervous and uncertain in approaching discussions with their parents of things that are important to them. They are apt first to test the mood of the moment by what seems like trivial conversation or quite a bit of verbal meandering. If you consistently tune out of such conversations with your teens, you may find that they rarely get brave enough to swing the discussion around to what they *really* want to say and instead beat a hasty retreat. Patient listening gives teenagers a sense of your acceptance and receptivity and sometimes leads to unexpected revelations or requests for advice.

(5) *Learn to listen at times when there hasn't been a request for a discussion.* Teenagers don't always announce the fact that there's something on their minds. If you are available as a listener at seemingly odd moments during the time you spend together, whether it's while you're raking leaves or bathing the dog or standing in line for a movie, you may be surprised to find that it's soul-baring time for your teenager. Be willing to listen, realizing that you don't need to have an answer right there and then, and you'll be much more likely to have your teenager feeling comfortable in approaching you under other, more convenient, conversational circumstances. If you break away from these odd-moment talks, you may make it much harder for your teenager to talk with you at times when you feel like listening.

(6) *Effective listening is an active rather than a passive process.* To listen with understanding requires an expenditure of energy and effort, yet many of us are so used to listening passively, whether to a spouse, the television, or a cocktail party conversation, that we bring the same attitude towards listening to our interactions with our kids. To listen actively, we must do more than just hear the words that are spoken: we must be sensitive to the emotions behind the words, we must watch for nonverbal clues to the meaning of the discussion, and we must be willing to listen with open minds that don't cut off communications because of our own preconceived notions. If we succeed in these things, we then are practicing the *art* of listening.

When Silence Is Golden (And When It's Not)

If your adolescent suddenly becomes silent and withdrawn from you, it's very tempting to think that this is a sign of problems brewing. Should you confront your teenager to find out what the trouble is and offer your advice? Should you ignore the silence, waiting for it to fade away as a passing phase in your adolescent's life? Or should you be grateful for the silence as a kind of truce, seeing it as something of a tranquil oasis? The answer, of course, depends on what's behind the silence.

In some circumstances, silence is a sign of constructive forces at work in your adolescent's life. Like everyone else, teenagers need privacy and space to sift through their own thoughts, and the wall of silence they erect to serve this need is healthy and protective. In fact, this type of silence can be a sign of creativity and growth in your adolescent, or it can be an opportunity for the adolescent to consolidate his or her experiences. It can also be a much-needed time for planning (that is, looking to the future) and for healing (getting over something troubling that is now past). If your teenager is realistic and responsible, and if the silence isn't accompanied by abrupt behavioral changes — avoiding friends, refusing to take phone calls, skipping most meals, and brooding or crying excessively, for example — it's best to avoid intruding too strongly into your child's privacy.

Parents also need to recognize more pernicious forms of silence and withdrawal. Silence can mask anger or pain for anyone, and teenagers — often less skilled than adults in dealing with these feelings — may retreat into a shell of silence to avoid having to cope with these feelings directly. Adolescents also sometimes use silence as a cover-up: that is, they imagine that their silence will protect against the discovery of some behavioral transgression that they want to keep hidden, such as trouble at school or drug experimentation. In other instances, prolonged silence and withdrawal may be a sign of depression or intense psychological conflict. In all of these situations, parents obviously need to do more than simply sit passively waiting for the teenager to start voluntarily communicating again. The trouble is, however, that your gentlest prodding may be seen as snooping, and your well-intended questions (meant to rescue rather than punish or pressure your child) may nevertheless be met by a blanket denial of anything being wrong, even if it is. Here no simple formula can be offered, and parents must rely on their intuitive judgments about their adolescents much more than on any help from other sources. By following the guidelines for communications offered earlier in this chapter, you can at least inform your teen of your interest (or your concern), your availability, and your intention of helping, if you can, in a positive rather than punitive manner.

One other facet of silence deserves mention. Parental silence has its place, although few of us recognize its utility. Obviously, refraining from incessant criticism of your child and avoiding offering your unsolicited opinion on every trivial issue gives your teenager more of a chance to be his or her own person and lends more weight to your words when you speak. Likewise, you can probably earn a little more respect as a parent if you can stifle the urge to comment negatively on things you don't enjoy or don't understand that are meaningful to your teens. Here, studied silence may be more helpful and diplomatic than brutal honesty.

At the same time, we must realize that parental silence can be interpreted as a sign of our approval or endorsement. Thus, teenagers may mistakenly assume that when we're silent on a given issue we're actually giving them free rein to do their own thing. Another potentially confusing pattern is a parent's resorting to silence only to avoid conflict with a teenager, a sort of "preserve-the-peace-at-any-cost" posture. It is at once both an abdication of our responsibilities and a troubling sign to our children of the most insulting stance of all: that we just don't care. The bottom line here is that we must be just as careful in choosing silence as in choosing the words we speak — both are part of the process of communication.

Practical Pointers in Communicating with Your Teen

(1) Don't talk down to your teenager.

(2) Don't pretend that you understand exactly how your teenager feels, because the chances are that you don't.

(3) Don't be afraid to admit you're wrong.

(4) Incessant criticism will only lead to defensive responses, not the changes you'd like to see.

(5) Cool off before you talk. Anger is generally destructive to communications and often leads to saying things one doesn't really mean.

(6) Don't pretend to have all the right answers, or to think that *your* right answer is the *only* solution there is.

(7) Don't try to win arguments with your teenager; instead, try to understand why you're arguing and see how you can transform the argument into an expressive discussion.

(8) Try not to be hypocritical.

(9) Try to see things your teenager's way, but don't let yourself be pressured into agreeing to something you'll regret later on.

(10) Be honest in what you say to your teen, but couch your honesty in a way that won't be destructive to his or her feelings.

(11) Avoid issuing ultimatums and commands except where absolutely necessary; these have a surprising tendency to backfire.

(12) If you won't listen carefully to what your teen has to say, the chances are that he or she won't listen carefully to you.

(13) Avoid overkill. Browbeating your teen just to make a point is a losing proposition.

Setting Limits

Setting consistent, realistic limits for adolescents to follow is one of the trickiest, yet most important, aspects of parenting a teen. In seeking to establish their own sense of autonomy and identity, adolescents are apt to rebel against rules set down by parents, stretching them to the breaking point and beyond. Sometimes there's no rational explanation for this rule breaking except to see the reaction it provokes and to say, "There—that *proves* you can't treat me like a little kid anymore." So parents approaching the task of setting limits for their kids are well advised to avoid posing limits as rules. While there may not seem to be much beyond a semantic distinction here, we believe that the way limits are communicated to teens has a great deal to do with how the limits are eventually handled.

If your limit setting is done in a tone or manner that suggests Moses bringing the Ten Commandments into your living room, you place a direct challenge in your teen's lap. The forbidden becomes enticing and exciting precisely because you've forbidden it. Likewise, if you announce a severe penalty for breaking a rule you've laid down, you may only fuel your teen's determination to flout you. Sometimes the dangerousness of the transgression is exactly what gives the adolescent the sense of satisfaction in trying it on for size.

In contrast, when clear, consistent limits are discussed by parents and teens not as rules but as guidelines, the teen is given a greater sense of responsibility and is more likely to respond by acting more responsibly, too. This doesn't mean that you should be offhand about limit setting — "By the way, Tom, it would make us happy if you came home by four A.M." — but it does suggest that by defining limits in a positive, rather than negative, way, you can prevent a lot of problems.

Here's a specific example to consider. Your fourteen-year-old son has just announced that some friends of his were smoking marihuana at a party last night. He was afraid to try any, but he asks you what you think. Do you respond by saying: "Good thing you didn't smoke that stuff or I'd have killed you if I found out!" or "You know we won't allow any drug use in our family"? Or "That stuff is dangerous to your health; before you know it you're hooked and your whole life is ruined"? These natural responses (which we've heard many times in family therapy situations) are each examples of limit setting that isn't likely to be effective. In contrast, saying something like "It must have been hard for you to say no to your friends. That's a real sign of maturity. I'm certainly glad you could use good judgment about it; you know we don't believe using drugs is very wise" is much more likely to result in a teen's feeling reinforced for doing the right thing *by his or her personal choice, not by parental edict.*

As we all know, it isn't always easy to set limits that our teens will follow. At times, it seems as though adolescents test limits just to get us angry or upset. But there's another side to the story, as many teens will reluctantly admit.

> Don, an eighteen-year-old, brazenly announced to his parents that he was driving to a concert "where everyone was going to get high." Instead of forbidding him to go, or saying that he couldn't drive, Don's parents asked if he wanted them to confis-, cate his car. Much to their surprise, Don said, "Yeah, I'm really afraid that Willy's going to get in a fight when he gets drunk. Are you sure I can't have the car?" When his parents affirmed their decision, Don said, "Thanks — I appreciate that," and went off with a smile to notify his friends.

Many therapists are aware that a good deal of seemingly impulsive, even destructive behavior by teens is actually a call for help to their parents. Some adolescents who get into drugs leave empty bottles and pill vials around their rooms and start using drug jargon in conversations with parents (or on the phone) in an attempt to test limits. The parent who remains blind to this limit testing may wind up with a drug-addicted child, while the parent who takes swift, firm action, as we will discuss in Chapter 8, may find that having clear, definite boundaries in place resolves the issue — the drug experimentation stops.

To be certain, there are times where the goal of limit setting through carefully designed communication must be superseded by survival concerns. Self-destructive behavior cannot be allowed to go on until a solution can be negotiated; parental action is required promptly and decisively. The rigidity of limit setting, the duration of the time over which limits will apply, and the severity of the limits all depend on the nature of the behavior in question. In most situations where self-destructive or malicious behavior is involved, though, additional help will be required to make any meaningful change — parental limit setting won't be enough.

Keeping Your Cool

(1) Yelling is not an effective means of communication even though it may momentarily make you feel better.

(2) If you're furious with your teenagers, it's better to get them out of your sight than to try to talk in the heat of anger. When logic prevails, communicate.

(3) Don't be baited by your teens. When they get foul-mouthed, temperamental, and argumentative, avoid the temptation to respond in kind. This type of behavior often is used to distract parents from their agenda. No one can win in this sort of shouting contest, and by avoiding provocation you can help preserve your own sanity.

(4) If you do lose your temper — as we all do at times — be big enough to apologize to your teens when you calm down. This may help them feel better and sets a good example, too.

The Art of Compromise

Communicating isn't much of a problem when you're in agreement with your teen or when you're both doing something you enjoy. It's when there are differences of opinion, or tasks to be done, or conflicting interests to be handled that difficulties arise. How you handle these problems is in part a reflection of your negotiation skills.

It's certainly simple enough to take the army sergeant's approach: "When I say 'jump,' you ask how high!" The trouble is, while this works for the military, it *won't* work for you. Not only is it unlikely your teen would follow your orders obediently; even if he or she should, doing so would be self-defeating, since you would deprive your child of important lessons to be learned from reaching compromise solutions.

Compromise implies some give on both sides, but it doesn't require giving up. You might feel, for instance, that your sixteen-year-old daughter is too young to spend Easter vacation at Fort Lauderdale, but you'd be willing to let her go with one of her girlfriends to Tampa, where she can get a suntan and practice her water-skiing while staying with Aunt Phyllis and Uncle Steve. Or when your fourteen-year-old son announces that he wants to hitch-hike three hundred miles to his brother's college campus to attend the homecoming football game, a compromise might be reached by getting him to agree to take the train if you foot the bill.

Compromising may also entail negotiations about the specific responsibilities your teen will take on, as shown by this exchange:

TEEN (*age 16*): C'mon, Dad, you know I've saved up enough money to buy that used car. Why can't I get it now?

FATHER: It's not just a matter of having the money to buy the car. There's also the cost of your insurance and the cost of running the car, too. But more importantly, I'm not convinced you're a safe enough driver yet.

TEEN (*sarcastically*): Oh, great. How will I ever get to be a good driver if I only get to drive for an hour a week?

FATHER: Well, I just might have a solution. If you pass the driver's ed course at school next semester, I'll pay half your insurance and let you get your car. Meanwhile, between now and then you can earn the money for your part of the insurance.

TEEN: That's not what I was hoping for . . . but it sounds fair. OK, you've got a deal.

While there are ingenious compromises where everyone can get exactly what he or she desired at the start, to compromise is usually to sacrifice a bit of what you want in return for something. With parent-teen interactions, compromise generally represents a kind of cooperation in which both parties must be flexible. Your own flexibility towards your teen will usually be reflected back to you by your teen's behavior — so remember, when your teen wants something very much, give some consideration to his or her viewpoint if you want to be treated with consideration when there's something important on your mind.

PART TWO

Problem Solving

6

Sex and Other Facts of Life

.

"If you really loved me, you would. That's the way people prove they love each other."

"I swear we won't go all the way. I'll stop whenever you tell me to."

"You're still a virgin? Something must be wrong with you."

The lines teenagers use to entice their partners into sexual relations haven't changed much over the years, but other aspects of adolescent sexuality are considerably different than they used to be. *Fact:* By age fifteen, 23 percent of girls are no longer virgins; by age eighteen, this figure rises to 57 percent. *Fact:* Unintended pregnancies among teenagers occur in epidemic proportions today, totaling an estimated one million pregnancies in 1982. *Fact:* One in three sexually experienced teenagers are so frightened, disappointed, or guilty they can best be described as "unhappy nonvirgins." Clearly, despite the finding that more adolescents are becoming sexually experienced, and at younger ages than ever before, teenage sex is hardly the blissful paradise adults often imagine it to be.

The Teenager, Sex, and Society

American teenagers live in the midst of a cultural double bind when it comes to sexuality. All around them they see evidence that sex is glamorous, fascinating, and fun, as dramatized by Hollywood and best-selling novels, as diligently discussed by countless articles in popular magazines, as portrayed subtly (and not so subtly) by Madison Avenue and the lyrics of their favorite rock songs. If they missed *American Gigolo* or *Endless Love* or *Risky Business* at the movies or on cable T.V., chances are they've seen other cinematic offerings with equally direct sexual themes. They may wake up in the morning to Marvin Gaye singing "Sexual Healing" on the radio, or driving home after school the car radio blares out the Pointer Sisters' number one hit "(I Want a Man with a) Slow Hand." These songs, and others like them, leave little to the imagination and offer an implicit cultural endorsement of sex as a fact of life. The result is, of course, that teenagers are piqued by the mystery and allure of sex. Moreover, these societal messages about sex repeatedly hint at the erotic energies of adolescence as a peak, delectable experience, and celebrate the sexiness of youth in contrast to the flagging sexual prowess of advancing years. The adolescent experimenting with sex is seen as a free spirit, a happy-go-lucky adventurer, while the middle-aged adult doing the same thing is regarded somewhat unsympathetically as trying to recapture an impossible remembrance of things past.

At the same time, while we tell our teenagers that they're no longer kids and have to hurry to prepare themselves for life as adults, we also tell them in no uncertain terms that they should wait to have sex until they're older. They should wait, adults say, because they're not ready yet; they should wait because they're not able to handle the responsibilities; they should wait because it isn't right; they should wait for the right person; they should wait so they won't risk pregnancy or venereal disease. Today, more than ever before, teenagers are skeptical of these adult admonitions to wait, seeing them as a sort of collective hypocrisy aimed at preventing them from having fun, making their own decisions, and acting grown-up. "What's wrong with having sex at sixteen if I'm ready, willing, and able?" one girl asked. "If I'm responsible enough to drive a car, why aren't I responsible enough to have sex?"

The result of this cultural double-bind is that teenagers turn more than ever to their peers for support in making their sexual choices. And the increasingly predictable peer-group message says, "Try it, you'll like it."

Pubertal Passages: Physical Aspects of Sexual Development

Puberty generally starts in early adolescence and takes one and one-half to two years to reach completion. The physical growth and maturation of puberty is triggered by an awakening of a preset "time clock" in a specialized region of the brain called the *hypothalamus*. Gradually, hormones secreted by the hypothalamus activate the acorn-sized pituitary gland, which sits just below the brain, to produce increasing amounts of two other hormones that stimulate the testes or the ovaries. As a result, these organs grow and substantially increase production of their own hormones — most notably, testosterone and estrogen, respectively — which directly control many of the ensuing biological changes of this developmental stage.

In both sexes, puberty results in an acceleration of growth of the long bones of the body, causing the "adolescent growth spurt" that can add to your clothing bills and transform a normally proportioned 5′4″ thirteen-year-old into a gangling 6′1″ fourteen-year-old. The adolescent growth spurt usually occurs earlier in girls (the average age is around thirteen) than in boys (the average is about fourteen and a half), creating many awkward scenes at seventh- or eighth-grade dances, where the girls, especially if they're wearing high heels, may seem to tower over their partners. Both sexes share equally in the appearance of acne as an undesirable side effect of the hormonal juices actively flowing in their systems.

In girls, the most visible change of puberty is breast development, which begins at an average age of twelve and reaches completion at about age sixteen. Menstruation typically does not start until six to twelve months after discernible breast growth has occurred. In the early stages of puberty, girls begin to accumulate a higher percentage of body weight as fat under the skin, and some researchers believe a certain amount of fatty tissue must be present before menstruation will occur. For this reason, adolescent girls who stay very lean because of vigorous exercise (especially activities like long-distance running or hours of training each day in gymnastics or ballet) or who diet fanatically to stay slim may not begin menstruation at all (a situation called *primary amenorrhea*) or may stop having periods completely (*secondary amenorrhea*). Other physical changes in girls during puberty include growth of the uterus and enlargement of the vagina, development of pubic and underarm hair, and the onset of ovulation, marking the beginning of their reproductive capacity.

Puberty in boys is accompanied by growth of the testes and penis, development of pubic and underarm hair, facial hair growth (and later, growth of hair on the chest if genetic makeup so dictates), deepening of the voice, and increased muscle development. Sperm production begins at puberty and boys first experience "wet dreams" (nocturnal ejaculation) during this time. Because some of the male sex hormone, testosterone, that causes these changes is broken down by the body into estrogen, many boys also undergo a temporary enlargement of their breasts that may last for a year or two and that embarrasses them considerably. Although this condition, technically called *gynecomastia*, affects as many as 60 percent of teenage boys at one time or another, and will ultimately resolve itself without any treatment, it can occasionally cause such profound psychological anguish that surgical correction is required.

There is little question that the hormonal surges of puberty play a role in activating sexual feelings during adolescence. Boys begin to get erections much more frequently than they did before; girls develop sensations of vaginal warmth or tingling and also experience vaginal lubrication (wetness), which is a physical sign of sexual arousal. However, as the noted sex researcher John Money explains, "The correct conception of hormonal puberty is that it puts gas in the metaphorical tank and upgrades the model of the vehicle, but it does not build the engine nor program the itinerary of the journey."

The timing of the onset and completion of puberty varies widely. Some boys and girls have completed this process by eleven or twelve, while others don't begin puberty until their fourteenth or fifteenth birthdays. While it's not much fun for a boy to be the class "shrimp" or for a girl to be less well endowed than her girlfriends, this variability is a normal feature of biological events and in most instances is not a harbinger of later physical appearance. The proverbial ninety-pound weakling of the ninth grade may wind up as a muscular varsity linebacker by his senior year; the girl who feels like a shapeless wonder in the tenth grade may wind up voted "sexiest" in her senior class poll. As a general rule of thumb, unless no signs of pubertal development are apparent by age sixteen, medical attention is unnecessary. Things will usually work out smoothly by themselves.

Psychological Aspects of Adolescent Sexual Development

While it's very clear that sexual feelings do not first arise during adolescence — younger children show signs of sexual curiosity and sexual arousal long before the teenage years — adolescence is usually accompanied by a heightened degree of interest in sexual matters. This is not controlled by biological forces only, but reflects the normal psychological development of the adolescent interacting with peer-group and cultural influences.

In contemporary American society it is hard for a teenager to miss the pervasiveness of sexual themes. The allure of sex, as seen by the teenager, comes partly because sex is an element of the adult world (and is therefore a sign of being "grown-up") and partly because it is forbidden and presented as a mysterious, dangerous force. As adolescents struggle with their personal journey towards maturation, most of them regard sex as a proving ground, a challenge, or at least something to learn about to be better equipped to deal with the world of adulthood.

Peer-group pressures typically reinforce these psychosocial factors by pushing teenagers towards becoming sexually experienced, although a few peer groups (some influenced by religious fundamentalism) maintain traditional sexual values and warn girls against the risk of "getting a reputation."

Teenagers give many reasons for participating in sex, including these reported by the researcher Robert Sorenson after conducting a national survey: for physical pleasure, as a means of communication, as a search for a new experience, as an index of maturity, as a challenge to parents, as a challenge to society, as a kind of reward or punishment, as an escape from loneliness, and as an escape from tension. In addition, some adolescents use sex to procure a sense of intimacy or love (just as adults sometimes do), while other teens use sexual behavior to express their rebelliousness.

> *A fifteen-year-old girl:* My mother was always lecturing to me, "Don't do this, don't do that, be a lady." I got so tired of hearing her tell me what to do, it was great to throw it in her face by sleeping with different guys, especially guys she didn't want me to go with.

> *A sixteen-year-old boy:* My parents are both so uptight about sex, they really don't understand where kids are at today. My old man gave me a birds and bees talk last month and after he stammered about it for a while I said, "Relax, man, I've been doing it since I was fourteen." It blew his mind.

Not all teenagers are comfortable with pressures to become sexually experienced, of course. Many adolescents are troubled by concerns about what's normal sexually — is it normal to have sexual fantasies? is it normal to masturbate? is it normal to enjoy oral sex? and so on. Others are anxious about their sexual anatomy (boys' concerns about penis size and girls' about breast size predominate). Some adolescents feel uncomfortable even thinking about sex, let alone participating, because of religious beliefs. And for still others, the biggest obstacles seem to be social in nature — embarrassment, awkwardness, fear of appearing foolish or doing the wrong thing, and so on.

Still, there is little question that today most teenagers feel that it's OK to have sex with someone you care for (not just someone you love) and many sexually inexperienced adolescents worry that something is wrong with them. At the same time, many teenagers who *are* sexually experienced are dissatisfied or disappointed and unsure about how to proceed.

Sex Education: Where, When, How?

If you've waited until your child is a teenager before broaching the facts of life, you've already missed the boat. The most effective sex education occurs as a continuous process from early childhood on, not as a hurried lecture from a parent just before an adolescent's first date.

Assuming you've already had occasional discussions about sex with your child in a manner appropriate to her or his age — covering such information as sexual anatomy, facts about reproduction, and sexual behavior — what do you do next? This checklist may give you some ideas about topics to discuss with your teen.

(1) Be certain both girls and boys understand menstruation.

(2) Talk about masturbation — teenagers are often surprisingly worried about this topic and harbor many myths about the imagined "dangers" of this relatively universal act.

(3) Discuss the interpersonal aspects of sexual relationships, stressing the need for responsible, nonexploitive conduct when it comes to sex. This means that both sexes must understand that forcing someone into sexual activity or deceiving them about sex is both morally wrong and a sign of personal immaturity. Likewise, irresponsible sexual activity such as having sex with someone when you know (or suspect) that you have a sexual infection is just as exploitive as the use of force.

(4) Include some mention of sexual feelings — where they come from, what responses they produce in the body, and how variable they can be.

(5) Talk matter-of-factly about specific types of sexual activity, including kissing, necking and petting, and sexual intercourse, being sure to give your teenager a chance to ask questions as you go along. This is a good time to also explain that intercourse is not the only way of attaining sexual pleasure or reaching orgasm. Note that it's best to avoid using the term *foreplay* in your discussions with teens, since it implies that intercourse is the logical pinnacle of sexual activity and that anything else is simply preliminary to the main event.

(6) Be certain that both boys and girls are aware of available contraceptive options, including abstinence as a method of preventing pregnancy. Being sure that your teenagers are well informed is *not* tantamount to giving them permission to experiment: in fact, informed adolescents are *less* likely to rush prematurely into sex than their uninformed friends may be.

(7) Discuss the recognition and prevention of sexually transmitted diseases (see Chapter 7 for specific information). Playing ostrich on this topic is inexcusable in light of the currently high rates of such infections among teens.

(8) Educate daughters about protecting themselves from rape and be sure sons understand that using force or intimidation in sexual situations is not only cruel but criminal. Both sexes should realize that rape is an act of violence, not a sexual act.

(9) Inform your teenager that (a) everything printed about sex is not accurate; (b) sex in movies and novels is often unrealistic and exaggerated compared to real life; and (c) "having sex" is not necessarily a sign of maturity or the road to immediate bliss.

(10) Most important, be sure to let your adolescents know that you're willing to discuss sexual matters in an open, straightforward manner — and that if you don't have the answer to a question they ask, you'll either find it or refer them to someone who can answer it.

If you've *never* discussed sex with your teenager, don't try to cover the entire subject in one sitting and don't deal with your dilemma by simply leaving a book around the house where he or she will be sure to find it. If you feel embarrassed discussing sex, or if you think that your teenager knows more than you do, think again — your teen is likely to be more uptight than you and far less accurately informed than you imagine. Discuss things as openly as you can, admitting to your uneasiness if you have any, because only in this way will you really be able to help your adolescent absorb factual information about sex in the context of your own personal values. You might explain, "I never had this sort of talk with my parents when I was a kid, and I haven't rehearsed what to say. So you may notice that I'm a little nervous. But I'm not nervous because I think sex is wrong or dirty but because it's important to me that you understand what I'm trying to say." On the other hand, if you are hopelessly paralyzed every time you try to muster up the courage to discuss sex with your teen, and your spouse can't help you out, the next best thing is to call for help from a family doctor, a trusted teacher, a guidance counselor, a member of the clergy, or a relative your teen respects. Whatever approach is best for you, don't assume that sex education is unnecessary in this day and age, because making informed, responsible sexual decisions requires that adolescents are not just guessing in the dark.

Patterns of Adolescent Sexual Behavior

There is little question that a sexual revolution has occured in the last twenty years and that teenagers have been in the vanguard of this trend. Traditional values of love, sex and marriage have been largely replaced by a "new morality"; peer-group pressures to become sexually experienced are intense; and the wide availability of contraceptives and abortions has conferred a relative sense of freedom on adolescents in making their sexual decisions. Despite these changes, many teenagers are unsure of themselves in sexual matters or are troubled by inner conflicts about sex. To understand what is happening here, and why it's happening, a few statistics may be in order.

— Today, almost as many teenage girls have experimented with masturbation as have teenage boys: the numbers are approximately 75 and 85 percent, respectively. In contrast, in the era of the Kinsey studies, published in 1948 and 1953, boys outnumbered girls by about 4 to 1 in ever having masturbated.

— "Necking" and "petting" — sexual touching that stops short of intercourse — was reported to have occurred in more than 80 percent of teenagers by age eighteen, according to Kinsey and his colleagues. Today, this remains a principal sexual outlet for about one third of teenagers, but many others have abandoned petting as "too timid" or "just fooling around" and instead go on to intercourse.

— While Kinsey reported in 1953 that only 5 percent of sixteen-year-old girls and 14 percent of eighteen-year-old girls were no longer virgins, the most recent research shows that at age sixteen, 38 percent of American girls are experienced with intercourse, and by age eighteen, this figure rises to 57 percent. In fact, in the 1970s alone the rate of nonvirginity among teenage girls rose by some 50 percent.

As these statistics show, more teenagers are becoming sexually active, and at younger ages, than ever before in our society. However, to guard against developing a view of all teenagers as consumed by voracious, insatiable sexual appetites, a few other observations may be helpful too. First, many adolescents who are no longer virgins have intercourse quite infrequently. (In a recent survey we conducted, more than one-third of the sexually experienced teenagers had intercourse less than once a month.) Second, the lower age of first sexual intercourse really isn't a sign of teenage promiscuity, because most adolescents have sex exclusively with one partner over a period of time rather than "sleeping around." Third, some teenagers — particularly those who tried intercourse out of curiosity, as a form of experimentation — find that once the initial mystery is gone, and they have proved to themselves they can "do it," the actual experience is far less intriguing. Thus, they go for long periods of time without having sexual intercourse, perhaps waiting to meet the right person.

While teenagers are more accepting of premarital sex than ever before, and act accordingly, some flies remain in the proverbial ointment. For example, of those with experience in sexual intercourse, about one third of both sexes can be called "unhappy nonvirgins" for one or more of the following reasons: (1) sex didn't measure up to their expectations; (2) sexual problems prevent them from enjoying themselves and may actually lead to severe anxieties; (3) sex becomes a matter of contention and manipulation within a relationship ("You're not interested in *me*, you're just interested in my body"); (4) pregnancy scares (or an actual pregnancy) or worries about a sexually transmitted disease override the pleasure derived from sex; and (5) guilt rears its head. Even in an era of

liberated feelings about sex, guilt or anxiety·about all forms of sexual behavior lingers. In fact, about half of all teenagers report negative feelings
about masturbation at least some of the time.

Despite the sexual revolution, not every teen has been conscripted.
Many adolescents are still sexually inexperienced, even sexually naive,
either by deliberate choice or by virtue of not having a willing partner.
These teenagers are not abnormal in any sense — although they may *feel*
that they are — and are not necessarily doomed to a life of sexual in-
adequacy or unhappiness because they're "slower" than other kids their
age.

Love and Infatuation

The columnist Ann Landers says that teenage love is really just
"two sets of glands calling to each other." A psychiatrist, Warren Gad-
paille, on the other hand, states that "love during adolescence can be real
and intense." Which view is more accurate? Is teenage love usually just a
convenient excuse for a sexual relationship? Is teenage romance mainly
just a dress rehearsal for the "real thing" to be found in adulthood? Or is
it possible that love during adolescence can be as authentic as love experienced and expressed by adults?

To answer these questions, we must begin by acknowledging that
adult person-to-person love takes many different forms. All adult love relationships are not reciprocal, stable, or even lasting. In fact, love in
adulthood can sometimes show more dependency and hysteria than maturity or resilience. These same observations apply to teenage love. Not
all adolescent love relationships are apt to qualify as "authentic" love.
Some are more of a social charade than a vehicle for genuine feelings.
Other teenagers experience an impassioned, soul-stirring version of love
that changes their lives and brings them quite a bit closer to adulthood
and maturity.

How can you, as a parent, tell the difference? How can you help your
teenager distinguish between these different forms of love? The answer,
unfortunately, is that it's a difficult task that can often be done only in
retrospect, not while the flames of love are burning. The reason is that
love can't really be defined in very precise terms. The best definition
we've seen comes from Robert Heinlein, a science fiction writer, who
says, "Love is that condition in which the happiness of another person is
essential to your own." But two psychologists, Elaine and William Wal-
ster, note, "The only real difference between liking and loving is the
depth of our feeling and the degree of our involvement with the other
person." Keeping in mind these inherent difficulties, the following questions may nevertheless be of some help.

(1) Do the lovers show genuine caring and respect for each other, or is their relationship constantly marked by selfish demands, manipulative pouting, and stormy confrontations?

(2) Does your teenager integrate the love relationship into the rest of his or her life, or do all other activities become subordinate? If your adolescent drops hobbies, stops studying, and in general seems totally preoccupied with a romantic attachment, it's not a very healthy situation.

(3) Does your teenager-in-love avoid all of his or her friends in order to spend time only with the loved one? If so, the "love" may be more stultifying and possessive than growth-enhancing.

(4) Is your teenager enjoying a love relationship based in present realities or is it more a figment of dreams and fantasies? While all lovers may be indulgent in their thinking, a fantasy love is ephemeral indeed.

(5) Does the love enhance your teenager's view of himself or herself, giving a sense of self-confidence and value? Or does the love lead to a constant sense of unworthiness or failure?

(6) Does your romantic adolescent seem to have little or no objectivity towards the loved one's flaws? If so, don't despair — after all, Chaucer wrote that "love is blind," and this blindness is a relatively universal phase of love. Over time, reality will surface spontaneously, so don't try to fight it — it's a losing battle that will only make your teenager think you're biased and unfriendly.

(7) Can you remember how you felt when you were hopelessly in love? Doing so may help you grasp the intensity, the sensitivity, and the emotional high your teenager is experiencing.

What about distinguishing between love and infatuation? While infatuation is a superficial, short-lived emotional state based more on wishful thinking than on reality, in truth, infatuation often looks very much like love while it's happening. Although infatuation is really a counterfeit version of love, you won't be able to convince your teenager of this fact while he or she is caught in its hypnotic tugs, so it isn't worth trying. Here, too, the passage of time will inject a strong dose of reality as an effective antidote, while your entreaties will be blithely ignored.

Though parents may think differently, most teenagers don't view sex as the most important part of romance. According to a 1979 survey conducted by the psychologist Aaron Hass, less than one-third of teenagers felt that sex was a "very important" part of a romantic relationship. In the same survey, approximately 80 percent of fifteen- to eighteen-year-olds said that they had been in love at least once. Hass commented, "We need to avoid getting caught in a rut of lightly dismissing teenage emotions because of their youthful source. Denying that teenagers can be in love with someone may also be an attempt to avoid a realization that he or she is growing up and becoming less focused and dependent on parental relationships as a source of gratification."

Specific Strategies for Positive Parenting

(1) *Take an active role in teaching your adolescents about sex.* This cardinal rule, which applies to fathers as well as mothers, is the cornerstone of prevention. Teenagers consistently say that they want to be able to talk with their parents about sex but feel they can't or shouldn't. The only way to change this is to initiate such discussions yourself. *Teenagers whose parents discuss sex with them openly and often are more likely to wait to have intercourse until they're more prepared for it and are also more likely to use contraception when they first have intercourse.*

(2) *Give your child permission to say no.* Giving permission is different from giving an order. Kids may rebel against being told, "You shouldn't have sex," but they're more likely to feel good about saying no if they understand why it may be a wise option. One way of approaching this subject is discussing the lines teens use to talk a partner into having sex. For instance, you might tell your adolescent, "If someone tells you, 'You would if you really loved me,' you can be sure that's only a line — real love is never proved by having sex." Doing this can lead to a more general dialogue about when and how to say no that can help teens rehearse responses that may be comfortable to use later on.

(3) *Avoid scare tactics and prudishness in your advice.* Frightening stories about venereal disease or "what-if-you-get-pregnant?" threats are not the way to win your adolescent's trust or confidence in your good judgment. Promulgating a code of sexual conduct more applicable to Victorian England than modern society either will push your teen into rebellious action in just the opposite direction to the abstinence you'd like to see *or* will lead to his or her becoming a sexually repressed adult. Instead, be flexible and realistic in what you have to say — and if your own inhibitions show, acknowledge them.

(4) *Help teens understand that sex is not just a matter of genital union.* Many teenagers and adults acknowledge that holding, cuddling, caressing, kissing, and other forms of sexual interaction are more sensual and exciting than having intercourse. To see sex and intercourse as synonymous is to take a narrow, restricting view of what sex actually encompasses. While total sexual abstinence is unrealistic (and probably unnatural) for most teens, choosing from among sexual options that do not involve intercourse provides teens with alternatives that don't force them into all-or-none choices about their sexual behavior.

(5) *Don't pry into your adolescent's sex life — respect your teenager's privacy.* This doesn't mean you've got to allow your fourteen-year-old daughter to entertain her boyfriend in her bedroom behind locked doors, but it does mean that your adolescent's personal privacy should be respected. Don't demand to know what happened sexually at every date, don't push for "true confessions" — instead, let your teenager know that if he or she is being sexually active, or is *thinking* of becoming so in the

future, precautionary steps towards responsible sexual behavior are in order.

(6) *Let your teens know that they can come to you to discuss any type of sexual problem they're facing or any sexual concerns they might have.* Not only will this allow your adolescents to ask questions, which is healthy in itself, it will also make it easier for them to come to you about disturbing events such as being propositioned by a teacher, being molested, or being upset by something they've read or seen.

(7) *Try not to overreact to questions about sex.* If your teenager asks what it's like to be pregnant, don't assume she already is. Answer questions factually and add something about your feelings or personal values, too, but don't cut off conversation by becoming accusatory or leaping to conclusions that may be totally false. Similarly, if you don't know an answer, don't fake it — find out.

7

Dilemmas of Adolescent Sexuality

We have already seen that adolescents today are subjected to considerable pressure to become sexually experienced. Rising to the occasion with a predictable degree of self-control, eight in ten males and seven in ten females report having had intercourse while in their teens. Despite this relative ubiquity of adolescent sexual activity, teenagers often view sex as something of a problem — at times, a problem of monumental proportions. In this chapter, we will examine the various facets of adolescent sexuality that are most likely to be problematic and offer suggestions for parents whose children may be struggling to confront and find solutions to these issues.

Whose Life Is It, Anyway?

A dose of realism is necessary whenever parents wonder what their adolescents are thinking and doing about sex today. The chances are that your teenager isn't a 1950s-style virgin, to whom French kissing and fondling "above the waist" on a first date would be shockingly intimate, or a character from *Fast Times at Ridgemont High* to whom orgies and oral sex are already passé. Instead, there is much more likelihood that your teenager, like most adolescents, is fascinated by sex, or even preoccupied with sex, but somewhat uncertain or even frightened when it comes to making personal sexual choices. As a result, teenage sexual behavior often occurs impulsively and by default rather than deliberately and by logic.

Nevertheless, it would be just as foolish for parents to try to orches-trate the sexual behavior of their teens as it would be to allow teenagers to direct the family budget. While this statement doesn't mean that parents shouldn't ever offer advice or set rules about teenage sexual behavior, it does suggest that a certain degree of adolescent autonomy in sexual matters is a requisite, and realistic, necessity for healthy maturation. In other words, teenagers need to be given room to make their own sexual decisions because doing so is a necessary part of growing up. The adolescent who completely avoids these decisions risks a developmental gap that may later cause adult sexual difficulties, since the sexual learning that ordinarily occurs during the teen years is a pivotal component of subsequent sexual identity.

All of this is to say simply that while parents might be more comfortable if their teenagers were perpetually sexually abstinent, such control would most likely produce a whole generation of sexually stunted, psychosocially handicapped young adults. Thus, the most cogent piece of advice we can offer parents about sex and teenagers is to acknowledge the teens' right to develop their own sexual thinking and to translate it into sexual decisions within a framework of responsibility and knowledge.

The Contraceptive Question

According to studies at Johns Hopkins University, more than half of sexually active teenage females aged fifteen to nineteen didn't have any contraceptive protection the first time they had intercourse, and more than a quarter of these females *never* used birth control. In fact, only a third of sexually active, unmarried teenage females use contraception regularly. It's no wonder that the Alan Guttmacher Institute in New York predicts that four out of ten girls who are now fourteen years old will become pregnant in their teens.

Given such odds, it might seem sensible for parents to distribute birth control pills to their teenage daughters and condoms to their teenage sons at breakfast each day. But such an Orwellian answer is hardly practical or appealing to parents, not to mention the teenagers themselves.

How do you proceed with your teenager? As we mentioned in the last chapter, educating your adolescents (girls *and* boys) about reproduction and contraception is the logical starting point, but by itself it won't work if it is just an abstract, theoretical discussion. Your teens should know that if they've even vaguely entertained the notion of being sexually active (even just once, to "see what it's like"), they should have an available means of birth control *in their possession* for use at the appropriate time.

Will this encourage them to have sex when they're not ready for it? Possibly — but on much safer terms than might otherwise occur. Will your teenager see this as your tacit consent to their sexual experimentation? No more so than they would see you providing a seat belt for their car as a signal of approval of drunk driving or being in an accident. Teenagers understand safety and precautions as distinctly different from danger; you should be able to see this distinction too.

It is hypocritical for parents to tell their teenagers to be responsible about their sexual activity but to treat possession of a contraceptive device as an illicit act. You don't have to rush your twelve-year-old daughter to the gynecologist to be fitted for a diaphragm, but you should be realistic enough — or informed enough — to know if your teen is "seriously dating" or is otherwise close to being sexually active and to act accordingly. Dire threats won't work here — you only fool yourself (although you may manage to frighten your teen in the bargain). You must come to grips with the reality of the situation, and we suggest that this is best done by helping your teen make an intelligent choice of birth control method.

What is there to choose from? Abstinence is the perfect contraceptive, but as we have already seen, it seems to have limited appeal to adolescents today. Like any other contraceptive method, if it's not used, it won't work. While it can be beneficial to your teen to be reminded that it's perfectly permissible to say no, the option of total abstinence is unlikely to be a viable one over the span of the adolescent years. The real choice — that is, the realistic choice — must then be among other available contraceptive methods.

There is very little doubt that the pill is the most reliable reversible method of birth control available today. While the pill requires a prescription and has a number of undesirable side effects, the most serious health risks of its use (dangerous blood clots, heart attacks) are exceedingly rare in adolescents and, on balance, the safety of the pill is substantial when viewed in the context of the health risks of teenage pregnancy. The pill is not a good choice, however, for a teenage girl who is not yet sexually active or who has only very sporadic sexual activity. This is partly a matter of overkill, and partly a reflection of the fact that many physicians believe it is not wise to have an adolescent take the pill continuously for a long period of time (say, three years or more) without a "rest period" to let the reproductive system function on its own without the suppressing effect of the hormones in the pill.

Intrauterine devices — IUDs — rank just below the pill in terms of reliability, but they are not generally a good choice for teenage females. For one thing, insertion of an IUD is apt to be quite uncomfortable in adolescents; in addition, IUDs cause more problems (higher risks of bleeding, cramping, infection, and so forth); and finally, IUDs are expelled (that is, pop out of position) at an alarmingly high rate in adolescents. As a practical matter, other choices will usually be better.

The use of a vaginal spermicide — a foam or cream or suppository containing a chemical that kills sperm — is a particularly suitable and convenient contraceptive method for teenagers. These products do not require a prescription and have no significant side effects (minor annoyances, such as local allergic reactions or genital burning may occur but are short-lived). What's more, they can be conveniently (and discretely) carried in a purse or glove compartment so that they are available when needed, and their use does not require any particular expertise. While they are not perfect in their contraceptive efficacy, with a failure rate of approximately 15 to 20 percent, they have the additional advantage of providing the female at least partial protection against gonorrhea.

The diaphragm, now enjoying something of a resurgence as a contraceptive choice among college-age females, is about equal in effectiveness to the spermicides mentioned above. In fact, a diaphragm must always be used in combination with a spermicidal jelly in order to work properly. It has no side effects, but some females find positioning the diaphragm in the vagina to be either unpleasant or difficult. Another more troublesome problem is that the diaphragm can slip out of position during sexual intercourse so that it doesn't provide the full barrier effect that it's meant to. Finally, a lot of teenage females who've been fitted for a diaphragm have gotten pregnant when they found themselves unexpectedly in a sexual situation ... and their diaphragm was in a bureau drawer at home.

A much-ignored, but very useful, method of birth control is the condom, subject of innumerable adolescent jokes. The fact is, however, that condoms are particularly useful for several different reasons. First, they are both convenient and safe. Second, they provide both partners with a substantial degree of protection against sexually transmitted diseases. Third, they can easily be used in combination with another method (such as foam), providing an effectiveness essentially comparable to that of the pill. (Used alone, consistently, the condom has a failure rate of 10 percent.) Finally, they involve the male adolescent in both responsibility for and awareness of contraceptive needs — something that researchers agree is a major step towards the reduction of unwanted teenage pregnancies.

The rhythm method and its various offshoots have no place at all as contraceptive methods for adolescents except for those whose religious beliefs dictate against the use of any other approach. The reason is a simple one — the failure rate of the rhythm method is unacceptably high, especially in adolescents. Likewise, douching is another extraordinarily poor method of birth control, with failure rates of 40 percent or more, and withdrawal (also known as *coitus interruptus*) is even less effective.

If your teenage daughter "forgets" to use a contraceptive or otherwise is inadequately protected during sexual intercourse, one other option should be mentioned, although this is not suitable for frequent use. The so-called morning-after pill, which can be begun up to seventy-two hours after unprotected intercourse, will prevent pregnancy in more than 98 percent of cases. The disadvantages of this treatment are that it frequently causes nausea and vomiting and alterations in the menstrual cycle, and its safety is not yet fully established. However, in special situations (such as rape or leakage of a condom) as well as in those "I forgot" cases, the availability of this option can be quite reassuring.

Sources of Sexual Turmoil

Previously, American teenagers struggled with sexual issues primarily in terms of a participatory question: Do I or don't I? Today, the complexities of adolescent sexuality seem to be far beyond such a simple formulation, leading to an exaggerated hodgepodge of conflicts and stresses affecting the lives of many teens on a day-to-day basis. Here are some examples of the commonest sources of sexual turmoil teenagers have to contend with at the present time.

Although most adolescents have become comfortable in disgarding traditional sexual values to the point that they condone premarital sex in the context of affection, if not outright casual or recreational sex, there is much ambiguity in the etiquette of initiatory sexual behavior. This is because sex role definitions have become far less clear than they were a few decades back, when it was a case of boys trying to "get all they could" from their female partners, while girls were trying to toe the fine line between being sexy and affectionate and being "loose" and "cheap." Today, many teenage males say that it's perfectly all right for their female partner to initiate or push for sexual activity, while another sizable number is obviously scared, or at least subdued, by this reversal in traditional roles. Similarly, while some teenage girls continue to be comfortable in the coy or innocent role of earlier generations, many adolescent females are becoming more sexually assertive in ways perceived by their male partners as pressuring or pushy. The following remarks from teenage boys are self-explanatory:

"I wasn't really ready for a sexual relationship but she kept telling me I didn't know what I was missing and I must not really love her."

"Every time we had sex it was like she was the local movie critic, giving my performance a rating of 1 to 10. What right did she have to do that?"

"I really got turned off to sex when she'd want to make it
when I just wasn't in the mood."

On the other hand, today's more liberated female adolescents are more
likely to expect to be full-fledged partners in sexual relationships than in
the past. As a result, they are apt to say what's on their minds (both in
terms of what they want and when they want it) and act accordingly.
And they are often likely to look upon the macho male as an anachronis-
tic relic while seeing the more androgynous contemporary teenage male
model as more flexible, more attractive, and even more sexually desirable.

This blurring of sex roles is expressed in other forms as well. For example, today's teenage females are far more likely to discuss their sex
lives — and their sex partners — among themselves than at any prior
time. As a result, teenage males find themselves the topic of discomfiting
locker-room talk in an ironic reversal of past practices, and they don't
like the feeling. While boys have discussed the comparative breast sizes
of their girlfriends or dates with great glee, when the tables are turned
and girls discuss how well hung their dates are, the boys recoil from embarrassment. It is also embarrassing to many teenage boys to find that
their partners are considerably more knowledgeable about sex than they
are, since the notion persists that the male should be the sexual expert.

Another source of sexual distress arises for teenagers whose parents
heartily endorse the notion of adolescent sexuality as a healthy part of
growing up and who consequently push their teenager towards becoming sexually experienced. In some instances, this action can result in a
reversal of typical parent-teen positions vis-à-vis sexual behavior: the
parent says, "Do it, it's good for you," while the teenager says, "I don't
think I'm ready yet." In other cases, well-meaning but shortsighted parents may put undue pressure on their teenagers to discuss their sexual experiences with them, losing sight of the teen's need for privacy in this
intensely personal area of life. The adolescent in a single-parent family
may be particularly likely to face this scenario, since the parent may feel
a compulsion to talk about his or her current social and sexual relations
and may encourage the teen to do so as a form of justification for the parental behavior.

Some teenagers are deeply troubled by sexual myths and random bits
of misinformation. The sixteen-year-old boy who thinks nocturnal emis-
sions are a sign of impending malignancy, the fourteen-year-old girl who
is afraid French kissing can lead to pregnancy, and the seventeen-year-
old girl who is convinced her masturbatory pleasure will doom her to a
life of frigidity with men are all victims of the same basic process. As we
discussed in an earlier chapter, assuming that because today's adolescents are more active sexually they are also more knowledgeable is like

believing that because teenagers eat out more often than they used to they know more about nutrition or fine cuisine.

Sexual turmoil can come from a number of other directions, not all of which represent new or different situations from those that have gone on in the past. Just ask any girl who has been several weeks late getting her period after having intercourse without contraception (or her partner, if she's told him) and you get a quick idea of what turmoil can be like. On the other hand, this is not likely to be as psychologically shocking an experience as being raped or being the victim of incest, which can produce lifelong aftereffects. While the latter types of victimization may be shocking and give you the sense that it can't happen to *your* child, the unfortunate facts are that rape and incest occur frequently and cut across class lines, occurring in all segments of society. Seemingly less serious forms of sexual victimization may actually be even more insidious: being intimidated into sexual acts by a date or friend (which may or may not be a form of rape, depending on the actual events involved) can not only be traumatic and degrading but can also give the victim a sense of personal failure in several different respects — believing they should have seen it coming, believing they should have resisted more forcefully or emphatically (and that their failure to do so makes them a "willing" participant to at least a certain extent), and believing that they must keep quiet about what happened so as not to look foolish or hurt their partner. *In all of these situations where sexual victimization has occurred, it is mandatory to provide your teenager with professional counseling to assess the harm that's been done and to implement measures to prevent long-range sequelae. DO NOT ACCEPT YOUR TEEN'S DENIAL OF ANY NEED FOR COUNSELING OR ANY PSYCHOLOGICAL DISTRESS, AND DO NOT DELAY IN GETTING SUCH ATTENTION QUICKLY.*

Several other areas also may cause anxiety about sex for adolescents. Teenagers are likely to be both preoccupied and fascinated by the body changes that accompany their pubertal development, and they frequently have problems when comparing their own sexual apparatus with imagined norms. Even if they have reached a relatively comfortable degree of acceptance of their own physique, they may be anxious about how a sexual partner will react to them, worrying not only about matters of size but also about mundane aspects like sweat, body odors, acne, body hair, and other aspects of physical closeness. Another cause of concern for many teenagers is that of sexual fantasies. Adolescents typically have creative imaginations and the sex fantasies they experience range across a broad number of partners and scenarios. A teenager may be quite frightened to find that his of her erotic fantasies feature a best friend of the same sex, a well-liked schoolteacher, or even a parent as a sex partner. Similarly, teens may be frightened by being aroused by fantasied scenes of "kinky" or violent acts, not realizing that these imaginary excursions can be outlets for pent-up psychic tension. Parents can offer re-assurance that such fantasies are *not* determinants of actual behavior, just as having a fantasy of robbing a bank doesn't indicate that a criminal life is just around the corner.

Many adolescents seem to have an approach-avoidance conflict over sex. While they'd love to have the sense of fun and excitement that being sexually active would bring, they have a host of different worries. This representative sampling will give you an idea of some other types of concerns teenagers voice today:

> "I can't find anybody that I care enough about to have sex with."

> "I just can't be sure I won't get herpes from someone else, and who wants to take that risk?"

> "My last boyfriend was going around with other girls behind my back even though he told me I was his only love — now I feel used and sad."

> "I'd be embarrassed beyond belief if he wanted to kiss me down below."

> "I keep wondering if I'm as good a lover as her last boy-friend."

> "I don't really have any interest in sex — it just leaves me cold, and that worries me a lot."

> "I don't think my girlfriend has ever had an orgasm, which probably means I'm doing something wrong."

> "My biology teacher rubbed his hand under my sweater and tried to get me to have sex with him in return for an 'A' and I don't know if anyone will believe me if I tell them."

> "I can't wait until I get to college because then I'll have my own room without parents around so my boyfriend and me can take our time instead of always rushing."

If your teen is having problems dealing with sexuality, qualified pro-fessionals are available to help. Sex counselors and sex therapists can provide reassurance, factual information, and straightforward sugges-tions for overcoming sexual difficulties of many kinds. In general, these are not problems it's wise for parents to try to solve for their teens, but short-term sex counseling — often involving only a few sessions — is quite effective.

What You and Your Teen Should Know about Sexually Transmitted Diseases

Infections that are spread by sexual contact are now known as STDs — sexually transmitted diseases — rather than by the old term, venereal diseases. And while you might be tempted to skip this section because of its "distasteful" subject matter, it would be a big mistake to do so. STDs are running rampant in America today, especially among the teenage population, and unless you have the necessary facts at your fingertips, you may not be able to offer your adolescent appropriate advice or guidance on this touchy subject.

Public health statistics in 1984 estimate that there are two million new cases of gonorrhea annually in the U.S., along with 500,000 new cases of genital herpes, 2.5 million cases of nonspecific urethritis, and 80,000 new cases of syphilis. More than half of the people affected are between the ages of fifteen and twenty-four, and most, if not all, of these diseases are preventable. Moreover, since STDs are not always spread by sexual intercourse (most can be spread by oral sex, petting, or even kissing), even if your son or daughter is still a virgin they're still at risk for contracting one of these unpleasant infections. Thus, the intent of this section is to provide a brief rundown on the salient facts you need to know.

Gonorrhea is relatively easy to detect in males, in whom it typically causes a puslike discharge from the tip of the penis and painful, frequent urination. However, fewer than half of females with gonorrhea have any symptoms, and when symptoms occur (vaginal discharge, burning or pain with urination, or abnormal patterns of menstruation) they are sometimes quite mild. This is particularly troublesome because untreated gonorrhea in females can cause serious complications, including permanent sterility. Gonorrhea is diagnosed by a culture (a test done by a physician or nurse using a cotton swab) that tries to grow gonorrhea bacteria in a laboratory. Treatment is a large dose of penicillin G, which is almost 100 percent effective.

Syphilis, which affects males more than females, is fortunately relatively uncommon today. The earliest sign of syphilis is a painless sore (chancre) that typically appears on the genitals or near the anus but can sometimes occur in other areas such as on a finger, on the lips, or in the mouth. The chancre usually begins as a reddish pimple that ulcerates and forms a round sore surrounded by a pink rim. Untreated, the sore heals in about four to six weeks, giving the false impression that the problem has gone away. Next, the infection passes to a stage called secondary syphilis, which can start up to six months after the chancre heals. Common symptoms in this stage include a pale red rash on the palms and soles, sore throat, fever, and aching joints. If the disease is still untreated, a latent stage occurs where the infection invades tissues such as the spinal cord and brain; in the most devastating stage of late syphilis, serious heart problems, eye problems, and brain damage can occur. Syphilis is usually diagnosed by blood tests (although it can also be detected by examining fluid from a chancre under a special kind of microscope) and is effectively treated with penicillin.

Genital herpes is an infection caused by a virus (herpes simplex virus, type 1 or 2) and is marked by clusters of small painful blisters on the genitals. The first episode, which is usually most severe, is typically accompanied by fever, headache, painful urination, and tenderness in the groin. The blisters burst within four to six days and form reddish wet sores or ulcers, which heal within another week or two. However, when healing occurs the herpes virus actually burrows into nerves near the base of the spinal cord, where it remains in an inactive state. Repeat attacks of genital herpes occur — sometimes only once or twice, but sometimes dozens of times — and are annoying not only because of physical discomfort but because they are a time of contagiousness, too. Genital herpes is particularly problematic in females for two reasons. First, it can be unwittingly transmitted to a newborn baby during delivery, causing death or serious damage to the baby's brain in many cases. Second, genital herpes appears to be linked to subsequent development of cancer of the cervix in some women. Genital herpes can be diagnosed by blood tests (to detect antibodies) or cultures (to detect the virus); unfortunately, however, there is no known cure at the present time.

Nonspecific urethritis (NSU) is an inflammation of the male urethra caused by an infection other than gonorrhea (most commonly, a bacteria called *Chlamydia trachomatis* is the culprit). The symptoms are basically similar to gonorrhea (discharge from the penis, painful urination) but usually are somewhat milder. Although this STD is easily treated with tetracycline or a number of other antibiotics, it is commonly transmitted to infected males' sex partners, in whom it can lead to sterility.

There are a number of other STDs that can affect adolescents, including pubic lice ("crabs"), which are tiny parasites that attach themselves to pubic hair and cause intense itching; hepatitis B (occurring commonly in homosexual males); and trichomonas vaginitis, a vaginal infection caused by a one-celled parasite that produces a frothy vaginal discharge, an unpleasant odor, and itchiness around the genitals. A detailed discussion of these and other less common types of STDs is beyond the scope of this book; instead, we would like to address the things that can be done by teenagers (or anyone else) to foster prevention of STDs. *We urge all parents to discuss these issues openly with their adolescents or to be sure adolescents have an opportunity to learn about these issues either from a sex education course or a health care practitioner.*

(1) *Prevention starts with having proper information.* Knowledge of the symptoms of STDs may keep a teen from exposing him- or herself to

an infected partner and can aid in deciding when to seek treatment. Ignorance is NOT bliss; it's asking for trouble.

(2) *Being cautious in sexual relations can help minimize the risk of infection with an STD.* Caution in this case can be looked at in several different ways. First, being selective in choosing one's sex partners is a key step in prevention. Studies repeatedly show that having lots of sex partners increases the risk of STD. Second, using contraceptive methods that lower the chances of getting an STD (condoms and vaginal creams, foams, or jellies) is another big step in the right direction. Third, if there is any doubt about whether a teen does or doesn't have an STD, he or she should be cautious by abstaining from sex and getting medical advice. Finally, caution requires realizing that none of the preceding steps can guarantee that one won't get an STD.

(3) *Seeing is believing.* Looking (at both oneself and one's partner) is the best way of finding out if there is any sign of sexual infection. Explain to your teens that they don't need to announce what they're doing or use a magnifying glass, but if they see a genital rash, discharge, or sore they should immediately stop what they're doing and make arrangements to get a medical exam.

(4) *Honesty is always the best policy.* Teens need to know that if they have (or think they have) an STD, it's important to tell their sexual partners. While many teens may understandably be worried about their partner's feelings or their own personal embarrassment at learning the news, the dangers of these infections (and the possibility of their continuing spread if left untreated) far outweigh these relatively minor social inconveniences.

(5) *Get tested, treated, and rechecked as promptly as possible.* Quick diagnosis and treatment reduces the risk of serious complications of an STD, but anyone who's had such an infection should be sure to check back for further testing after the initial treatment because in a few cases, treatment doesn't work completely. In addition, there is sometimes a "Ping-Pong" effect between partners where one person gives the infection to the other, then gets treated, and unknowingly catches the infection back from the untreated partner. For this reason, it is usually advisable for a teenager being treated for an STD to urge that his or her sex partner also be tested.

Straight Facts for Parents about Homosexuality

Few topics are as apt to produce a gut-wrenching response in parents as the possibility that one of their children may be homosexual. The typical reactions that one hears — "Where did we go wrong?" "It can't be true . . . it's just a passing phase," or "Let's get to a doctor to see if it can't be fixed" — are those of despair, guilt, and anger combined. Despite our cultural biases towards homosexuality which tend to view it in stereotyped terms (effeminate hairdressers, "butch" females, maladjusted psyches), the fact is that approximately 10 percent of American males and 3 percent of American females are homosexual, and most of these people don't fit the stereotypes at all. Indeed, many of these individuals realize they're gay sometime during adolescence, although they may try hard to keep this feeling hidden from their families out of shame or fear of rejection. And until parents come to recognize that homosexuality is not an illness, but is simply a normal variation of expression of human sexuality, it is likely that some adolescents will continue to worry about their sexual preferences in just the same vein.

Some homosexuals say they had discovered being gay in childhood, sometimes as early as age five or six, while others didn't recognize this aspect of their personalities until adulthood. The most common pattern for gay males, however, is to come gradually to awareness during the teenage years of having the same-sex preference, perhaps because before this time we are all so strongly conditioned to think of ourselves as heterosexual.

Some people discover they're homosexual only after a long process of conflict and confusion. Others "know" they're gay — or "different" — instinctively, while still others may suspect that they have homosexual proclivities but struggle against them, never really succeeding in fitting into the heterosexual mode they yearn for. While no single pattern governs, it is safe to say that the teenager dealing with homoerotic impulses is apt to be frightened, uncertain, and worried about just what's going on. The chances are that such a teenager won't confide in a parent about this, but if this occurs, try to listen carefully and don't pretend to have the answer.

The teenager who announces to you that he (or she) is gay and is tired of keeping it secret is still your child. You can either react in a knee-jerk reflex of anger and indignation — just as your teen probably feared you would — or you can try to be loving and understanding. Here's how one eighteen-year-old female recalled her mother's reaction to her disclosure of her homosexuality:

MOTHER: I'm not sure I understand, Beth. Are you saying you're homosexual?

BETH: Yes. I've just started to realize it myself.

MOTHER: Do you think it's just a phase?

BETH: I'm sure it's not.

MOTHER: I have to say I'm pretty shocked. And scared, too, I guess. This won't be easy for you.

BETH: I know, Mom, but it's not something I can control.

MOTHER: Of course you can't. And I won't let it change anything between us. I'm glad you trusted me enough to tell me. And I'm always here if you need me. It may take some time, though, for me to adjust to the idea — and I can't guarantee I'll fully accept it. But I'll try.

To love and to understand doesn't mean you must approve of or endorse your teen's feelings, but it does say that you care. The following facts may be of assistance to you in dealing with such a situation.

(1) Researchers do not agree on the causes of homosexuality, but they don't know what causes heterosexuality either. In any event, most of sexual identity seems to be complexly determined by a number of factors interacting together, not just by a single aspect.

(2) Homosexuality is not an illness (the American Psychiatric Association officially took this position in 1974) nor are homosexuals psychologically disturbed. While there are certainly some homosexuals who are deeply troubled, there are plenty of heterosexual rapists, murderers, and generally maladjusted people; sexual orientation is *not* the determining factor.

(3) Homosexuals are not usually recognizable by their appearance, mannerisms, or occupational choice. There are many gay men and women who are doctors, lawyers, accountants, athletes, teachers, truckdrivers, and so on; most of them keep their sexual preferences private and are never thought to be "different" by colleagues or friends.

(4) Many advances have been made in the last decade in civil rights for homosexuals and in increasing acceptance by society, but homosexuality has its drawbacks, too. Higher rates of sexually transmitted disease are found in homosexual men, primarily because of a more promiscuous pattern of sexual behavior. Certain jobs in the government or military are closed by law to homosexuals, and homosexuals clearly are discriminated against in ways that range from the subtle to the overt in many aspects of everyday living. Not everyone is apt to be accepting of the out-of-the-closet homosexual; in fact, your teenager may find that some of his (or her) friends suddenly disappear when they learn about this.

Because this is a topic that deserves more discussion than space permits here, interested parents are referred to the following sources for additional reading: C. Silverstein, *A Family Matter: A Parent's Guide to Homosexuality* (McGraw-Hill, 1978), and B. Fairchild and N. Hayward, *Now That You Know: What Every Parent Should Know about Homosexuality* (Harcourt Brace Jovanovich, 1979).

Beyond the Sexual Double-Bind

Like many parents, you may be troubled by the notion of your teenager becoming sexually active at too young an age. Most authorities agree, for example, that thirteen- or fourteen-year-olds are not really ready for the responsibilities of having sexual intercourse, nor emotionally equipped for the types of intimate relationships that we generally believe are ideal for sexual interaction. At the same time, it now seems inevitable that large numbers of older adolescents — eighteen- and nineteen-year-olds — will be sexually active whether we approve or not. To pretend this won't happen to your child is to take an ostrich-eye view of the world.

The tough spot for parents is in coming to grips with the possibility that teens in mid-adolescence — fifteen, sixteen, or seventeen years of age — may choose to be sexually active. We strongly believe that, except for the least psychologically mature in this group, there is nothing inherently harmful about this. In fact, despite emotional protestations to the contrary, it now looks as though becoming sexually active during these years *in a responsible manner* may actually be beneficial to growth and development and may set the stage for a healthier sexual existence as an adult. While each parent will have to think about these issues and decide how to deal with them in their own family situation, our advice is to avoid the "damn-the-times, forbid-the-unspeakable" attitude and instead enter into an open dialogue with your teenagers to let them know how you feel. This may mean that you voice reservations, outright approval, or ambivalence about teenage sex, but at least your child will see that you're trying to be open-minded and honest. No previous generation of teenagers has had the benefits of this approach.

8

The Drug Mystique

— According to the National Institute on Drug Abuse, 64 percent of American teenagers have experimented with illegal drugs before they finish high school.

— A startling 40,000 teenagers are injured each year in auto accidents caused by alcohol, with many of them crippled, paralyzed, or permanently disabled.

— In almost every high school across the country, a wide variety of illegal drugs are sold and used each day.

Frightening, isn't it? Just a few generations ago, parents of teens didn't have to face these problems. Today, no matter how much you may want to fool yourself by thinking "*My* kid won't be involved," the majority of teenagers *do* try drugs, and those who don't are under strong pressures that can weaken their resolve.

Fortunately, parents don't have to sit back passively and watch what happens. Understanding why teens turn to drugs and mapping out a plan for realistically controlling such behavior, you can take a giant step in the direction of prevention. To do this, though, we must begin by examining the role of drugs in our contemporary society.

A Cultural Overview

The scene is a cocktail party in an affluent suburban community. The people mingling happily on the flagstone terrace and occasionally drifting into the handsomely furnished colonial home are a group of successful, vibrant, middle-aged professionals. Among those in attendance are three doctors, two lawyers, a psychologist, a banker, and a judge. On the buffet, right next to the Jarlsberg cheese platter, is a silver dish with a dozen neatly rolled joints of marihuana.

At the very same moment, a group of businessmen are wrapping up a dinner meeting in Boston, completing plans for a $15 million shopping mall. On their way out of a fashionable French restaurant, one man asks another, "Do you have any coke to spare?"

The next day, the league-leading St. Louis Cardinals baseball team makes a terse announcement at a hastily called press conference. Starting outfielder Lonnie Smith will be out of action indefinitely as he seeks treatment for a previously unsuspected drug problem. He was batting .311 when this decision was made.

These actual events and countless others like them that play out each day indicate the pervasiveness of the drug problem in our society. It's no passing fad we're dealing with, either. In the last two decades, our society has undergone major changes in its tolerance for use of illicit drugs.

In the early 1960s and before, drug use was generally regarded as a deviant act. With the radicalization of adolescents in the 1960s — in part, in rebellion against the Vietnam war — drugs began to appear on college campuses across the country, and the wheels were set in motion for a major shift in attitudes. Although at first the hippies and flower children who flocked to Haight-Ashbury in San Francisco and followed Timothy Leary's admonition to "Turn on, tune in, and drop out" were simply regarded as weird misfits, the Woodstock generation began a general glamorization of drug use as a recreational act that has mushroomed far beyond any social forecaster's early guesses.

In looking back today, we find that adolescents of the 60s staged one of the biggest coups ever to occur in the annals of intergenerational war. Middle and upper class youth borrowed from bohemians and ghetto residents the concept of taking mood-altering drugs and literally created a counterculture that eventually transformed the drug taboo to an accepted societal ritual. In fact, moderate drug use has become the practice and play toy of the masses. In 1962, only 4 percent of the general population had ever tried an illegal drug. Two decades later, one third — 33 percent — of all Americans aged twelve and older have engaged in such experimentation.

A change of this magnitude cannot be easily explained, but a number of factors contributed to shifting our societal thinking about drugs. To begin with, the 1940s and 1950s saw tremendous advances in medical pharmacology that paved the way for America to become a pill-popping society. Antibiotics, tranquilizers, steroids — the so-called "wonder drugs" — became widely used and widely seen as beneficial. Well-intentioned parents who didn't want their children to suffer any physical miseries began to stock their medicine chests so they could offer immediate relief for any discomfort. As a result, children were indoctrinated to believe that there was a potent pharmacological cure for their every ache and pain. Teething gels, cough syrups, nose drops, aspirin, diet pills, salves, ointments, and a host of other chemical substances were enthusiastically embraced. "Better living through chemistry" became a popular notion.

At roughly the same time, adults began using prescription medications far more than they had in the past. There were pills to go to sleep, pills to pep you up, and pills to calm you down and relieve the tensions of the day. No-Doz (concentrated caffeine) sold briskly on college campuses at exam time; amphetamines were rumored to be even better in helping you stay awake and alert. Younger adolescents who noticed these trends didn't really expect to use these drugs immediately, but began to think of them as something used by "grown-ups."

As the Vietnam era took shape, and male teenagers gradually became aware of the possibility of being sent off to combat, a new form of hedonism spread. Enjoy immediately. Do not delay. Tomorrow you might come home in a body bag. Dissatisfaction with the adult world mounted as campus protests and sit-ins were met by unyielding college presidents and insensitive police. The generation gap was stretched to its breaking point; rebellion was *de rigueur*.

By the late 1960s and into the 1970s, other elements began to come together to alter our society's attitudes towards drugs. For one thing, it became readily apparent that the old warnings that drug use of any sort would cause insanity, criminal behavior, and dire health consequences were simply not true. (To a generation that felt they'd been lied to about Vietnam and Watergate, this came not as a surprise but as a reinforcement of prior distrust, a reaffirmation of the "Don't trust anyone over thirty" mentality.) For another, some of the adolescents' most visible role models began to glamorize their drug use. Rock stars like Janis Joplin (who carried a bottle of Southern Comfort with her everywhere and frequently drank during performances) and Jimi Hendrix were in the forefront of this movement, and the lyrics of many rock songs related to the drug experience. Various rock groups openly encouraged drug use during concerts, and audiences were all too happy to oblige. The "contact high" was first experienced by teens attending rock concerts — the cloud of marihuana smoke which enveloped the audience was often so intoxicating that it wasn't necessary to actually smoke a joint to get high. Rock concerts also became places for drug generosity — many a kid would roll and light a joint of marihuana and then pass it around to people sitting nearby. Few teens could turn down the offer in the midst of the electronic throbbings of the music and the flashing, multicolored, mesmerizing light shows.

As teenagers used drugs to emulate adults and "act more grown up," a new phenomenon began to appear. The hippie generation, now slightly aging, took jobs, got married, settled down, and became parents. Already knowledgeable about the drug scene (unlike their own parents), this generation began to experience a strong urge to stay young. For many adults in their thirties or even forties, recreational use of drugs had thus become even more appealing as a way of rejuvenation, of revisiting their youth, of denying graying hair and bulging midriffs.

Today, drugs are so widely available in our society that Professor Norman Zinberg of Harvard University said recently, "Nobody in the United States is more than one handshake away from virtually any drug they want to get." Cocaine has become the "in" drug to use, and despite its expense it's being used widely. By 1982, when it made the cover of *Time* magazine, cocaine use had doubled in the adult population over what it had been just three years earlier. Cocaine is bought and sold on Capitol Hill, on the floor of the New York Stock Exchange, and on school playgrounds. We truly live in a democratic society.

Peer Pressure and Other Perplexities

According to researchers at the University of Michigan who conducted a national sampling of 170,000 high school seniors at 130 public and private schools, one out of five has been a *daily* marihuana user for at least a month at some point during high school, and 41 percent admit to having consumed at least five drinks in a row at least once in the last two weeks. These staggering levels of teenage substance abuse are in large part a reflection of peer pressure that adults have trouble comprehending.

"I was thirteen when drugs began to appear at parties," Ellen told us. "At first I kind of shied away because I was afraid of them. But when all of my best friends started using, I felt like I was a baby if I didn't try, so I did." (Ellen, now fifteen, smokes marihuana "four or five times a week, usually after school," and also takes Quaaludes, Valium, and LSD. She says she'd like to try cocaine, but her friends can't afford it.)

Bill describes peer pressure of a slightly different sort. "When I was fourteen, some friends and I formed a secret club. We held special meetings and did a bunch of things together. One of the other guys brought some weed to a meeting and said we'd all smoke to prove that we were tough. I didn't want to, so I left. The next day, I was told that I'd been voted out of the club. They said they didn't want a sissy." (Bill, now seventeen, has managed to stick by his guns. He has not taken any drugs and is proud of it.)

For Carl, peer pressure appeared in a different guise. "My girlfriend pulled out a joint and said, 'Let's have a party.' I really didn't want to, but she kept telling me that it made for great sex — and if I didn't want to join her, she'd find someone else who would." (Carl now smokes marihuana every weekend, and has also tried a few other drugs, including cocaine. He makes about $100 a week dealing drugs to friends of his younger brother, who is thirteen.)

Peer pressure operates in many ways. Its central message is "Do what we do to prove you're one of us, otherwise you're on your own." Some teenagers are notoriously in need of support from their peers, of getting a sense of belonging and acceptance that eases their separation from the family. To risk rejection from their peer group is tantamount to psychological suicide. And, unlike sexual behavior, the ritual of drug use often begins in a group setting, reinforcing the impression of a shared experience, a common bond of friendship. To "do drugs" with one's friends proves a teen is trustworthy, compatible, and "with it."

The rituals of drug use can create a strong feeling of camaraderie, even among strangers, in a manner akin to the pleasant ambiance found at a neighborhood tavern. In the tavern, a toast where someone shouts, "I'll drink to that!" can unify a group immediately. To teenagers, the shared rituals of drinking or using drugs also provide a form of status, a source of social acceptance, and a way of avoiding the dreaded sensation of being "different."

Fortunately, peer pressure regarding the use of drugs and alcohol operates as a restraining force, too. While the occasional recreational use of mind-altering substances is seen as acceptable, chic, and sophisticated, the extreme by-products of addiction and alcoholism are viewed with contempt and disdain. The implicit attitude is that sensible drug experimentation requires moderation — being in control of the drug experience, rather than letting it get control of you. One seventeen-year-old summed this up in describing what happened to a friend. "Joey was stupid and weak. He couldn't handle what he was doing, and he turned into a junkie. No one wants to be around him now."

Not all teenage peer groups are drug-oriented, and if an adolescent's best friends abstain from drugs the chances are much greater that he or she will avoid drugs too. Peer pressures can work in either direction. But if an adolescent's friends are all experimenting with drugs, sooner or later he or she will probably be enticed to try. "What's the matter? Are you *afraid* or something?" is the kind of challenge most teens can't resist if it's repeated often enough by friends.

The Great Escape

Trying to discover why adolescents use drugs is a little like trying to figure out the economy. There are many possible explanations, most of which sound quite plausible, and you can call on statistics from a number of different studies to "prove" almost any point you'd like to make.

In our two decades of working with teenagers, we have found the single most common denominator in adolescent drug experimentation is a simple one: teens are looking for a way to escape from the everyday world around them. In many cases, these kids want to escape boredom; they see drugs as exciting and *different* compared to the other things they do. In fact, the very language that describes drug use — "taking a trip," "getting high" — suggests this element of countering boredom. The illicitness of drug experimentation contributes to this aura; beyond this, the user's *expectations* of excitement are also a powerful factor in the equation. Interestingly, other teens use drugs to escape problems and tensions — that is, they use drugs for their tranquilizing, soothing properties. Here's how one high school junior describes it: "I started smoking pot when my parents separated and things got pretty tense at home. It was a good way to relax, to get a kind of mellow feeling that replaced the knot I felt in my stomach."

Today's teens feel they're under an unusual number of pressures, and they're probably right. They're expected to do well in school. They've worried about the oil crisis and a faltering economy. They know about inflation and unemployment and ecological problems. They've read that our Social Security system is teetering on the brink of disaster. They're not sure they'll be able to ever live as well as their parents do. And they are fully aware of the risks of nuclear war. Is it any wonder that escaping from these pressures is appealing?

Drugs can provide another type of escape for teenagers, a combination effect, so to speak, since it works in two ways at once. Adolescents generally feel that using drugs proves they're sophisticated, knowledgeable people; thus, drugs provide an escape from being seen as naive or childlike. Secondly, drug use allows teenagers to escape from feeling that they're "nobodies." It gives them an instant sense of status and identity.

It's interesting to note that adolescents who don't need to escape from boredom or tensions don't often get as deeply involved with drugs as those who need to escape. This doesn't mean they don't try drugs at all, because many teens experiment a few times to satisfy their curiosity and to assuage their peer group, and then stop. Instead, these are teens who typically find excitement in their lives from other challenges, such as athletics, music, theater, or academic performance. Such teens dissipate many of their psychological or physical tensions in more productive ways and do not need to use chemicals for such purposes.

Other Reasons Why Teens Experiment with Drugs, Alcohol, and Tobacco

Adolescents are drawn to drugs for a variety of reasons that go beyond the need to escape. Here is a list of some of the more common ones:

(1) Drugs provide pleasure and make them feel better.

(2) Many drugs, including alcohol and marihuana, lower the adolescents' inhibitions and make them feel less "uptight."

(3) For teenage boys, drugs and alcohol provide a way to test their masculinity. This is especially valued by those who aren't talented athletes, since our society provides few other rituals or challenges that can "prove" one's manliness.

(4) Drug use is a way of expressing alienation, disaffection, and rebellion.

(5) Many teens incorrectly believe that drugs possess mind-expanding properties that will make them more creative or insightful. Thus, they use drugs to find an altered state of consciousness.

(6) Drugs are easily accessible and relatively inexpensive.

(7) Drugs and alcohol are seen as enhancers of sexual feelings. The lure of imagined aphrodisiac effects of illicit substances is hard for many teens to resist.

(8) Using drugs is a way to prove they're "mature" or "grown-up."

(9) Some adolescents use drugs as a cry for help. Pressured by their peers but confused or even frightened by their drug experiences, they really want their parents to intercede and forbid such behavior. This form of experimentation can also be a symptom of internal psychological problems such as depression or severe anxiety.

(10) Drugs are forbidden; what's forbidden seems enticing. A combination of curiosity and risk-taking is involved.

In addition to these factors, it's important to realize that teens are caught in a cultural double-bind when it comes to drug and alcohol use. Beer commercials on television emphasize that drinking is something "good buddies" do together. Liquor advertisements often have a note of sex appeal. The "Marlboro Man" is unquestionably macho. Dean Martin has made a career out of being tipsy (or at least pretending to be); for the younger generation, Cheech and Chong glamorize marihuana use while ridiculing the uptight adults who want to stamp it out. "Head shops" — stores where drug paraphernalia are sold openly — though being outlawed in many communities, continue to exist. With messages like these all around them, it's no wonder that many teenagers feel that total abstinence is hardly an option.

Strategies for Positive Parenting

Perhaps the most important starting point for positive parenting regarding illicit drugs, alcohol, and tobacco lies in the role models we provide for our children and the values we teach (by example as well as by words) long before they reach the teenage years. One of the most effective commercials we've seen in the antismoking campaign illustrates this premise.

> A young, attractive father is sitting with his six-year-old son in a park on a beautiful, sunny day. He takes out a pack of cigarettes, casually selects one, lights it, takes a long, satisfying drag and then innocently puts the pack down. The little boy, in a perfect imitation of his dad, reaches for a cigarette to duplicate his father's behavior.

Children who see a parent take a drink to relax or know that their parents use tranquilizers, sleeping pills, or other medications are already preprogrammed with a lowered resistance towards using drugs as teenagers. In fact, an adolescent who has at least one parent who smokes is almost three times as likely as the child of nonsmoking parents to begin using tobacco.

The next strategy of positive parenting, which also should begin before adolescence, is providing effective drug education for children. To do this, of course, you must begin by educating yourself. (Chapter 9 in this book, "A Parent's Primer on Teenage Alcohol and Drug Abuse," is a good starting point. Other useful resources are listed in our bibliography.) By learning the basic facts about drugs, alcohol, and tobacco, you position yourself to teach your children what drugs are, why they're used, and how they can be avoided. This involves more than just teaching scientific facts: it requires that parents instill values and attitudes regarding adolescent drug use as well as a repertoire of skills aimed at fostering self-discipline, self-esteem, self-control, and self-awareness. Teaching of this sort must be a continuing process, not a one-time lecture, but it can pay important dividends to your child later on.

The process of drug education need not be confined to the home. Check with your school system or church to see what resources they have available. If they don't have specially trained personnel to provide preventive education, try to contact others parents to initiate such a program. Many organizations (listed in the Appendix) can provide assistance and materials for such an undertaking. But these programs are needed in grade school, before drug experimentation begins; in the high school years their preventive value will be minimal.

When you talk with your kids about drugs, you may be regarded suspiciously. Here's a checklist of dos and don'ts that may be of help:

(1) *Be open and direct in what you have to say.* Beating around the bush isn't very useful.

(2) *Scare tactics don't generally work in keeping teens away from drugs.* While this doesn't mean that you should ignore reality, don't put

too much emphasis on health risks or the chances of being sent to jail, because most teens won't believe it anyway.

(3) *Give your teens ammunition for recognizing and dealing with peer-group pressure.* Explain what peer pressures are and how they operate. Talk about giving in to such pressures as a form of weakness, emphasizing that being one's own person — sticking by one's own decisions — is a sign of strength.

(4) *Set clear limits and explain what will happen if these limits are ignored.* Over and over again, teenagers tell us that their parents never really told them what to do and what not to do when it came to drugs and alcohol. If you're totally opposed to a teen's trying any illicit drug, make your position very clear. If you don't mind having an older adolescent use marihuana occasionally, say so. But specify that this is the only drug use you'll tolerate and explain exactly what consequences there will be to violating this rule. Keep in mind that a minor penalty ("No T.V. for two nights, Charlie") tells your teen it's a minor matter, while a stiff penalty ("You'll lose your driver's license for two months") not only gets your teen's attention but probably will have some deterrent value of its own. But be sure your limits are expressed with a sense of love and caring, rather than hostility. You don't want to challenge teens to break the rules.

(5) *Let your teens know that you're available when they need you.* But if you really want them to come to you with their thoughts, questions, or problems, you must not yell at them or act hurt and shocked at what they have to say. Stay calm and keep an open mind.

Beyond education, there are other important steps parents can take with their teens to help them negotiate the temptation of drugs. The first is to provide a family atmosphere of warmth and acceptance. Researchers agree that changes in the basic nature of the American family have contributed significantly to drug problems. A strong family support system and a sense of family combat this trend. (This *doesn't* mean that all teens who use drugs have family problems, however.) Next, provide your teens with alternatives to the drug experience, such as:

(1) *Physical activity and awareness.* Sports and exercise provide a perfect foil to drugs for many adolescents. They can serve as a form of tension release, can enhance body awareness, and give a sense of group participation and camaraderie.

(2) *Sensory awareness.* Instead of turning to chemicals to alter perception, try other approaches. Music and art can "turn people on," if they'll only let themselves get involved. A trip to the beach or a day in the mountains can expand sensory horizons; the television set can't.

(3) *Close interpersonal relationships.* These are both more satisfying

and more lasting than drug effects, and tend to reduce the inner tumult in teens' lives that sometimes lead to drug use as a form of coping.

(4) *Challenges.* Bolster your teens' self-esteem by giving them attainable goals. Introduce them to chess, bridge, or other similar games requiring skill and concentration. Enroll them in a wilderness training program such as Outward Bound. Get them involved in community action programs, or training a pet, or any other situation that will teach responsibility at the same time it tests their mettle and prevents them from getting bored.

(5) *Activity in their religion, if this is appropriate to your personal values.* Many studies have shown that teens who are more involved in religion are more likely to avoid drugs than their peers. While religion is hardly a cure-all for the drug problem, it helps give an extra edge of stability to your teen's life.

Finally, get active at a community level. Parent-initiated groups have played a major role in getting drunken drivers off the road and providing telephone hot lines for information and crisis counseling about drug and alcohol abuse. Interested and involved parents *can* make a difference: rates of drug experimentation by teenagers seem to have reached a peak prior to 1982 and are now beginning to decline.

It is unrealistic to believe that we can eradicate the drug problem in America in easy fashion. There are economic and political issues involved as well as issues of the psychology of drug use. But we can take heart by realizing that our teenagers are willing to listen to us if we make sense and don't panic, as recent surveys are beginning to show. Daily cigarette smoking by high school seniors dropped from 29 percent to 21 percent between 1977 and 1982, according to studies from the University of Michigan. Daily marihuana use by high school seniors declined from 10.7 to 6.3 percent from 1978 to 1982. While the battle against drugs is slow and frustrating, it appears now that the tide may be turning at last.

9

A Parent's Primer on Teenage Alcohol and Drug Abuse

Adolescents use drugs and alcohol in many different ways. We have already discussed the whys and wherefores of teenage experimentation with drugs, pointing out that this is now such a widespread practice that the drug-naive adolescent is statistically in the minority. Experimentation, however, refers to occasional and casual use of illicit substances and is a distinctly different situation from two other patterns of adolescent drug use that are far more frightening. They are *drug abuse,* in which the frequency of drug use or the effects encountered from the drug(s) being used produce harmful effects on a person, and *drug addiction,* in which a person develops a strong physical and psychological craving for a drug after repeated use, and experiences withdrawal symptoms if the drug is not taken regularly.

The National Institute on Drug Abuse estimates that more than a million American teenagers abuse drugs each year. An additional 750,000 adolescents can be classified as alcoholic. Parents need to know how to detect drug abuse by their teens and what to do about it if we are to make a meaningful dent in these statistics.

Detecting Drug Abuse by Your Teen

Probably the most frequent question parents ask about adolescent drug abuse is "How can I tell?" There are no sure-fire methods, but the following signs and symptoms of drug abuse can serve as a guide.

(1) Diminished alertness and inability to think clearly

(2) Slow, slurred speech

(3) Sluggish behavior, lack of energy, and excessive sleeping or drowsiness

(4) Prominent mood changes, especially irritability, wide mood swings, and depression

(5) Deterioration in school performance

(6) Diminished drive and ambition; lackadaisical attitudes about life in general

(7) Frequent infections

(8) Weight loss and decreased appetite (except for marihuana users, who tend to get the "munchies" and may gain weight)

(9) Cessation of menstruation

(10) Yellowish-brown discoloration of the skin of the thumb and forefinger (in heavy marihuana smokers)

(11) Needle marks on the arms or legs (on those injecting narcotics or other drugs)

(12) Bloodshot eyes (in marihuana users and alcoholics)

(13) Dilated pupils (Constricted, pin-point pupils can be a sign of narcotic use.)

(14) Excessive, chronic coughing

(15) Frequent headaches

(16) Hyperactivity (common with cocaine and amphetamines)

(17) Prominent anxiety reactions, paranoia, or hallucinations

(18) Chronic runny nose and red, irritated nostrils (in cocaine users)

None of these signs or symptoms is irrefutable proof of drug abuse, but if several are present they should certainly raise parental suspicion. In addition, if your teen suddenly drops his or her friends in favor of a new crowd, or becomes a loner, consider the possibility of drugs as the cause.

To tackle the drug problem intelligently, you need to have accurate facts at your disposal. Here is a summary of current information on illicit drugs that are most frequently abused by teens.

Alcohol Alcohol is sometimes overlooked as a drug of abuse, but we have chosen to list it here because we believe it definitely fits in this category. An estimated 1.5 *million* teenagers are problem drinkers, with half of this number — three-quarters of a million teens — believed to be full-blown alcoholics. Researchers in the field are no longer surprised to see seventh or eighth grade students who consume several bottles of wine or a fifth of hard liquor every day; in the last fifteen years, excessive alcohol use has crept down to increasingly younger age groups.

As a drug, alcohol is a powerful depressant to the central nervous system, meaning that it disrupts the normal workings of the brain. The precise effects depend on the amount of alcohol absorbed into the bloodstream, which in turn reflects the amount of alcohol consumed, the rapidity with which it is taken, the weight of the person, and the amount of food in the stomach (alcohol is absorbed more rapidly when no food is present, leading to higher blood alcohol concentrations). One or two drinks consumed slowly — over an hour or more — produce only mild behavioral changes and often serve as a "social lubricant," helping people relax and feel more at ease. Larger amounts of alcohol, or even two drinks chugged rapidly, begin to affect judgment and physical coordination. Boisterous behavior, slurred speech, "tipsy" balance, and impaired reaction time begin to appear. With four or five drinks consumed in an hour, people invariably become drunk, although they may protest that they're feeling fine and perfectly in control of their actions.

Drinking means more to the teenager than just indulging in the pleasurable effects of alcohol. It has its own cultural symbolism, signifying being "one of the gang" and being "grown-up." Its use in these symbolic ways guarantees a particularly dangerous side of teenage alcohol use: drinking mixed with driving.

Driving while intoxicated is particularly common in teens for three reasons: (1) they are inexperienced in handling both drinking and driving, and thus have less of an experiential base to draw on in making judgments about either activity; (2) they're trying to impress their friends by how "mature" they are; and (3) they don't think that getting arrested for drunken driving or having an accident could happen to *them*, only to someone else. But statistics from the last decade have shown quite decisively that up to 60 percent of those killed in drunk driving accidents are teenagers and, whenever the legal drinking age is lowered, auto accident rates for teens go up substantially. We can't stress enough the need for parents to insist their teens do not drive when drinking — regardless of the amount consumed.

Teenagers don't see the health effects of heavy alcohol consumption right away, but they can develop liver damage (cirrhosis, alcoholic hepatitis), pancreatitis, chronic gastritis, alcoholic heart disease, degenerative arthritis, and brain damage in their twenties or thirties if their abusive drinking pattern persists. These health risks are heightened in the great majority of alcohol-abusing teens who get involved with other drugs as well. In addition, heavy drinking disrupts normal sex hormone production in both males and females and is likely to lead to serious difficulties in sexual functioning.

Abusive drinking also leads to a number of behavioral problems (although admittedly, it is sometimes hard to tell what is cause and what is effect). Truancy, fighting, encounters with the police, disruptive family behavior, and generally poor impulse control are the hallmarks of teenage problem drinkers. Impaired school performance is almost guaranteed by a haze of alcohol; social isolation and depressive episodes are also seen.

If heavy drinking is suddenly stopped after physical dependency has set in, a full-blown alcohol withdrawal syndrome occurs. The most prominent features of the mild version of this syndrome include shakiness, irritability, agitation, insomnia, anxiety, sweating, and a rapid pulse. About one-quarter of alcoholics also have hallucinations during withdrawal, but they usually clear within a week. A smaller number have convulsions ("rum fits") within the first day or two after the cessation of drinking, and about one-third of this group have DTs (delirium tremens), a condition marked by delirium (confusion, fluctuating disorientation, and hallucinations) and tremors accompanied by high fever, rapid heart rate, and elevated blood pressure. Although DTs are relatively rare in teenagers, they may be seen in those who have been regularly using barbiturates or tranquilizers along with substantial amounts of alcohol. *DTs are a life-threatening condition that requires immediate emergency medical attention.*

Marihuana Marihuana (pot, grass, weed, Mary Jane, hash, Maui Wowee, Acapulco gold), which comes from the *Cannabis sativa* plant, is the most widely used mind-altering substance in America other than alcohol. It is the first illicit drug most teenagers experiment with, probably because of a combination of its wide availability, its comparatively low cost, its pleasing "high" and its relative safety. First-time users often do not get noticeably intoxicated from smoking pot, but with repeated use it produces a transient "high" marked by a sense of relaxation, an alteration in time perception (time seems to pass more slowly), an increased heart rate, feelings of euphoria or elation, and a sense of heightened sensory awareness.

Marihuana is *not* an addictive drug, although those who use it heavily over time can become psychologically dependent on it. Early claims that marihuana was completely safe have now been exploded by numerous studies, but the early arguments by opponents of marihuana of dire health consequences have also been shown to be greatly exaggerated.

If it is used on an *occasional* basis — less often than a few times a week — adverse effects are relatively few. Anxiety attacks (panicky feelings and hyperexcitability) occur in 1 or 2 percent of users; "flashbacks" (recurrences of the marihuana high without using the drug) are even less frequent. The greatest physical danger seems to be that driving and other machine-operating skills are impaired because of decreased alertness, impaired complex reaction time, and visual distortion. While there are no reliable statistics on auto accidents caused by marihuana, a number of experts believe that tens of thousands of these preventable car crashes occur annually, with thousands of deaths involved. According to various reports, about 40 percent of high school students sometimes drive while "high" from marihuana.

Heavy marihuana use is another story. To begin with, the active chemical ingredients in marihuana accumulate in the body over time, particularly in tissues such as the brain, the testes, and the liver. Studies have shown that sperm production is lowered by chronic heavy marihuana use, and levels of the principal male sex hormone, testosterone, can be depressed. (Because testosterone plays an important role in male pubertal development, this effect may be of particular concern to parents and teens alike. Unfortunately, despite its wide use in the adolescent population, no investigations have yet been conducted to see if marihuana interferes with puberty.) Recent evidence suggests that heavy marihuana use can disrupt normal menstrual function in females, and it has been conclusively shown that the active chemical component of marihuana crosses the placenta in pregnant women and enters the circulation of the developing baby.

Chronic marihuana use also damages the lungs and lowers resistance to infection. Since marihuana smoke has many of the same constituents as tobacco smoke, some experts feel that prolonged, heavy use may lead to lung cancer. But perhaps most disturbing of all, scientists agree, is that very frequent marihuana use can lead to the so-called "amotivational syndrome," marked by passivity, lack of ambition or motivation, and reduction of active involvement in living.

On the other hand, it now appears that early reports of brain damage due to chronic marihuana use were in error, and support for the idea that marihuana causes birth defects (based on animal studies) has not been forthcoming. What is clear is that marihuana is far from innocuous in its effects, although the occasional user is quite unlikely to encounter these problems.

Recently, the National Academy of Sciences issued a report, prepared by a blue ribbon panel, on marihuana and health. According to Dr. Arnold Relman, a member of the panel and editor of the prestigious *New England Journal of Medicine*, "In its painstaking review of the published data, the committee found much reason to worry about the widespread use of the drug — *particularly among the young* — but not enough hard evidence to answer many questions about the extent of the risk [emphasis added]."

"Uppers" (Stimulants: Cocaine and Amphetamines)   Cocaine ("coke," "snow," "Big C," "powder") is clearly the "in" drug of the 1980s, although teenagers are not as likely as adults to plunge nose-first into coke since it costs about $100 to $150 a gram (about a teaspoonful, or enough for two people to use for a few hours). Nevertheless, 16 percent of high school seniors surveyed in 1982 admitted to experience with coke, and

6.9 percent of teens aged twelve to seventeen had used it at least once.

Cocaine is extracted from the leaves of the coca plant and can be either inhaled ("snorted"), smoked, or injected. It produces a temporary — twenty- to thirty-minute — state of hyperstimulation marked by euphoria, a sense of power, and intense alertness. To some, it is the "ultimate high," giving the user feelings of supreme competence, mastery, and perfection. Its appeal is heightened by its reputation as the "Rolls Royce" of drugs (partially because of its use by celebrities, models, and sports figures) and its purported effects as a sexual stimulant.

Occasional use of cocaine hasn't been studied in detail, but new scientific findings are rapidly causing a reassessment of the drug. Perforation of the nasal membranes is the most common finding. But far more disturbing is the fact that cocaine has a high addictive potential, although it was once thought to be free of this risk. Mercury Morris, the former Miami Dolphins' football star now serving a twenty-year prison term for dealing coke, describes its draw in graphic terms: " 'Enough' is never present in your reasoning. You've had enough when it's gone, and when it's gone you want some more."

Heavy use of cocaine leads to appetite suppression and weight loss, insomnia, suspiciousness, hallucinations, and anxiety reactions. Depressive reactions occur commonly when the cocaine is stopped. Worst of all, perhaps, is that the person who gets hooked on cocaine loses control of his life and becomes a slave to the snowy white powder that gives him a supercharged jolt. Teenagers who are frequent users almost invariably must steal to support their expensive habit, and those who don't steal sell drugs as a way of raising money.

If you discover that your teen has used cocaine, swift parental intervention is called for. It's important that teens be made to recognize the destructiveness of this drug before they're dependent on it.

The amphetamines constitute the other major type of drug in the stimulant category. Known in street parlance as "speed," "pep pills," "bennies," "dex," "crank," "splash," or "crystal," these drugs are also dangerous due to their high addictive potential. Occasional sporadic use of amphetamines (taken by mouth) doesn't seem to have particularly serious consequences. The principal effect of the drug is to heighten alertness and overcome fatigue, although complex judgments may be adversely affected. Injected or inhaled, amphetamine causes more intense sensations, sometimes described as a "flash" or "rush." If mixed with other drugs, or taken in excessive doses, "mainlining" (injecting the drug intravenously) can result in hyperactivity, poor impulse control, hallucinations, irrational (sometimes destructive) behavior, and occasionally a condition in which the "speed freak" is unable to move or speak. Death due to overdose can also occur.

The amphetamine addict is susceptible to a number of effects, including a sizable risk of suicide. Brain hemorrhages and irregular heart rhythms can occur, blood vessel damage is common, and liver disorders are frequently encountered. Paranoid delusions, severe weight loss and malnutrition, and disturbances of sexual function round out the unpleasant picture of this condition.

Fortunately, amphetamine use among teenagers seems to be declining at present. Nevertheless, the high risks of "speed" are not to be ignored.

"Downers" (Depressants: Barbiturates, Methaqualone, Tranquilizers)
The barbiturates — drugs like phenobarbital (Luminal), secobarbital (Seconal), and amobarbital (Amytal) — are an important part of the street drug scene. Widely available and relatively inexpensive, they are used either alone (to reduce anxiety, to "relax," to slow things down) or in combination with other illicit drugs to tone down their excessive stimulant action. Barbiturates are dangerous any way you look at them. To begin with, they are the most common drugs used to commit suicide. Accidental deaths due to the combination of alcohol and barbiturates are not unusual; the barbiturates are also highly addicting. As with alcohol addiction, withdrawal from barbiturates can be dangerous, so medical care is strongly advised.

Methaqualone, previously sold under brand names such as Quaalude, Sopor, and Parest, is a sedative that is particularly popular among adolescents, possibly because of its supposed aphrodisiac effect. The truth is that methaqualone actually *impairs* sexual performance, although its disinhibiting effects may lower ordinary sexual anxieties and thus make a user *feel* sexier. Like barbiturates, methaqualone is addicting and dangerous, although many teens seem convinced the drug is innocuous. Especially when it is mixed with alcohol, marihuana, or heroin, death can occur either through cardiac arrest or respiratory failure. Chronic abuse of this drug typically produces a picture of impaired coordination, unsteady gait, inability to concentrate, memory problems, poor judgment, and emotional apathy. In late 1983, legitimate U.S. pharmaceutical houses agreed to stop manufacturing this drug completely because of its high abuse potential, but since most of the methaqualone reaching street users was illicitly produced, this dangerous drug will continue to be available for years to come.

In contrast to these classes of depressant drugs, tranquilizers such as Librium and Valium are less widely used by teens and are somewhat safer. Valium, in particular, is used in the drug subculture to treat complications of drug experimentation, such as a bad LSD trip. It is also sometimes used to ease the letdown after a long bout with stimulants such as amphetamines or cocaine. Rather than giving a true high, Librium and Valium leave their users feeling "spacy," "floating," or "mellow." While these drugs have a high abuse potential, they are not usually addictive.

PCP (Phencyclidine)   PCP ("Angel dust," "hog") is difficult to classify because it can act as either a depressant, a stimulant, or a hallucinogen depending on how it's taken and the dose used. It is one of the most dangerous drugs being used by teens, although it's widely available. PCP causes bizarre behavioral effects that can include a tendency towards violence, impulsive behavior (including self-destructive acts like suicide), and an intense sense of depersonalization. Teens high on angel dust have walked off the roofs of tall buildings thinking they could fly like Superman; turned viciously on their friends, sometimes killing them; and used autos like Sherman tanks attacking enemy lines. PCP used in low doses sometimes produces a sense of elation and feelings of power and intense sensory perception, but it also commonly causes paranoia, distorted vision, illusions, muscle incoordination, and flashbacks. In high doses, it can cause convulsions, coma, or extreme hyperactivity. All users risk having serious mental breakdowns from this drug, including acute psychotic reactions that require hospitalization and intense treatment efforts. Unfortunately, these psychotic episodes have sometimes been permanent.

Psychedelics   The use of psychedelic drugs such as LSD ("acid"), peyote, mescaline, and similar substances has been on the decline among teens in America in the last few years. While these vary in their chemistry and their specific actions, they all affect brain activity so that users are inundated by flooding sensations of color, sound, touch, and smell. In some cases, frightening hallucinations occur; in others, the hallucinations may take on religious overtones or seem to reach into the depths of the universe. These drugs are particularly insidious because they break the user's contact with reality and can precipitate acute or long-term psychiatric problems. Flashbacks can also occur and tend to be unpleasant and frightening.

Narcotics   So much has been written about the dangers of narcotics like heroin and morphine that we won't devote much space to repeating what parents already know. These highly addicting drugs produce withdrawal symptoms once physical dependence develops. These include runny nose, shaking, sweating, nausea, vomiting, abdominal pain, muscular aches and pains, chills, insomnia, and, occasionally, convulsions. There is general agreement that narcotic addiction is linked to criminal behavior such as theft and prostitution (which provide a means of purchasing drugs to avoid withdrawal symptoms) and it is also clear that there are numerous adverse health consequences to long-term narcotic usage. If you find out that your teenager is involved with these drugs, don't wait to work things out — get professional help immediately.

Inhalants   Teenagers have one sector of the drug abuse scene pretty much to themselves: the inhaling of industrial solvents found in paint sprays, gasoline, dry cleaning solutions, airplane glue, lighter fluid, spot remover, or fingernail polish in order to get "high." These readily available, inexpensive products are completely legal, unlikely to raise adult suspicions, and quick-working to boot. Fumes can be inhaled either from a soaked cloth or a plastic bag or aerosols may be sprayed directly into the nose and mouth. The "high" is brief — generally lasting only a few minutes — and it doesn't leave much of a hangover. Headache seems to be the worst common aftereffect.

These seemingly innocuous habits of inhalant use are dangerous for two reasons. First, there is potential physical toxicity from repeated direct contact with these chemicals, particularly in the high concentrations that must be used to get an effect. Some of these products are actually poisonous, and more than 100 deaths a year result from their use. Second, and perhaps even more disturbing, is the fact that the kids who use these inhalants — particularly those in elementary school and junior high — characteristically progress to using other drugs.

Older teens disdain glue-sniffing as a "babyish" thing to do but may become involved with another type of inhalant. This is a drug called *amyl nitrite* (known as "poppers" or "snappers" in street parlance because it comes packaged in glass pearls or vials which give a popping or snapping sound when broken open), which first gained prominence in the male homosexual community but is now enjoying relatively widespread use on college campuses. The drug is often used during sexual activity because of its mild, but short-lived, sensory amplification and subjective effect of seeming to slow down the passage of time. Amyl nitrite is now most commonly obtained not as a drug but in the guise of room deodorizers under names like Bull, Rush, Kick, and Bullet. It causes headaches, nausea, and dizziness due to a drop in blood pressure and a slowing effect on the heart, but it is not addictive and doesn't seem to have serious health consequences or effects on behavior.

Dealing with Drugs: A Reality-Based Approach

What do you do if you discover your teenager has gotten involved with drugs? You must begin by carefully assessing the situation in several different ways while avoiding angry, outraged reactions that are likely to cut off honest communication with your child. First, find out what drug (or drugs) your teenager has been using. Next, get an idea of the frequency involved — was this a one-time thing, a sporadic occurrence, or has it already become a regularly established pattern? Find out why they felt the need to try the drug (curiosity? peer pressure? tension? school problems? escape from boredom?) and what their reaction has been to the drug experience. Finally, if at all possible, try to discover where they got the drug. It's one thing if they got it from a friend, but quite another if they're buying from a stranger, since this may mean they have access to drugs of considerable danger. In gathering this information, the manner in which you ask questions is critical. Try not to be accusatory as you inquire, keeping questions as nonjudgmental and straightforward as you can. "I want to know where you're buying the marihuana" has a greater chance of being answered than "Who's the damn pusher selling you this junk? I'll bet it's Doug, isn't it? I never liked that punk."

If your teen tells you that he or she has just experimented with a drug once or only a handful of times, be circumspect and realistic in your response. Many adolescents "try" drugs like alcohol or marihuana to see what they're like and to "prove" to their friends that they're grown-up enough to make their own decisions, and then discover that it's no big deal. Now able to say they're experienced, these kids feel more comfortable in saying "no" when offered such drugs again. If this is the situation you're dealing with, you can encourage and reinforce their decision to be abstinent and give them a sense of your confidence in their judgment. If, however, this doesn't seem to apply to your teen — if he or she tells you that they *liked* getting high and they intend to experiment further — you've got a difficult decision to make.

Some parents will tolerate moderate social use of marihuana as long as it's confined to weekends and isn't mixed with driving. Other parents can't live with endorsing such a permissive position. Before you react precipitously in either direction, think through the issues as they apply to your teen, not in an abstract, philosophical sense only. If you really believe your teen will use marihuana only casually, without becoming a compulsive user, it may not be worth risking the polarization that can occur with a parental edict banning any and all chemical substances. The fact that *you* didn't feel the need for drugs when you were an adolescent really serves no practical purpose here and won't be very persuasive: the reality is, times are substantially different. On the other hand, some teens certainly look to their parents for setting definite limits, and if you seem too nonchalant about drugs, they may deliberately escalate their usage to test you.

Similar quandaries face parents in regard to teens and alcohol. Do you completely ban drinking until age twenty-one, as some state legislatures are doing? Do you introduce teens to alcohol under your own supervision, prohibiting drinking outside the home until they've reached a certain age (say, eighteen) and have demonstrated that they can hold their liquor? Or do you endorse their drinking if it's done in moderation and only at times when they're not driving? There is no single "right" answer for everyone. Parents must decide what to do in these situations partly based on knowledge of their teen (how mature? how trustworthy? how impulsive?) and partly on their own comfort level. Setting standards for behavior that are dissonant with your own personal beliefs and values is not generally a wise thing to do.

For teens experimenting with reasonably safe, nonaddicting drugs on an infrequent basis, who are unwilling to promise to stop completely (or if you don't want to put them in the position of having to break such a promise, which can be counterproductive), you may want to reach a negotiated settlement while keeping the matter under advisement. One good way of doing this is to suggest a compromise of sorts: the teen can continue to experiment, but only if he or she does so no more than twice a month. If the adolescent agrees to this offer and then goes on to more frequent drug use, this is powerful (and objective) proof to you and to your teen that there is more of a need for drugs than was originally believed. This means it's time to discuss corrective measures, before things get out of hand.

Suppose, though, that you discover that your teen is abusing drugs in a more substantial way, using one drug several times a week, or using several different drugs, or experimenting with a dangerous drug or one with high addictive potential. While you should begin by assessing the situation as previously outlined, there are a number of other considerations that should come into play.

(1) Does your teen have a realistic understanding of what he or she is doing?

(2) Can your teen honestly tell you that he or she has not been dealing (selling drugs)?

(3) Is the drug used by ingestion or smoking, rather than by injection?

(4) Is the pattern of drug use strictly recreational, with no element of compulsive need?

If any of these questions has a "no" answer, you've got a major problem on your hands that requires professional attention. As well intentioned as you may be in wanting to help your child, you must be able to realize that this is not time for amateur assistance. In fact, even if you happen to be a mental health professional with experience working with adolescent drug problems, your teenager needs the benefit of an objective counselor or therapist who is not emotionally involved in the situation.

Once a teen has become a drug abuser, the only realistic treatment goal is abstinence. But for this objective to be attained, the teen must be willing to accept responsibility for his or her behavior and make the effort to stop using drugs. A therapist, no matter how competent, can't bring about cures by simply waving a magic wand. This means that if your child refuses to stop using drugs, the possibility of a residential treatment program or hospitalization should be strongly considered.

In dealing with drug or alcohol abuse, it is critical that parents realize that lying becomes a characteristic pattern, so you need to have better assurances than your teenager's word that he or she is abstinent. This can be partly achieved through laboratory testing to detect the presence or absence of many illicit drugs in urine samples, thus providing a more reliable means of confirming or denying continued drug abuse.

At the same time, treatment should be directed at identifying and correcting the underlying problems that led to the drug abuse in the first place. This can't be achieved in just a few sessions of therapy; it usually requires an intense look at both your teen's psyche and the nature of your family's interactions. As uncomfortable as it may be for you to have your parental practices scrutinized and possibly criticized by an outsider, this is often exactly what is needed to help your teen.

If your adolescent voluntarily has told you about a drug problem, it's a reasonably good indicator of three things. First, your teen recognizes the *existence* of a problem, which is no small matter in itself. Second, your teen is asking for help, which is also a positive sign. Finally, it's an indication of your teen's trust in you, which can be viewed as an important factor in breaking out of this self-destructive behavior pattern. On the other hand, if you discovered your adolescent's drug abuse by yourself or from a third party, your teen's initial reaction to your questioning is of considerable significance. If he or she denies that there's a problem, it's a fairly strong indication that they have no intention of trying to stop and also shows that the family will be of little help in curbing the drug-abusing behavior.

While you can't take responsibility for treating teenage drug abuse by yourself, there are specific steps you can take to be of assistance in this situation.

(1) *Remove all psychoactive substances from the house.*

(2) *All family members should curtail their use of nonprescription drugs, no matter how casual or infrequent.*

(3) *Keep lines of communication open.* This will only work if you don't engage in constant recriminations and blaming.

(4) *Avoid making your teen with the drug abuse problem a scapegoat for all the problems in your family.*

(5) *Until you're convinced all drug abuse has stopped, don't permit your teen to drive.* This means banning access to the family car and taking away your teen's driver's license.

(6) *Don't make your teen a prisoner, but don't let him (or her) get into situations where drugs will be readily available.*

(7) *Take strict control over all money your teen has.* Seizing bank accounts, taking away credit cards, and putting your teen on a strict budget with total accountability for every penny spent may not be pleasant, but it costs money to buy drugs.

(8) *Don't force your teen to leave home.* Throwing drug-abusing adolescents out only pushes them closer to a life of addiction.

(9) *Find a competent therapist to work with your teen.* See Chapter 22 for more details.

(10) *Recognize that short-term drug abstinence doesn't always equate with long-term success.* Some drug-abusing teens respond to the temporary pressure exerted on them by their families and therapists, but then surreptitiously relapse. Don't assume that everything's fine; keep a watchful eye.

(11) *Adopt a detailed, concrete plan for your teen's rehabilitation.* This should include plans for activities that can provide an outlet for your teen's energies and capture his or her interest. Schooling and vocational needs should also be assessed. But be sure that you make such plans in conjunction with your teen, not by yourself.

A final word for parents regarding teenage drug or alcohol abuse seems in order. There are no easy answers to these difficult problems, but it's senseless to feel that you've failed because your child has gotten involved with drugs. Instead, focus on rehabilitating the drug-dependent teen, recognizing that there are many factors outside your control that may prevent the outcome you desire. In some cases, you just can't save someone bent on self-destruction, but at least you'll know you've tried.

10

$\mathcal{S}chool\ \mathcal{D}ays,\ School\ \mathcal{D}ays$

School occupies a central place in the lives of most adolescents, but the school experience has undergone some major changes from what it used to be. Teens work at computer keyboards, get videotape feedback on their oral presentation skills, have homework assignments in sex education, and take minicourses on topics like "The Twenty-First Century as Portrayed by Major Science Fiction Writers." Even the sports scene has undergone considerable change: girls' basketball has shed its old-fashioned rules and become a fast-paced, aggressive game; new varsity sports like soccer and gymnastics have sprung up; and coaches worry about what to do when their team captain shows up for a game stoned on drugs. Yet despite these changes, as the French proverb says, "The more things change, the more they stay the same."

As in days gone by, the school experience aims to prepare students for what lies ahead. Contrary to what some teenagers think, there is life after high school, and it can be long and meaningless for the ill prepared. School provides a chance to develop skills and talents in both academic and nonacademic pursuits, to learn what one does well, and what one enjoys. It does this by teaching facts, teaching ways of thinking, and socializing students to be aware of and cope with the complexities of modern life. Hopefully, school days also give teens a sense of how much there is to learn in life and the motivation to learn it.

114

Getting Educated for Fun and Profit

In many ways, school is a microcosm of the working world. The student rises early to catch a school bus at a specific time. Classes usually begin at 8:30 or 9:00. A break for lunch occurs at noon. Students interact with teachers and fellow students, some of whom they like and some they don't. They work for rewards that come not in the form of dollars but in letter grades, signifying degree of mastery and achievement (eventually to be translated into dollars). A typical day ends with a bus ride home or with participation in some extra social or athletic activity that is not required by the school, but highly encouraged to form a well-rounded individual. Homework is done each night to prepare for the following day. By this description, high school mimics the work world more closely than college does because, though college requires more personal responsibility, class schedules are less structured and allow for more freedom.

An analysis of data released in 1983 by the U.S. Census Bureau on personal income provides some interesting insights on the economic impact of completing high school. The median income in 1981 for American male high school dropouts twenty-five and older was $11,936 versus $16,989 for those who completed their high school education. Over a normal adult working lifetime, this translates into an earnings gap of almost a quarter-million dollars before making adjustments for inflation. For American females of the same age, high school graduates earn 40 percent more, on average, than high school dropouts. Clearly, then, completing high school has quite tangible economic rewards.

In pursuit of an education, students also taste bits of adulthood, like coexisting with authority figures, following rules and regulations, and the politics of social interactions. That's why parents often fare better if they relax their grasp during the first year or so of high school, letting their teen learn the intricacies of these situations for themselves. Even if Jimmy isn't making straight A's, or has — for some unknown reason — chosen the vocational/technical course of study rather than science/engineering, he is learning invaluable lessons about assuming responsibilities, accepting the consequences of one's actions, and aspects of his personality in relation to his peers.

By the start of your teen's junior year in high school, though, certain difficult assessments must be made. Is your child college material? Does he or she wish to attend college? Have any talents emerged during the pursuit of extracurricular activities that might make your teen better qualified for an artistic career, or an athletic one? Where does your child's academic skill seem to lie and how can it best be honed after graduation? Answers to these questions and dozens of others need to be decided a few years before graduation because of the deadlines for certain procedures needed for shaping a student's post–high school future. Adolescents may change their major halfway through college, or drop out of the sculptors' school their parents sent them to after only three months, but without setting certain gears in motion back in high school they might never have had the opportunity to see what college or art school was all about.

Reaching these types of decisions requires a lot of input from parents, as well as their guidance in directing the teen to sources that can provide the information the parents may lack. Diane thinks she might want to become a doctor. Bombard her with information about the profession if you can. Tell her how many years of school it will take, the kinds of subjects she must study, what her grades must be to be accepted at a medical school, the kind of schedule she will have as a doctor, the types of doctors there are, the range of salary she could make. The more information given, the more informed the decision. Encourage Diane to speak with some doctors and learn first-hand how they got to where they are and how they feel about it. Go with her to a medical school and arrange for her to speak with some medical school students. Suggest she volunteer in a hospital and see the environment at close range. Many parents don't stop to realize how critical the career decisions made in high school may later turn out to be. With each decision about their future, teens close some doors behind them. How sad to see doors closed on rooms never glimpsed, on rooms the teen may later regret having overlooked.

Deadlines seem to be the bane of the high school senior's existence. There are deadlines for scholarship and loan applications, deadlines for admission applications to colleges, deadlines for standardized exams such as the SATs. Ideally, your teens should have enough maturity and sense of responsibility to chart and meet these deadlines themselves, but they are probably also caught up in an explosion of social engagements. High school seniors have generally reached driving age and many are permitted to drive to school. They can date without being chaperoned, they may be busy with a grueling sports schedule, or suddenly find the difficulty of their schoolwork has increased substantially as they take higher-level courses to prepare for college. Whatever the reason, the alert and concerned parent would be wise to keep an eye on deadlines and requirements, providing nudges or help as needed for meeting them.

Grade Pressures and School Performance: Is It Okay to Be "Average"?

Many parents want their children to earn straight A's or honors grades throughout their school careers. Never mind that we barely managed a B average and consistently brought C's home in English. Our ninth grade daughter should be a dean's list student who writes stories for her English class that rival D. H. Lawrence and solves algebraic equations in the blink of an eye.

Well-intentioned parent that you are, not even your child is perfect Worse yet, he or she may be a C student, barely managing to be "average." Now what do you do?

You can put intense pressure on your teen to be a better student, to work harder, to bring that grade average up to B's at least. You can review all the great persons throughout history who were such geniuses that they found high school boring and got low grades. You can fault the school and its teachers for their inability to educate your child and transfer him or her to a school you think is better qualified. Or you can make a sensitive assessment of your teen (with the help of teachers and test scores) to decide exactly what his or her level of competency and ability is and whether he or she is reaching it. If your adolescent is doing the best he can, and the best he can do is a C average, you should be proud of him. He is achieving at the top of his own personal scale, not an easy task for any of us.

The tough part of all this is determining your teen's *real* potential. Consistency of achievement level emerges as a critical factor, so you need to have a solid idea of your child's school performance from a young age. If Ted has always whizzed through history and social studies classes, but brings home a D in history the first quarter of his sophomore year, you would be justified in expecting a much better performance from him. He has already proven from his past record that he not only can do it, but seems to have a special aptitude for the subject. Look for extenuating circumstances causing the "fall." If, however, Ted has always struggled with math classes, working incredibly hard for B's, and then gets a D in his first algebra class, you are clued to his lack of understanding or native ability in this subject and the possible need for a tutor or special help from you for him to learn it.

All but the most extraordinary students will have an easier time mastering some subjects than others. By learning your teens' academic strengths and weaknesses you can help bolster their egos when they do poorly in one area by reminding them of their special talents in another. Jack may be average in Spanish but able to put together a car engine in record time. Nancy may burn every meal she prepares in home economics but understand geometry theorems faster than any of her classmates.

Unfortunately, the area your teen displays exceptional competency in may not be given much importance at the school he or she attends. As noted earlier, many schools stress certain activities over others; sports over academics, for example, or performing arts over vocational skills. Appreciation of these skills by parents can help overcome these slights, and sometimes a training program in addition to the high school classes is necessary. If your child's high school does not offer much training in music, for example, or computer programming, you might want to enroll him or her in a Saturday class at the local community college or arrange for individual lessons. If cost is a problem, you will find many college students willing to trade lessons for something you can provide.

It is more than just OK to be average. It is perfectly acceptable if being average is the limit of your teen's ability, if being average makes your teen happy, if being average gives your teen time to pursue other interests having no bearing on school. *Average* is not an inherently negative term; it signifies only the category most of us fall into. The average teen is in good company.

Homework

Sooner or later, everybody gets it — schoolwork to be done at home, to intrude on sand-lot baseball, a dip in the lake, a favorite television show, or any of the activities that mark freedom from the schoolday routine. Maybe that's why so many students put it off, scribble it down on the morning bus ride to school, copy it from a friend during lunch, or just don't do it — homework offends their concept of school time. "School owns me for six hours each day; why should I give it my evening hours, too?"

Many high school schedules now provide study halls to help overcome that problem. Ideally these are silent, unstructured periods when students can study or do homework for any class they choose. In reality, study halls in many schools are rowdy opportunities for an hour's free-for-all. Even with serious study halls, homework can build to the point where some of it must actually be done at home, and parents (wisely) tend to become the overseers of the task.

You're undoubtedly a veteran of the old after-dinner refrain, "Arnold, have you done your homework yet? You know you can't ____ (fill in any enjoyable activity) until it's all done." And, of course, the even more familiar reply, "I don't have any homework tonight." How can parents know for sure and what can they do to help motivate their teens to finish homework?

You can get a good idea of quantities of homework by either attending an open house at the school early in the year or talking to some teachers on an individual basis. Your teen's friends may also give you a clue by talking about the number of papers they have to write or the worksheets to be completed. In some report cards, space is allotted for detailed comments on performance, and incomplete homework assignments may be cited.

Students planning to continue their education beyond high school need to learn good study habits, so it may be helpful to arrange a kind of schedule for the completion of homework. Parents can help their teens develop discipline by setting aside certain hours and a definite area in the home for this purpose. Adolescents should have a desk or table to work at, if possible, in a quiet part of the house. If you have several children, the study area can be shared in shifts if necessary. Peggy does her homework from 4:00 to 5:00 P.M. and Mike does his from 7:00 to 8:00 P.M. A special time and separate area for doing homework tends to eliminate lots of excuses, such as "I couldn't do my math problems because my sister was making cookies on the kitchen table," or "Every time I started to write my essay, Dad would yell for me to do something for him." The family learns to respect "study time" as the teenager learns good study habits.

Another recurring concern to parents is how much help they should give their teens in completing assignments. It's easier than you may think to get roped into the Tom Sawyer method of fence painting, and find that as you're showing Gail how to work through algebra equations you are actually doing all her problems for her. Whatever help you offer should fall along the lines of directing teens to think through the problems for themselves. You are a guide toward the solution rather than a source of the solution itself.

Try to avoid the "we never did it like this when I was a kid" syndrome, which only encourages the undermining of your child's respect for his teacher's methods. In the school building, the teacher is in command; he or she is the professional hired to be in charge of educating. Maybe they don't do division the way you remember it, but they didn't have pocket calculators when you were in school either, or computer terminals. The old way is not necessarily the better way.

Refusal to do homework can be met with a variety of consequences on the part of the parent, ranging from a reminder that failure to maintain grades at about the level reached last semester will result in suspension of driving privileges for one month, to one hour's less television for each homework assignment not completed. You know what sorts of rewards and punishments your teen responds best to and how specific you must be to motivate his or her behavior. Some teens react most productively to a "free rein" statement like "You know best how much work you must do to earn the kinds of grades you want, so I'll trust you to be responsible for remembering to do your homework and letting me know if you ever need help." Others need their parents as strict overseers of their study habits.

Whatever the situation, parents should know that the Coleman Study, a recent report on high school education in the United States today, found that students who had greater amounts of homework generally developed greater self-discipline. In addition, schools that assigned more homework rated higher in terms of academic performance than others with less of a homework load. Thus, while homework may be the cause of disgruntled moans from teenagers, it also seems to be an important ingredient in helping teens develop independent study skills and better academic proficiency.

School as a Social Event

The social side of school is not to be scorned, for it provides an unsurpassed environment for learning social skills and developing personality traits. Social events also inject an element of fun into school, providing a powerful motivator for attendance. Certainly learning about computer language and the evolution of the cosmos can be exciting, but the chance to eat lunch with the most handsome boy in the tenth grade is often the deciding factor in getting kids out of bed in the morning.

The social side of school ranges from seeing friends during and between classes to attending school-sponsored dances and parties. A school with a well-balanced program of social events provides its students with enough opportunities to socialize outside classes that socializing does not intrude too heavily into the educational process. Students attending rigidly run institutions that provide little or no outlet for social activity often spend class time trying to make friends or get a date. Notes are passed, whispers exchanged, and Archimedes' principle goes unnoticed on the blackboard.

Social events also give parents a chance for closer involvement with school faculty and their teens' peers. Dances and parties for young adolescents require chaperones, and schools are usually happy to accept the volunteer services of parents. The social functions of older adolescents may require the organizational skills of a parent, or help with transporting some of the party paraphernalia. Even if your assistance isn't needed, volunteering is a nice show of support to your teen that you encourage participation in social events as well as academic pursuits.

Of course, the social side of school can predominate in a student's life, requiring parents to step in to restore a healthy balance. The main purpose of school is to educate, so when teens become social butterflies to the point that learning is impeded, it's time to clip their wings a bit. Regulating the hours and nights of the week your teen is permitted to attend social functions is often enough to keep the academic side in order.

Extracurricular Activities

Like social events, extracurriculars complement the strictly academic side of school, providing channels for the development of talents that might not be tapped by classroom subjects alone. Extracurricular activities can range from archery to chess to the school musical to an oil painting exhibit, anything that falls outside the normal daily school curriculum and requires the student to stay after school or attend a weekend function.

We asked a few high school students to discuss what they thought were the benefits of participating in extracurricular activities, and were surprised by the responses many of them had:

"They look good on my college applications."

"I like the clubs because I can run for office and be president or vice-president."

"Sometimes you get out of school to travel for meets."

"They keep me away from my crummy home."

"I met a lot of foxy girls."

"You get your picture in the yearbook more times."

These explanations seem to be far afield from the notion of participating in such activities because they're fun, but the truth may be that fun often takes a back seat to some other item on a teen's agenda, such as being with the right crowd, doing something to advance one's status with peers, or getting a leg up on the college admissions process.

Whatever reasons teens have for joining, parents need to be aware of the time-consuming nature of some of the extracurricular activities and whether this is affecting the quality of their teen's schoolwork. A lead part in a play, for example, can require three- or four-hour rehearsals five nights a week, so that only the best organized student could pull it off without neglecting academics a bit.

Students often have to make some difficult choices at the beginning of the school year. If Larry tries out for the football team, and makes it, he won't be able to join the math club. If Eileen debates this year, her Saturdays will be occupied, and she can't cross-country ski with the club. If Malcolm meets with the black pride group, he won't have time to co-chair the Saturday night dances. Parents can help their adolescents realistically appraise and budget their time, so they don't overextend themselves and add further to the pressures school can create.

Athletics and Competition

Involvement in sports is a perennial part of the school experience, although not all teens have the talent, size, and inclination to win a spot on the varsity team. To become a top athlete is, for most teens, an arduous task requiring long hours of training, willingness to stretch themselves to the limits of their endurance ("no strain, no pain, no gain"), and enough dedication to make it through the times when improvement is hard to see.

Unfortunately, some parents push their adolescents into athletic endeavors to satisfy their own egos. This is a mistake of monumental proportions if your fifteen-year-old son would rather be doing the staging for the school play than learning to pole-vault or play middle linebacker. The reluctant teenage athlete who feels pressured by parents into competitive sports not only may be unenthusiastic about the activity but also may feel like a failure because he or she can't perform up to parental expectations. This sense of failure may be heightened when parents deride their kids for not trying hard enough or for giving up, when giving up may be exactly what they want to do. In fact, this applies to top teenage athletes as well as those who never make it to the limelight. Let's listen to a sixteen-year-old former tennis champ's story, told in her own words:

> I guess my problems started when I won the "12 and under" bracket in the state tournament. My dad became convinced I was good enough to reach the pros if I just worked at it for a few more years. So it was practice, practice, practice all the time — four or five hours a day. By the time I was 14, I'd won 24 tournaments and my trophy cabinet was full. Dad drove me to a different city each weekend, and he kept close tabs on the national rankings, waiting for my name to appear. The pressure was really starting to mount. So last year I was ranked second in New England and I lost a big tournament in the first round. He got furious with me, said I wasn't playing up to my potential. All I wanted to do was lead a normal life, have a boyfriend, relax a little. So one day I just told him I was quitting, and I haven't picked up a racquet since. I'm a lot happier now, but I know he's disappointed in me — but I don't care. I've got the rest of my life to live.

To be sure, there are many benefits that can come from participation in athletics. Teens can gain coordination, strength, and stamina (obviously good for their health), increased confidence and self-esteem, a sense of teamwork, a chance to demonstrate leadership potential, and awareness of what good sportsmanship is all about. Sports can also lead to good friendships and give teens a chance to test themselves in challenging situations. But there's another side to the story, too.

Let's visit Vince Lombardi High School for a moment. Here, the principal philosophy is "Winning isn't everything, it's the only thing." When this belief infiltrates teenage athletic competition, the positive effects sour and pressures to perform well during a game mount to excruciating levels. The stars, those who can survive the pressure and turn in stellar performances, acquire the laurels and the adoration of their school. Those who buckle under pressure or who tried out for the sport because they thought it would be fun are confined to the bench to wait out the season. Their confidence and self-esteem lessen with each game that passes them by. They learn only that they haven't the hunger for the throat that would make them superb athletes, and that to the victor go the spoils.

Parents can't usually do much to reverse the "win at all costs" attitude that pervades many high schools (and creeps into junior highs a bit, too). This philosophy filters down from the top ranks of the professional teams that search colleges for athletic stars, so the colleges search the high schools for the young up-and-comings. Big money can be made by a college with a superb athletic team as they sell the rights to televise their games. Top high school athletes can earn full-tuition scholarships and perhaps a car or a luxurious apartment if they are good enough to be wooed by schools with a hefty athletic budget. So the pressure is on for the high school athlete to perform and for the high school to have a winning record, because the scouts might overlook a superjock playing on a losing team.

Fortunately, many high schools provide intramural team competition to help divide the intensely aggressive or talented athlete from the student wanting some enjoyable exercise. Your teen may be better suited for intramural competition, where one team from the junior high or high school competes with another team from the same school on a fairly low-key level. Budgets for intramural sports have decreased recently, however, and the variety of sports available is probably diminishing. In lieu of school-sponsored sports activities, you can always check the local YMCA for intramural competition or try to organize some neighborhood pickup games.

Whatever the degree of the competition, teens usually enjoy having parents attend at least a few of their games to show support for and pride in their endeavor. It is probably wise to avoid playing assistant coach with your kids and instead let the actual coach be the person in authority. A few tips do no harm and show your interest, but bad-mouthing the coaching techniques will only discourage your teen's faith in his or her coach and destroy the vital coach-athlete relationship.

If your teen seems destined to become one of the high school athletic stars, make it a point to remind him or her periodically of the importance of academics. You might cite statistics showing how difficult it is to make the professional teams, and remind your son or daughter of the need to read and write proficiently no matter what their career choice. Yes, it is possible to receive special dispensations from teachers throughout high school and college so excellent athletes pass their classes without doing the work, but one day these deficiencies will emerge and may hamper that person's endeavors for the rest of their life.

We wish equality between the sexes were so pervasive we didn't need to say this at all, but change occurs slowly so we'll make a special point of it. Girls can benefit as much from athletics and competition as boys can. Schools are gradually acknowledging this as they strive to create programs and competition specially for girls' teams. Your daughter should not be made to feel odd or unfeminine because she enjoys and/or has special abilities in athletics. Research studies and observations are proving that masculinity and femininity have little relation to athletic or nonathletic abilities. Females are coming increasingly close to breaking male records in certain swimming and track events, and making great strides in tennis, golf, basketball, and many other sports. Scholarship and prize money for, as well as media coverage of, women's events still lags behind men's, but this will change only as more parents encourage their daughters from a young age to participate in athletics.

Even when parents are encouraging, however, some girls who look promising in junior high abandon athletics in high school, often because peer pressure is at work. It's OK for girls to be cheerleaders but if they play guard on the basketball team they might have trouble getting a date for the prom. Parents need to be doubly supportive in cases like this to make up for the peer group's negativism. If she hangs in there, she'll probably make lasting friendships with a few of her teammates to allevi- ate the loneliness of being different. Happily, in lots of schools as much status accrues to girls with outstanding athletic ability as it does to boys. In any event, health, attitude, energy, strength, endurance, and flexibil- ity are traits available to everyone, male and female, and the pursuit of them is everyone's right.

Parent-Teacher Relations

"If only I had the time to visit with Billy's teachers" is a common lament among today's working mothers and fathers. For obvious reasons, many school activities open to parents occur during the weekday when working parents cannot attend. Alternatives exist, however, for getting to know your teen's school and teachers without attending every planned parent function. You may miss Stefanie's lead in the ninth grade rendi- tion of *The Cherry Orchard*, but you can still arrange time to discuss with her math teacher her failing grades on recent tests. Teachers understand that parents have myriad responsibilities. You'll be surprised how many teachers will agree to meet with you after work or discuss your teen over the telephone.

More than anything, you want to communicate a caring attitude to your adolescent's teachers, letting them know you support them and are genuinely concerned about your child's education. When both teachers and students know parents care about performance, motivation to suc- ceed usually increases. Several high school teachers we spoke with complained of feeling alone, as though the students have been abandoned and the teachers existed to save them. This burden can quickly assume an unbearable weight as teachers realize they have access to a student for only a few hours each day. Parents may feel the same burden. "He's at school all day. What can I do to change him?" Frequent, honest communication between parents and teachers can lift that burden.

For parents who have the time and desire to become more politically involved in school policy, running for PTA president or as a school board member provides political entree. Don't expect your teen to heartily congratulate the endeavor, though, because your activities will probably receive some sort of public attention and your teen may be ribbed about everything you do.

In developing a relationship with teachers, try to remember they have been hired as the experts in educating your child. We've mentioned this twice earlier but can't stress it enough. Your teens need to believe in the efficacy of their teachers. If you belittle their abilities, it is doubtful your teen will respect them enough to learn from them. Parents who think they can do a better job teaching than most of their children's teachers ought to return to school and get a degree in education. Sure, you can explain to your adolescent that teachers will no doubt range in ability and teaching style. Teens will have personality conflicts with some of them and be bored by others. Teachers are people just like the rest of us. They occupy positions of authority in your teen's world, however, so adolescents must learn how to tolerate their frailties.

Specific Strategies for Positive Parenting

(1) A positive, healthy attitude towards school begins with a child's first exposure to it. Day care, nursery school, kindergarten all contribute to the child's impression of education. The attitude of the parents towards school and education is another important factor and is communicated to the child in nonverbal as well as verbal methods. If you feel positive about the value of an education, your teen is likely to copy that attitude.

(2) Stay in close, consistent contact with your teen's teachers, work load, and performance. You might ask to see the book report your son's been working on or offer to help with a research project. Direct exposure to your teen's work helps you to better assess the accuracy of the teacher's grades or reports, and lets you spot potential problems and correct them quickly. Assign a certain time — whether once a day or once a month — to discuss school issues with your teen. This shows them you give school enough priority to schedule it in and ensures periodic communication on the subject.

(3) Communication with the parents of your teen's friends about school can broaden and refine your perspective of the entire school environment. "Does your son complain of the strictness of Mr. Miller?" "Is your daughter also having difficulty making good grades in Mrs. McGee's class?" Discussing these issues with other parents may help put your mind at ease by showing you what you need to worry about and what you don't. Considering the complexities of school and adolescence, doing this can be well worth it.

(4) Watch carefully for early signs of a lack of interest in school. Causes for this can range from boredom to lack of comprehension to poor eyesight. The sooner the problem is resolved, the less likely the teen will be turned off to school permanently. The slow learner and the unusually bright student can both be aided by tutoring; in the first instance, to reiterate the information in a comprehensible fashion, in the second to supplement the material to keep it interesting.

(5) Early in your adolescent's junior year, compile a timetable of deadlines to be met for entry in your teen's chosen post–high school training program. When must applications be completed, financial aid forms submitted, auditions performed, interviews conducted? If you and your teen put this information in an oversized calendar form, it can be posted in a high-visibility area (like near the refrigerator) so you can remind each other of upcoming deadlines. Much of the information about forms and deadlines needed should be available through the school guidance counselor or in college catalogues found in almost any library.

(6) Above all, try not to be overbearing where school is concerned. Hang loose, be patient, sit back a bit, and remember that the schoolhouse is not the only arena for achievement in an adolescent's life. The average pupil in academics may be the star student in violin class. Use whatever accomplishments he or she has to help your teen feel good. This burgeoning self-confidence will aid your teen in every endeavor — from scholastic competition to skateboarding — by building ego strength and a solid sense of competency.

11

Schooltime Blues

The high school years are supposed to provide teenagers with a variety of educational and social experiences that will prepare them to become competent, literate individuals capable of handling the challenges of adulthood and of making positive contributions to society. Unfortunately, such lofty goals are not universally achieved. Disciplinary difficulties, problems with educational methods, and social pressures all conspire to make school a less than optimum experience for many adolescents. In this chapter, we will look at what problems exist, and what parents can do about them.

Recognizing School Problems before They Explode

How would you react if you received a phone call at work that your son had just received a week's suspension from school for smoking marihuana in the boys' bathroom? What would you do if your teenage daughter nonchalantly announced that if her grades didn't improve she'd be ineligible for the all-state women's track meet and the college scouts wouldn't get a look at her athletic performance? How would you cope with a special delivery letter from the junior high school principal asking why you hadn't responded to any of his notes requesting a conference about your teen's chronic truancy (you had received no notes and had no idea your child was skipping classes)? Would you be angry, flabbergasted, hurt? Would you feel duped, or could you see such a disaster coming although you had done nothing specific to counter it?

How could you have helped prevent situations like these from occurring in the first place? The major stumbling block in troubleshooting a teen's problems in school is that your accurate knowledge about your child's behavior and academic performance at school is limited. For better or worse, teens stand or fall on their own merits in school, an area of life where the teens, not the parents, are in complete control. Parents who choose to become informed (by volunteering at school, for example) are a step ahead of other parents who rarely or never set foot in a school. By being accessible to teachers and administrators, such parents are perceived as allies in the task of educating the teens and develop first-hand knowledge of how the school runs, what seems to work and what doesn't.

Educators are likely to communicate with involved parents more promptly and informally about anything concerning students than with parents who are unfamiliar names on a roster. Let the teachers and/or guidance counselors know at the start of each school year that you want to know quickly about any problems. This parental involvement translates into accurate information for parents that is necessary when confronting teenagers about school problems, and may help short-circuit difficulties before they need disciplinary or academic action. Parents' interest and involvement in the teens' schools send out clear messages that they care, that they value education and want to help the teens and educators maximize the learning experience. Teens may pretend to be embarrassed at their parents' interest, or say they are impinging on teenage territory and denying them privacy, but numerous studies have shown that kids whose parents are involved in school functioning do better academically, have better attitudes, and are more successful students than children of uninvolved parents.

Teenagers can experience problems on every level of their academic lives—intellectual, social, and behavioral. Since they tend to be very close-mouthed or even deceptive about themselves, it is often difficult to determine what is problematic and what is not. Many teens honestly believe that to admit to school problems is to admit failure as a person. They may play cat-and-mouse games with their parents, dropping tidbits of information but never revealing the whole picture almost as if they were baiting their parents, daring them to help. Others make up elaborate lies to deny anything is wrong and may intercept mail sent from school or alter report cards to hide the fact that problems exist. Some admit to difficulties but try to blame peers or teachers ("The teacher hates me because I'm creative," or "They didn't vote me into the club because they think I'm too academic and they're just a bunch of social snobs!"). In any case, parents must decipher what is really going on.

Parents should try to be alert to nuances of teens' behaviors, be observant without being intrusive, be perceptive without being hysterical, and be assertive without being threatening. Teenagers having school problems are rarely happy or satisfied with the status quo, may be hostile or sullen, seem depressed, bored, listless, frequently uncommunicative, volatile, secretive, and evasive when it comes to talking about day-to-day events. They may expend much energy putting down teachers, peers, or coaches, for example, and overreact (crying or screaming in rage) to innocent questions like, "How was your day, dear?" or "Why haven't you called Nicole lately? You used to be such good friends," or "Will we need to buy you any equipment for your soccer practices this year?" Teens on the brink of having to admit to and deal with school problems may also seem to spend their lives putting things off, falling into an "I'll do it later" syndrome. This then becomes a vicious circle of not confronting problems at their sources which preprograms failure and the need to make up silly excuses or blatant lies to cover up the failures.

You needn't be investigative reporters to recognize teens' school problems before they explode. But you must be supportive parents, even if what you discover is startling and disturbing. An all-too-human reaction to stress leads many parents to withdraw their support from these teens just when the kids need it most; parental statements such as "I can't deal with him anymore" or "How could he do this to me? That's not the way we brought him up to be!" may be typical. To let your anger cut you off from your teens, however, is counterproductive; it's better to aim for a combination of communication, awareness, negotiation, and respect. Be knowledgeable about your teens' academic programs, the schools' values and goals, learn about the teachers and their reactions to different types of teenagers, and whether their complaints are fair. Become acquainted with some of your teens' friends to get insight into peer groups and how they operate in school, and to help you assess whether they may be involved in the problems. Try to find out if your demands are placing too much pressure on your teens and check whether your perception of the trouble spots matches your teen's. Doing these things requires tenacity, tact, and a major commitment to help your teens in spite of their protests and denials. You may not feel like the most popular parents in the world if you take this course of action but considering what can happen to students allowed to flounder and drown in their problems, there really are no alternatives.

Flunking and Other Facts of Life

How many times have you said to your teens, "Nobody's perfect" and then yelled and screamed about a mistake they made? It's silly, but parents do it all the time. Somehow, at the back of our minds lurks a desire for perfect children — one reason why school failures are so threatening. Rational parents should be able to admit that there are degrees of failure and that flunking does not necessarily doom their teens to academic or social oblivion, nor mean they are "bad" kids or "lazy good-for-nothings."

How can parents who are not professional educators determine the seriousness of teens' flunking? Assessing the number of failing grades, the kinds of courses they are in, and the pattern of failing grades within a larger academic picture helps. A look at the student's academic records will yield reliable clues and will distinguish between a one-time failure and "flunking out." If your teen is in tenth grade and received a failing grade in physics at midterm but all A's and B's in the other subjects, that F may only reflect that he or she hasn't quite mastered the rigors of lab work and weekly quizzes. On the other hand, if your teen failed everything except physical education, the seriousness of the failures warrants your immediate attention and intervention. Was truancy the reason? Were behavior problems, rather than skill-oriented academic deficiencies, the cause? Or is the student having personal problems that are affecting academic output? It's possible that physical or learning disabilities haven't yet been diagnosed and need correcting.

When a teenager fails a subject, some parents are unwilling to listen to the teen's side of the story. Other parents react defensively by confronting the teen's teachers, blaming the system, and making a martyr out of their child. These parents fail to acknowledge that no teen is perfect, no teen is uniformly good at everything every semester. Variables must be accounted for in all teens' academic performances: interest, ability, commitment, how well they like the teachers and vice versa, the teachers' skills and talents, other tasks besides school the teens must routinely handle, the status the teen and peer group assign to schoolwork, and the status the teen's family assigns to schoolwork.

It is very hard to fail everything in school. In fact, most teachers bend over backward to avoid failing their students. If your teen brings home a report card with all F's, it indicates a serious problem that goes beyond academic capabilities and requires immediate investigation.

Teacher Troubles

The stereotype of the self-sacrificing teacher willing to give his or her entire life to the education of children, a model of self-discipline and self-control mirroring the standards by which our children are to live their academic lives, morally above reproach and accorded respect just by virtue of his or her position, exists primarily in fantasy. Today's junior and senior high school teachers are often not much past their student days themselves; they are in a profession that has lost a significant number of its more experienced members to industry, where salaries are higher and emotional and physical stress is lower. Teachers often enter the profession with high ideals and incredible commitment to youth, only to burn out within a few years because of overcrowded classrooms, poor facilities, inadequate teaching materials, inflexible school policies, and kids who would rather be somewhere else. Of the teachers who stay, some flourish and are incredibly successful not only with the good students but with teens who have scholastic difficulties, managing to be creative and functioning within any limitations the school system erects. Others can remain and coast — using the same teaching plans from year to year, and not allowing for students' individual differences — either because they're tenured or no parents have complained enough to get them to change. Some teachers have reputations for being fair, others for being unfair and playing favorites. Some teachers make certain students their pets from year to year, and seem biased against other types regardless of their academic performance or behavior. All teachers are not created equal, and it's likely that sooner or later all teens will experience some conflicts with their educators. The kinds of teacher troubles teens are likely to encounter depend not only on what the teens do but on the skills, personalities, and personal biases of the teachers.

Schooling is not a win-or-lose battle between students and everyone else. All too often, however, the types of students who do have academic or discipline problems perceive their educational experiences as a battleground between opposing forces: themselves and the teachers who have "fingered them" and exposed their shortcomings. When parents are asked to become involved, either by teens seeking allies or by school personnel needing parental help in devising solutions to the problems, there is in reality only a limited amount those parents can do. Fair or not, in school situations, teachers and administrators are in the catbird seats. Parents cannot undo what the teens have done, cannot deny the fact that teachers say the teens are at fault. Parents may feel attacked by the educators, believe that the teachers or administrators are wrong or the school's rules too harsh, and may come in fighting. These reactions may be typical of parents whose teens are in trouble, but they are counterproductive.

Parents can, however, do a number of things to assist teens in trouble at school. You can gather enough information to help you negotiate within the limits of the school policies. Obtain a copy of the discipline code and the academic requirements for either the grade level or the particular course in which the teen is having problems. Also, obtain a copy of the students' rights and responsibilities within that particular school, because this will enable you to assess correctly whether your child is really at fault or it's more a case of teacher overreaction.

Analyze your own attitudes about the school. Many parents have unrealistic expectations about what the school can do for their teens, naively believing that teachers alone are responsible for motivating students to study and learn. Education is a cooperative effort between family and school, and teacher troubles occur more frequently when the parent part of the equation is missing.

Arrange a conference to see your teen's records on file at the school. The Freedom of Information Act gives you the right by law to be allowed access to such documents. (Any school that refuses to do so can be stripped of federal funds!) School records indicate academic standing, reveal teachers' assessments of the student's strengths and weaknesses, and will help you understand why your teen is having trouble.

Parent-teacher conferences are recommended as the next step. Since parents can become intimidated or flustered in such situations, it is useful to prepare a series of questions ahead of time. Some of the things that might be asked are:

(1) Please describe the trouble my child is in.

(2) How long was he (she) in trouble before you contacted me (and, if it was more than a few weeks, why did you wait so long)?

(3) Is my child the only one in class having these problems (causing these problems) or are there others? Is he (she) part of a group that is disruptive (if discipline is the cause of trouble)?

(4) How has my teen reacted to being told he or she is in trouble? How did you deliver this information? Are other school personnel involved in this situation?

(5) What do you feel should be done to eliminate the trouble he (she) is having?

(6) Is there anything I can do to help you and my child solve the problems?

(7) What is the worst thing you see happening if my child continues as is?

(8) How will the problems you and my teen are experiencing affect his (her) school record? Will your assessment be part of the permanent record?

(9) Are you willing to come to a compromise if we can work out the details?

Questions like these are obviously difficult to ask, but they are just as difficult for a teacher to answer without feeling somewhat threatened by a parent's assertive approach to conflict resolution. Therefore, during the meeting it's important to indicate support of the school and your willingness to reinforce its work. Civility is contagious and might even positively affect the teacher's attitude towards your teenager — especially if the nature of the trouble between them is due to personality conflicts and unrealistic expectations complicated by poor communication.

Teachers are occasionally inflexible in their demands of students and overreact when rules aren't followed exactly.

Melanie, a junior, received a failing grade on her English term paper because she handwrote it in pencil instead of the required ink. Her failing grade gave her no credit for its content.

Teachers can also be unaware of certain biases they exhibit in their treatment of students.

Phyllis received a C in algebra during her freshman year. The teacher, a man, noted on her report card that her infrequent class participation had lowered her grade. Phyllis said he ignored her in class and called only on boys despite her frequent volunteering to answer.

The parents of both these students arranged conferences. The math teacher was unaware of his antifemale bias, since none of his students had previously confronted him about it. He changed Phyllis's grade to more accurately reflect her achievement and began calling on her in class. Melanie's parents discovered that the English teacher was willing to regrade the paper if it were recopied.

You need to discuss the outcome of such conferences with your teens. Ask them the following questions: "Can you or will you do what it takes to reverse the situation? If you don't make an effort to ease the situation are you willing to live with the results? Had you ever communicated with your teacher about the problem before it got to the point of explosion? How do you feel about what the teacher told me?"

Speaking with teachers or administrators doesn't always lead to solutions of teacher troubles. You may need to consult the superintendent of schools or school board members if you can prove your teen is being treated unfairly. Sometimes, bringing in outside consultants such as educational psychologists or counselors may be effective. They may find the teen has a previously undiscovered learning disability that needs special attention. Or they may determine that the teen merely has poor study skills, never having learned to take notes or organize homework time, and needs some direction to develop or improve them. They may suggest that the teen would do better in an alternative-school setting offering more flexibility in scheduling and choice of courses than in a traditional classroom environment. Various educational options exist and must be objectively considered if they're to prove useful to you.

If you are a part of your teen's problem-solving efforts, you need to stick to a productive approach that will serve the best interests of the student but not contradict or conflict with the rules of the school. Chances are good that if parents try to cooperate with teachers, students will too.

Cheating

There are as many ways to cheat as there are students in a school and, like it or not, your teen has probably tried at least one of them. This does not necessarily doom your teen to a life of dishonesty or juvenile detention. It does signal a child who may be having difficulty handling any of a number of pressures related to peer-group practices, heavy academic or athletic schedules, job responsibilities, family hassles, or self-image problems. Or the teen may simply be taking the easy way out.

Teens who cheat cannot or will not organize their lives well enough to be prepared for school responsibilities; cheating is an attempt to hide this fact. Cheating is more than just copying someone else's test questions, making crib sheets for exams, agreeing to "fix" sports events, or faking illnesses to avoid making class presentations. Cheating is an attitude, a way of pretending you are doing what is expected of you without actually doing it. It's a habit that, like any other, can get out of control, blinding teens to other options whenever confronted with pressure situations.

If your teen has been caught cheating, determine from school personnel:

(1) how often the cheating has occurred,
(2) how long it took before they decided to notify you,
(3) whether the teacher sought an explanation from the student,
(4) whether cheating is prevalent in the teen's peer group,
(5) whether the school has a student honor board that reviews cases of cheating or whether such issues go directly to administrative personnel.

This may have been a first offense and happened because the student had a full-time after-school job and literally fell asleep studying the night before the test. Or your teen may be a chronic offender, warned several times by the teacher about cheating and now faced with suspension from school. Clearly, these two situations need to be dealt with differently, so parents should not automatically censure their teens and threaten to punish them when they learn of an episode of cheating. Instead, be prepared to listen, to find out if there were extenuating circumstances, and evaluate your next actions based on this assessment.

It is unlikely your teen is proud of cheating, and it is just as unlikely you will accomplish anything productive by withdrawing your understanding and support. It is the rare teen who will believe the adage that "by cheating, you are only cheating yourself," so it doesn't do much good to utter platitudes. It *is* important to state your parental disapproval and disappointment but then you must help your teen develop strategies to avoid the need to cheat in the future. Some of these strategies are:

(1) *Help your teen organize time better.* Teenagers can unwittingly waste enormous amounts of time, leaving assignments to the last minute. Limiting phone calls, car privileges, T.V. or stereo time until homework has been done is fair and workable. You might also list the things your teen does daily and compare it to what he or she would have to do to get studies completed and have leisure time.

(2) *Try to find out why your child cheats.* Your teen may think of him- or herself as too dumb to learn, so he or she uses cheating in place of thinking. Your teen may be scared to fail, and so risks cheating for a good grade rather than really studying and perhaps not getting those high marks. Cheating may be a mark of bravado in your teen's social circle, and it really has nothing to do with how well your teen is learning. Your teen may cheat to please you, believing that if he or she is anything less than perfect your love will stop. Or your teen may honestly believe cheating is OK, perhaps having picked up subliminal messages from parents who are less than 100 percent honest in their daily lives. These issues need open discussion, but don't be afraid of laying down the law.

(3) *Teach your teen that it is all right to be imperfect, and that it may be necessary at times to ask for help.* Do not equate help-seeking behavior with weakness or lack of intelligence; instead, equate it with strength of character, maturity, and honesty. Sometimes it's necessary to be a little idealistic and optimistic when we talk to our teens, even though they may balk at this type of talk. They will secretly appreciate the support and internalize it at some point in their lives.

Cheating should not be condoned but the cheater should not automatically be condemned.

Discipline

According to the Gallup polls of public attitudes about education, lack of discipline in the schools has been rated the number one concern in every year but one since 1969. No wonder. In junior and senior high schools across the country, homeroom teachers confiscate a literal arsenal of knives, brass knuckles, and guns. Not only boys are guilty of aggressive misbehavior — teenage girls fight, spit, and assault their teachers in violent fashion. Add to this the disciplinary problems surrounding teenage drug use (students actually smoke marihuana joints in hallways or classrooms, daring their teachers to stop them) and the older, more familiar scenes of harassing teachers by walking in late, cursing, sleeping through class, and simple clowning around, and you begin to understand the pervasiveness of the problem. And, if you think this description applies only to inner-city schools, think again — even parochial and affluent suburban schools are sorely tested by disciplinary problems.

Your first reaction may be that this is a problem for someone else to worry about, but educators don't agree. One school principal put it this way, "Parents can't just park their kids at school all day and expect both discipline and teaching. The more time and energy we spend policing students, the less time and energy is left to plan, to teach, and to learn." Many teachers echo this sentiment, adding that if school becomes a battleground over disciplinary matters, the inevitable result is a lowering of educational standards and loss of competent teachers who simply give up in the face of insurmountable odds.

A history teacher with thirteen years' experience who recently retired to become an insurance agent confirms this view: "I chose teaching as a career because I loved the thrill of getting through to students, helping excite them about the world of ideas. But after being assaulted three times in the last two years, and realizing my role was really that of a zoo-keeper, I decided to call it quits."

Concerned parents and educators agree that no simple answers are available. Since many teens make a game out of breaking rules to challenge authority, one logical starting point is to place responsibility for formulating and enforcing rules on the teens themselves. This approach uses peer pressure to maintain disciplinary order and has worked quite well in some settings. The major problem with this approach occurs when model students, who are not themselves disciplinary problems, are put in charge of this system so their trouble-making classmates don't really feel pressure from people they consider their peers.

An effective answer to disciplinary problems at school must begin with appropriate standards and values learned at home. Self-discipline — the elusive ingredient that's *not* always present when the school bell rings — simply doesn't develop unless teens see some reason for it and some benefit to them. The discipline we use with our teens at home and the consistency with which we apply it is the principal source of the self-control teens exhibit outside the home.

There are deficiencies in our schools, however, that create an environment in which dissatisfaction leads to troublesome behavior. In many cases, there are simply no payoffs for following the rules. Boredom is often a major problem either because the curriculum is not up-to-date or because teachers are so overworked they have little time for innovation or creativity. Overcrowded classes, poorly kept physical plants, and inadequate recreational facilities also contribute to disciplinary dilemmas. As a result, even the teens who have good self-discipline at home may find it more interesting or prestigious at school to ignore the rules.

If discipline is a problem at your teen's school, what can you do? You can organize a parent group to lobby for monies to hire someone like a crisis-intervention specialist who can mediate student-teacher problems. You can speak to the teachers' union representatives in your school and offer your support and assistance in devising a solution. If your own teen is part of the problem, you must be willing to admit this, confront the reasons for the discipline difficulties, and try to determine if you as a parent have been unwittingly contributing to that teen's need to break the rules. You can also try to mobilize public opinion about the larger situation and try to involve the media to get results. But do something; discipline should never be allowed to become so overwhelming an issue that it interferes with learning.

Social Sorrows

The social aspects of schooling are often more problematic and traumatic to teenagers than are academic rigors. Unfortunately, parents tend to forget what it was like trying to find a place in the social sun and so may belittle or minimize their teens' social agonies.

You cannot protect your teens from the pains of growing up, nor shield them from teenage romantic crushes that end up crushing them. You cannot get them accepted into clubs that have chosen to exclude them; you cannot make positions for them in honor societies or on cheerleading squads for which they don't have the credentials. Nor, in fact, should you. What you should do, however, is be accessible if your teens want to tell you about these situations.

In order to do this, keep the following facts of teenage life in mind:

(1) Social life can make or break a teen's self-esteem. All the adulation and love in the world from one's parents may not mean as much as acceptance by one's peers.

(2) Being a social outcast can seriously influence any teen's academic performance in school. Teens who don't fit in with a crowd may become lazy, bored, uninterested, or sloppy about their schoolwork because they are preoccupied with remedying the deficiencies of their social lives.

(3) Romantic problems can definitely affect a teen's schoolwork. The girl whose boyfriend dumped her or the boy who was turned down one too many times by the girl of his dreams are likely to become moody and depressed and show no interest in school, obsessed with thoughts of lost opportunities for romance. Romantic entanglements teach their own lessons, however, which may be just as valuable as school lessons.

(4) Teens who can't fit in with one social group may choose another group to hang out with but may never really be comfortable there. They may seem to have perpetual chips on their shoulders, and may badmouth the group they really wanted to be accepted by. They are often very negative in their outlooks about school.

Social matters *do* count and do have repercussions beyond next weekend's dates. Teenagers who experience lots of social sorrows during their junior and senior high school years lose out on two counts: they don't have much fun, and they don't develop the sense of group identity that usually precedes a burgeoning sense of confident individuality. If your teens are having undue problems with peers, don't tell them, "It doesn't matter; ten years from now no one will care." Instead, try to explore the following topics:

(1) Why do you think nobody likes you? What proof do you have?

(2) What would you change about yourself to get accepted if you could? Why do you think that would make a difference?

(3) What is the best thing about you? Does anyone else know about that part of you? How would you let someone see that side of you?

(4) Is there anything we can do to help you or would you rather we not mention this anymore?

(5) Have you ever told any of the kids you'd really like to be friends with about how you feel?

(6) How would you describe your ideal friend? Your ideal social life? Your ideal school life? Does your actual life correspond to these ideals?

(7) Do you like everyone you meet? If you don't, then why do you expect everyone to like you?

(8) Would it help you to talk to a counselor or therapist about your social problems at school?

These kinds of questions stimulate the teens to think positively and realistically about themselves and can help parents decide whether the social sorrows are transient, serious, or genuinely debilitating to the teens. If the latter is the case, we suggest you seek professional help from the school or from a private source.

Truancy

Truancy is a major problem in many secondary schools today. When students skip classes or entire days of school, everyone loses — the kids fall behind in their academic work and may drop out if the amount of makeup work seems impossible to deal with, and if their school is public, rather than private, the school district loses federal and state funds that are tied to the number of students actually attending classes each day. In New York City and other large metropolitan areas, this problem has become so serious that truancy officers ride special vans or buses in a search for truants, with the intent being both to get these phantom students back in the classroom and to notify their parents in hope of enlisting their involvement in dealing with the problem.

Parents often don't realize their teens are skipping school and react with surprise, embarrassment, and anger when they find out. Sometimes they admit to feeling powerless to control their adolescents, and sometimes they simply don't care. In other cases, parents equate chronic truancy with criminal behavior, which is certainly not always the case, and refuse to come to their teens' assistance.

Although the reasons motivating truancy are varied and complex, they all seem to involve little positive return from class attendance. Skipping school thus becomes either an exercise in recreational therapy (e.g., playing video games, shooting baskets, roaming the streets) or an attempt to make some money (either through legitimate activities like a daytime job, or in street-wise hustling in pool parlors or card games, or in illegal acts ranging from drug transactions or shoplifting to stealing cars and committing muggings). In either case, skipping is more exciting to the chronically truant teen than the boredom of the classroom.

What should a parent of a truant do? Mrs. G., whose son Tony had been cutting classes since age thirteen, said:

> It's impossible at first. You're afraid to admit there's a problem since the kid's actions reflect on us. Or so I thought at first. The trouble was that I was wrong. If I had faced it long ago it never would have escalated as much as it has.

Parents should confront their truant teens and open a dialogue. The following statements can be useful opening lines in dealing with these ticklish situations:

(1) "I know lots of things in school are imperfect. Can we discuss the things that are bothering you the most?"

(2) "If you don't plan to go to classes, can you think of some ways to spend your time that might be legal and acceptable substitutes?"

(3) "Have you been feeling well lately?" (Physical problems such as lack of energy due to anemia or poor nutrition or poor eyesight can be contributing factors to the frustration with school that often leads to adolescent truancy.)

(4) "How do your friends feel about your truancy? Are you just skipping school to be one of the group?"

These sorts of queries are nonthreatening and reflect a willingness on your part to be objective and hear your teen's point of view. The discussions that ensue may help both of you think about the reasons for the truancy and what might be done to overcome these problems. Once you've talked this over thoroughly with your teen, a joint visit to the school guidance counselor may be in order. It may be possible to work out practical solutions that will make school more appealing to your teen — for instance, dropping several academic subjects and replacing them with vocational training, or switching courses so as to get in classes with particularly stimulating teachers — but in the final analysis, even being your teen's ally won't eradicate the truancy unless he or she wants it to change.

Dropouts

While a dropout is clearly no longer an active student, it may be that he or she would like to be back in school under the right circumstances but doesn't know how to go about it. Some teens may be embarrassed to go to school because they don't have appropriate clothes to wear; others fear reprisals from teachers; and others have left because they feel that school is a dead end. Complex personal problems also contribute to the dropout rate — alcoholism and drug abuse, coming from an abusive family situation, personal illness, and so on. Whatever the underlying reason(s), if your teen has decided to drop out of school you can play an active part in triggering some blunt discussions about alternatives. Here are some questions you can ask:

(1) "Being out on your own can be difficult for anyone — even for me. Have you ever found this to be the case?"

(2) "When I was in school there weren't too many kids who dropped out. Can you explain what it's like to be out of school at your age?"

(3) "What would an ideal week be like for you? Does school fit in at all?"

(4) "How do you spend your time? Do you have fun? Do you find life interesting? How would the kids in school be spending their days?"

(5) "Sometimes my boss is hard on me. What were your teachers like?"

(6) "Sometimes things don't go right for me. I argue with my friends, I don't have enough money to do what I want, I get a little bored. Do you ever feel that way?"

Your teen may be reluctant to talk about these issues with you at first, but keep trying. By drawing parallels with your own experiences you are saying to the dropout that you can empathize with him or her and by asking for information you may get a better grasp on how to proceed. The key thing is to discover if there's any reason to encourage reenrollment in school or to pursue alternatives that don't leave the teen to his or her own devices.

As parents of dropouts you are the school's best ally. You can fill in missing details of possible reasons for the teen's decision to quit school, you can be an active participant in any plans to reenroll, and you have the right to make sure that if your teen had real or imagined problems with teachers or other students in the past that appropriate steps will be taken — including provision of counseling services, where necessary —

to help the teen avoid them once he or she is back in school. You can also give permission for your teen to become involved in alternative school options such as work-study programs, which might serve your teen's needs better than traditional school.

Dropping out is not necessarily a dead end for your teen. If you become a part of the solution (even though you may find you've been part of the problem) there is a much better chance your adolescent will succeed the next time around in school.

Special Students: Learning Disabilities, Gifted Teens, Underachievers, and More

Thousands of children in the United States today have special educational needs. Depending on the nature of their handicapping conditions, their schools are required by Public Law 94-142, "The Education of All Handicapped Children Act of 1975" to provide these students with free, appropriate public education that includes special education and related services in the least restrictive environments.

The law defines handicapped children as mentally retarded, hard of hearing, deaf, speech-impaired, visually handicapped, orthopedically impaired, or otherwise health-impaired children with specific learning disabilities. Learning disabilities are disorders in one or more of the basic psychological processes involved in understanding or using spoken or written language. Students with specific learning disabilities may exhibit severe discrepancies between achievement in school and intellectual ability in one or more of the following areas: oral or written expression, listening and reading comprehension, basic reading skills, mathematical calculation, and reasoning. For example, learning-disabled kids' writing and reading is frequently characterized by reversals, substitutions, and omissions of letters and sounds; their attention spans may be short or they may be very distractible; they may have problems remembering left and right; they may have coordination deficiencies, may have problems focusing their eyes on a page or finding their places when reading even if their eyesight is 20/20, and so on. Students may be learning-disabled because of visual, hearing, or motor handicaps, mental retardation, emotional problems, environmental, cultural, or economic disadvantages.

As you read this, you may suspect that your teen is learning-disabled but has not yet been diagnosed. Your teen may have been kept back in school, or may have exhibited behavior problems that caused numerous suspensions, but for some reason your school district never conducted an evaluation to determine if that teen had a handicapping condition. As a parent you have the right to request such an evaluation, usually called an Initial Evaluation Program (IEP). P.L. 94-142 states that the IEP must be conducted by a multidisciplinary team consisting of special-education teachers or specialists, school psychologists or educational diagnosticians, one or more regular classroom teachers, a physician and/or a school nurse, a school counselor or social worker, other specialists such as speech pathologists or physical therapists if applicable. If a specific learning disability is suspected, the regular classroom teacher and an educational diagnostician at the minimum must be present.

Because P.L. 94-142 specified that special students should be educated in the least restrictive environment, many schools are "mainstreaming" — placing students with special learning needs in regular classrooms with nonhandicapped students. The spirit and intent of P.L. 94-142 is to lessen and obliterate the impact of the handicap label on the students; foster understanding among other students of the problems handicapped kids must overcome; desegregate the special students (who prior to this law tended to be educated only with each other, apart from the mainstream) and give them the chance to function in environments that do not necessarily cater to their unique needs, thus building confidence in their abilities to function in the world of the nonhandicapped.

P.L. 94-142 also decreed that special students have access to special services. This included academic instruction provided by special teachers when necessary; corrective and supportive personnel, equipment, and material resources: for example, transportation, corrective services such as speech therapy, audiology, physical and occupational therapy, psychological services, recreational activities, medical and counseling services. The same support services available to nonhandicapped students have to be available to handicapped students: physical education, career and vocational education, college and job-placement counseling, and aptitude testing services.

Parents of teenagers who require special educational services are generally more intimately involved with their teens' schooling than are parents of nonhandicapped children. The reason for this is that parents must give their consent to any changes in a child's educational program that require special services. Specifically, the parents' procedural rights include:

(1) written notification prior to any school evaluations of the teens' handicapping conditions or prior to any changes (or refusal to change) in the educational programs already in place;
(2) the option to arrange for an independent educational evaluation of their children;
(3) the examination of all school records about the teens;
(4) participation in all meetings to plan individualized educational programs for the students in question;
(5) giving written consent to placements in special programs;

(6) due-process hearings if the parents disagree with the school's assessments or procedures.

With so many parents' rights mandated by law, how could problems arise? In practical terms, involvement requires parents to be totally informed of these rights, totally cognizant of their childrens' unique educational needs, and certain that these needs are correctly assessed and dealt with by the particular school district. Many commentators have dubbed this process as "negotiating the special education maze," a feat that requires extraordinary perseverance. Although all fifty states have mandated education for special students, certain districts have better services than others. Suburban districts of 5,000 or more enrollment tend to excel, as do those in large cities or in areas where the schools are close to universities with training programs for teachers of the handicapped.

Negotiating with teachers can be difficult at times, especially if your teens are mainstreamed and it seems that the classroom teachers are less than sympathetic to their plight, or worse, not fully trained to handle special students. In such cases, parents must be active advocates for their teens. Doing this demands close contact with the schools, a willingness to share information about the kids with school personnel, perhaps keeping your own files on the teens' academic progress to compare periodically against school records, and comparing school reports with what you observe at home. Parents are a vital link in the educational partnership.

Gifted teens are yet another category of special students. In 1978, Congress enacted the "Gifted and Talented Children's Education Act" under Title IX of the Elementary and Secondary Education Act. Funds were thus allocated for state programs and model projects for gifted students, but the act didn't provide specifically for gifted children with handicaps. Up to now there has been a great deal of opposition to the notion of special programs for gifted and talented students, partly because the United States has such an intense belief in democracy that many people see provisions for gifted and talented students as somehow antithetical to the notion of equal education for everyone, a violation of our egalitarian tradition. Most people don't think gifted students need any special considerations because the myth is that if they're lucky enough to be smart, they have no other problems. In reality, many of these students have problems as serious as those of their handicapped and learning-disabled peers. They are, in fact, the other end of the continuum of capabilities of students. Many gifted students flounder in school programs that either don't challenge them at all, don't challenge them appropriately, or worse, don't even identify them as gifted.

Who are the gifted and talented students? They come from all walks of life, all races, religions, national and regional groups. They seem to be equally spread between both sexes and can be found in every socioeconomic group. Sometimes the special students we discussed earlier are gifted; sometimes gifted students have incredible behavior problems and are underachievers. They are not all the stereotypic genius reading Shakespeare at age two and doing quantum physics at age seven. In most areas of life, gifted students are indistinguishable from their "normal" peers.

Of the many dictionary definitions of giftedness, the one that seems most accurate says that giftedness includes not only endowment and talent but drive and the opportunity to express one's talents. In 1972, the United States Office of Education defined gifted children slightly differently, saying that these were people capable of high performance, including achievement and potential ability in any of the following areas (singly or in combination): general intellectual ability, specific academic aptitude, leadership ability, visual and performing arts, creative or productive thinking, psychomotor ability. They did not mention the opportunity factor identified in the definition we prefer. In fact, the overwhelming majority of the approximately 5 percent of the total school population who are gifted and talented are neither adequately identified nor nurtured in their homes. Most parents are unaware their children are gifted; many of these potentially gifted students fail to develop because of lack of stimulation, lack of role models to emulate, and lack of opportunity to acquire the motivation to succeed.

Some of the problems of gifted and talented teens have to do with labeling, the stigma of having others call them "brains" or "eggheads" or "stuck-up snobs" — a problem not unlike those of handicapped students who bear the brunt of similar labeling processes at the hands of insensitive "normal" peers. As a result, many gifted and talented students opt for social acceptance, hiding their unique capabilities and keeping their probing intellects to themselves. It is easier to be average than it is to be "special," and it can be stated unequivocally that adolescent females tend to try to hide their giftedness more than any other group.

Gifted students also can suffer at the hands of insensitive or untrained educators.

(1) Junior and senior high school teachers may inaccurately interpret the gifted/talented teens' tendencies to ask more complex questions, pushing for answers beyond the capacities of the average teachers to respond as somehow equivalent to threats to their authority within classrooms or showing off, and may try to extinguish those curiosities in favor of conformity to a different norm or learning style.

(2) Junior and senior high school teachers may harbor certain myths about gifted and talented students: that they are all fast learners, that they are equally bright in every subject area, that they all test very high on standard I.Q. tests, that their rate of learning is constantly accelerat-

ing with no plateaus, that they love school and would rather be there than anywhere else. Such myths cause many truly gifted/talented students to be overlooked.

Parents can pose yet another set of problems:

(1) Parents may be so proud of having gifted/talented teens that they will encourage them only in the areas of intellectual development, forgetting that all teens need the opportunity to develop social skills.

(2) Conversely, parents may feel intimidated and threatened about the teens' skills and may transmit these negative feelings to those teens, who then lose the support they need so badly from the home environment.

(3) Parents may harbor unrealistic expectations about what their gifted/talented teens can accomplish with their lives. This is especially dangerous if the parents try to live vicariously through these teens, and the teens don't deliver in spite of their abilities!

Some of the major problems gifted teens exhibit in school are the following:

(1) They may be hypercritical of other students who don't think or act the way they do.

(2) They may be overdependent on adults (i.e., their favorite teachers) and afraid to take risks because they are very self-critical.

(3) They may be underachievers because of boredom, frustration with busywork, poor study habits, and poor self-images.

(4) They may rebel and become discipline problems because their gifts and talents are not adequately channeled and challenged.

(5) They may gravitate towards older friends, a tendency that can be especially problematic during the junior high school years.

(6) They often express feelings of inferiority (in part due to their own high expectations and those of parents and significant others).

Clearly, gifted/talented students cannot necessarily make it on their own. Schools should not ignore the special needs of this minority group. In the words of a teacher at New York's Bronx High School of Science, "We hadn't realized until recently that giftedness is a kind of handicap ... bright kids need a structured and challenging environment just as much as deaf kids need an atmosphere sensitive to their special needs."

The underachievers of the junior and senior high schools, teens who don't work up to their potentials according to the educators' assessments, come from all segments of the school population. Underachieving can be a signal of a number of problems:

(1) The school is not doing its job to challenge and motivate its students, and learning is not rewarding enough.

(2) The social status of the underachiever is greater than that of the competent learner.

(3) The parents aren't giving their teens positive feedback for school performance so the teens stop trying.

(4) The teens are suffering emotional problems, such as depression that make it impossible to achieve anything beyond the bare minimum for school regardless of the teens' intellectual capabilities.

(5) Underachieving is a cry for help. The teens need parental attention or teachers' attention, and this is a way to elicit it.

Underachievers tend to make everyone a bit angry — teachers get frustrated by their inabilities to motivate these teens, parents get aggravated by the teens' poor grades and nonchalant attitudes; the teens themselves don't really want to be known as underachievers but the pattern becomes so ingrained it's hard to break out of it.

Motivating underachievers should be the job of the schools, but the reality is that teachers may not have the time to provide these students with classwork appropriate to their learning styles. This is where parents can fill in the gaps. Sometimes it can be a matter of making magazines available that might stimulate your teen's flagging interest:

> My son was in an English class studying satire. He couldn't handle reading Jonathan Swift and I knew he had to write a paper. So I went out and bought him a copy of *Mad* magazine and we read it together. He thought I was crazy at first but it really got his brain moving. He told his teacher and she adopted the idea in class. He passed and even began to do work!

Sometimes a parent can help by reinforcing the few things the teen is interested in, and discussing (and implementing) ways of linking these things with school work:

> My daughter was completely involved in designing and sewing quilts, and her school had no home ec. program. She hated to read and spent all her spare time quilting. I talked to her history teacher and asked if I could develop and teach a unit on quilting in the history of America, even teach quilting if necessary. My daughter was furious at first but helped me write the curriculum. She actually got the message that there's more to history than memorizing dates, and she taught our unit the next term to underclassmen.

You don't have to be a professional educator to be a potent motivator!

The opposite of the underachievers, the overachievers, can be just as frustrating; they try to do so much they cannot possibly succeed at everything. They may feel pressured into trying by parents who expect too much of them, or out of allegiance to teachers they are hoping to impress, or by peer pressure if their social groups are comprised of the school's doers and shakers. They may come on very strong in school, may try to politicize things, may try to manipulate situations to get everything done. Generally, they cannot delegate responsibility and come across as pushy and brash when underneath they may be just the opposite.

Then there are the nonachievers, the teens whose entire schooldays are devoted to getting away with doing just about nothing. It is not that they don't work up to their potentials — they don't work, period. They stay in school for a variety of reasons: their parents make them, they are too young to quit legally, they genuinely like school. Unfortunately, many of these teens are automatically passed from grade to grade and many graduate without having really fulfilled the minimum requirements.

Motivating nonachievers is probably the most difficult task for both teachers and parents. The key is to get the energy such teens devote to not working redirected to schoolwork. Parents need to be strong enough not to allow their teen to be passed to a higher grade level just because he or she is too old to be held back. It is important to get these kids tuned into the notion of accountability — that they have the responsibility to try at least to learn something while in school, that this is their job. Sometimes, such teens can be victims of the expectation exchange in which parents are unrealistic in their demands so their kids simply stop trying to please; this attitude eventually creeps into how they cope with school.

Gimmicks or challenges rarely work to motivate nonachievers. Blunt honesty that surprises or disarms them can and may be the first step in breaking the habit the teens have fallen into. Exploring options is another useful approach — perhaps the teen is eligible to switch to another school in the district, perhaps a change from an academic to industrial arts curriculum will do the trick. It is possible to motivate nonachievers, and parents' input does make a difference in the long run.

Getting educated is a job, an art, and a chore. It is not an easy task, and the school years are fraught with many unseen dangers and stumbling blocks thrown in the paths of adolescents' intellectual and social development. Schooltime blues are inevitable; how teenagers cope with them depends in large part on the support of friends, teachers, *and* parents.

12

Social Skills, Risk-Taking, and Self-Esteem

The psychological development of the adolescent is a complex process. Teens react to themselves, to their families, to their environments, and to ordinary and extraordinary life stresses in a number of ways. In later chapters, we will examine some of these special situations that produce psychological conflicts or crises for teens and their parents. Here, we focus on the normal psychological vicissitudes of the teenage years.

The Adolescent's Ego and Other Fragile Matters

The ego is an invisible part of each of us that consists of a sense of self-identity combined with an awareness of how our feelings and thoughts relate to those of others. During adolescence, the ego is a little like a yo-yo, bouncing up and down as teens feel alternately secure and confused about who they are and how others see them. Understanding what makes your teenager tick is often best accomplished by realizing where the "ego yo-yo" is in its excursions — on the ascent or plummeting.

We have already mentioned the extreme sensitivity of the typical adolescent. In part, this sensitivity stems from the fact that the teenager's ego is not yet securely anchored, making him or her highly susceptible to self-doubt. Teens look to important people in their lives for approval and encouragement to help overcome this ego-uncertainty; failing to find it, they worry that they're not worth much, or that they're lacking in character, drive, talent, popularity, or some other magical ingredient.

The teenager whose ego is consistently weak relates to the world in tentative, uncertain, self-effacing ways. Like the ninety-pound weakling of the ads, who gets sand kicked in his face and stands powerlessly by, the ego-deficient adolescent approaches life with numerous anxieties, passivity, and little sense of control. When something good happens, such a teen may decide it's due to luck, not hard work, skill, or determination. When something not so good happens, the teen may think it couldn't have been helped — it was preordained. Because of this attitude, teens with poor ego strength are less likely to work towards improving themselves, since they believe what happens to them is more a matter of fate than anything else.

Adolescents can develop stronger egos in a number of different ways, with encouraging, supportive parents being a prime factor in this process. But the flip side of this phenomenon should be looked at, too, because *too* strong an ego, like an overmuscled body, can have negative effects and interfere with smooth functioning. Teenagers whose egos get so overblown that they are too impressed with their own importance can be in for later rude awakenings. Until this happens, though, they may literally bristle with arrogance and unknowingly antagonize almost everyone they come in contact with. Intriguingly, parents seem to be among the last to recognize the overdeveloped adolescent ego. Among the key warning signs are:

(1) a "know-it-all" attitude that is often expressed in arrogant behavior;
(2) a persistent need to be the center of attention;
(3) consistent insensitivity to the feelings and needs of others;
(4) a pattern of selfishness in dealing with family and friends;
(5) intolerance for others;
(6) inability to admit being wrong.

Teenagers may have a firm sense of identity in certain areas but feel relatively bumbling in others. The proficient student who is self-assured in class may be transformed into a childlike worry wart at social events. That take-charge leader on the athletic field becomes tongue-tied and intimidated by any mathematical endeavors more advanced than measuring first-down yardage. The computer whiz has trouble carrying on a conversation with a date unless they discuss bytes, ROMs, and disk-drives. This doesn't mean there's something wrong — it just takes time for other competencies to develop. How parents can assist in this process is something we'll now discuss.

Parents as a Source of Self-Esteem

Adolescents get feedback on how their personalities are developing from a few primary sources — parents, friends, teachers and/or employers. Few teens have developed enough insight to assess themselves accurately, and most fall on the side of being overcritical. They seek these "significant others" as mirrors to reflect their true image back to themselves. Depending on the parents' style of communication, they can reflect a crisp image that expands the teen's understanding of him- or herself, or an amusement park distortion that shatters their teen's self-esteem.

Feelings of self-worth are the essence of an adolescent's sense of identity. Psychologists realize that low self-esteem can lead to a variety of problems, including delinquency, depression, and drug abuse, while high self-esteem seems to preprogram teens for success. Thus, it's important for parents to encourage — rather than undermine — their children's belief in themselves, but accomplishing this can be a tricky task. One way to achieve it is by supporting teenagers in developing a sense of responsibility. To be effective, you've got to be willing to let teens make their own mistakes without condemning them for failure. Only in this way — perhaps with a bit of gentle prodding — will teens see that performing a task poorly should not be justification for relinquishing responsibility for that task.

Parents who try to live for their teens will be met with resistance and resentment. Adolescents want to prove their competence, which they can only demonstrate by doing things by themselves. We cannot take our teens' hurts from them, protect them from the abuses society may inflict, go on their first date with them, or turn down the marihuana joint passed to them at a party. Parents who are supportive of their adolescent's increasing autonomy, though, make it easier for the teen to have confidence in his or her ability to maneuver through the mazes of life and increase their odds of avoiding future mistakes.

Joan, a high school freshman, tells her mother that a senior has asked her for a date. Joan has had some previous dating experience with freshman boys but never with anyone older. Joan's mother could react in several ways. She might forbid her to date the senior, although Joan has not asked for permission, just brought up the topic for discussion. A more effective response that would encourage Joan's own assessment of the issue would be, "From the way you're telling me about this, it sounds like you're not sure you want to go out with him. Do you like him?" Joan can then explain what type of person he is, how long she has known him, etc. Her mother might add, "It sounds like you're a little frightened about a date with him. Maybe you aren't feeling completely comfortable because the age difference might keep you from having things in common. I would feel better with you dating someone closer to your own age, but I haven't met this boy yet and I trust you to make the right decision."

Joan may ultimately decide to date the senior, but her mother's response has accomplished two goals vital to preserving and supporting

Joan's self-esteem. She has been open and honest with her daughter about her own feelings — without forbidding the date. From this, Joan can see that her mother trusts her judgment. Her mother has also acknowledged what she sensed were Joan's own feelings. Later, if the date fails and Joan feels childish and out of place, she has been prepared for some of these feelings and told they are a natural reaction to that type of social situation. Joan is less likely to feel like a failure because of the date and can view the outcome from a healthier perspective.

Parents can aid their teens' self-esteem in another, direct way. Teens often complain that their parents embarrass them. The house is messy when friends drop by, Mom sings along with hit tunes on the radio as she drives the boys to a football game, Dad goofs around at his son's parties, acting more foolish and immature than any of the guests.

Kids who are proud of their parents can't help having more pride in themselves. Although struggling to break free of parental dependence, kids still want their parents to make a good impression when meeting their peers. This usually translates into parents' adopting a style of speech and clothing that does not try to imitate youth, and displaying a pleasant interest in the teens' activities without sounding condescending or nosy. Kids don't want to be embarrassed by their parents any more than parents want to be embarrassed by their kids. If you make a few concessions to accomplish this, your teenager will probably be more willing to shower and put on clean clothes before your dinner party.

Here are a few other specific suggestions for enhancing your teen's self-esteem.

(1) *Avoid criticizing your teen incessantly.* Constant criticism tends to negate self-esteem by giving adolescents the idea that they're failures. While constructive criticism is sometimes required, if it's delivered in gentle, supportive terms rather than in a belittling fashion it won't have this negative impact.

(2) *Take an interest in what your teen does.* This is concrete evidence that your teen's accomplishments are important. When parents pay little or no attention to what teens are doing — in school, in sports, in hobbies, and so on — it can make teens feel that their achievements are trivial or meaningless. Few things deflate self-esteem as quickly as the thought that one's "big success" doesn't amount to anything.

(3) *Show your teens that you believe in their competence.* The best way of accomplishing this is by giving adolescents age-appropriate responsibilities and then stepping aside to let them be carried out. Parents who do *everything* for their teenagers miss this opportunity and impede the development of the teens' self-esteem.

(4) *Whenever possible, let your teens make their own decisions.* Be available to support them if they've chosen unwisely, but remember, by

defending their right to be wrong you've given them the courage to think for themselves — an essential part of a solid self-image.

(5) *Help your teens recognize the difference between things they can change and things beyond their control.* Like anyone, adolescents can be easily frustrated by battling windmills — and when the windmill wins, they feel as if they've failed. Teaching your teen to avoid feeling personally reponsible for everything that goes wrong is synonymous with shoring up their self-esteem.

(6) *Help your teens to be realistic in their goals.* Too many unrealistic aspirations, or a single unrealistic goal that dominates your teen's life, can set the stage for a major shock to self-esteem. Helping your son or daughter select goals that are attainable, rather than far-fetched, is an investment in their developing sense of personal worth.

(7) *Be generous with your love.* There is no better nutrient for the growth of self-esteem than this.

Social Skills I: Having (and Keeping) Friends

The peer group is that ubiquitous entity that gets blamed for most of the ills that befall youth. Why does it instill so much terror? In reality, it is nothing more than the group of friends your teenager enjoys being with for an extended period of time. Is it so different from your own social circle, the people you play bridge with, invite to a pool party, visit on holidays? Friends provide adolescents with experience in social situations, support during attempts to break away from parental control, and vital feedback about developing personality.

A gap forms as adolescents pull back from their dependence on parents. They don't wish to run to Mom and Dad every time they have a problem or feel lonely, because that would be resorting to childlike behavior. They must leave childhood behind if they are to enter a satisfying adulthood. When Mom, Dad, sisters, and brothers are no longer desired for their companionship and advice, adolescents need friends of their own ages who are confronted with similar issues and locked in the same struggles for independence.

Teenagers attempting to form firm identities and struggling to become autonomous are often riddled with self-doubts and lack self-confidence. Friendship networks help erase these feelings of weakness because they provide a testing ground for social interactions, personality development, power, charisma, cooperation, generosity — all the personality traits and skills that ultimately form the identity of a mature teenager. To deny your adolescent this opportunity because you disapprove of the appearance or behavior of some of those friends is to thwart his or her development. Teens generally know how parents and siblings perceive them, and it is imperative that they be allowed to find out how people closer to their own age and circumstances feel about them too.

Teens will make mistakes, sometimes hurting or humiliating others. But the peer group, for the most part, takes care of itself. Popularity (according to a recent poll of teenagers) depends on friendliness, enthusiasm, enjoying jokes, initiating activities, attractiveness, and status. Kids who are nasty or have no sense of protocol are soon ostracized until they learn the proper peer approach.

Parental interference in this social beehive is usually resented, but parents who observe their teen making repeated mistakes in social interactions might casually mention what they have noticed. Marion (age fourteen) seemed to have difficulty making friends in junior high and spent most of her evenings and weekends alone in her room. Her mother, curious about Marion's hibernation, volunteered to chaperone a dance that she persuaded her daughter to attend. She soon discovered part of Marion's problem. Her wardrobe (much of it handed down from her older sister) was obviously outdated, and her hairstyle looked childish. Her mother helped Marion buy some new clothes, took her to a hair stylist, and showed her how to use makeup so that it was more flattering. Marion's peers didn't jump up and take notice overnight, but gradually she found she was making more friends and becoming more active socially.

Over time, teenagers often surprise parents with their good judgment in friends, so unless your teen is endangered by the relationships, it is usually best to keep quiet when you meet some friends you don't approve of. Forbidding a friendship is often the wax needed to seal it. In a poll, 88 percent of teenagers said they would continue seeing a friend of whom their parents disapproved. Kids want to be as different from their parents as possible; when a parent doesn't like someone, the teenager feels obligated to defend and love that person. In time, most kids will see through a friend who lies or is involved in undesirable activities and will move on to someone else. Especially in early adolescence, teens encourage and then reject several strings of friends before finding the two or three people compatible enough to form a long-term relationship with.

Teenage friendships are also sometimes stormy — marked by arguments, periods of silence, and then making up and feeling good about each other. (In other words, it's a little like being married.) These types of interactions are important proving grounds for your teen's interpersonal skills and should not be interfered with. Teens need to discover for themselves what the consequences of certain actions are — what happens when they break a promise, or when they're jealous, or when they entrust someone they barely know with "confidential" information — and it's far better to learn these things sooner, rather than later. At the same time, the joys of friendship provide important lessons about trust and plain fun. But you have to live them to learn from them.

Social Skills II: Relating to the Opposite Sex

Thanks to the general lessening of sex-role divisions and stereotypes, today's teenagers are freer to make friends among the opposite sex. Groups of boys and girls attending a movie together or going ice-skating are in a comfortable forum for learning about each other without one-on-one dating pressures. In fact, one of the pressing questions teenagers must face is: How can you tell when you're really on a date?

For thirteen-year-olds like Karen, Stacy, and Julie, wandering around a fashionable suburban shopping mall gazing in windows, being on a date meant that three male friends were somewhere on the premises either playing video games or "goofing around." Eventually, these six would meet, share some refreshments, and part company once again. The girls all agreed that this sort of dating was complex business.

At the other end of the spectrum are two relatively "new" phenomena: girls phoning boys and asking them out, and amorphous dating of the "maybe-I'll-see-you-at-the-party-tonight" variety. In the first category, girls no longer seem totally constrained by custom in waiting for boys to take the initiative in asking for a date. While it's certainly not a widespread practice, this sharing of date-initiating responsibilities is no longer a rarity. And, yes, in many cases when a girl asks a boy out — *she* foots the bill. The second type of newer dating style is really a nondate. The concept seems to be "strength in numbers" — by getting together casually in a group, two teens who have some interest in each other can meet and spend their time together. The boy is spared the ordeal of picking up his date (and being scrutinized by the girl's parents), while the girl is spared a lecture from her parents about her poor taste in boys. And if the relationship doesn't work out and they find they don't like each other as much as they thought they would, they can part as casually as they came together.

Despite these variations from more traditional dating patterns, some aspects of dating have remained pretty much the same. Teens report that they date for recreation, to enhance status, to find a good listener, a good friend, or a possible spouse. They learn about intimacy and emotions, how to express themselves, and how to handle being hurt as well as how to cope with infatuation. They learn flirting and games of attraction. And, contrary to what many parents think, most teenagers believe that warmth and friendship are more important in a relationship than sexual intimacy.

Parents can do little during this period but watch the mating game unfold and set a few guidelines for conduct (curfews, type of dating activity). If a relationship is moving towards sexual intimacy, however, no curfew will stop it. As sixteen-year-old Patty explained, "My mother has a fit when I'm a few minutes late from a date. As though we couldn't do all those things *before* eleven o'clock that she's afraid we'll do *after* it."

Parents often have ambiguous feelings about their teenager going steady. When a son or daughter sees one person exclusively, the parents usually get to know that person better and the chances of indiscriminate promiscuity decrease. But going steady also narrows the experiences of dating and relationships, confines the person to one partner while leaving little opportunity to explore other types of friends. Teenagers often find the concept of going steady attractive because it provides the kind of psychic attachment a strong husband-wife relationship can provide — security, love, commitment — all critical to the vulnerable adolescent.

Unless you feel your son or daughter is being physically or psychologically abused by the steady relationship, it's best not to interfere. A young adolescent's moods swing wildly and rapidly. The Juliet of his life one week may be Katharine the Shrew the next. Forcing two young people apart who feel they love each other often accelerates the drive into each other's arms.

Social Skills III: Dealing with Adults

Parents have a right to expect certain behaviors from their teenagers when in the presence of other adults. They should be courteous, respectful, and considerate when an adult is treating them similarly. It is not always necessary for teenagers to agree with adults, however, and it's important not to mold your kids into "people pleasers" who deliver the proper phrases and actions to make adults like them at the expense of their own integrity and self-expression. "People pleasers" often harbor animosity and resentment towards the adults who like them because they sense they are not appreciated for their real selves but for their well-acted performances. Teens need to learn tactful ways of disagreeing with adults, and should be encouraged to cultivate conversational skills in order to be able to communicate with adults as well as their peers.

The average teenager will at some point try to avoid adults as much as possible, barely tolerating teachers and relatives, giving parents the silent treatment. Teens may feel that adults can't possibly understand what a teenager's life is like, but they won't even bother to try to get those adults to understand. "They treat me like a kid," one sixteen-year-old complained of his aunt and uncle. "They ask me how school is and tell me how much I've grown. They don't have a clue to what I'm really like. They didn't even know I was driving and had bought my own car." Had he written them a letter or phoned them when he got the car they would have known, but like many teens, he assumed no responsibility for communicating his news. Teens want adults to care about them; the problems occur when the social skills are absent.

Since the world still consists of people of all ages, it is necessary for an adolescent to learn how to interact with all types of people. Because the adults who affect teens' lives are often authority figures, it may be hard for the teen to separate the person from the role. Parents can highlight this distinction by saying, "Mr. Tomlin did not suspend you because he doesn't like you. He is not a vindictive person. You broke the rules and Mr. Tomlin is paid to enforce them. Try not to take it in a personal way." Teenagers will be more open to understanding and accepting adults if they can separate their job functions from their personality. Adults do not plot to make a teen's life miserable, but often perform jobs that require conformity to rules teens may be trying to break or ignore as part of their striving for independence.

Social Skills IV: Snafus, Embarrassment, and the Art of Saving Face

Because adolescents have a brief, or nonexistent, history of coping successfully in social situations, the slightest faux pas can assume the magnitude of a major social catastrophe. As adults, when we say or do something that turns out to be embarrassing, we console ourselves with the knowledge that we have seldom (if ever) made that kind of mistake in the past and probably won't in the future, or if we have made the mistake previously we survived it. Adolescents, though, have little to fall back on. They rarely say, "Well, I've handled that type of situation better before. I'm not socially awkward. I merely made one error." They are in the process of being inaugurated into the real world, and failure or success at maneuvering gracefully in social situations is much more significant the first few times around. Simply stated, teens lack perspective.

Adolescents are always extremely self-conscious. In the process of developing a self, locked into a body undergoing rapid and sometimes frightening changes, adolescents scrutinize themselves intensely, trying to understand who and what they are. Their preoccupation leads them to the false conclusion that others are equally preoccupied with watching them, convincing them that any social error will be permanently etched into the brains of all those who witnessed it.

To hide this sensitivity, some teenagers adopt a cool, detached stance, trying to remain aloof from society's rules. They believe that by defying the rules, they don't have to worry about following them correctly and may save themselves from embarrassment. That's why Mike won't put his napkin on his lap when he goes out to dinner with you, or use the correct fork for his salad. He rebels against the requirements of etiquette that make him feel uncomfortable and incompetent.

Parents can provide the objectivity a teen lacks when a particularly embarrassing situation has occurred. Sandy, sixteen, landed a date with a boy she'd had a crush on for months and spilled a Coke in his lap at the movie theater. She was mortified. "I can't bear to face him again," she said, refusing to take his phone calls. "I don't want to go to school. I'll run into him." Sandy's father acknowledged her feelings and then tried to get her to consider the situation from her date's viewpoint. "Did he seem mad? What did he do?" Sandy finally began to understand that her date accepted it as an accident, didn't seem to think any less of her because of it, and was probably calling to ask her out again. "If it would make you feel better, you could offer to have his pants cleaned," her father added. With this approach, Sandy learned that embarrassing accidents happen to everybody, don't doom one to a life of ineptness, and that there are ways of trying to compensate for an accident. Sandy's parents never teased her because they knew it was a serious problem to her, and recognized that she felt very badly about it.

Risk-Taking as a Primary Act of Adolescence: Its Implications and Rewards

"Nothing ventured, nothing gained" befits the risk-taking attitude of the average adolescent. How else to exercise new-found skills, to chart the boundaries of acceptable behavior, to try on new identities before choosing the most comfortable? Risk-taking is a kind of scout sent ahead to check the safety of the path an adolescent is about to embark on. If risks aren't taken, the personality hesitates to emerge because it has no idea what it is emerging into.

Risks manifest themselves in three major areas: verbal, behavioral, and attitudinal. Verbal risking often includes swearing or talking back to a parent or adult in authority. For the first time in many adolescents' lives, they begin to feel independent enough to disagree with their parents. The dozens of opposing viewpoints that have been quelled in the past may burst out of angry adolescents with the fury of an erupting volcano. They may call you names, say your argument is stupid, raise their voices to ear-splitting decibels — all to test their powers of manipulation and intimidation. They're too big now to be thrown over your knee and they know it.

You definitely don't need to join in the fray, hurling verbal abuses back at your teen and reducing the disagreement to a cat fight. It may strain your mettle, but the best approach when pulled into adolescents' verbal muscle-flexing is to stay calm and reasonable, making it clear that you will not participate in any further discussion until they control their emotions and their tongues. Your teens need to know that it is OK to disagree with you, but it must be done maturely. They wouldn't like you swearing at them and calling them names; why should you accept that treatment?

Try not to take such verbal outpourings too personally. Adolescents, like everyone else, just have to let off steam to somebody, and parents are convenient, if unwitting, scapegoats. If verbal abuses fail to get either your attention or the desired outcome from you, your teen will soon learn other less volatile methods of communicating.

Behavioral risk-taking is of even more importance to adolescent development. Whether your teen begins to experiment with new styles of dress, rebels against household chores, smokes pot, or rides a motorcycle, rest assured that some form of risk-taking will come to the fore — or something's drastically wrong. These types of new behaviors are ordinary ways of asserting independence and satisfying curiosity. In one sense, such risk-taking is a bit like testing the water before plunging in: it allows teens to see what something feels like before they decide if they like it. Risk-taking also lets teens check the consequences of their behavior — "What will happen if I. . . ?" If the consequences are not enjoyable or rewarding (throwing up and waking up with a pounding hangover after drinking too much, for example), and parents don't blow the incident out of proportion by "absolutely forbidding" a repeat performance, the behaviors usually return to normal in due time.

While you shouldn't try to regulate your teens' lives so tightly that they become afraid to take risks, parents do need to inform their teenagers of any life-endangering or irrevocable consequences to their behavior. "Going along with the guys" may be fine in some things, but foolish if "the guys" are breaking the law. Riding a motorcycle may be a scary but acceptable risk if safety precautions are taken, but it's asking for trouble if your teen won't wear a helmet. Riding into the city with friends may be fun, but hitchhiking with strangers is another story entirely. Relying on your adult insight to explain probable consequences of risk-taking encourages self-responsibility in your adolescents. These insights need to be stated firmly. "I am strongly in favor of the motorcycle helmet laws. Hundreds of teenagers die each year from head injuries sustained in motorcycle accidents. If I saw you riding without your helmet, I wouldn't hesitate to report it to the police." Declarations like this make it crystal clear just where you stand on the topic. The decision is still theirs, but now they can make informed choices.

Attitudinal risk-taking emerges through both verbal and behavioral channels. Margaret (age seventeen) decides agnosticism is a more enlightened religious philosophy than Presbyterianism and refuses to accompany the family to church on Sundays. Kevin (age sixteen) thinks the two-party system is immoral and rallies for the third-party candidate, never missing an opportunity to bring up politics at the dinner table so he can scathingly denounce his father's beliefs. These attitudinal changes are a "trying on for size" session to help adolescents select a wardrobe of their identity. Margaret already knows what Presbyterianism is and means; Kevin already knows what Republicans and Democrats stand for. They must broaden their experiences, adopting other philosophies and beliefs to decide the best one for themselves. Again, a parent who does not escalate these attitudinal shifts into full-scale conflicts may find in a few months that Presbyterianism and the two-party system have returned to their teenager's ideology. If this doesn't occur, however, it is important for parents to accept the autonomy of their children and tolerate (if not celebrate) the freedom of their life choices.

Not all risk-taking is designed to defy adult authority. Some of the riskiest actions an adolescent can take are those that confront existing peer attitudes. Consider the shy thirteen-year-old who risks running for homeroom representative; the football quarterback who risks taking violin lessons; or the prom queen who fights to organize a girl's basketball league. This sort of bucking of the existing peer expectations is a positive sign in an adolescent and points towards a strengthening of the ego and identity that has less need to conform than to express its true self. The power of your child's own convictions are dictating his or her behavior. Whether or not success is attained in the risky endeavor is secondary to the courage summoned to take the risk. We learn by failing, too.

All things considered, it is healthier and safer for limits to be tested during adolescence than later in adulthood when the games played have higher stakes. Lance (twenty-two) went through high school and college without risking much, for the most part adopting his parents' philosophies and lifestyle as his own. He never got in trouble, achieved good grades at Harvard, and landed a high-paying job with a top-notch airplane manufacturer. A few months into his job, though, he began to question the pat existence his parents had prepared him for. He couldn't shake the nagging feeling he was missing something. He dropped his steady girlfriend from college, and began dating a hairdresser and socializing with a wilder crowd. The hairdresser convinced him that he would look "real punk" with a blue streak dyed into his brown hair and said she'd do the job for nothing. Three days later he was fired from his job for "improper appearance." Had he tried this prank in high school, the principal might have called him in, probably met with his parents, and given him a chance to explain the streak and get rid of it. Employers, as Lance found, are seldom so lenient and the consequences of his delayed risk-taking will haunt him for years on his employment record.

Specific Strategies for Positive Parenting

(1) Feelings of self-worth are the essence of an adolescent's personality development. Do whatever you can (without condescending, patronizing, or fawning) to encourage your adolescents' belief in themselves. You can help build teens' self-esteem by praising them whenever possible and by giving them responsibilities that show that your regard for them is not just a matter of empty words.

(2) Be aware of the seesaw mood swings of your adolescents and their extreme sensitivity to criticism. They may resist your sympathy and understanding but want you available on demand to listen to their problems. Encourage them to express their feelings by being empathetic and by helping them find their own solutions, not telling them what to do. Indicating that you sometimes feel down or exasperated is another good way of helping. For instance, you might try something like "I understand your anger because I feel that way too when people ignore me."

(3) Don't assume teens' social problems as your own. You can't face difficult social situations for them; they must learn these vagaries by themselves. Adolescents don't often want — or need — solutions, just someone to support them as they move towards self-responsibility.

(4) Avoid labeling, which has a way of confusing a teenagers' actions with their personalities. Your son may do a bad, or good, deed but that doesn't make him a bad or good person. If we cannot separate our actions from our personal worth, one mistake has the power to shatter our self-esteem.

(5) Respect your adolescents' privacy. Paradoxically, as they become more social, they'll need more time to themselves to write letters, make phone calls, contemplate the universe. Allow them this solitary time; it can provide a much needed chance for the kind of reflection that enhances personality growth and identity formation.

13

The Antisocial Adolescent

Teenage behavior, almost by definition, is erratic behavior. Many parents of seemingly "model" children lament the volatility of their adolescents' emotions and the inconsistency of their behavior. It's hard to predict when the sweet and considerate teenager you're seeing will suddenly be transformed into a sullen, selfish ogre, or worse, an abusive, violent, or self-destructive one.

Not only do adolescents behave erratically and unpredictably, adults and communities respond to them unpredictably, too. This is not because we are a normless society — on the contrary, we set high standards for our teens — but because we are an inconsistent one. For example, some families tolerate wide behavioral and mood swings in their teenagers while others punish the slightest departures from rigid rules. Some schools tolerate deviations from socially acceptable behaviors so students who commit petty thefts or deface property may receive no more serious punishments than letters to their parents and warnings not to repeat the behaviors. Other schools prosecute such teens and involve them in the criminal justice system.

It is estimated that tens of billions of dollars are spent annually to repair acts of teenage vandalism and to run the juvenile court system and programs aimed at rehabilitating antisocial or delinquent youths. Yet we are not seeing positive results from our efforts, and long-term solutions seem elusive. The family can be an enormously positive force in preventing antisocial behavior from turning into delinquent behavior. Parents can and should learn to recognize antisocial patterns in their teens and understand how to channel such behavior into more productive and responsible pursuits.

Recognizing Antisocial Behavior

No specific behavior is always abnormal in itself. However, when it occurs in the wrong place, at the wrong time, among the wrong people, or to an inappropriate degree, almost any behavior is likely to seem abnormal.

The following case illustrates this point.

> A healthy, active thirteen-year-old who showed considerable talent in sports activities, Jimmy became hooked on Bible study and fascinated by his skill in memorizing biblical passages. He gradually fell into the habit of prefacing every comment he made — at home, in class, on the gridiron or the basketball court — with a biblical quotation. His parents, who at first thought his religious interest was laudable, began to get uncomfortable, and then distraught. His friends all deserted him. His teachers finally suggested he see the school psychologist as his classroom participation was disruptive and not easily controlled.

As this example shows, antisocial behavior takes many forms. It can be aggressive — directed towards self, others, or institutions — or passive, as in social or psychological isolation. When antisocial behavior is defined in the context of group activities, any action that disrupts, hurts, annoys, or prevents people from participating in the group is considered antisocial.

The terms *antisocial* and *delinquent* are often used interchangeably but should not be. *Juvenile delinquent* is a label used by the judicial system to classify those individuals who have violated state or local statutes and end up involved in a court proceeding. By definition, teenage juvenile delinquents are considered antisocial, but antisocial adolescents are not necessarily juvenile delinquents.

Antisocial behavior is not always destructive. The teenager who is a chess freak and spends all her time plotting game strategies rather than going out with friends clearly isn't harming anyone and certainly isn't delinquent. What looks like antisocial behavior may just be an expression of a teenager's narrowly focused range of interests. Unfortunately, such teens may be considered eccentric, eggheads, oddballs, or snobs by peers who don't really understand them, and the teens themselves might not even be aware of their impact on others.

There are other times when self-imposed isolation may signal that teens are having problems. Many adolescents who abuse drugs or alcohol are locked into antisocial patterns. The abuse becomes a way to hide or escape from problems too painful or frustrating to confront any other way. Substance abuse makes it easier for teens to turn inward, away from peers and families, since it dulls awareness of their relationships with others. (Drug and alcohol abuse are also major contributing factors to juvenile delinquency, since they have the potential to lead to violent or destructive acts.)

Short-term episodes of relative isolation and withdrawal are not unusual during adolescence. These are often triggered by a specific event — the breakup of a romance, poor performance in school, rejection by a group of erstwhile friends — and this sort of isolation serves a therapeutic purpose, allowing emotional wounds to heal and helping the teenager decide what to do next. It is only when these episodes stretch out over time — lasting months rather than weeks — that you should be concerned about the possibility of a psychological disturbance requiring the diagnostic services of an expert.

There are relatively minor forms of antisocial acts that are commonplace among teenagers. These include fighting, playing pranks, making nuisance phone calls, loitering, goofing off in school, talking back to adults, being purposely impolite, and disrupting ongoing group activities. While you might think that such behaviors are simply a normal part of growing up, studies have consistently shown that they may be antecedents of more serious types of deviance that can become actual delinquent acts. On the other end of the spectrum are the antisocial behaviors so often referred to as *delinquency.* These are typically malicious, destructive acts that cause a great deal of harm to others and cost the United States in excess of $16 billion a year. They include vandalism against school property (a 1982 government publication cited 42,000 incidents *per month,* affecting one in four schools, for total yearly repair costs in excess of $200 million), petty theft, auto theft, drug and alcohol abuse, muggings, homicides, and sexual assault. Many of these acts occur because the teenagers have difficulty controlling their impulses and their anger. But in some instances there is no real malice involved — just a total lack of comprehension of possible effects or consequences. In other words, these teens are notoriously ill-prepared to be responsible for their own behavior.

When malicious antisocial acts occur, it does not necessarily mean that a teenager is "bad," "hopeless," or a "misfit." It does not necessarily mean that the teenager is doomed to a life of crime. What it does indicate is that these teens are likely to be out of synchronization with some aspects of their home, school, community, work, or social environments. Prior to confronting them it is useful to determine if any of the following situations might be contributing to the antisocial outbursts:

(1) *Disparity between the teens' abilities and the actual demands of their environments.* For example, a teen may be failing in school because of deficient reading skills or excessive absences. To the teen who is so far behind, it may seem that there is no way the work can be made up. If he

or she is unwilling or unable to seek help, that teen's frustration, anxiety, and anger are expressed through antisocial channels — vandalizing the school that is causing so much pain.

(2) *No apparent "payoff" for behaving or operating within the norms.* For example, a teen who needs money to take his girlfriend to the senior prom gets a night job at a fast-food restaurant. His friends routinely rip off the school's lockers or break into cars to get items they later fence for pocket cash. They are always in the black; he struggles to get by and is exhausted too. He joins their gang because the payoffs are greater and he feels the ends justify the means.

(3) *Low self-esteem.* Many teens are unsure of their value to their families and friends. Malicious antisocial behavior can be a way of calling attention to themselves, creating status where none seemed to exist before. That their actions might be harmful to others and themselves may not be considered a drawback, for the overriding needs are to belong, to be accepted, and to be noticed.

(4) *Problems controlling anger and impulsive acts.* Teenage boys especially tend to strike out physically at others when they feel powerless to get their way by other means. These adolescents often lack verbal skills and believe in a distorted version of the "actions-speak-louder-than-words" model of living.

Identical forms of antisocial behavior may fulfill very different functions in different people. For some it may be a way of getting into a peer group or showing friends that you're with them all the way. It may be a way of thumbing a teenage nose at adult authority. Antisocial behavior may serve some teens by confirming their personal identities, or by helping them attain otherwise unattainable goals. For still others, it may be the ultimate means of coping with failure or frustration.

Antisocial behaviors can be malicious or benign, occur as isolated incidents or part of long-standing patterns. Antisocial adolescents may be quite conscious of what they are doing and why, or blissfully ignorant of the impact of their acts on others. Parents must examine antisocial behaviors in the context of the teenager's total environment. If not, we cure only the symptom, not the disease.

Fear of Failure, Fear of Success

Teenagers often find themselves paralyzed by fears. Caught somewhere in the murky ground between idealism and realism, they have only vague notions of what success means and what penalties are attached to failure.

In the teenager's mind, to fail at something means you have let someone down and exhibited your weaknesses or imperfections. It may mean you become labeled as incompetent — a loser, lazy, "not working up to your potential" — which shows that you are not in control of yourself. As a result, teenagers have difficulty accepting failure as part of life. Since failure can be so devastating, to request help to overcome the failure can be nearly impossible. Fear of failure, then, can lead to a self-perpetuating cycle which encourages isolation, further failures, and the unwillingness to try new things or to take reasonable creative, social, or intellectual risks.

Fear of success is harder for most adults to understand. Whatever accounts for success — skill, hard work, luck, personality — we tend to think of success as giving a sense of satisfaction and a glow of well-being. Adolescents don't always see it this way, however.

> Linda was a bright, vivacious fifteen-year-old who consistently excelled at mathematics. Her knowledge of computer programming was quite advanced, and her analytical thinking qualified her for a spot on the school's math team, which won second place in a statewide contest. When she started going out steadily with a classmate who was just an average math student, she dropped out of her calculus class and began getting B's in geometry. When pressed by her parents about this, she said, "Who wants to be a brain, anyway? They never get to have fun." Further discussion revealed that she was afraid of being better at math than her boyfriend.

Thus, success can create problems for teens, just as failure can. In fact, once the immediate impact of success wears off, teens may experience any or all of the following reactions.

(1) *A sense of loss.* Once a goal is reached it is no longer there to aspire to; it is, in fact, lost. Energies concentrated on achieving the goal now must be used in different ways which can be very scary, because once again the outcome is unknown.

(2) *A fear of what others will think.* The opinions of peers are so important to teenagers that they often worry that certain successes will alienate them from the group. Most adolescents realize that success can lead others into bad-mouthing them, making fun of their achievements, or being intensely jealous — and they may not want to pay this price.

(3) *A fear that further successes may not occur, or if they do, somehow they won't be as good.* This is both a fear of the unknown and a fear of self, of maintaining social or economic skills, and expanding them.

(4) *A fear that being successful will lead others to expect the teen always to reach a similar result.* In other words, many teens feel that by

being too successful, they make it impossible to match themselves. This is perhaps the biggest problem high-achieving teens face.

Fear of failure and fear of success should be discussed openly with teenagers. For instance, you might bring up the topic by saying, "I've noticed you don't seem to be as proud of your success in physics as I am. I remember how scary it was to be good at something academic — I was always worried that my friends would make fun of me." Parents can be supportive by acknowledging how oppressing such fears can be, while also taking several steps to bring a new perspective to these issues.

(1) *Defuse such fears by bringing them out in the open and discussing them in detail.* What functions do they serve? What triggers their occurrence? What might help to make them better?

(2) *Examine your expectations regarding your adolescent.* Are they realistic and flexible, or do they place a great deal of pressure on the teen's shoulders? Have you communicated these expectations clearly to your teen? Does your teen see your expectations as unrealistic — if so, why?

(3) *Give your teens permission to fail — as long as they're trying.* There are constructive lessons to be learned from failure, and failure can spur people on to impressive accomplishments if they don't give up and stop trying. The Wright brothers failed in many attempts at making a flying machine; Winston Churchill was widely regarded as a political failure early in his career; Willie Mays got only one hit in his first twenty-six major-league at-bats. As long as failure doesn't become a way of life, it's nothing to be ashamed of.

(4) *Give your teens permission to succeed by letting them know that they're not expected to be perfect.* It may be necessary to use some humor to get this point across if your teen doesn't accept a more straightforward statement. For instance, you might try something like, "Perfection in our family is almost extinct — about the only place we look for it is in Grandma's apple pies," or "I used to expect people to be perfect but I learned a long time ago that your mother and I are the last of a dying species."

(5) *Make it clear that you love your teens even with their fears, and you're willing to accept them unconditionally.* This means you'll refrain from the urge to say "You're just being silly," replacing it with "No matter how silly or illogical you think your fears are, they're real to you — so I'm here if you want me to help you deal with them."

(6) *If these fears are so overpowering that they really paralyze your adolescent, find competent professional help.* No matter how good your relationship with your teen, it's not a do-it-yourself project.

Loneliness and Isolation

Teenagers are usually portrayed in movies as hanging around together, doing things in groups — at the beach, at rock concerts, at the playground, at the neighborhood pizza parlor. But this impression can be misleading because it doesn't show the degree to which some adolescents experience an intense sensation of loneliness, even in a crowd. To these teens, and to others who have no crowd or group to call their own, the adolescent years can seem to be an incredibly isolated, painful existence. While imagining that other teenagers are all comfortable with their friends and easily able to handle the banter and interplay of group dynamics, these adolescents feel like social misfits who won't ever connect with or be understood by their peers.

Teenage loneliness and isolation take many forms. In some instances, the problem is caused by a condition that makes social interaction with peers awkward — as with some physically handicapped adolescents, or those with a chronic illness that seriously restricts mobility. In other cases, the loneliness is a byproduct of our geographically mobile society. A teenager who has just moved to a new school for the third time in five years may be leary of establishing close friendships or may have a tough time being accepted by the "in" crowd because of being seen as an intruder. If no one takes the time to befriend a teen in such a situation — or even worse, if someone tries to be friendly and the teen commits some grave social gaffe — the sense of rejection by one's peers may be hard to avoid. In still other cases, teens who are unable to adjust to the demands of group interaction become isolated either by choice or by being deliberately ostracized. This was what happened to fifteen-year-old Laura, who lived in a small, tight-knit suburban community, after she informed her parents that two of her friends were dealing drugs. When police arrived at school and made their arrests, word quickly got out about who had squealed. Suddenly, Laura became labeled an undesirable friend by all the teens who knew her. Her next year and a half in school was a sheer agony of social isolation which was only ended when her parents sent her to live in another state with an aunt.

Loneliness and isolation should not be confused with the adolescent's need for privacy. Teenagers who cannot cope with the demands of their everyday lives will isolate themselves in attempts to insulate themselves since they don't have the necessary skills to do otherwise. These teens may be unable to develop friendships because of fear of rejection or because of personality problems that make it impossible for them to trust or share with someone as equals. In other instances, the adolescent who opts for isolation is obsessed with some activity — long-distance running, stamp collecting, computer programming, doing drugs — that replaces the need for person-to-person contact.

It is important for parents of lonely or isolated teenagers to acknowledge their childrens' feelings. Instead of blaming them for their behavior, put yourself in your adolescents' shoes and remember how difficult it was to reach out to others when you weren't very sure of yourself. Talk things over with them and offer advice but don't pretend you have an instant solution. It's just not that easy.

If the loneliness and isolation are due to skill deficits — the teen really doesn't know what to say on a date, is afraid to make a phone call, is scared of a teacher, is hurt by a friend and can't tell him — it is possible (if your teen will let you) to practice these skills through role-playing. For example, you can say to your teen, "Let's assume I'm the other person, and you try to tell me what's on your mind." You can rehearse all the various scenarios your teen is imagining (plus a few of your own invention) so when your teen goes from rehearsals to the real thing, he or she feels adequately prepared.

Another useful strategy is to pretend to be your teen and let the teen play the role of the other person. This can provide insights from at least two different directions. First, your teen gets the benefits of your role model as an example to possibly follow (or at least to see how *not* to act). Second, there is much to be learned from seeing things from the other person's perspective, which this sort of reverse role-playing can help to achieve.

If all else fails, get counseling for your teen. Do not allow loneliness and isolation to become such ingrained patterns that your teenager becomes an adult who perpetually lives with loneliness, too.

The Phobic Child

Everyone, including teenagers, encounters fears in certain aspects of their lives. A car swerves closely by as we're crossing the street, and our hearts start pounding. We feel nervous and uncomfortable before going onstage to lecture to a group. A college entrance interview raises anxiety levels and causes uneasy anticipation. These are, of course, completely normal responses to the stresses and strains of everyday life. But the teenager who is terrified of the dark, or is so afraid of dogs that he or she refuses to walk outdoors, or who always panics before taking a test is likely to be suffering from a condition known as *phobia*, a useless fear that may paralyze its victims and cause them to live in a world of dread and uncontrolled anxiety.

Dr. Joseph Wolpe, a professor of psychiatry at Temple University, has found that phobias can develop either suddenly, based on a single frightening experience, or gradually, evolving out of a series of events. "A person's susceptibility is not affected by how intelligent or athletic or capable he or she is," he notes, and the existence of a phobia doesn't mean that someone is mentally unstable.

In contrast to useful fears, which serve to alert us to potential danger of one sort or another, phobias can interfere with everyday functioning. As with other psychological conditions, there are varying degrees of severity. In the most serious cases, the phobia disrupts lives either because it is directed at an everyday situation (e.g., going to school or riding in a car) or because the phobic person becomes obsessed with his or her fear. A girl who is terrified of snakes ordinarily has no problems (unless she's in a reptile house at the zoo), but if she becomes so subjugated by her fear that she won't go outside or open a closed door because she's afraid that a snake is lying in wait for her, the situation is quite different. Fortunately, most adolescent phobias are of the milder, more manageable variety. In fact, phobias that don't materially interfere with a person's life do not generally require any sort of treatment.

People who are phobic are frequently misunderstood by those of us who don't share these intimidating fears. For example, many phobic teens are thought to be antisocial because they try to mask their fears by manipulative, controlling behavior or by social isolation and withdrawal. What is actually happening is that phobic kids are often embarrassed by their fears and want to hide them. It is easier to pretend to be obstinate, dumb, or snobbish than to admit to being unable to control a part of your emotions. The ultimate solution to the prospect of confronting their fears seems to be to withdraw completely and isolate themselves: the isolation provides a safety net.

How do you deal with a teenager's phobia? Whatever you do, don't try to force the issue. You don't teach a child to overcome a fear of water by throwing her into a pool. You won't cure claustrophobia by locking a teen in a closet. You don't throw grease on a fire if your intention is to smother it.

Although phobias sometimes go away spontaneously, they can also worsen over time. To avoid this possibility, consult with a professional who can assess the seriousness of the problem and tell you if treatment is indicated. Look for a counselor who will be able to explain the teenager's phobic problems to the school or place of work and help get the entire environmental system involved in the teen's recovery. This is important because phobic children and teens are sometimes subject to intense peer ridicule and to being misunderstood by teachers and other adults. Because few of us suffer the intense fears of the phobic person, there is always the danger that the phobia will not be taken seriously and will be laughed at, scorned, or disbelieved.

Fortunately, a variety of short-term behavioral therapies exist that are highly effective in dealing with phobias. Teens no longer need to suffer in silence with the burden of these useless fears.

Juvenile Delinquency

American society is a bit peculiar in its response to juvenile delinquents. On the one hand, we tolerate and even encourage glorified images of alientated youths whose social lives revolve around gangs, drag racing, and rumbles. On the other hand, our society fears its juvenile delinquents and wants to either get rid of them or at least get them out of sight.

This ambivalence is heightened by the fact that we tend to be confused about just what juvenile delinquency is. While legal definitions lump together young offenders who decorate subway cars with colorful graffiti with other teens who commit violent crimes, our sensibilities tell us that these are really not equivalent situations. We also know that many juvenile delinquents have never been reported to the police, much less caught or successfully prosecuted, so they remain free to commit their violent or criminal acts within a society that seems virtually powerless to stop them.

The psychological perspective on delinquency suggests that such antisocial and criminal behavior reflects a teen's failure to have learned the essential controls that most other young people do in the course of growing up. If they lack socially approved skills, they get gratification from breaking rules rather than following them.

Unfortunately, many adults use the terms "juvenile delinquent" and "juvenile delinquency" to describe any teenager whose behaviors are sufficiently different from the norm to arouse suspicion or alarm. This leads to false labeling (especially in school) of teens who may not be delinquent at all but who may just fit an image made popular by media.

There are different categories of delinquent behavior just as there are different kinds of phobias, or different manifestations of antisocial activities. *Impulsive* delinquents are those who typically engage in stealing, whose actions are accompanied by insecurities, anxieties, and unhappiness. *Unsocialized* delinquents don't have those requisite internal controls, often come from homes with overstrict or erratic parental discipline and a lack of family cohesiveness. They tend to be more violent than the impulsive delinquents. *Socially* delinquent teens are those whose behavior actually conforms to the standards of the immediate social environment — e.g., youth gangs — but violate the norms of the dominant, law-making culture. No matter what category a teenage delinquent falls into, punishment per se has been found to be the least effective way to deal with the offender. In fact, putting a teenager in jail greatly increases the odds that problems will continue, so this can hardly be seen as a corrective solution. Instead, family-like community settings, or treatments in mixed groups of nonoffenders and offenders have been found to be promising alternatives.

It is doubtful that we will ever be able to eradicate delinquency entirely. However, if adults can be sensitive to the unmet needs of those teens who turn to delinquent acts to gain status, self-esteem, acceptance from peers, or who do illegal and destructive things to call attention to their emotional voids, perhaps the antisocial delinquents will begin to trust the adults, seek them out, and eventually see payoffs in living a straight life.

Breaking Through

Antisocial adolescents build imaginary walls around themselves to insulate them from situations they are poorly equipped to deal with. The walls may be responses to fears, in which case isolation, loneliness, or even phobias may result. When they are responses to serious family problems, social injustices, or labels others put on the teens, the walls insulate them from society and make it easier for them to engage in law-breaking, delinquent acts. The walls block communication.

How to break through is determined in part by the problem your teen has, by the nature of his or her personality, and by the teen's willingness to meet you halfway. Some parents will choose to do the job alone, others will need the assistance of professionals — therapists, police, lawyers, teachers, clergy. No matter what the task, however, we suggest the following:

(1) Define the problem as you, an adult and parent, see it.

(2) Define the problem as you believe your teenager sees it.

(3) Ask your teenager to define the problem and compare notes.

(4) Do not engage in combat. This means avoiding shouting matches or even physical battles with your teen, no matter how provoked you might be. In combative situations, you give up whatever vestiges of parental control you might still have — not a wise proposition.

(5) Express your love for your teen (even if you hate his or her behavior). We've already mentioned this several times before. The key thing is to let your teens know that while you're rejecting or condemning their troublemaking behavior, your love for them is as strong as ever.

(6) Determine if, and how, your teen would like to see you intervene in the problem situation.

(7) Write down the ways you would like to intervene in the problem situation and compare notes.

(8) Decide what the possible consequences are if things stay as they are.

(9) Ask yourself what good might accrue from change.

(10) Find out what are your viable sources of assistance.

You should not expect miracles, but if you make the effort to get to know your teens better, if you define problems and explore options, and if you can communicate love and understanding, then you should see improvement, if not total resolution. Whenever a parent reaches out to a child, even if that child is 6′ 2″ with a criminal record, the effort is nine-tenths of the solution.

14

Miscellaneous Matters

The little things in life can matter a lot. Like the pebble in your shoe when you're out for a jog, they aren't likely to do major damage but they can certainly be irritating in the long run.

We don't have many pat answers to the issues raised in this chapter. As in the rest of this book, we offer items for consideration, a chance to review some potential pebbles and consider ways to remove them before they become irritating. The areas we touch on here are the stuff of everyday life with a teenager, a few of the aggravations that try your patience and wisdom as a parent.

Driving

It is a rare teenager who does not spend every spare moment after the passage of his or her sixteenth birthday plotting, preparing, and pleading for a driver's license and a car. "I gotta be mobile," a young friend confided, "or they'll leave me behind." "They," of course, refers to the peer group one must be mobile with. A license and access to a car are status signs to the adolescent, symbols of independence and autonomy, a chance to seize responsibility by the wheel and drive it into the sunset.

Insist that these road warriors take — and pass — their high school driver's education course. These classes are not only a safe, effective way to teach rules of the road and provide driving experience, but in almost all states, successful completion of driver's education reduces the teen's insurance premium. If there's no class available (this is one of the first electives to be cut when school budgets dwindle), it might be worth the investment to sign your teen up with a professional driving school. Several of the national department stores offer this service at reasonable rates. The cars used for this type of training are safer than your own (the teacher has a set of controls to override the student's in an emergency), and the teachers are probably more relaxed with their students than you would be with your teen. After all, they teach driving for a living. The average parent teaches driving skills two or three times in his or her life.

Set specific guidelines for the use of the car. When is it available? Where can the teen take it? Who puts in gas? Who washes it? Who maintains it? Most teens are only too happy to wash and wax the family auto, fill it with gas and check the oil, if they get to use it on Friday night. Also be sure to be specific about which abuses will result in suspension of driving privileges — while you may not worry about a parking ticket (if your teen pays the fine), a speeding violation is another matter. One safety precaution we believe should be mandatory (and one that is insisted upon by driver's education trainers) is use of the seat belt. Parents can set a good example by always using seat belts themselves and by insisting their teens do, both as drivers and passengers. In fact, the best policy to follow is to require that *all* passengers riding with your young driver have their seat belts fastened before foot touches gas pedal.

Once your teens hit driving age, they will not only be driving themselves but will be riding with friends who are driving. You won't have much control over the competency or sobriety of these chauffeurs, so make a point of telling your teens to call you anytime they think their ride home might be unsafe, and that you'll gladly pick them up or pay for the taxi. No parent wants their teenager to risk his or her life by getting into a car with an unreliable driver (or attempting to drive under the influence of alcohol or drugs) just because the teen was afraid to disturb Mom or Dad.

Teenage driving has a bright side, too. The adolescent driver is usually happy to run errands, pick up Grandma, take Tony to the Boy Scout meeting, or use any excuse to get out on the road. Teens also come in handy by sharing the driving burden on long road trips — like family vacations.

Telephone Use and Abuse

A good friend of ours had just about reached the end of her telephone cord in trying to enforce a few basic rules of telephone use with her two teenagers. They spent hours tying up the phone lines with conversations to friends who lived just a few blocks away. They made numerous calls outside the local call area that almost doubled the monthly bill. They encouraged friends to call late at night so they wouldn't be hassled by parents complaining of their monopolizing the phone (instead, the parents were awakened after midnight by the phone ringing). Finally, Suzanne gave her teens an ultimatum: either abide by the rules or buy your own phone and number.

The kids never even considered abiding by the rules — the chance to have their own telephone line was too appealing. So Suzanne went with them to the telephone service center to talk about price. The teens' fantasies about two designer phones (one in each bedroom) and a private line with unlimited calls were soon shattered when they found out the cost. There would be connection fees and phone rental fees and usage fees and tax. Their part-time jobs at Kentucky Fried Chicken would hardly cover the expense. They soon settled on a basic black rotary dial with a measured-service two-party line. And Suzanne was most pleased to see that they began setting their own rules of use to keep their phone bills to a minimum.

If Suzanne had not been willing to let the girls pay their own way, she had one alternative open to her — restrict or eliminate phone use. Some parents set a timer by the phone and restrict every incoming or outgoing call to a set number of minutes. Other parents limit their teens to a specified time when they can use the phone: 7:00 to 9:00 P.M. on schooldays, and until 10:00 P.M. on weekends. Another alternative is to ban telephone access until homework has been completed. In stubborn cases, key or combination locks are available for phones, to restrict use and let parents monitor all outgoing calls.

Increasingly today, teenagers use telephones in troubling ways. You may discover, for example, that your daughter has been making prank calls to classmates at odd hours and hanging up without talking. Or you may find that your thirteen-year-old son has been calling the New York City Dial-a-Joke number, or even worse, that he's run up a considerable bill using a service that gives sexy messages over the phone — for a price. Other teenagers have gotten into trouble by gaining access to another customer's long-distance dialing code numbers and using them to talk cross-country — which is stealing. Obscene or harassing phone calls have not gone out of style, either.

These are not simply mild annoyances, because these telephone misbehaviors can escalate and explode in your face. While there's no such thing as a "telephone user's education course" at school, you should be sure to warn your kids about what constitutes appropriate use of the phone and what doesn't, and you should be prepared to take firm action at any signs that your rules are being disregarded.

Personal Grooming

Remember the sixties? That renowned era when nobody bathed or washed or cut their hair, when the quality of a pair of jeans was directly proportional to the number of patches and rips? When college boys stopped worrying about acne because every male had an abundance of untrimmed facial hair? By sixties standards, today's designer jeans and polo shirts are operating-room sterile, and the task of cleaning up today's youth is not nearly as great. One father even complained his kids were too neat. "They have all their jeans dry cleaned and change shirts about three times a day. The cleaning bills are eating me alive. And my daughter has to have her hair trimmed (at about forty dollars a visit) once a month or it doesn't 'lie right.' Whatever happened to scuffed sneakers and ponytails?"

As discussed in other sections of this book, puberty brings many bodily changes with it, among them an increase in body odor and body hair. You might want to mention the need for deodorant at this time and discuss shaving with sons and daughters. Oil production is increased also, so hair needs shampooing more often and faces must be washed several times a day. Adolescents are sometimes so caught up in other changes taking place — their school, social life, or sports activities — that they don't pay as much attention to personal appearance or clothing as they should. Other teens never stop thinking about it, and seem to have two extra appendages — the comb and the mirror.

Parents can act as another type of mirror to teens, reflecting how they appear to the rest of the world. Without insult or sarcasm, a parent can describe the teen's appearance with phrases like "You're dressed very casually and comfortably for tonight, but we're going to a formal restaurant. I think it might be more appropriate for you to wear dress pants and jacket." Statements like these are less likely to alienate or hurt the teen, since you are not disparaging his or her taste, only directing it down a more appropriate path. Calling your teen a slob or an idiot for dressing a certain way only strengthens his or her resolve to continue rebellious grooming habits and patterns.

Try to keep in mind that many young adolescents need to be taught some basic rules about personal grooming and clothes. Most of them haven't had much experience making their own decisions about these things until adolescence — Mom or Dad usually picked out the appropriate clothes to wear, told them when to bathe and brush their teeth. Take some time to explain that people are judged by their appearance. This may offend your teen's idealistic sense that people should be appreciated for who they are, not what they wear, and you can agree with that philosophy in theory. But in reality, clothes and grooming are often the first impressions we have of a person. If these impressions are unfavorable we may not take the time to get to know them on any more than a superficial level.

Some adolescents won't listen to reason (at least from adults) and in spite of your protests refuse to stay clean and dress appropriately. You can't force your teens to do either, so explain the alternatives (which can be any you feel will be effective). For instance, the teen might not be allowed to attend the function with the family if he or she is not dressed fittingly. Or they don't get an allowance that week. In general, it is best not to be too strict with teens, letting them learn proper personal grooming for various situations by trial and error. You may not be too happy about the styles of clothes that are popular, either, but unless the teenagers are dressing for an important event — like a college or job interview — give them some freedom in developing their own tastes and experimenting with fashion. The leather jackets and white T-shirts of older generations weren't exactly a class act either, but the wearers managed to graduate into business suits and dresses when the time was right.

Neatness

It's not uncommon for a teen to be a fanatic about personal cleanliness yet sleep in a bedroom hogs would find inviting. Erma Bombeck has foolproof advice for parents of teens who won't keep their rooms neat — close the door and let them fend for themselves. This won't work, though, if your teen shares a room with other siblings or their sloppiness overflows into other rooms of the house. Here are a few things you can do to try to improve things a bit:

(1) Enforce a rule that the teen must entertain members of the same sex in his or her room. At least that way, they'll have to clean off enough of the bed for two people to sit on it.

(2) (For stout-hearted parents only) warn teens that parents are not slaves or lackeys or personal servants who clean up after their children. Then stick to this strategy. If teens throw their clothes over the dining room chair, simply pick up the pile and throw it into their room. If they leave a kitchen full of dirty dishes and empty soda cans, pick up the mess and gingerly deposit it on their desk. The more cramped and stench-filled their bedroom becomes, the more motivated the teens are to change their slovenly ways.

(3) Implement a reward system for neatness around the house. (This usually works more effectively than punishing teens to get their cooperation.) For instance, a week's neatness may translate into a monetary bonus to their allowance, a reprieve from other unwanted chores (such as taking out the garbage), or a specified number of points to be accumulated towards a major purchase they want to make. This is bribery, but it works!

(4) When two children share a bedroom, the fine points of neatness

must be negotiated, often with written requirements. This ensures that the responsibility for the tidiness of communal rooms is justly shared, and the person with the lowest tolerance for messiness doesn't automatically become the maid.

Language

"Yesterday my sixteen-year-old told me I looked 'pretty bitchin' and I slapped him. How was I to know 'bitchin' meant good?" Maybe in your heyday the cool words were *swell* or *groovy*, or *far out*. Today things that are good are "bad," eating too much is "pigging out," being surprised or amazed is being "blown away." And today's youths pepper much of their speech with a variety of not-so-innovative four-letter words that even the most out-of-touch parents will easily recognize.

Each generation creates its own language barrier, a unique method of communication that keeps adults at a distance and binds teens to other teens who understand the language. This is by no means harmful and can help give adolescents their first sense of a separate identity. How much "jive" talk or "Valspeak," though, should you have to listen to in your own home?

Every parent has the right to require that certain types of language not be used in their home. You may consider curse words to be disrespectful or you may not want younger siblings to be exposed to them. For whatever reason, make it clear to your teen which words will and will not be tolerated, and specify the punishment to be meted out for failure to obey. Teens are too old to have their mouths washed out with soap, but they'll probably respond even better to having to wash down the bathroom or not getting the car Saturday night. Remember that your teen will be more likely to obey your rules if he or she can also follow your example. Words off-limit to adolescents should not be a major part of your own verbal repertoire unless you want to be labeled a hypocrite, with good reason.

Beyond the definitely nonnegotiable vocabulary you will not tolerate, list the slang words you are neither annoyed by nor happy with. A simple, effective response to heavy use of incomprehensible slang is "I don't understand what you're saying, so I can't consider your request. When you can translate that into plain English, we'll talk about it." Teens have to learn to tailor their language to their audience — not to hamper communication, but to enhance it. You wouldn't use polysyllabics to talk to a four-year-old. Neither should your teen use adolescent-era slang to talk to you — if he or she wants you to respond favorably.

Language use, including verbal mannerisms such as "uh" and "like" — filler words — can quickly become habit. You have a responsibility to point out any irritating gestures to your teens as they may be unaware they are doing it, and these disconcerting quirks can hinder their chances in an educational or job atmosphere. We are judged not only by what we say but how we say it. The person who fills in natural pauses in conversations with "uh" and "like," who says, "she goes" when "she says" is meant, is viewed (according to several psychological surveys) as being less in control and having lower maturity and self-esteem than the person who can state his ideas clearly, concisely, and unfalteringly.

Teens with language and communication problems that are not caused by physical handicaps (such as impaired hearing, cleft palate) and do not require actual speech therapy (such as stuttering) are often helped by joining the school debating club or taking a public speaking class. Keep listening to your teen (even though wading through the "hip" talk is frustrating) to determine whether his or her communications methods are so poor they need help. Most teens outgrow their love affair with slang, but some have a deep anxiety about speaking and may hide their fears behind a wall of slang terms, trendy speech patterns, or constant cursing.

Money Matters

Oh, yes it does, and the sooner your teens learn that money matters, the more responsible they'll be with their (and your) finances. There's a problem here, though, since teens can't learn to handle money unless they have some to handle. Parents often make the first investment in this education by providing children with an allowance, usually a payment for chores done around the house. Other parents don't make an allowance contingent on anything; regardless of behavior, the child gets a predecided sum of money each week. Giving children spending money helps them learn its value as consumers — what it will buy, how much things cost — but not as earners.

Ideally, an allowance is *earned.* The difficulty of the tasks required to earn the allowance needs to be geared to the age and ability of the child. By the time a child reaches adolescence, the amount of the allowance will have increased along with the size of the duties required to receive it. Teens thus learn the value of work, that money is not doled out without reason, that earning money takes time and effort. The intricacies and negotiations of allowances serve as an excellent training ground for a teen's first job, and usually help the teenager appreciate the expenses parents incur raising a family.

Knowledge about family expenses can also be shared directly. Discuss budget items such as the mortgage payment, the phone bill, the utility costs, medical and dental expenses with your adolescent. You need not perform an internal audit with your son or daughter in order to give them a general sense of costs of living. Several teens we talked to discussed their shock at the cost of the basics when they moved away from home. Many had not even gone grocery shopping and had no base of comparison for prices of food, housing, and clothing. "I never looked at price tags when I went shopping with my mother. She would just tell me whether we could afford what I wanted or not. But I found out when I got my own apartment. I couldn't afford anything!" a nineteen-year-old girl told us.

One other aspect of money matters should be mentioned. The financial habits your teenagers develop will stay with them for life, so encourage saving and planning from an early age. Let your adolescents open their own savings accounts; give them help in figuring out a weekly budget; and give them a chance to buy things on their own. If they've set their hearts on a Walkman stereo, don't buy it for them — let them save for it and purchase it with their own money. And don't be too free with credit cards for your teens. The cards can give them the impression that money grows on trees.

Jobs

To work or not to work? On the one hand, a part-time job can disrupt school studying, social life, and participation in extracurricular activities. On the other hand, a job teaches a teenager the value of money, and responsibility and commitment to an employer. The dilemma of working versus not working must be solved through careful assessment of the unique traits of each individual teen. Ask the following questions:

(1) Can the teen handle the extra time and energy the job would take? Are his or her grades solid? Is time already budgeted efficiently?

(2) Will their social life and development be impeded?

(3) How badly does the teen (or your family) need the extra money? What is the money planned for? To move out, buy a car, an engagement ring, drugs, college tuition?

(4) Consider the teen's age, maturity, and future plans when trying to decide on the best type of job for them. Teens hunting for their first jobs usually have to take anything they can get, but after they have gotten a bit of work experience, they can be more discriminating in searching for a job that will add to their future marketability and experience.

(5) Explain to the teen about recommendations and references, their importance, the effect of building on early experience to broaden job skills and increase wages. Every job, from hamburger slinging to news-

paper reporting, needs to be taken seriously because it all becomes part of the teen's employment record and helps prospective employers make decisions about hiring.

(6) Establish rules of hours to be worked and when, including any activities you decide should *not* be disrupted by the job (such as chores, school, church). These preferences should be discussed *before* the teen goes job hunting, so he or she can gear the hunt to your expectations. You'll need to be flexible, however, and allow exceptions to your boundaries that are beyond the teen's control.

All in all, the majority of teens find their work experiences informative, fun, interesting, and profitable. At an important time of growing independence from parents, working teens are able to feel more financially responsible for themselves and display high self-esteem and confidence. They also get the benefits of a nonacademic form of education, which is no trifling matter.

Parties

You've already watched your kids grow from pajama parties to camp-outs to pizza parties to boy-girl parties. But adolescence is where the fun really begins. Not only do parties take on a new degree of social seriousness, they are fraught with potential trouble spots — drugs, alcohol, sex, gate-crashers, and maybe even theft or violence. What's a parent to do?

For younger adolescents, parents need to ask what type of party it will be (how many people? boys and girls? overnight?), who will chaperone it, the hours it is to last, and the chaperone's views on drinking and drugs. Will you let your teenager attend a party given on a school night? Will attendance at a party be considered a reward, and in that case, what must the teen do beforehand to be allowed to attend?

These same issues must be considered when throwing a party at your own house. Will you allow cigarette smoking? liquor? drugs? boisterousness? a loud stereo? lights out? locked doors? How do you plan to control these situations? Explain to your teen (in advance of party night) that you plan to check in every hour, perhaps, and will (after a certain number of warnings) call the police if the behavior isn't stopped or the offending guest banished. We strongly suggest that everyone at the party be told that drugs or alcohol brought on the premises, or destructive behavior, will result in an instant end to festivities. In our opinion, it's better to be seen as a strict parent than as a pushover.

Older teens are more difficult to interrogate about partying activities. They often have their own wheels and may forget (conveniently) to tell you about the party they are going to at the Abelses' house while Mr. and Mr. Abels vacation in Maine. As mentioned in the driving section, encourage teens to call you if they feel trapped at a party where activities they don't wish to participate in are taking place. Your teen may not have expected that marihuana joints would be passed around at Doug's party, but figures he has to stay until his ride is ready to leave. You can bail him out of an uncomfortable spot if you are ready and willing to come take him home (even if it means meeting at a house a block away so the other kids don't see his parents picking him up).

Curfews

The ideal curfew teaches teens reasonable, responsible hours of activity outside the home but is not enforced so rigidly that it begs to be broken. The teen arriving home five or ten minutes past the curfew on occasion need not be reprimanded. A simple reminder of actual curfew times usually does the trick. But adolescents who consistently swagger in an hour or so past curfew (with or without excuses) clearly show they are not yet mature enough to handle staying out that late and need an earlier curfew until they can prove understanding of and adherence to it. One angry parent simply added up the minutes her daughter had been late for curfew over the last month and set the curfew time that much earlier.

In discussing curfews with teens and parents we found that curfews seem to work best when:

(1) The purpose of setting a curfew is clearly explained to the teens. Curfews aren't punishment — they're a check on the safety and dependability of your teen. If you have requested that your teen be home by 11:30 P.M. and he still hasn't showed up at 12:30, you've got a legitimate reason to begin worrying and calling around to locate him. Teens who can consistently adhere to curfew are proving they are trustworthy, dependable, and deserving of other freedoms and ways of being treated as an adult.

(2) Whenever teens sense a curfew might be missed, they should call home to inform parents of the situation. It's better to call at 10:30 P.M. and explain why they will miss the 11:00 P.M. curfew (or request an extension), than to try to sneak in at midnight past parents who've had an hour to worry and get angry about their tardiness.

(3) Flexible curfews work better than across-the-board curfews. The most successful system seems to be setting a general curfew time for nonspecific activities, such as 9:30 on school nights and midnight on weekends. This is then coupled with flexibility and room for negotiation for special events. If a party doesn't start until 9:30 and the hostess lives half an hour away, it would be ridiculous to insist your teen be home by

11:00. Reasonable, flexible curfews are often heeded better by teens and have the added bonus of teaching the art of negotiation and compromise. Treat your teen like an individual and the same respect will be returned.

Vacations

The family no longer cheers when you announce the annual trip to Avalon, New Jersey. Sally wants to go white-water canoeing with the Adventurers' Club. Jeff will miss a week of football practice. You've heard about spouses opting for it, but whole familes taking separate vacations?

A variation of this theme is the family that agrees on the dates and place for a vacation but, once they get there, argues over the activities. Jack wants to hear some jazz bands. Tracy's into architectural tours. And Mom wants nothing more than six uninterrupted hours on the beach each day.

Here are your options:

(1) Let the kids go on their own vacation: (a) with another family; (b) with relatives; (c) with an organization; (d) if old enough, with a group of peers.

(2) Let kids stay at home: (a) with relatives or friends; (b) if old enough, alone.

(3) Take different interests into account when planning the vacation: (a) pick a spot that has something for everyone; (b) invite a teen's friends along for companionship; (c) compromise — "You go with us tonight, and we'll take you to your choice tomorrow."

A vacation should be a time of relaxation and enjoyment, a special chance to reunite with your family in pleasurable activities. Hassles are to be avoided, so don't hesitate to pursue any of the above options if you think they'll bring peace of mind to all involved. Parents tend to relinquish vacation times begrudgingly, remembering with warm sentiment the great vacations the family enjoyed when the children were younger. You can't force your kids to have a good time with you, and trying to force them only breeds resentment. It may ease the pain to think of this "separate vacations" time as a temporary phase too soon replaced with large family vacations that include sons-in-law, daughters-in-law, and grandchildren.

Family Chores

"Chores." The word connotes visions of the never-ending stream of back-breaking tasks required to run a 315-acre farm. Who will milk the cows each morning at dawn? Who will bale the tons of hay? Who will feed the chickens?

The number of families in the United States today in which chores really mean hard physical labor is small. But even in the average suburban household or city apartment there can be dozens of minor duties and tasks necessary to keep things organized and running smoothly. And just because the jobs are less physically taxing doesn't mean they need any less attention or organization to ensure they are completed. Like the chores on a large working farm, the chores in a middle-class two-story house must be divided equitably, overseen carefully, and kept flexible enough so they are not resented to the point of not getting done.

Every member of the family should be responsible for some aspect of household functioning. If seventeen-year-old Chris must cut the grass each Saturday, then thirteen-year-old David should also be assigned a task suited to his age and abilities (like hosing out the doghouse). Adolescents are extremely sensitive to unjust allocation of duties and will resent either you, the "pampered" sibling, or the task itself if they feel they've been treated inequitably.

Your attitude towards chores also needs to be flexible — to a point. Adolescents seem happier with tasks if given a bit of freedom in accomplishing them. Rather than mandating that the laundry must be washed on Mondays, the garage cleaned on Thursdays, the car washed on Saturdays, simply explain the details of the task to your teen, how many times per week it should be done and let them fit it best into their own schedules. Everyone has noticed that some days he or she feels like doing particular types of jobs more than on other days. Teenagers are no different. Given a time span in which chores must be done, they will learn how to budget time and schedule activities accordingly, feeling more independent and responsible as they do.

It's important to outline specifically what you wish each task to encompass, at least until the job descriptions become ingrained. Don't say merely, "Wash the car," and then become angry when it hasn't been waxed and the carpet hasn't been vacuumed. Writing a checklist can help ensure that the teen covers all the areas required. This also helps teach younger adolescents the importance of following directions.

Some families work better if everyone blitzes the house at one time — on a Saturday morning, for example — in a version of the "misery loves company" syndrome. This doesn't leave much flexibility among individual members to work at their own leisure, but it brings a sense of teamwork to the family. Scheduling problems can make this approach cumbersome, though — so if your teens consistently have to miss activities with their friends to help you with this type of housecleaning, you might want to reconsider the wisdom of your approach.

In the interest of equality, you may want to rotate chores among various family members. This way, everyone gets a chance to do the things they don't mind (dusting the furniture, for instance) as well as the things they hate (cleaning the bathroom). But if a teen has outside employment and is using part or all of the salary for items normally bought by parents, less time will be available for chores, and tasks should be geared to time and energy available. Explain your rationale to all your helpers so no resentments or hard feelings pop up.

Lastly, try to make household chores fun. This may sound impossible or unlikely, but if parents display a positive attitude towards working around the house, the tasks won't seem as burdensome to the kids. Remind each family member he or she is not alone. Taking care of the house is a team effort and a responsibility they can and should be proud to accept.

Babysitting

Parents are often surprised to find that the teen who despised babysitting for brother or sister is delighted to accept sitting jobs from neighbors and family friends. The difference is simple — the latter is a *job* that offers a certain status, some pay, the chance to run a different house, and the extra respect children will often give a stranger that they wouldn't dream of giving to a sibling. But before you permit teens to babysit, you must be sure they're ready to handle the responsibilities involved.

Here a few things you will want to cover with your teens before they do any outside babysitting:

(1) They should always give you the name, address, and phone number of the family they're sitting for and a projected time they'll be home.

(2) Once on the job, they should get information (in writing) about the destination of the parents who've hired them (including a phone number), as well as a list of names and numbers for emergency situations (e.g., doctors, police, fire department, relatives or friends).

(3) Specific instructions regarding their duties must be obtained: should they bathe or feed the kids? are there pets who need special care? what time do the kids go to bed? are there any special routines to follow, like giving a dose of bedtime medicine or a mandatory bedtime story?

(4) There are some "don'ts" for the babysitter to remember, too. Don't talk incessantly on the telephone while working — even after the kids go to bed. Don't allow friends over to visit. Don't open the door to strangers. And don't leave a mess — be sure to clean up after yourself as well as after the kids.

(5) Last but not least, the babysitter — whether novice or experi-

enced — should realize that it's perfectly all right to call you if they need advice or help. After all, what's a parent for?

Electronic Games (and Computer Addicts)

You probably already know the sight. In arcades, bowling alleys, shopping centers, and other spots, teens stand quietly hunched over video screens, joysticks and control knobs clutched in their hands, intently blasting invading hordes of space creatures out of existence. Games like Pac-Man, Donkey Kong, Centipede, Frogger, and dozens like them have become a part of the nation's landscape, far better known to today's adolescents than Monopoly or Scrabble had been to their parents. And, unlike these board games of yesteryear, modern videogames have voracious appetites for quarters. For all but the experts, it's easy to spend ten or fifteen dollars in an hour of video recreation.

Adults have reacted to the videogame mania with predictable ambivalence. Some have joined their kids in becoming skilled players and heartily endorse the pasttime. Others object vehemently and believe these games have major negative effects on teens. One father described his worries as follows, "These games are deceptive. They look like good, clean fun, but they're really addictive, expensive, and a waste of time. My son was spending three hours each afternoon at the video parlor, and his grades went down as a result. He also managed to spend four hundred dollars — his entire summer earnings — in these machines before I put a stop to it."

Some psychologists have echoed this father's concern, pointing out that electronic games can be so hypnotic to teens that they block out the rest of the world, diverting adolescent energies and attention from important developmental tasks. And physicians have acknowledged that marathon stints with these games can lead to eyestrain, headaches, blisters, and callouses.

Other experts see a beneficial side to the video revolution. For one thing, they point to studies showing that these games improve eye-hand coordination (in fact, they've been used by the military for this purpose). There is also mounting evidence that the complexity of video games fosters inductive reasoning and parallel processing (evaluating many variables simultaneously). Others note that the games encourage competitive spirit and provide kids with a sense of catharsis — a chance to get rid of everyday frustrations and tensions by escape into a light-flashing, musically programmed fantasy world. Still other adults are relieved by the fact that teens hooked on videogames generally avoid drugs and booze, which would only detract from their skills in playing these games.

Computers are more difficult to compete with for attention. Computer magazines have published several articles reporting the development of a kind of love affair between the computer and its programmer/operator. Master/slave relationships also abound.

Teens with little or no prior authority or control over anyone or anything are suddenly given sophisticated equipment they can order about at will, telling it what to do and watching it respond efficiently and without complaint. The feelings of power can be awesome and overwhelming — similar to what other teens feel after buying their first car.

Because computer technology poses a challenge to teens, more advanced computer hacks may try to prove their knowhow by breaking in, electronically speaking, to the large computer systems of businesses, hospitals, universities, laboratories, or even government agencies. Serious damage may be done in these situations in terms both of the economic cost of repairing such systems after they've been vandalized and of destroyed records that may be irreplaceable. Teens who spend a lot of time at the computer console must understand that abusing the computer by gaining unauthorized entry to another computer is a form of breaking and entering that is a criminal act and may have repercussions far beyond their imaginations. As Representative Ron Wyden of Oregon observed, "For some reason, some teen-agers who would never knock down an elderly woman on the street and empty her pocketbook see nothing wrong with tapping a few keys on a computer terminal, thereby wiping out that same woman's retirement savings."

We don't know exactly what directions new technology in computers will take, but we can be fairly certain that more and more teens are going to become computer-literate in the years ahead. This means that the number of adolescents who are so fascinated by the power of computers that they virtually become wedded to the keyboard will increase — producing just one more source of parental concern.

Short of repeating, "It's only a machine, it's only a machine," and constantly reminding your adolescent that people are important, too (even if they won't do your bidding after you push a few buttons), there isn't much to be done. This is a new, technological, computerized age we live in. Once they've glimpsed those city lights, you'll have a hard time keeping them down on the farm.

PART THREE

Crises

15

Crisis Resolution and Beyond

It's relatively easy to be a loving, understanding parent when your teenager is playing by the rules you've set. The crucible of successful parenting is not how you handle yourself when times are good, but how you respond to major problems that suddenly appear. Your aptitude for thinking quickly, submerging your own feelings in the interests of helping your teen, and maintaining a steady course even when things don't resolve instantaneously is the real acid test of successful parenting.

A General Approach to Crisis-Solving Skills

When a major crisis appears in your adolescent's life, you must begin by defining its dimensions in a number of different ways. Foremost, you must discover if the situation is an emergency that poses a potential threat to life or health. If your teen has taken an overdose of sleeping pills, you don't have time to sit and discuss the meanings of this act or talk about options of how to proceed. In many other crisis situations, though, there is no imperative to act within the first few minutes after learning of the problem, so that a very different approach can be taken. You should recognize that the emergency nature of a crisis may not apply to your adolescent alone; find out at the outset if anyone else is involved with them in case others may be in danger of one sort or another and their parents don't know it yet.

From this point on, the emphasis should shift for a while to listening to your teen to get as much information as you can about the situation.

191

What's the problem? When and how did it begin? How serious is it? Who's involved? How certain are your adolescent's facts? Your initial responses will dictate, to a large degree, just how honest your child will be in giving you the full story, so keep your emotions under control. Likewise, in most crisis situations the adolescent comes to you with a sense of fear and anguish — don't feed into this by responding with the "I-told-you-so" lecture that will alienate your teen from you, confirming his or her worries that you can't really be relied on to help. The teenager who feels rejected by parents in a time of crisis is a teenager who may go off the deep end in a desperate attempt to find a solution, even if the solution is as drastic as running away or attempting suicide.

Since most crisis situations do not require immediate mobilization for action, avoid jumping to any hasty decisions. Instead, take a bit of time to reflect on the available options, weighing the advantages and disadvantages of each. In many instances, a consultation with an appropriate expert may be in order (e.g., a lawyer, a physician, a teacher, a guidance counselor) since you may not really be in a position to recognize all the options that exist. To guard against undue emotional influences on their thinking, spouses should discuss matters together and consider the possibility of talking with a third party — one of their own parents, a trusted friend, a sibling — in devising the strategies that will be followed.

Once you've decided on a course of action, remember that your teenager needs to be involved as well. Discuss things together, outlining the basis of your reasoning but leaving the door open to modify plans if your teen comes up with an angle you hadn't thought of. In some cases there may be only one possible way to go, but most crises have alternative solutions, so try to give your adolescent a chance to express his or her feelings on the matter.

> Thirteen-year-old Diane had come to her mother late at night to say she needed to talk. After a hesitant start, she spilled out a horrifying story: her Uncle Harry had been abusing her sexually for more than a year. Frightened into silence by threats that he would kill her if she told anyone, Diane had stoically tried to keep quiet but now found herself living in a nearly perpetual state of panic and shame.
>
> Her parents reacted to this news with shock and anger. How could Harry, with whom they'd been quite close, have done such a thing? Their initial reaction led to an angry confrontation at Harry's house, with Harry's denial of the accusation rapidly changing to a tearful confession and a plea for understanding. "Please don't report this," he begged; "it'll ruin my life." They reluctantly agreed, perhaps out of family loyalty, on the condition that Harry would seek psychiatric help.

Diane wasn't happy with this arrangement. She felt that Harry should be reported to the police, and pointed out that she thought he might be molesting other children besides herself. When her mother asked if she realized that filing formal charges would require divulging what had happened to nonfamily members, Diane blurted out, "Good. I'll feel better if I can get it out, anyway."

The parents decided, after some soul-searching, to follow the course of action Diane suggested. Diane's guess about Uncle Harry's involvement with others proved to be correct, and Harry eventually was convicted and sentenced to a state-run sex-offenders' treatment program. Diane, with the assistance of a psychologist who saw her weekly for two months, emerged from her ordeal feeling healed and confident. Her parents were amazed at her composure when she testified in court and were delighted to find that she returned to being an active, normal teenager.

In dealing with crises, it is often difficult to admit that easy solutions are truly rare. Facing up to the realities at hand may also require admitting that resolving the crisis may be painful in a variety of ways — in fact, possibly more painful for you, as parents, than for your teen. Once a course of action is decided on, however, stick to it unless new evidence shows that it won't work or an alternate plan presents itself that clearly offers a better chance of success. The trials and tribulations of the early going may be especially distressing, but may be a necessary path towards healing.

How to Avoid Panic, Pressure, and Prejudice

Many high school locker rooms have a well-worn sign displayed that says, "When the going gets tough, the tough get going." If athletics are in many ways a metaphor for living, we can learn a lesson from this adage that is applicable to crises like the ones we're discussing here. To react to a crisis with panic is to lessen materially your chances of successfully dealing with the situation. Instead of panic, a tough resolve is called for that can instill much-needed confidence in your teen and also help you think clearly. Parents who respond to their children's crises with angry, emotional outbursts are just as caught in the panic trap as parents who throw up their hands and give up when a tough situation appears. Remember, you are essentially embarking on a vital rescue mission — and panic can undermine even the best-planned rescue attempt.

Parents sometimes react to crisis in their adolescents' lives by deciding that it's time to reassert their authority as autocratically as they did when the teen was a young child. In falling into this somewhat reflexive pattern, parents are apt to pressure their teenager into seeing things their way, not recognizing that doing this poses no real solution at all, although it may temporarily give a false sense of security. The pregnant fifteen-year-old is not apt to regress to nursery school behavior, even though she may accept parental pronouncements without protest as a form of self-punishment. The sixteen-year-old boy who's been caught stealing autos is not going to change suddenly because of a stern lecture delivered by dad. Pressure from parents is hardly optimal in dealing with crises, just as panic doesn't work very well either.

In previous chapters, we have repeatedly pointed out that the major behavioral problems of adolescence must be evaluated in context to devise effective coping strategies. An approach that works with one teenager won't necessarily work with another, since you are dealing with different personalities, different circumstances, and different impacts on the teenager's life. One thirteen-year-old boy may see a suspension from school as the world's major catastrophe, while another sees it as a great chance to hang out on the streets, pick up some pocket money, and have some fun. One sixteen-year-old girl is mortified at being pregnant, while another finds it inconvenient but no big deal. Clearly, then, the approach to crisis situations must be individualized to fit the needs of each person.

As steps are being taken to bring matters under control in one way or another, avoid prejudicing your interactions with your teenager because of the crisis. If you allow the crisis to cast such a dark cloud over your relations with your child that he or she feels totally rejected or worthless, you seriously diminish the chances of effecting a permanent solution. Solving one problem, only to have a barrier erected between you and your teen, is almost a guarantee that another problem or crisis will crop up soon. We don't suggest "forgive and forget" as the best way to go (most of us are all too human for this to work) but we do urge an attitude of forgiveness. Constant recrimination can leave your teen feeling indelibly stigmatized, and hence more apt to think, "I might as well screw up because they expect me to anyway." Forgiveness and love can work wonders in resolving crises even though no one forgets what happened. In fact, if we forget what happened we may easily fall into the same trap again. Remembering what happened and what it felt like is a good way of ensuring that the important lessons of the crisis won't be soon discarded.

Guilt Is Not the Answer

It's incredibly tempting to use any mistake your teenagers make as grist for the mill when you're trying to get them to see things your way.

When a major crisis arises, the magnitude of your adolescents' blunder is a quantum leap beyond everyday mistakes, so the temptation is even stronger to remind them of how stupid (or thoughtless or immature or reckless) they were in order to obtain their complete attention and obedience. But inducing guilt in your adolescents by constant reminders of how they got into hot water and how you rescued them is likely to backfire over the long run. In fact, while your adolescent's complete obedience might be temporarily comforting to you, it would actually result in an untenable situation in which your teen would be the loser.

Despite this fact, many parents use their adolescents' guilt as a powerful weapon in establishing control after a crisis has arisen. To maximize their authority, these parents actually nurture guilt to ensure it will grow and embed itself in the teenagers' minds. This is an insidious form of vindictiveness that borders on child abuse. No one wins when an adolescent is made to feel inadequate and worthless, and the long-range consequences in terms of the child's battered ego may be significant. Family therapy may be required to break this pattern of parental guilt-induction if it occurs over a long period of time.

What can be done to be certain the crisis won't reappear in one form or another? While there are no guarantees or foolproof methods, your best bet is to treat your teenager with love and respect rather than with distrust and derision. We all have made mistakes in our lives and experienced crises in one form or another; often what we remember best from these is the compassion and understanding extended to us by another person who helped us get through this trying time. You might want to make a habit of saying things like these to your teens once you've weathered a crisis:

(1) "Remember how it was before we learned to talk about our problems? I do, and I hope we're never tempted to shut each other out again."

(2) "Parents sometimes forget what it's like to be a teenager. Please remember to remind us from time to time."

(3) "Would you mind if we asked for your advice or opinion every now and then?"

Your relationship to your teenagers through the crisis and beyond can be a catalyst to their learning something unique about themselves and about you; your behavior during this time can also provide a superb role model for coping skills that just may turn out to be one of the most valuable lessons your child learns while growing up.

"I got pregnant when I was fifteen," Cindy told us. "It was a stupid, thoughtless thing to do. But what I learned from the experience — besides the obvious lesson of using contraception — was that my parents were on my side when I needed them. I was amazed that they never got mad at me, never shoved my mistake in my face; they just helped me think things through and find a solution that felt right to me. I'll never forget what that meant, and I know that will help me be a better parent when I have kids of my own."

Restoring Family Equilibrium

Like a stone thrown into a pond, a major crisis involving you teenager produces ripple effects on your family system. In the initial going, when parents mobilize to meet the crisis head-on, a lot of tension may build that doesn't get outwardly expressed. Once it's clear that the crisis is no longer an acute threat (action has been taken to ameliorate the problems as well as can be) these pent-up tensions may begin to emerge and influence the ordinary relationships between family members.

The aftermath of the crisis may include strained relations between spouses or rebellious behavior by a younger sibling anxious to get his or her share of the spotlight of parental attention. Another common pattern is a general stigmatization of the teen who has been in the crisis, with other family members blaming the teenager for anything that goes wrong and avoiding contact with the teen as though distance will be protective. Realistic recognition of the dynamics of what's occurring and some attention to remedying the situation, however, can restore a reasonable degree of family equilibrium in short order.

Ordinarily, the first step is to be honest with your other children about what has happened and what's being done about it. Secretiveness may be necessary if you're dealing with a teenage pregnancy or a suicide attempt, but in many cases siblings will quickly recognize that something's wrong and will want to know what it is. Unless they're very young and would be completely unable to comprehend the nature of the problem, honesty (not necessarily down to the last gory detail) will be better than allowing their imaginations to run wild. At the same time you can explain that this is a private family matter, not something to be discussed at school or with friends.

The restoration of family equilibrium usually occurs more smoothly if all family members get a chance to ventilate — that is, to talk about the feelings they're having in relation to the crisis and how it was handled. A detailed postmortem is not called for, but simply pretending that life goes idyllically on without acknowledging the disruption is not likely to be realistic or helpful. At the same time, you as parents need to guard against allowing the family to make the teen who caused the problem into an all-purpose scapegoat.

Restoring family equilibrium is, in the final analysis, a matter of healing, just as crisis resolution itself is an ongoing healing process rather than a single stroke of action. The trick is to recognize that time itself is a great healer, sometimes working better than all the medicine in the world. Allowing your family to heal its rifts in a gradual manner rather than trying to force everyone to behave in a certain way *right now* is a wise approach indeed.

Learning from Experience

From your teenager's viewpoint, the only real benefits that come out of a crisis are the lessons that are learned. One of the principal lessons the teenager can learn is that parents can be counted on to help, no matter how serious things may seem to be. Another prominent lesson should come from understanding the circumstances that led up to the crisis — what happened, why it happened that way, and what could have been done to prevent it from happening. Your teenager may need help here in putting together the pieces of the puzzle, because try as they might, not all adolescents are sufficiently analytical or mature enough to recognize how a problem originated or how things might have been handled differently at various points along the way to keep it from escalating into a full-scale crisis. The idea here is not to force your teens to see things your way but to help them gain a greater degree of insight into the results of their own behavior. Such insight will not always cross over to other areas in their lives, nor will it guarantee that they won't repeat the mistake (since some teens will out of obstinance, stupidity, or deliberate destructiveness), but those who don't learn from the past are indeed doomed to repeat it.

Parents can also learn something from how the crisis was handled. Were you completely satisfied with your own performance, or were there things you wish you could do over? Did you respond to the crisis in a calm, collected manner or did you lash out with anger and resentment at your teen? Did you listen to your child's point of view and take his or her feelings into account in formulating a solution, or did you arbitrarily impose your judgment because you figured you knew what was best? Did you avoid dumping a lot of guilt on your adolescent's shoulders? Did you lecture incessantly or did you give your teen room to express his or her feelings? In short, did you treat your teen as you would have wanted to be treated in a crisis? If not, look carefully at what happened and try to see where there were problems, devising strategies for improving your role if the need should arise again.

Long-Range Planning

Despite how you may feel as a crisis is painfully upon you, with time the nature of the crisis will pass and the pain will recede to vague memories. In itself, this isn't necessarily good or bad — it's simply the way the human mind works to let us deal with the vicissitudes of everyday living. But rather than just sitting around waiting for the passage of time to heal your hurts and the agonies of your teenager, you can take a more active role by doing some long-range planning to minimize the chances of this same type of crisis repeating itself in your lives.

A good place to begin is by making an accurate appraisal of the nature of the crisis you've just gone through. Is it possible it was an isolated occurrence that's unlikely to happen again, or was it more of a "tip-of-the-iceberg" phenomenon, indicating that other problems may still be present and require attention? Certain types of adolescent problems, such as depression or drug-dependency, won't typically disappear just because you've helped your teen through one crisis caused by them. In other instances — a teenager caught plagiarizing an English paper, for example — the crisis may be part of its own resolution since the anguish of getting caught becomes a strong deterrent to subsequent attempts to beat the system.

This raises an interesting question for discussion. What sort of punishment, if any, should be meted out to the teenager who's gotten into a crisis situation? If your seventeen-year-old son caused an accident while driving under the influence of drugs he obviously needs to be prohibited from driving alone for a while, but should you also take away his car keys and ban him from driving Aunt Sarah to the shopping center to get her weekly groceries? If your fourteen-year-old daughter got pregnant and had an abortion, would it be wise to ground her for a while so she can't go out on dates? From these examples, you can readily see that punishments are not always appropriate to crisis situations. In some cases, punishments are useful ways of setting limits by taking away privileges until they've been earned back. In other cases, your punishment may have a certain deterrent value of its own. But often it is best to resist the urge to impose a harsh penalty on your teenager — "I'll show him [her] who's boss" — since the traumas of the crisis may already have functioned in much the same way as punishments.

There are several other issues that should be of far more importance to you and your adolescent in terms of long-range crisis resolution. First, you need to assess the impact of the crisis on your teenager, recognizing that his or her immediate reactions don't always indicate what the lasting effects will be. In some instances, the adolescent will go through a phase of denial in which he or she pretends the crisis never happened. This is not an attempt to fictionalize life, but is instead a very common psychological defense mechanism that permits people to cope with un-pleasant, stressful, or threatening circumstances. In fact, parents may cling to such a denial mechanism more tenaciously than the adolescent does, especially when the type of crisis has been particularly embarrassing or upsetting. Another common reaction to a crisis is a period of depression or melancholy that sets in once the problem is seemingly solved. This can be a type of mourning over the illusions shattered by the crisis or it can be a simple case of giving up ("Life's too difficult to deal with") and subsequent withdrawal. A third pattern sometimes encountered is a phase of anger and frustration that appears when the crisis is seemingly over. This may result from suppressing many feelings while faced with an acute crisis. After the crisis has faded, pent-up reactions may explode with a vengeance.

In each reaction pattern described above, it is important to recognize what's happening and move beyond it to better integrate the crisis into your lives. You and your teenager both need to go on living, but you also need to readjust your expectations, your cautionary flags, and your patterns of interaction based on what occurred. The goal actually consists of two parts: preventing recurrences of crisis situations and minimizing the chances that the crisis you've just gone through will leave permanent scars. Both parts of this long-range goal of crisis resolution can best be served by enhancing communications with your teenager, the first and most effective step we know towards problem prevention.

16

Ground Rules for Parents Getting a Divorce: How to Save Your Kids

If a divorcing couple can be likened to warring nations, then in this simile the children of divorce are in the position of civilian populations, exposed to the ravages of a war they did nothing to create.
— *Joseph Epstein,* Divorced in America

You don't need to read sobering lists of statistics to know that more Americans than ever are divorcing. A quick tally of your neighbors, co-workers, relatives, and friends provides a pretty accurate picture of the rate of divorce in the U.S. today: Nearly one out of every two marriages is destined to end this way if present trends continue. One million children are affected by divorce each year. While the pain and agony of these children of divorce is difficult to quantify, researchers agree that family breakups typically create an atmosphere loaded with potential problems.

If divorce looms in your future, but you shudder over its possible effect on your adolescent, be heartened. A divorce need not split the ground under your adolescent's feet. All teenagers will feel some tremors, but a few basic preventive techniques can help them escape any earthquakes.

Marital Tensions and Their Impact on a Teenager

About ten years ago, when divorce started becoming widespread in the U.S., most of what was written about the children of divorce concen-

200

trated on the preschool or elementary school child. Perhaps social scientists believed that by adolescence a child could grasp the "adult" concept of divorce and this understanding would allay the trauma of having the mother and father live apart.

Since those early studies, it has become clear that age does not automatically lessen a child's pain over his or her parents' breakup. Even children in their twenties and thirties (many with children of their own) express emotional upheaval and sometimes seek professional counseling at being told their parents are planning to end their marriage.

But the negative effects on children, including teenagers, don't begin *after* the divorce. The tensions that exist in a marriage — sometimes for years — take a toll on the children in a number of different ways. First, marital tensions create a sense of unhappiness and helplessness in all children. Teenagers, especially, may feel they are causing the problem, seeing their own conflicts with parents as a major factor contributing to marital discord. Second, parents who are having trouble relating to each other characteristically devote less energy and attention to their kids. The adolescent is apt to see this as a form of rejection, a lessening of parental interest or love. Third, parents in dissonant marriages are likely to take out their hostilities on their teens, who are marvelous (if unwitting) targets for such venting. Finally, an atmosphere of simmering marital tension puts a Damocles sword over the teenager's head: the thought of divorce becomes a constant worry. The adolescent may react by trying to mediate arguments or becoming a marriage counselor, offering encouragement and suggestions for preserving family unity, and shouldering an immense sense of failure if things don't work out.

> A fourteen-year-old girl: "I saw it coming but I didn't want to. I kept thinking how I'd become a 'child of a broken home' and what that meant. If only I could find a way to fix it. Every time one of my parents said they wanted to talk with me about something, I was sure it would be the official announcement. But it was about six months before their plans for divorce finally came into the open."

Squabbles and marital tensions cannot be hidden from an adolescent, but neither should your teen be given a ringside seat. Too much discretion and your son or daughter will feel isolated and excluded, maybe even deceived; too much exposure of your own indecisiveness tosses the adolescent to and fro in the same excruciating turmoil you feel — but with no control over the outcome.

Divorce is a frightening word to adolescents, conjuring a dozen different questions. "Where will I live?" "Who will I see most?" "Will we have enough money to get by?" "Will I have to go to a different school?" "If Mom or Dad remarries, how will I get along with a stepparent?"

Later, the adolescent may come to realize that divorce was a wiser solution than a lifetime of bickering and tension, but a teenager's initial reaction to the news of a parental breakup is almost always shock and denial.

With this in mind, it's easy to see why parents will subject their children to months of arguments and marital tensions rather than make a final decision to get a divorce and proceed with the legalities.

Separation Is a Strain, Not a Solution

> A sixteen-year-old boy: "My folks hated each other. At first I was relieved when they separated. But separation didn't stop the fighting; it just complicated it."

You and your spouse have been agonizing for weeks about whether to file for divorce. You both know that you can't go on living like this, searching for opportunities to hurt each other, feeling anxious when you have to share the same part of the house for any length of time. Your nerves are frayed, your appetite diminished. The pressure to make a decision is so massive it has paralyzed your ability to act. You need a respite, a rest, and suddenly it comes to you that you can separate temporarily, buy yourselves some time, get out of each other's hair long enough for an answer to make itself clear.

A separation, in which one partner in the marriage moves to a different location for either an indefinite or a set length of time, is only a decision to postpone the decision. It may be just the time-out needed for married persons who are not parents, but when children are involved, a separation often amounts to cruel and unusual punishment. Adolescents have a strong need to know where they stand in relation to their parents and to the world at large. They need limits and boundaries and rules to help them navigate the confusing sea of maturity. Parental separation rarely provides any rules or limits; it places issues of critical concern to adolescents (like custody, school-year residence) in limbo, and hovers over their lives like menacing shadows.

Perhaps worse than the unanswered questions, a separation encourages what often amount to false hopes of reconciliation. "For over a year I plotted and schemed to get them back together. They weren't officially divorced, so I thought the only thing keeping them apart was their own stubbornness," one eighteen-year-old boy told us. "Of course every time one of my plans would work, and my parents would be thrown together at a school function or a soccer game, my hopes were high and my disappointment great. I shouldn't have put myself through those ups and downs, but I couldn't give up until they finally filed with the courts."

If you and your spouse feel you absolutely must attempt separation before deciding on something as final as divorce, it is best if you first detail the terms of that separation. You can agree, for example, that the separation will last three months, that the children will stay with their father during the week and their mother on every other weekend, that the mother will move out of the house by a certain date but confine her new residence to within a ten-mile radius of the home, etc. The amount of financial support can also be negotiated, as well as the frequency and forms of communication between parents. Of course without a legal contract, it would be difficult to force either spouse to uphold his or her side of the verbal bargain. But attempting a fair division of responsibilities and agreeing to a deadline for deciding about the divorce is far superior to an impulsive separation that, like the first chapter in an Agatha Christie novel, leaves a great number of key issues dangling.

Preparing Your Children for Divorce

You and your spouse have decided your differences are irreconcilable; divorce is your only solution. How do you tell the kids? And when? The children should be told as soon as you are sure about the divorce, and you and your spouse have had time to (1) control your emotions enough to present the news calmly and rationally; (2) research the custody options for presentation to them. If you have more than one child and their ages span a wide range, it is best to explain it to each one individually. Both spouses should still take part in each presentation, but in this way you can gear the level of the explanation to the age and maturity of the child. For children who are close in age, thirteen and fifteen, for example, telling them either separately or together has its advantages and disadvantages. The response of the adolescent told separately might be less inhibited than if a sibling were gazing on. Other teenagers like the feeling of immediate support they get from having siblings close to their own age in the same room with them. This decision requires your personal judgment of your children's needs and personalities.

Before the adolescent is called into the conversation, it is imperative that you and your spouse thoroughly review what will be said, who will say it, the reasons you wish to give your child for the divorce, and how you will reassure the child that the divorce will not alter his or her individual relationship with either parent. You and your spouse should agree on the handling of all these points beforehand. Do not use the explanation of your divorce to your teenager as another excuse for an argument. The energies of both of you need to focus on the child at this time, not each other.

How is an adolescent likely to react to the news? Younger teens will probably start to cry, showing their fear, uncertainty, and disappointment. Older adolescents are more likely to sit quietly, fighting back all emotional urges (anger as well as sadness) until they have escaped to the privacy of another room. Some teens react in stunned silence; others have a million questions. Whatever reaction occurs, respect your adolescents enough to allow them their private ways of adapting to the news. Your conversation can be resumed in a few hours.

Some outspoken teens express their anger or upset with vehement immediacy. Try not to take the insults and rantings too personally, remembering that a quick verbal outpouring of feeling is better than stifled emotions that slowly boil only to finally escape in steamy bursts of drug or alcohol abuse, promiscuity, or antisocial behavior. Be prepared for the fact that your teenager may size up the situation and quickly and impulsively take sides with one parent or the other. This is more apt to be a form of self-defense than a reliable indicator of his or her true feelings towards each of you. It may be useful for you to say something like "I understand how hurt and betrayed you must feel and I can't blame you for it," or "I'm sorry if we disappointed you," since these messages tell your teen that you understand the depths of his or her emotions and are willing to talk about it, even if you are the target of a lot of temporary hostility.

Of all the practical details of the divorce that should be covered with an adolescent, the most important fact both parents need to communicate is their continued love for their children. A divorce does not sever the love or bonds between parents and their children; the parent-child relationship can never be removed by legal decree. The reaction of a seventeen-year-old boy sums it up very well:

> "I remember my dad saying over and over again, 'No matter what happens between your mother and me, I am still your father and you are still my son. Nothing anybody does can change that or stop that. My love for you continues stronger than before.' Even though I felt those things inside, I needed to hear him say them. I began to realize it was as hard for my parents as it was for me. They hurt too."

Custody and Other Quandaries

When a teen is involved in a custody decision it is a complicated and sensitive situation. Clearly the adolescent's own preferences for custody should be considered, since he or she is old enough to deserve some voice in the decision (the timbre of that voice varying from teen to teen). An adolescent forced to live with a parent he or she refuses to tolerate might run away from home or display a rebellion so pervasive that the postdivorce life of both parents is made miserable.

Adolescents also require reasonably detailed explanations of the final custody decision if all persons involved are to be fairly happy with the arrangements. Discuss the pros and cons of living with either parent. Would neighborhoods and school districts change? Would one parent have more free time to spend with the teenager than another? Parents who strive for rational reasons as the basis for their custody agreement, rather than emotional pleas, tend to devise arrangements considered in the long run to be more equitable to all concerned.

A realistic appraisal of the future lives of the family members also helps in creating an effective custody plan. If you know, for example, that seventeen-year-old Donna leaves for college in four months, then vacation, holiday, and summer months custody will be the primary considerations, as well as assigning the financial responsibility for various aspects of her education. For thirteen-year-old Bobby, however, whose future appears less clear in the crystal ball, custody discussions should encompass which parents attend which school functions, whether both parents will reside in the same school district, whether or not both parents will work and at what hours, and similar issues. The larger the number of contingencies you both uncover and discuss before attorneys join the discourse, the less chance after the divorce of misunderstandings that sometimes escalate into a return trip to the courtroom.

The four main types of custody are joint, sole, divided, and split. Joint custody, in which a child lives most of the year with one parent but both parents share in practical, philosophical, and financial decisions about the child's upbringing, is rising in popularity today. The more traditional sole custody grants the lion's share of moral responsibility for shelter and upbringing of the child to one parent (in the U.S. it is usually the mother) with the other parent often required to provide some degree of financial support and allowed a number of visiting privileges. In divided custody, the child lives with one parent for a set period during the year and with the other parent for the remainder. Split custody is possible only in a family of two or more offspring, because the children are divided between the parents, the father assuming sole custody of the boys, for example; the mother custody of the girls.

Coparenting, another term frequently used in recent years as a variation of joint custody, extends the range of the parents' commitment to the continued sharing of their child's upbringing after the divorce. Although the terms *coparenting* and *joint custody* are often used interchangeably, joint custody tends to focus on legal issues like rights of visitation and place of residence, while coparenting involves the child's nurturance and love, socialization, recreation, religion, and other sociocultural aspects of raising the child.

Each type of custody has its drawbacks and benefits. Sole custody places such a heavy burden of responsibility on one parent that it can exhaust her or him, causing resentment that is often expressed to the children. From the adolescent's point of view, sole custody denies him or her the benefit of two opinions, two judgments in important decisions about the future. Sole custody can be necessary, however, if one parent shows no interest in raising the child. Decision-making is also likely to be expeditious since the other parent need not be consulted.

Divided custody often has logistical problems that make it an impractical choice. If either parent moves out of the original school district, the adolescent may have to switch schools—an extra adjustment that is especially hard for peer-oriented teens. Some parents divide custody between the school term and summer vacation, but adolescents often object to leaving their school friends during the summer. A variation of divided custody which puts less strain on the adolescent (but more on the parents) is the "bird's nest plan" in which the teenager stays in one house, but the parents alternate their residency there. This is a viable solution only if both parents live and work fairly close to each other (something many newly divorced couples try to avoid).

The split custody option (more popular in Europe than in the U.S.) forces children to suffer not only the breakup of their parents' marriage but the division of sibling attachments as well. Brothers and sisters often provide each other with invaluable solace as they experience the same emotional strains of divorce at the same time. In cases where there is a wide gap in the children's ages, however, and neither parent feels equipped to take custody of all the children, split custody may be the only practical alternative.

Decisions are made together in joint custody and coparenting and should be unanimous, so the mother and father must be able to communicate in a nonhostile manner — not always easy after a divorce. If unanimous decisions cannot be reached by the parents, the courts may be again consulted, involving additional attorney's fees and often interminable time lags. An uncontested divorce between two mature, friendly partners, however, lends itself well to a successful joint custody arrangement.

Overall, joint custody combined with coparenting offers the most potential for an egalitarian division of parental duties and responsibilities while preserving the philosophical unity of the family despite its physical division. Adolescents, perhaps more than any other age group, need (and sometimes demand) wisely rendered decisions as well as reasonable limits set on their behavior. Parents of adolescents often complain that they felt as if battle lines had been drawn the instant their child turned thirteen. Joint custody and coparenting allow divorced parents to continue combining their forces in the pursuit of the best interests of their children.

Ventilation versus Valor

"The better part of valor is discretion. ..."
(Shakespeare, I Henry IV, V)

No matter how amicable your divorce, some tranquil afternoon your ex-spouse is going to do or say something so unconscionable you'll feel unable to restrain your anger. Your natural first reaction will be to vent those feelings to the nearest available body, most likely your teenager.
Don't do it.

Stretch your four-letter vocabulary to its limits, see how many pieces you can reduce your wedding china to, scream into your pillow — but don't force your adolescent to be your audience. Chances are that Tom, Jr., witnessed enough emotional outbursts as your marriage was dying — he doesn't need his memory refreshed by a solo performance.

If you make the mistake of force-feeding your adolescent with jugs of your homemade emotional turmoil, one or all of the following is likely to result.

(1) Your teen may seem to agree with you, but actually sympathizes more with the parent who is being criticized. This is partly a reflection of the adolescent's sense of fair play — since the other person can't defend himself (or herself), the teen's natural instinct is to take his or her side.

(2) Your bitterness and anger may be so frightening that it drives your teen away. Runaways are discussed in another chapter, but the shock waves of a divorce motivate many of them to take that first step. Don't shake your adolescent's world with your temporary anger, no matter how strong it may be.

(3) Your teen may run to your ex-spouse's home. This is a variation of the second point and sometimes more difficult for the deserted parent to accept. "How could Mary leave me for her father, when I kept warning her about how awful he was?" She may have wanted to judge for herself.

(4) Your teen may feel unable to cope with your anger and be worried about your mental health. This may lead to questioning your judgment in *all* matters, leaving teens to rely on their instincts rather than your guidance or advice.

(5) Your teen will accept your emotion-laden judgments as fact. This response is the most insidious because it can unnecessarily and irreconcilably drive parent and adolescent apart. Words, once said, cannot easily be reclaimed. Your uncontrolled outburst may echo in your adolescent's mind forever.

Anger and frustration may not be the only emotions you'll want to vent concerning your ex-spouse. Loneliness may overwhelm you, guilt over the divorce engulf you, or sentimentalism invade you when a song on the radio or a whiff of cologne resonates with memories of happier times with your ex-spouse. Be careful not to share these feelings with your adolescent either; if they are as fleeting as most divorced person's, they serve only to tease your teen into thoughts of parental reconciliation. Don't lead your child on unless reuniting becomes a very real possibility. Teenagers often grasp at the least substantial of straws, especially since their notions of love and romance are drawn more from fiction — with those "they-all-lived-happily-ever-after" endings — than from fact.

While we're on the subject of ventilation of feelings, you and your ex-spouse won't be the only persons occasionally needing a way to release the valve on your emotional pressure cookers. Your children have sensibilities of their own. The age-old pendulum swings both ways, and the surprises and inconveniences of life after the divorce can host swarms of parasitic emotions like hurt, rage, depression, and disappointment.

How should the divorced parent respond when an adolescent complains that the other parent has hurt or angered him or her? Swallow the impulse to rush to your child's side and take up arms against that insensitive clod you used to be married to. Your innocent thirteen-year-old may be playing the Divide and Conquer game (see Chapter 4) with greatly increased odds of winning now that the blade of divorce has severed Mom from Dad. As in the nondivorced family, you can destroy that game by keeping communications between you and your ex-spouse as open and objective as possible. A certificate of divorce does not prohibit you from contacting the other parent to discuss your teen's complaint rationally.

The Aftermath of Divorce

Some divorcing couples mistakenly believe that the moment the court declares the marriage ended, all their trials and tribulations end too. Unfortunately, this is not the case. Not only do divorced parents find themselves in situations they hadn't really imagined — dealing with lonelinesss, worrying about social skills, facing economic strains, and watching many of their married friends desert them — the fact is that children often have a harder time after a divorce than they'd had before.

The family tensions and insecurities of a divorce situation are particularly difficult for adolescents to face. Teens ordinarily establish their own independence and identity using their family as a frame of reference; when the family unit is shattered, it's like breaking your only compass when you're trying to find your way out of the woods. As a result, many teens regress temporarily, reverting to less mature, less "adultlike" behavior and thinking to try to deny the reality of the divorce. It's almost as if by becoming childlike again, they can turn back the hands of time. Other teens seek to escape from the pain they feel by turning to drug and alcohol use. Still others mask their inner hurting by retaliating outwardly with impulsive, irresponsible behavior aimed at making parents notice them. This type of "acting out" behavior also releases anger that the adolescent may not be able to communicate in any other way.

Here are comments from several teens while in the immediate post-divorce period:

> *A sixteen-year-old boy:* "I think my dad is a real bastard. He didn't even try to save the marriage; it was like he wanted to get free. I don't know if I'll ever be able to really trust him again."
>
> *A fourteen-year-old girl:* "There's no way I'll ever get married. It can't be worth the agony that we've all gone through. And the worst part is I don't think my parents ever really worried about *my* feelings — it was all a big, selfish game."
>
> *A thirteen-year-old boy:* "What hurts the most for me is that my dad didn't even want me to live with him. He said I'd be better off with my mom, but I know he just didn't want me around."

As these comments show, many teens are severely distressed by divorce and harbor resentments towards one or both parents that linger on instead of quickly going away. Adolescents are not immune to feelings of parental rejection; these may be directed at the parent they're living with as well as at the parent who has left their home. Teens often feel manipulated, bribed, or coerced by their parents during the postdivorce adjustment. One parent asks "innocent" questions — "Is your mom dating a lot now?" — and the teen feels like a spy. A parent offers to buy some new clothes for the teen — and he or she thinks, "You can't buy my love this way." A parent says angrily, "Maybe you'd rather live with your father! I'm doing the best I can," and the teen feels guilty. It's a complicated time with few easy answers.

Researchers agree that one of the most prominent effects of divorce on adolescents is to leave many of them with an intense fear of their own future marital failure. While the reasons for this are not entirely clear, it may reflect the teenager's sense that if his or her parents could fail in marriage, practically anyone can. Beyond this, while most teens are understanding about divorces that occur early in marriage, they have a difficult time seeing how a couple married for fifteen or twenty years can suddenly discover it isn't working out. "Why did they have to wait until *now* to do it?" a sixteen-year-old girl plaintively asked. "I could've had my own car this year and I was planning to go to a good college. Why couldn't they work it out? They must've had rough times before." A fourteen-year-old boy offers a similar refrain. "I don't understand how they could let it happen. They never tried marriage counseling or anything; they just got lawyers. That's a hell of a way to ruin four lives."

Fortunately, there may be a new trend emerging in divorces in

America today. In a growing percentage of cases, friendly feelings, cooperative interactions, and open lines of communication are being maintained by former spouses, allowing them to raise their children in a less destructive atmosphere. Shared child-rearing responsibilities and amicable relations between ex-spouses seem to translate into far less trauma for teens, with postdivorce recovery occurring more rapidly than in families where anger, resentment, or power struggles continue after the marriage is ended. "Friendly divorces" can offer an important answer to minimizing the problems a divorce will cause for your teen.

Specific Strategies for Positive Parenting

(1) Recognize that marital problems inevitably create ripple effects that your teens will feel. Do whatever you can to make certain that the difficulties you and your spouse are having don't divert your attention from your children's needs.

(2) Don't drop hints about divorcing prior to the final decision; wait until you and your spouse have unequivocally made up your minds before announcing the news to the children. Why provoke worry and anxiety in your adolescent if the two of you are ultimately able to succeed at the marriage? An adolescent need not and should not participate in your every doubt.

(3) Be realistic about your situation. Plan the details of the divorce and your postdivorce relationship with your spouse using logic and a spirit of joint bargaining. An amicable divorce will go a long way towards reducing the negative impact on your children.

(4) Try to involve your ex-spouse with you in some form of mutually cooperative child-rearing. Doing this will minimize your teen's worries of rejection and provide a reasonable sense of stability while other changes are occurring.

(5) Praise your ex-spouse as a parent if at all possible. Negative comments about your former spouse only hurt your teens or make them take sides.

(6) Don't turn your adolescent into a substitute spouse. Sometimes you'll feel as if an ocean of emotions has deposited you on a lonely beach, and the temptation will arise to seek solace from your teenager. Seventeen-year-old Jason's shoulders may look strong, but they won't support a parent for long without sustaining some damage.

(7) Avoid competing with your ex-spouse for your children's love and loyalty.

(8) Watch your child closely for signs of trouble during the postdivorce period. Dejection, denial, and hostility are common reactions that can escalate to full-blown depression, running away, suicide attempts, or

drug abuse. Get professional help if necessary, or consider having your teen participate in a support group of other children of divorced parents. (Such groups can usually be located through local child and family service agencies.)

Going through a divorce isn't easy for anyone. But by careful planning and attention to details, you can take some deliberate precautionary steps that will reduce the stresses and strains your children feel and help them bounce back from this difficult phase of their lives.

17

ℰating ℘roblems: Obesity, 𝒜norexia, and ℬinges

Americans have several national passions — football, baseball, and food. While many of us love to eat, we clearly don't like to let ourselves get fat in the process. It is as if the permission to show we love food by being a bit overweight has been culturally withdrawn; some experts suggest we somehow have come to equate fatness with decadence and loss of self-control. This creates a double-bind: we want to eat and do eat because it's not only life-sustaining but pleasurable, but we feel guilty for our excesses and either bemoan our self-indulgences or go a step further and diet (or pretend to diet).

Teenagers are particularly vulnerable to cultural trends and mirror adult eating and dieting behaviors. Some teens, the lucky ones, eat normally and don't give food much thought beyond what tastes good or bad and what pleases them or doesn't: they know when they're hungry and when they're not. Other teens go a step beyond — since they equate hanging out at fast-food joints with social acceptance, they use food as a form of entertainment. But for a growing number of adolescents, the pursuit of thinness takes precedence, for they believe a thin person is guaranteed a problem-free life. Unfortunately, they fail to see that such beliefs are fantasy. Instead, trying to achieve their goals by the misuse of food, these teens often develop bizarre and unhealthy eating patterns and lose control to such an extent that disorders such as anorexia nervosa (the self-starvation disorder) or bulimia (a binge-purge problem) set in and seem to dominate their lives. Other teenagers use food as a screen to hide behind when the pressures of real life become too much to deal with. They may become overweight, even obese, and, ironically, cause

212

themselves still greater social pressures. For far too many of today's teenagers, the meaning of food and eating has become twisted. Parents may react with rage, frustration, or despair, but it doesn't have to be that way.

Of Junk Food, Eating Habits, and Good Nutrition

A recent study found that high school seniors don't know much more about nutrition than do sixth graders. Teenagers' eating habits are often both erratic and almost completely adapted to snacking instead of eating regularly scheduled meals containing foods taken from each of the four major food groups. This shouldn't come as earth-shattering news to most parents of teenagers, but it does point out an alarming national trend: our teenagers not only don't known the first thing about good eating habits; they don't seem to care.

There is an enormous amount of food propaganda aimed at adolescents because they are very impressionable individuals not yet completely skilled in evaluating the products they buy and because they spend a lot of money on food. Teenagers react in a fairly predictable fashion to advertising campaigns, so food and soft-drink commercials are pitched to a superficial level of image. Put yourself in your adolescent's place for a moment. You are watching a commercial for a particular hamburger chain. The teenage actors and actresses all have perfect complexions, great-looking bodies, and are either cheerleader types or jocks. They are sitting around a table eating burgers and fries and drinking shakes. The message, the image, is that popular, attractive people eat these foods and you should too. Or consider any of the soft-drink commercials: again, the teenage models are all talented, sexy-looking people who are great dancers and fabulous singers as well! You begin to internalize these images. In effect, you begin to equate the products with the popularity, sensuality, and talent portrayed in the thirty-second television spots and you buy into the message that by using the products you can be like the people on the screen. You purchase an item impulsively because you enjoyed the hype and you identify with the not-so-subliminal messages.

Despite this, teenagers rarely compromise their health from "junking out" or snacking. If we are going to be rational about all of this, we must acknowledge our input as role models: if we have poor eating habits, we really cannot expect our children to emerge magically in their teenage years selecting whole-grain breads and unprocessed foods. Also, we must try to maintain some emotional distance from eating issues: we wouldn't much care for someone monitoring every bite of food we take, so it's not likely our teens enjoy that kind of attention either. If we can be both rational and enlightened about nutrition, we can admit that though a steady diet of ketchup, french fries, and soft drinks is not particularly healthy, many foods we consider to be empty calories or nutritionally unsound are not so empty or unsound after all. For instance, even pizza has some nutritionally redeeming value: three slices at Pizza Hut contains 54 grams of carbohydrate, 25 grams of protein, and 15 grams of fat — 450 calories, roughly equivalent nutritionally to a lamb chop, string beans, and a small baked potato.

Food issues do not have to deteriorate into generational battles or cause family disharmony. Eating should be a pleasure, not an Issue with a capital I. Parents must realize and try to accept the fact that today's teenagers all junk out at some point. The bottom line should be whether your teen is healthy, and whether his or her eating habits allow a normal life-style or whether they interfere with day-to-day life so as to be harmful. Perhaps we should remember the infant and child care books many of us turned to when we were new at the job of parenting. They pointed out that children eventually choose a balanced diet if given the free choice of foods because a person's body demands certain nutrients and will crave foods containing them. If available to a young child, the foods eventually get eaten — but perhaps not in the sequence an adult would deem acceptable. Barring the presence of an eating disorder, this is really true of teenagers too.

Being Fat in America: The Teenager's Perspective

There is no law in the United States that says teenagers must be thin, well-dressed, and "with it" in order to be fully accepted participants in the American adolescent subculture. Yet most of our teenagers conduct themselves as though these were dicta to be followed rigidly. Many teens equate overweight with the ultimate curse of being a social outcast and use diet to avoid that imagined fate. If dieting fails to yield the desired results and make them Cinderellas or Prince Charmings, they set themselves up for an adolescence fraught with further hurts and traumas. Other teens use their excess weight to avoid social interaction with peers, blaming many or all of their problems on their obesity, never learning how to deal constructively with the challenges of adolescence. They turn for solace to food rather than family or friends and literally use their overweight to isolate themselves from others.

Adolescents can be insecure about how their bodies function and look, worrying endlessly about how others perceive them. Therefore, adolescents are particularly vulnerable to feelings of worthlessness and even depression when their bodies don't develop into replicas of the perfectly formed young men and women they have been staring at for so long in their teen magazines and on television. It's not bad enough that adolescents worry about the condition of their skin, their sexual anatomy, and their ability to attract members of the opposite sex — when a weight problem appears it adds yet another whammy to the list of adolescent concerns that are not easily dissipated by logic. A parent saying, "Don't worry, dear, we all had awkward periods when we were young" doesn't make it any easier for the fifteen-year-old girl who has never been asked to a school dance or the sixteen-year-old boy who is always the last to be picked for teams in gym.

Our unmistakable cultural bias against overweight people is perpetuated by a number of myths that regard obesity as a sign of flawed character, laziness, or sloppiness — a condition willfully self-induced and easily reversed by willpower. Teenagers, plagued with shaky self-images anyway, buy into this bias and often don't know how to react to obese peers who don't fit acceptable standards. One way of coping with the unfamiliar is to avoid having to deal with it, and many average-weight teens do this in terms of their reactions to overweight kids. They may be purposely cruel and insensitive, totally rejecting anyone who doesn't measure up to their physical standards. They may try to be friendly but end up being condescending. Interestingly, if and when friendship develops, body dimensions cease to dominate the relationship.

Certainly, not all overweight teenagers suffer rejection. Some are self-confident individuals who like themselves and are active and successful participants in all aspects of the typical teenage school and social milieus. Teens who have been heavy since childhood, whose parents or other family members are overweight, and boys tend to fall into this category. Unfortunately, girls and those who have recently become overweight don't fare as well.

One of the biggest problems obesity creates for teens is dating, which becomes a very frightening proposition. Overweight girls and boys may worry that their appearance will make them so undesirable that no one will want to go out with them. In addition to this fear of rejection, many also fear they will be ridiculed on dates because of their ample proportions. An even worse fear is that they will turn off their partners should any kind of intimacy evolve. Thus, the opportunities for interpersonal and sexual relationships that would in effect prepare the teens for adult roles may be completely shortcircuited by the obesity factor. In the long run, such teens may grow into adults who choose not to socialize at all.

There are, on the other hand, many adolescents who do not suffer discrimination from their peers as a result of a weight problem. Boys generally have an easier time with obesity than do girls because it is more culturally acceptable for males to be heavy-set. Consider for a moment the number of heavy male role models: power lifters, ultraheavyweight wrestlers, and the sports figures who are massive but muscular: football players, body-builders — all of whom are quite visible on weekend television sports shows. It is no wonder that pediatricians and physicians specializing in adolescent medicine report that few boys ask for diets to help them lose weight — instead they opt for exercise routines to change their body proportions. Also, boys are rarely coddled by parents when they gain weight. Whereas girls' parents worry about their daughters' figures and the ramifications of not being cute or pretty, boys' parents are more apt to say their sons are "solid" or "built." Girls' parents often try to protect their daughters and may unconsciously encourage them to avoid confronting underlying problems, substituting food-as-panacea habits for talking. Those boys or girls who are popular and socially or intellectually successful even though they may be extremely overweight are the teens who have learned not to use the weight as a shield or a cloak to undermine their own positive feelings, and not to let that weight serve as a negative cue to others. These are the teens who integrate their looks, personalities, and capabilities into a package that becomes a total image — one apsect does not need to dominate the others, or operate at the expense of the others.

Dieting, Doctors, and Drugs

In America, diet books are perennial best-sellers. Low-calorie foods are packaged and sold as gourmet delights. Since dieting is intrinsically unpleasant, a huge industrial network (including publishing, food, television, self-help) has evolved to package it and make it a palatable process.

Although the motivations adults have for dieting are diverse, ranging from prevention or elimination of health problems to the quest for the perfect body, teenagers diet for somewhat different reasons with slightly different goals. Some do it as a kind of sport, a game in which the rules are as arbitrary as the chosen diet plan. Some say they are dieting when they are not really: rather than changing their eating patterns and cutting calories they resort to the use of over-the-counter diet pills to curb their appetites or use laxatives to literally eliminate food from their systems or diuretics to get rid of the teenage curse — excess water weight. These chemical methods are popular with athletes (such as wrestlers) who must qualify for particular weight classes in order to compete. Teenagers use dieting as they would cosmetics or fragrances, attempting to make themselves more attractive to others, and switching "brands" (that is, changing the diet method) depending on what their friends are doing. Teenagers are prone to see themselves as imperfect in spite of what others tell them to the contrary, and many use diets to provide them with what they mistakenly believe is *the* panacea for all the problems they think were brought on by a few extra pounds. Teens who need to diet for health reasons or because they are really obese often do not do so, whereas teens who are average weight or even underweight may diet obsessively. In any case, dieting alone rarely yields major solutions to adolescent angst and is more likely to be a source of frustration for a teen. Teenage dieting is more than a fad; it has become a ritualized collective behavior.

Why do we do it? Dieting somehow absolves us of other guilts; dieting lets us have safe scapegoats, for, as William Bennett and Joel Guerin, authors of *The Dieter's Dilemma: Eating Less and Weighing More,* suggest, "If fat people did not exist, American society might have to invent them. They have become virtually the last target of guilt-free discrimination." Dieting lets us forget about other problems and lets us focus on bodies that need to be disciplined like naughty little children. Consider the case of Peggy Ward, who as a sixteen-year-old junior at Ringgold High School in Finleyville, Pennsylvania, was ordered by her band instructor to lose weight for the sake of appearance or lose her position as a majorette on the drill team. At 5'4" she had slimmed down to 129 pounds from 138 but was still barred from participating because she could not achieve the required goal of 126 pounds. An excuse from her doctor, which said that further dieting would aggravate her hereditary liver ailment, convinced school officials to let her work with the team at 127½ pounds. The end result? She lost interest in the activity and dropped off the drill team.

Dieting encourages us to focus on ourselves in a way that seems productive but is in fact is very shallow. Dieting gives us something to talk about when there is nothing much else to say.

Dieting has its own cult figures and cult books. Depending on your diet plan preference it could be Richard Simmons and his *Never Say Diet* book, any of Jean Nidetch's Weight Watchers tomes, Dr. Stillman's water diet, Dr. Tarnower's Scarsdale Diet, Judy Mazel's Beverly Hills Diet, the rice diet, the grapefruit diet, the Cambridge Diet Plan, the Southhampton Diet, the F-Plan Diet, the No Choice Diet, the Nine Day Wonder Diet, and so on. Since many of these books suggest contradictory things about what, when, and how to eat, which "expert" is a teen to believe? Adults don't even seem to know. Therefore, it is important that parents learn accurate facts about diets to help their teens make informed choices.

(1) *There is no such thing as a perfect weight for a person of a certain height.* The height-weight charts provided by insurance companies are simply statistics, not absolute goals. One person may weigh more than another and be the same height, but this difference may have less to do with fat than with the amount of muscle one has (muscle weighs more than fat) or the person's build (a large frame obviously would weigh more than a small frame). Very athletic teenagers who are heavily muscled are almost always very lean, yet may weigh more than less-active peers of the same height.

(2) *Different diets have different effects on a teen's body.* The follow-

ing information should be obtained about any diet: will it first reduce fat stores and then attack the muscle fibers (which could be hazardous to health given the adolescent growth spurts)? Will it affect their metabolism so that their bodies are depleted of essential minerals and moisture needed for continued good health and growth? Will the diet make them so weak that they will be unable to concentrate on schoolwork and participate in sports, or so hyper and "up" that they feel let down when the diet is stopped? Your role as a parent is to provide such information, since it is unlikely that teens will get it on their own. Teenagers would like to believe that a diet will work immediately to transform them into the person on the cover of the diet book, but they are rarely concerned with the long-term effects of the plan. Unfortunately, it is in the long term that diets can become dangerous for teenagers. Therefore, we strongly advocate that no long-range diet be undertaken by any teenager without prior consultation with a physician and/or a nutritionist who is a licensed practitioner. Realistically, however, we know that doing this is not always practical, so the importance of parents' getting correct information to teens is increased.

(3) *During adolescence there are many changes in body configuration and distribution of body fat, making weight problems difficult to assess.* Dieting may thus be unnecessary or even contrary to our natural biological processes.

Fact: The average percentage of body fat decreases from 16 percent to 10 percent in boys during adolescent development.

Fact: The average percentage of body fat increases from 16 percent to 20 to 24 percent in girls during adolescence.

Fact: Adolescent girls will not start menstruating until they have reached the minimal 20 percent body fat. If a teenage girl diets to eliminate her fat deposits, she either will not start menstruating or if her menses have started, they may stop.

Fact: Girls' and boys' bodies are not meant to look alike once adolescence has set in. For a female to attempt a diet that will render her shapeless is to try to contradict gender.

(4) *Most diet plans don't work.* Not losing weight on a diet does not always indicate a lack of willpower or "cheating." One theory states that our bodies have natural setpoints — the weights we stay at (give or take a few pounds) without really thinking about it — and that dieting tries to overcome the setpoints. The reason some of us gain weight after a diet, or experience a yo-yo of alternating weight losses and gains over and over again, is that these setpoints haven't been brought down (by a combination of reasonable exercise and reasonable eating) to allow the weight to stay off. Another reason diets fail is that teens choose eating plans that don't account for their nutritional needs (they forget they are still growing) and cannot possibly maintain them over extended periods of time without feeling awful.

(5) *There is a sensible way to diet.* Nutritionists and doctors agree that if a diet is to work for a teen it must be individualized to take into account the adolescent's growth rate, stage of development, and the average energy expenditure. The goal should be for gradual weight loss in order to prevent excessive fatigue. Since one pound of fat requires 3,500 calories to maintain, eliminating 500 calories a day from one's diet would lead to a weight loss of one pound a week — a weight-loss rate that is safe for teenagers both physiologically and psychologically.

If a moderate reduction in caloric intake is combined with a physical training plan, the chances of success are even better. Under this sort of regimen, a teen will be more likely to burn fat preferentially and build up muscle at the same time. One does not have to be an exercise fanatic to do this, either: something as simple as a consistent walking or jogging program, done at least three times a week for about thirty minutes each time (and building up to four to five times a week) will do the trick.

(6) *Drugs, diets, and teenagers don't mix.* Teenagers should not be permitted to take any drugs for appetite suppression or altering body metabolism both because it is risky and because it's ineffective, too.

Over-the-counter diet aids are found in most drug and discount department stores openly displayed with toothpastes and other personal products. As nonprescription items they are not regulated by the Food and Drug Administration. Most of these diet pills and reducing candies contain a substance called *phenylpropanolamine* (PPA), which is a decongestant also found in many sinus remedies, and chemically akin to amphetamines. PPA differs from the now heavily regulated amphetamines (the diet pills of choice from the 1930s through the 1960s) only by one oxygen atom, and it is often called the poor man's speed. PPA is a stimulant, and it is not a benign one. It can induce high blood pressure in people who have normal blood pressure; it has been known to produce anxiety and agitation as well as dizziness; it can cause gastric distress and even hallucinations on rare occasions. PPA is dangerous and has no place in a teenager's reducing plan.

More needs to be said about doctors and their role in treating adolescent obesity. You must choose the physician for your teenager very carefully because it is critical that such a person be attuned to your teen's emotional as well as physical state, and be sympathetic to what the teenager is experiencing, what the teenager is reacting to by overeating (if anything), what the family does vis-à-vis food, and so on. A pediatrician who devotes the majority of his or her practice to the care of young children may be unable to communicate on the right level with an overweight teen seeking help; an internist who has had little contact with teens may present too threatening a posture, too sophisticated an approach to treatment. The ideal choice is a physician who specializes in adolescent medicine, but they are few in number. Occasionally, a child psychiatrist will specialize in helping children with eating disorders, and if he or she works in conjunction with a nutritionist, this may be the person best able to help your teen. A physician's relationship with a patient is critical to the success or failure of any treatment program; if the empathy isn't right between the doctor and your teen, head for the nearest exit and seek professional help elsewhere.

If a doctor suggests that you put your teenager on a regimen of diet pills or injections to melt fat away, leave at once. This person is probably a quack or a get-rich-quick entrepreneur taking advantage of your anxieties. Such practitioners — who often have hundreds of patients undertaking such "treatments" — are unethical, and run the equivalent of diet-pill mills.

A good physician will spend time getting to know your teenager, time in which the physical and psychological reasons for overeating or incorrect eating will be explored. Such a physician should have a holistic approach to the teen's health, realizing that a teen's life operates on many levels: school, home, extracurricular, fantasy, all of which interact. A good physician will not accept total responsibility for the teen's success or failure with an eating/exercise program but will make clear the limits of what a physician can do to help and what the teen must do by him- or herself. A good physician will offer support but will not be a crutch, will be a resource while expecting the teenager to be in control of the final outcome. Rapport between physician and patient can make it much easier for a dieting teenager to reach a desired goal of weight, health, and fitness.

Anorexia Angst

Singer Pat Boone's eldest daughter has had it, poet Elizabeth Barrett Browning was alleged to have had it, singer Karen Carpenter died with it, fashion model Twiggy looked as if she had it, many people joke and say they wish they could have it for a week or two. "It" is anorexia nervosa, an eating disorder that begins with compulsive dieting and progresses through several stages of increasingly obsessive behaviors to a state of virtual self-starvation. Anorexia can lead to the death of its victims just as surely as cancer or heart disease can, and even in nonfatal cases is a serious hazard to physical and psychological health.

Anorexia nervosa is not a "new" disease. Physicians were aware of the syndrome and were writing about it as early as 1500. In 1874 the term anorexia nervosa was coined by Sir William Gull, who believed it was a refusal to eat accompanied by a revulsion for food and that it occurred in both males and females. The first accounts of anorexia in children were published in 1894. Over the years it has been considered a physical disorder, a psychological complaint, a combination of the two (sometimes called a psychophysiological disorder), and, most recently, an eating disorder. No matter how you classify it, it is serious.

The number of cases of anorexia among the adolescent female population has risen dramatically in the past decade, with current estimates suggesting that approximately one in 175 teenage girls are caught in its web. (Among boys, the condition is fifteen times less common.) Recently, the media have gotten on the eating-disorders bandwagon and splashy coverage of anorexia has resulted: news programs, a variety of magazine articles, and a huge number of fiction and nonfiction books have been published about anorexia, anorectics, and food obsessions. Many parents now rate eating disorders as a major worry, right up there with sex, alcohol, and drugs as potential threats to their teenagers.

It is not always easy to know when your teen has developed anorexia, especially in its initial stages. Because we don't really know what causes it, it is hard for us to take measures to prevent it. Part of the problem for parents lies in the erratic eating habits that are the norm for so many teens; another is the fact that we do not always take our meals together and can't monitor our kids' food intake. Yet another is the fact that so many parents condone the quest for thinness. What starts out as a well-intended cutback in calories to hone one's figure can get out of control and turn into a full-blown obsession; *when* that transition occurs, however, is notoriously difficult to pinpoint. It is important for parents to be aware that anorexia affects the total person, and is extremely disruptive to family harmony. Parents must also realize that feelings of anger and frustration are common reactions to their sense of helplessness if the teenager does not want their help in getting better. If anorexia is allowed to develop, its victim may seem to be under the control of some outside force that is destroying her or his logic, personality, and capabilities and is turning the teen into an isolated, withdrawn stranger. What really happens is that if the child is literally starving, a number of physical processes are set in motion that do, in fact, affect psychological functioning. Until that teen gets some adequate nourishment, no therapist will be able to help very much. In cases of severe anorexia, partial weight restoration must occur before really useful therapy can begin.

Being aware of signs and symptoms of anorexia is something every parent can accomplish. These occur as a constellation of behaviors rather than as one single thing; however, no two victims are exactly alike in their symptoms and behaviors.

(1) Your teen expresses (by words and/or actions) *an intense fear of fatness.* This will occur even when a significant amount of weight has been shed and the teen could not be considered fat by any stretch of the imagination.

(2) *Your teen is very thin, yet insists she or he is fat.* This reflects a

distorted body image that is one of the side effects self-starvation has on a person's psychological health. Many anorectics actually see fat where none exists and experience sensations of bloating in their abdominal areas. Many wear oversized, loose-fitting clothes to hide their imagined obesity.

(3) Self starvation leads to *hyperactivity*. Many anorectics exercise at a frenetic pace, often doing 600 situps at a clip, jogging five miles instead of two, swimming miles and miles daily even if not on a team.

(4) Many anorectics *no longer accurately interpret the body's internal cues about hunger* and insist they are not hungry though they actually are starving. They become obsessed with food, keep diaries of what they have consumed and the calorie count of each mouthful, choose to do the family's grocery shopping and prepare the food while refusing to partake in what they have created. They develop rituals about food and eating, often cutting their meager portions into minute pieces, arranging them in definite patterns on the plate, using their utensils in bizarre ways such as not letting the tines of a fork touch their lips. The preoccupation with food and the rituals may be a psychological defense aimed at covering up the intense physical hunger that isn't being taken care of.

(5) Anorectic females *often stop menstruating* as a direct result of self-starvation. Girls who are anorectic prior to the onset of their periods may delay their cycles indefinitely. This is a reliable diagnostic sign of anorexia when no other underlying physical causes can be found to account for lack of menses.

(6) *Behavior changes* that cannot be accounted for by any other physical condition are common. Anorectic teens crave privacy, isolate themselves from friends, refuse to partake in previously enjoyed activities, may develop rituals about everyday things besides food (like touching certain objects in each room, arranging things in specific order). All of this can alienate friends and loved ones and cause a great deal of emotional turmoil.

(7) *When anorexia is in its advanced stages (defined as when 25 percent or more of a person's original body weight is lost) other physical symptoms show up:* the teen is cold all the time, may have a slowed heart rate, may experience pain when sitting or lying down because the fat layers that ordinarily cushion the bones are depleted, may develop a fine coating of hair all over the body while losing the hair on her head, may experience insomnia, and may develop an inability to concentrate. These are all by-products of starvation.

A teenager does not become anorectic in a vacuum. Eating disorders generally reflect problems in a family system that need to be addressed and hopefully corrected. As we noted earlier, no one really knows what causes anorexia, but many therapists feel that certain communication patterns in a family combined with a certain type of child result in the development of anorexia. The type of child has been referred to as a perfectionistic, sometimes compulsive person who by family accounts has never given anyone a bit of trouble or cause for concern. The type of child has been dubbed "the best little girl in the world" by one commentator, and it is an apt title. The dean's list student who has always followed parents' advice and never shown any signs of rebellion is a prime candidate for this disorder. The family communication patterns often include: (1) few words of praise to the "good" child for her accomplishments; (2) a tendency for family members to second-guess one another regarding individual needs and desires so that they operate on assumptions about one another rather than on facts; (3) too little communication from parents to children on all levels so that children seek drastic ways to get parental attention. Anorexia is a very effective way to assert control of one's body, one's environment, and one's family.

In the past few years, increasingly sophisticated treatment approaches have proved useful in helping anorectics and their families. We believe the most desirable method is a team effort between family members and therapists and should include a significant component of self-help. Many hospitals now have nutritional-disorders units that are prepared to cope with the psychological as well as physiological needs of their patients. Most physicians now understand that weight gain must be gradual to be beneficial to the anorectic and will keep a patient hospitalized only until an agreed-upon minimum weight needed for reversing the self-induced state of starvation has been achieved. Parents of anorectics should be wary of physicians who opt for forced feeding or overfeeding, or who equate weight gain alone with "cure." Recently, doctors have discovered that the greatest strain is placed on an anorectic's heart immediately after lost weight has been regained, if the weight gain is too rapid. Careful long-term monitoring is critical. Weight gain opens the doors for psychological therapy and self-help to begin working. Nutritionists can be very useful in helping the anorectic reestablish normal eating patterns and will suggest individualized food plans to achieve that goal. A psychologist, social worker, or psychiatrist can provide counseling — what counts is that your chosen therapist gets along with your teen and wants to work with her or him. Therapy should not be thought of as punishment; it is a way to get out of the eating disorder maze.

Self-help groups consisting of people touched in any way by eating disorders are now thought to be crucial to the alleviation of anorexia. Such groups provide a safe, caring, noncensuring environment in which people can express their innermost thoughts and know they are not alone. If none exists in your area, you may have to start one and can contact your local medical society for suggestions, or you can contact any of the self-help groups listed in the appendix.

Anorexia is frightening and all too prevalent. Yet we must guard against labeling all teens who diet as anorectics and be careful not to become so hysterical about the potential dangers that we create a monster where none exists. A recent letter to the editor of *The New York Times Book Review* said,

My slightly overweight seventeen year old daughter acknowledged recently that her overeating habits are not due to hunger or pleasure but to a new and rare disease she calls "anorexophobia." An avid reader of young ladies' magazines, my daughter developed her refrigerator-raiding habits in answer to the deep need to reassure herself that she is not anorexic.

The mandate for parents, then, is to learn when eating behaviors become maladaptive and problematic as opposed to merely reflecting normal teenage eccentricities!

Binges, Bulimia, and Other Battles

A binge can be defined differently by different people, depending on whether they are in control of the binge or it is in control of them. Those of us who know when we're hungry and when we're full, and who can stop eating when we're full, may consider an elegant meal with wine, appetizer, soup, main course, and dessert a binge, a unique treat, an occasion to be shared with a special person. For others, a binge may be indulging in a food they haven't had for a long time, as when a college student comes home for Christmas vacation, can have as many of his mother's homemade waffles as he likes, and requests them every morning for breakfast until he can't stand the sight of them! That student knows when satiety has set in, and can then alter his eating to a more normal, varied pattern. For some of us a binge means a splurge, a spur-of-the-moment decision to dash into an ice cream parlor and order a double hot fudge sundae with all the trimmings. That binge is pure fun, gustatory delight, and guilt-free. Many adolescents binge with some regularity. They consume huge quantities of food: sometimes as a social thing (as at an all-night fraternity beer blast), sometimes out of boredom, as a tension-reliever, or as a way of dealing with hurts or frustrations. Some kids may become overweight or obese and suffer the emotional and social consequences of their obesity (as we have discussed) as a result of binge-eating habits. Some teens may binge one day, fast the next, and eat normally for weeks thereafter until they binge and fast again.

For some of us, however, to binge means to lose control of ourselves. For such people, food is not an aphrodisiac, not a delight, not a life-sustaining thing, but instead it becomes a narcotic, a drug, a poison. The thought, sight, and smell of food can turn those individuals into pawns, with food as their master. To binge becomes the focal point of their existence, an end in itself.

If and when a person's existence is dominated by the thought of food, if everyday activities are interfered with as a result of this obsession, if a person is concerned with weight control to an extreme, if a habit of binge eating followed by purging the body of the ingested food (by means of laxative abuse, self-induced vomiting, ipecac abuse), that individual is probably suffering from another form of eating disorder called bulimia (bulimia nervosa, bulimarexia).

Bulimia is on the upswing among both adolescent females and males and though the male-to-female ratio has yet to be established, it is known that females predominate. Bulimia too has recently received much media exposure, and with people like Jane Fonda admitting publicly that they have struggled with bulimia, others are admitting they too suffer from this eating disorder. Bulimia is not a discovery of the 1980s. The Romans routinely binged and purged en masse, having access to public vomitoriums. The difference between the Roman culture and ours, however, is public acceptance. What was accepted in ancient times is now regarded by most Americans as aberrant behavior.

Bulimia and anorexia have been called Cinderella's stepsisters, the flip sides of the same coin. In fact, many anorectics are bulimic at times, and some bulimics become anorectic. Both eating disorders involve established rituals: a bulimic will be likely to set apart a portion of the day to binge, and usually has only a limited amount of time in which to do it (generally around two hours or less). Often the intensity of a binge will be so strong that a bulimic will seem to be in a trancelike state when eating, perhaps not acknowledging any activity going on around him or her, perhaps going into a rage if disturbed. While the anorectic abstains from most foods but will consume quantities of low-caloric items that are "safe" and preferred, the bulimic tends to have food preferences too: they are often high-caloric, snack-type items that need little or no preparation (though there are exceptions — one person ate so many carrots for so many days she turned orange because of the carotene in her system). Bulimics also lose the ability to read their bodies' hunger-satiation cues correctly and can gorge, seemingly under the food's control, sometimes without tasting what they are consuming until (1) they run out of food; (2) the pain caused by overstretching of the stomach becomes unbearable; (3) feelings of guilt wash over them and cause them to stop; (4) the binge is interrupted by an external force — a phone call, a relative coming into the room, a barking dog.

Bulimics do great physical damage to themselves when they habitually binge and purge. Vomiting can upset one's electrolyte balance (causing potassium deficiency), erode the enamel of teeth, and cause damage to the esophagus. Ipecac, an emetic intended to be used only when vomiting is required as a result of accidental poisonings (and then only in minute quantities), has been used by the pint by many bulimics mindless of the fact that it is toxic. Bulimics are notorious laxative abusers and many take between 60 and 100 per day, damaging their intestines and bowel functions, often permanently. Salivary glands may enlarge when a person vomits regularly, and this enlargement gives a bulimic's face a puffy, "cheeky" appearance. People who induce vomiting by putting their fingers (or even an entire fist) down their throats may develop callouses on their knuckles. When these measures do not lead to weight control and weight loss, bulimics frequently turn to diet pills and abuse them as they do laxatives. Bulimics, like anorectics, then, are at high risk where health is concerned.

Bulimics are also at risk emotionally. They may become isolated from friends because they are afraid of what could happen if they were to share a meal together. They may steal food or money for food from the people they live with and, if caught, suffer the consequences of hostility and rejection. (This is now becoming a major problem in college dormitories.) Unlike anorectics, bulimics rarely *look* sick, so when the side issues of the messes, food bills, reeking bathrooms, and hoarding of food confront them there is less likelihood they will glean any sympathy from their accusers. Parents must recognize there is a lot of pent-up anger and frustration in bulimics, and understand that their behavior is as frightening to them as to the people around them. To blame or scold them is unlikely to solve anything.

A teenager does not become bulimic overnight. As was true of the anorectic, it can be said that bulimic behavior is typically an expression of problems in a family system that need to be addressed. It is not always possible to pinpoint what triggered the bulimia, but many therapists say that adolescent bulimics are more sensitive to self-esteem and self-image issues, especially vulnerable to the relatively new social pressure to be able to be a "total" individual able to carry on successful school, job, social life, and family commitments at the same time, with the same skills and intensity. It has been theorized that many bulimic females resent the fact that their mothers were forced to choose the lives of wives and mothers over those of career women; unsure of whether they will themselves be able to handle so many responsibilities, they find in food their panacea, their way of avoiding the questions, the realities of life. Many bulimics are outgoing people who can hide these anxieties quite well, and are often able to carry on what amounts to a double life: maintaining an apparently normal daily routine that masks the secret private rituals of binging and purging. The demands of this double life are tremendous and take a psychic and physical toll.

After a while, bulimia becomes an ingrained habit. But like any habit, it can be broken. A seventy-two-hour period of abstinence from gorging and purging to let the body begin to repair itself should be the first step in interrupting the binge-purge cycle. Some therapists have found that three weeks "off" is sufficient to break the hold of bulimia completely and put the locus of control back inside the individual rather than in the food, laying the groundwork for a return to normal eating patterns.

Supportive therapy is crucial and is similar to what is done for an anorectic, minus the hospitalization. Unlike the starving patient, a bulimic is not in need of nutritional supplementation, and the only reason a hospital stay might be indicated would be to provide an environment where binging would be impossible. A team approach to therapy includes psychiatrists, social workers, psychologists, and self-help, the latter often being the most critical component of that effort. When a bulimic hears from other bulimics ways to sidestep the urge to binge; how to keep binge foods out of the house; how to develop a network of people to call when the urge to binge comes on and why this works; alternatives to eating that have worked; and how to interrupt a binge and regain control, he or she is likely to believe them since they have been through the same experience. A bulimic who is prepared with information about the disorder and ways of coping with and counteracting it has nine-tenths of the battle won. Parents, friends, and relatives benefit from self-help, because to know that they are not alone can give them strength to deal with eating disorders. A word of caution: forcing someone into therapy usually does no lasting good. The bulimic must want help in breaking the habit before any sort of therapy will contribute to the solution of the problem. However, this fact must be balanced by the fact that a skillful therapist can help a person with bulimia find his or her own motivation to solve the problem.

There are many teenagers who are neither anorectic nor bulimic but whose eating habits and demands for certain foods can drive their parents crazy. Teenagers love to follow fads, so they may decide to do the health food routine one month, a Zen routine the next. Some will insist on wheat germ with everything, others will not leave the house until they have eaten their daily ration of Choc-O-Diles. As long as their food habits are not obsessive, as long as their health is not impaired, and as long as the teen is in control of what is eaten rather than vice versa, a parent might just as well sit back and watch.

18

Unintended Teenage Pregnancy

One million pregnancies occur annually among American teenage females. This is equivalent to a rate of 2,740 conceptions each day, or 114 pregnancies each hour, or one adolescent pregnancy beginning every 35 seconds around the clock. In fact, the U.S. has the dubious distinction of having the highest incidence of teenage motherhood among nations in the Western Hemisphere. With 52 per thousand (approximately one out of 20) adolescent females having babies each year, the American teenage birth rate is almost 60 percent higher than Great Britain's, double the rate of Sweden, and 17 times greater than Japan's.

It is pointless to pretend that unintended teenage pregnancies are not a problem of major proportions for our society today. It is also pointless to pretend that it can't happen to your child. Regardless of how you feel about the so-called new teenage morality, the fact is that pregnant teenage girls and fathers-to-be are a group of vulnerable individuals who must face some of the most difficult ethical, emotional, and intellectual decisions of their lives in deciding what to do about unintended pregnancy. Parents can and must help them in this process. To be of real assistance, you must be armed with accurate facts, keep control of your emotions, and be willing to be flexible.

Some Eye-Opening Facts on the Teenage Pregnancy Epidemic

— There are 30,000 pregnancies annually among teenage girls under fifteen years of age.

228

— Six out of ten adolescent females who give birth before they are seventeen will be pregnant a second time before their nineteenth birthdays.

— Although teenagers represent only 18 percent of sexually active females in the reproductive age group, they account for 46 percent of all out-of-wedlock births.

— Half of the premarital pregnancies among adolescents occur within six months after the first episode of sexual intercourse.

— Babies born to teenage mothers are nearly twice as likely to die in infancy as those born to women in their twenties.

Why is teenage pregnancy such a monumental problem today? A recent study by the Ford Foundation succinctly summarized many of the pertinent background factors:

[Teenage] mothers tend to experience poorer medical outcomes during pregnancy and delivery, larger family size and little family stability, inadequate education and vocational training, unemployment or intermittent employment in occupations with low wages and little mobility, and dependency on government services and support. The children of teenage parents tend to be less healthy, to be less adequate as parents, to achieve less academically, and to repeat their parents' patterns.

In light of these facts, it's not surprising that 400,000 pregnant teens opt for abortion each year, accounting for 35 percent of all abortions performed in this country. This is only the tip of the iceberg, though, since another 600,000 teenagers give birth each year, with the great majority of these children being born out of wedlock. Nine out of ten of these teenage mothers want to keep their babies.

Of those carrying to term, seven in ten receive no prenatal care during the first three months of their pregnancies. As a group, they are at great risk for miscarriage, toxemia, hemorrhage, complications at birth, and postnatal anemia. Their own growth may be stunted, since optimum height is not generally reached until four to five years after the first menses; in some pregnant adolescents the process of fusion of their own bones may not yet be complete. Their babies often suffer the complications that occur with low birth weights. Maternal death risks are 60 percent higher for pregnant girls under the age of fifteen than they are for older girls; in the sixteen-to-nineteen-year-old group the risks are 13 percent higher than for those who wait until their twenties to conceive.

Most teenage mothers who keep their babies drop out of school never to return. As a group, they tend to be overrepresented in the poverty statistics. Children born out of wedlock are more than twice as likely to be physically abused as children of married couples. But if the teenage parents under the age of seventeen do marry, their relationship is three times as likely to end in divorce as it would be if they waited until their early twenties to marry.

What about the young men who impregnate those adolescent girls? The stereotype is of self-centered, irresponsible, sexually overactive boys who generally take advantage of the girls and who have no inclinations to consider the consequences of their actions. A recent review of the literature about teenage fathers has proven this stereotype to be unfair and incorrect. Actually, many teenage fathers would like to play a role in making decisions about the pregnancy, but their efforts tend to be blocked by the girls' parents or neglected by social service agencies. Teenage fathers are at risk economically, socially, and emotionally much as teenage mothers are; they too tend to cut short their schooling, take lower-status blue-collar jobs, and enter the labor force earlier than do their peers who are unencumbered by the responsibilities of early parenthood and marriage. Another aspect that is often forgotten is the impact of an abortion on the prospective father: in some cases, the boy feels the loss more keenly than the girl, who may be relieved to get the pregnancy over with and go on with her life.

Why Teen Pregnancies Occur

Misinformation (or in some cases, complete lack of information) is the primary cause of unintended teenage pregnancies, according to most authorities. While studies repeatedly show that teenagers want to get detailed, accurate information about sex, few parents and few schools actually provide this to them. Only one-third of American secondary schools offer any form of sex education, and the courses that are given are often woefully incomplete. According to a recent survey conducted by the Sex Information and Education Council of the United States, only 39 percent of such courses discuss contraception! Since only about 10 percent of parents discuss sexuality with their teenagers beyond saying "Don't," it's not surprising that adolescents turn to their peers to fill in the gaps. Sadly, the information provided by peers generally perpetuates the myths and misperceptions about sex that contribute to the upsurge in unplanned teenage pregnancies. Saddest of all is the fact that many of these pregnancies could have been prevented if the teens had been able to reach out to their families and been met by information and support.

Another principal reason behind the teenage pregnancy epidemic is that many adolescents cling to belief systems that are incompatible with reasonable contraceptive behavior. For instance, some teenagers feel that birth control is unnecessary because pregnancy is unlikely or impossible. The following explanations are typical of this category:

— "She's too young to get pregnant."
— "She can't get pregnant 'cause it's just after her period."

— "I didn't think I could get pregnant because I never had orgasms."

— "I can't get pregnant because we never deep kiss."

Other adolescents don't use contraception because they see it as an immoral act (either from a religious perspective or otherwise) — a sign of promiscuity or lax moral standards. One sexually active fifteen-year-old girl put it this way, "If I used any birth control, it would be like planning to have sex in advance, and that would make me feel cheap." Adolescents also avoid contraceptives because they believe they will lessen sexual pleasure, reduce sexual spontaneity, or create problems such as health risks.

Some teenagers simply don't care whether they get pregnant or not. To these girls, getting pregnant can be an adventure that will prove their femininity, validate their adult status, and get them attention from their parents and peers. There are also those who use sex as a way of coping with problems, a way of lashing out at parents, and sometimes a way of ensnaring their parents in their predicaments and finally achieving something in common — shared misery! Surprisingly, many such girls are actually quite conservative sexually and believe in traditional female roles and the double standard.

Another factor contributing to unplanned pregnancies has to do with the fact that many adolescent boys as well as girls confuse the concepts of sexuality, love, and intimacy. It has been documented that younger adolescents think of sex as a very good way to get acquainted with one another, whereas older adolescents tend to reserve sexual intercourse for those relationships where commitment and caring were established. Also, too many adolescents ignore or discount the probability that any given act of sexual intercourse will lead to pregnancy, and too many of them assume the other is taking care of contraception when in fact neither partner is. Here again, the communication issue comes into play. Teenagers are unskilled in talking about their sexual feelings to one another because of embarrassment, because they don't have the right words to express them, because they don't know the right questions to ask, and because they incorrectly assume everyone else is more knowledgeable than they are and don't want to appear naive. Unplanned pregnancies can be the result of such missed opportunities for talking. For example, Carole had never seen a condom and so had no way of knowing for sure whether her partner was using one. Assuming he was, she decided to have intercourse and became pregnant as a result of one sexual experience. She assumed too much and didn't ask enough.

When contraception is ignored or discounted by sexually active teenagers, pregnancies are bound to occur and obviously do with some frequency. The choice to use contraception or not is clouded by many side issues: religious, esthetic, social, and parental. We have already suggested that if the unplanned teenage pregnancy explosion is to be stemmed, contraceptive use must be taught as a viable choice for even our younger adolescents. Interestingly, there is a very strong correlation between a teenager's age at first intercourse and the use of a birth control method: the longer the female postpones the first intercourse, the more likely she is to be protected. Also, teenagers whose parents discuss sex with them generally delay their first intercourse longer than do adolescents whose parents remain silent on the subject of sex. Teenagers who do not opt to use contraceptives have been found to consider themselves as *not* sexually active (many will say their first few sexual encounters were accidents and not likely to happen again); others seem to have less self-esteem and lower self-concepts than do teens who consciously protect themselves against pregnancy.

There really is little mystery as to the causes of unplanned teenage pregnancies. Our children are sexual beings and will experiment with sex in spite of our admonitions or desires to protect them. The best thing we can give our teenagers is the right to be responsible about their sexual activities and to do so we must contribute to their education by sharing our values, knowledge, attitudes, and beliefs with them. Since we know why teen pregnancies occur, we have the resources to help stop them.

Learning the News

The words "I'm pregnant," or "I got a girl pregnant" are among the most dreaded and feared revelations to make or to be heard. Teenagers and parents alike tend to react fairly predictably if the event was unplanned. On the parent side there is denial — the "it can't be" syndrome seems to set in first, followed by shock and anger, "How could you?" "I'm going to kill you (her, him)" and often accompanied by guilt: "Look what you've done to me, to our family. What will the neighbors say?" Punishment may ensue: "You get out of this house, I'm not going to support a whore," or "I'm going to ground you for the rest of your life" — all of which indicate the parents are out of control and temporarily incapable of dealing with the stress of the situation. Teenagers react with shame ("I didn't mean to do it") and guilt ("I didn't mean to hurt you") and often walk around in a state of shock ("This can't be happening to me") or fear ("What am I going to do next, who can I turn to for help?").

Learning the news does not have to be so painful if we can try to understand the situation objectively. The teenager is in trouble and needs help. The kind of help we can provide as parents falls into several categories: love and emotional support, medical attention, and practical guidelines to follow in order to come up with a solution to the problem pregnancy.

Instead of hurling epithets at the teenage fathers- or mothers-to-be, sit down and *be available.* Try to listen to what they have to say without immediately judging truth or falsehood, and if you are having trouble swallowing the information admit this but do so without rancor. Anger and retribution do little good and much harm. They can push the teens to run away, to seek abortions from disreputable practitioners, to try self-induced abortions that can cause death of the fetus and the mother, even to try suicide. Parental reactions have a much greater impact than might be imagined and realizing this goes a long way towards achieving the goal of everyone staying in control of their emotions.

The first thing to do is to make sure there really is a pregnancy. Ask your teens whether they have seen a doctor, been to a clinic, or spoken with a counselor. Find out whether a pregnancy test was done, at what point after the girl's first missed period, and whether it was done by a lab or with an over-the-counter, at-home pregnancy testing kit. Recognize that all pregnancy tests give occasional false alarms, and a missed period (or even several missed in a row) is *not* an irrefutable sign of pregnancy in adolescence. Make sure the teens have access to competent medical attention. This is important for the boys, too, as it is wise for them to be screened for sexually transmitted diseases that might endanger the pregnancy.

Ask your teens what they want to do. It is quite likely that their only reactions will be fearful ones and they may respond with "We'll do whatever you want us to do." Teens need to begin to assume responsibility for the consequences of their sexual behavior; do not be seduced into being complimented by their concern for your parental desires. The point is that the teens need to explore the pros and cons of continuing or terminating a pregnancy, and you need to help them establish the parameters of their decisions. You may have to give them facts you neglected to share with them before; you must share them now. The choices the teenage parents-to-be make will affect your lives, too, and you must speak up though you may not expect to have the last words.

Ask your teens what you can do to help. This may be the hardest thing for parents to do and the teens may react in disbelief at hearing this from the parents. Yet it can force the teens to confront their relationship with their parents and can foster communication on a serious level that has been missing for some time. Your teens may only want to hear that you still love them, or your teens may want you to help them arrange for an abortion; there is no way to predict the response. The point is that it is far more important to support the teens than to abandon them.

If you cannot tolerate the news, get professional help. It is better to admit you need a mediator to deal with the situation than to do something rash such as abusing your children or throwing them out of your homes. Many agencies are geared to assisting teens and their families in crisis; take advantage of them if you need to.

Discussing Options

We are fortunate to live in an era when it is possible for pregnant teenagers to have options, options that extend far beyond the obvious ones of choosing whether to have abortions (approximately 400,000 adolescents select this as the solution to unintended pregnancies annually) or have the babies (the choice of about 600,000 pregnant adolescents annually). The options that are available to our adolescents include lifestyle and education arrangements that would facilitate having and keeping their babies, and health care and support systems provided by hospitals or social service agencies that make it unnecessary for any teenagers to face the prospect of pregnancy or abortion alone and unassisted.

Discussing options must be done as rationally as is humanly possible. At the outset, you must tell your teens whether you see the situation as cut-and-dried or if you see room for negotiation. Obviously, for certain parents and teens the range of choices is limited — religious, ethical, and emotional values dictate that abortion is not permissible. Marriage may or may not be a viable option for many of the teens. If not, the options to be discussed will include whether the pregnant girl will remain at home and in school during her pregnancy or go to a school with a special program designed to prepare her for parenthood and beyond. The more difficult questions concern the options available once the babies are born. The teens can keep their babies and raise them with or without the help of family; they can have the babies and release them for adoption; they can have the babies and arrange for foster care until some future time when they can assume responsibility for the children themselves. Though it may seem premature to discuss day care arrangements for the baby at such a time, day care is at a premium and ensuring a spot in a licensed program may require several months' advance enrollment notice. Other options that need to be considered are the extent of the involvement of the adolescent fathers and their families in the support and care of the children. Since many teens do not marry even though they decide to have and keep the babies, this is a crucial area to be explored prior to final decision-making time. Clearly, it is much easier for adolescent mothers to plan to continue schooling or work if they do not have to shoulder the responsibility for children themselves.

In discussing these options it is very important that parents do not *dictate* final decisions. Ideally, the options must remain options, and — for better or worse — the ultimate decisions will have to be the teenagers'. The parents should not consider this period of negotiation as a battle for control; they would do better to perceive it as a fact-finding mission in which they are advisers and guides acting in the best interest of the adolescent parents-to-be, exploring options and locating resources to ensure the correct decision will eventually be made.

At the other end of the option continuum is the choice of abortion. Moral considerations aside, it is clearly a safe alternative (if done by licensed medical personnel within the first trimester) to the continuation of pregnancies to term, especially for younger adolescents, whose chances of having smooth pregnancies uncomplicated by major health problems for mother and baby are lower than average. Abortion may be viable if the pregnancy results from forcible rape, incest, or other coercive sexual experiences that so traumatize the mother that she is not psychologically equipped to handle the pregnancy. Abortion is clearly indicated if pregnancy in any way threatens the life of the adolescent mother, or if the teen is mentally impaired and unable to care for herself (much less an infant). Abortions should be considered if the teens' futures seem seriously jeopardized by full-term pregnancies, as might be the case of a girl going away to college on a full athletic scholarship, or about to enter military service, and so on. The abortion option may be considered because of economic necessity. The decision, once again, must be the teen's, though parental input is valuable and needed. Abortion is final; once the pregnancy is terminated there is no changing one's mind and the teen must be fully cognizant of the seriousness of this option.

Whatever options are discussed, it is crucial they give the teens the sense that there are solutions to the unplanned pregnancies that will work within the frameworks of their particular life-styles and eventual goals.

Decision Time

Decision time can be excruciatingly difficult for some teens and their families and relatively easy for others. The exploration of options prior to decision-making sets the stage for a logical and livable decision and should facilitate a quick decision so that the teens can get on with their lives.

Legally, a parent cannot stop a teen from having an abortion if the teen chooses this option. A pregnant teen (or any teen, for that matter) has the right to make all the basic decisions concerning her own health care and cannot be denied access to this health care. No state can interfere in a teen's right to an abortion prior to the thirteenth week of pregnancy; during the second trimester a state may intervene to require the procedure be performed in a hospital by a qualified physician to ensure maternal health. After twenty-four weeks of gestation, abortions are forbidden except when the mother's health is threatened.

The decision to terminate a pregnancy must be made with the knowledge that there may be emotional aftereffects. Teens should be told that they may experience a range of emotions from euphoria and relief to guilt, depression, and grief. Teens must also be told that one abortion does not make it impossible to have a planned pregnancy at some point in the future. Animosity may develop between the families of the teenage mother and father, especially if the boy wants the baby and the girl wants to abort the pregnancy.

The teens who decide to marry as a result of unplanned pregnancies will, one hopes, do so fully aware of the difficulties they may face as they begin to make a life together. The decision should be predicated on facts about the calculated risks — what are the chances they will be able to complete their educations, what are the chances they will be self-supporting, how will they care for their baby, what emergency resources will they have access to and so on. Even more important is the matter of personal affection and compatibility, for a loveless marriage forced by circumstances is preordained to later problems.

The girl who remains unmarried but wants to keep her baby must be asked if she is making the decision because of parental pressure or because she has a romanticized notion that a baby will give her someone to love and will be someone to love her back completely and adoringly (this is known as the "baby-doll syndrome"). Incredible as it may sound, a teenager's choice to keep a baby is sometimes influenced strongly by peer pressure — "My best friend is doing it, so I will too." Here's what one sixteen-year-old had to say on this topic:

> When I found out that I was pregnant, my first reaction was panic. But as I thought about it, I realized that this was really a blessing in disguise. I mean, my friend Mary has a six-month-old baby boy who's cute and cuddly, and she's a really neat mother. Now this baby'll belong to me and I'll be a good mother too. Mary and I can take our kids to the park together and watch them play.

There are a number of difficult questions that must be addressed if a teenager is leaning towards having and keeping a baby. Does she really know what it means to care for an infant? Can she project what the responsibilities will be over the long term? Is she expecting family support or will she have to rely on day care or a group-home living arrangement? How does she feel about receiving public assistance? Has she ever had to discipline a child, and how does she expect to react if her child becomes difficult to handle or emotionally disturbed and in need of special care? What would she do if the child were born retarded or physically impaired? What would she do if her pregnancy left her physically ill or permanently impaired? These probing, uncomfortable questions must be asked and answered prior to the final decision time because they inject a sense of reality and responsibility into an issue that often becomes clouded by fantasy.

The decision about keeping a baby is considerably different for an older teen than for a younger one. Few girls aged fifteen or under are capable of responsible parenthood, and fewer still will have a spouse to help them out. This typically means that you, the baby's grandparents, will be called on to function as surrogate parents — a role you may not want to assume for any of a number of reasons, including economic considerations. In such circumstances, unless a realistic plan can be formulated for taking care of the newborn, you may wind up with several miserable beings.

A decision to have the child and release it for adoption should be made only after the teenage parents have considered that they might want to contact the child at a later date. They must be aware of their rights as natural parents as well as the rights of the child, and they will need to decide if it is important to them that the child's records be sealed at birth or if they prefer mutual access and even contact with the adoptive parents. They must also consider whether it is realistic to expect that their child will be adopted quickly or if there is a real possibility the child might languish within a foster care system for some years, perhaps until it becomes an adult!

A number of other options exist regarding the adoption process. Although a majority of adoptions are arranged through social service agencies, in many states there is also the opportunity of arranging a private placement. (Since this practice is not universally legalized, however, you must check its status in your particular geographic area.) A physician, lawyer, or clergyman may be able to make arrangements for a non-agency adoption that includes payment for the mother's living expenses, prenatal and postnatal care, hospital charges connected with delivery, and legal fees. In addition, it is possible to arrange for your daughter to meet the prospective adoptive parents before deciding what she wants to do, and sometimes an agreement can be reached that gives her the right to later visit the child. On the other hand, private adoptions may be more problematic in some ways than an agency adoption — for example, the signed agreement may not give your daughter the right to change her mind — so have all of the arrangements checked thoroughly by your own lawyer.

Another factor that must be considered at decision time is the reaction of peers to the pregnancy outcome, be it abortion or birth. The teens must decide whether they can live comfortably with their choices regardless of their peers' possible disapproval. Teens often make precipitous decisions on the basis of what they assume their peers will think of them and are sorely disillusioned when the reality and the expectation do not coincide. Decisions must be made independent of the group norms, and bucking one's peers may be more difficult than coping with parental disapproval or outrage.

Decisions should be made only after the initial shock of learning about an unplanned pregnancy wears off, after the various options have been explored and probing questions asked and answered. The process leading to the ultimate decision can be educational and emotionally cathartic, and is imperative in helping the teens develop realistic attitudes about the impact of bearing and rearing children on one's life-style and life choices.

Looking Ahead — Sensibly

Unintended pregnancies don't have to mean the end of the world for the involved teens and their families. Because there are options available, many teens can continue their lives successfully and productively in spite of or even because of the birth of their children. What parents and teens alike must do is evaluate the events leading up to the pregnancies and potential reasons for them, and change whatever might have been dysfunctional in their lives to prevent repetitions. Looking ahead, then, involves looking backward with hindsight. Looking ahead also means discarding our illusions and fantasies — as parents we must stop pretending we can protect our children by inhibiting their sexual development and we must not blame them if they make sexual mistakes. Teenagers must be allowed to take responsibility for their sexuality and to do so with facts and input from their parents.

Looking ahead sensibly, then, means planning for the future. It means being available as resources for our teens, as support systems, and as advocates. It means understanding that parents may need help in coping with the trauma of unintended pregnancy and knowing there is no shame involved in getting counseling for all family members. Looking ahead sensibly means taking advantage of community resources, of education programs and self-help or peer counseling groups so that no one, neither parents nor teens, feels alone with insurmountable problems. Repeat episodes of adolescent pregnancies need not happen if proper protective measures are taken, and parents can be significant contributors to prevention. The key word is *sensibly;* the choices exist.

19

Runaways

Running away from home is deeply embedded in the American tradition. Literature's most famous examples — Mark Twain's Tom Sawyer and Huck Finn — are epitomes of a romanticized notion of the experience. During the Great Depression of the 1930s children left home in massive numbers to find work and their next meals. The flower children of the 1960s ran away to find life-styles that would be esthetically and morally superior to those of their parents. There is neither romance nor idealism motivating most of the runaways of the 1980s. The unknown dangers of running are often less frightening or debilitating than the family situations they are leaving.

The runaway problem is now a nationwide epidemic. One in seven teens leaves home without parental permission, which means approximately two million youngsters are considered runaways each year. Not all of the children who go do so willingly. Recent estimates suggest as many as one-third of them are "pushouts" or "throwaways" — teens whose parents have thrown them out of their homes for offenses such as misbehaving, eating too much, or becoming pregnant. The actual number of these children may be higher than the estimates, for such parents rarely report their children missing.

Kids are becoming homeless at younger ages than ever before. Runaway shelters report eleven- and twelve-year-olds seeking help, though the average age is 14.9 years. National surveys of these shelters show 64 percent of the teens processed are girls. They usually run not to seek "fun" and "adventure" but because their options seem severely restricted and running becomes their way of coping, of finding alternatives to an intolerable status quo

Why Teens Leave Home

According to the National Network of Runaway and Youth Services in Washington, D.C., five major factors occur singly or in combination in many of the families of children who run away:

(1) poor communication with parents;
(2) existence of or fear of abuse, neglect, or sexual exploitation by parents or relatives;
(3) unreasonable, excessively harsh demands or restrictions placed on teens by parents;
(4) problems or disruptions in family systems (separate from conflicts with teens);
(5) school-related problems.

That poor communication patterns within families is number one on the list of major reasons for running — it is found in more than half of these families — is not surprising. No one likes to be misinterpreted, or worse, ignored and discounted. Many parents use a rigid "either-or" approach to discipline which roughly translates into the message "Either you do what I say, when I say, and how I say or you (get punished, lose privileges, get thrown out of the house)," but do not recognize that this style of controlling the teen is a sure-fire way to undermine communication. The combination of seemingly unfair restrictions (from the teen's viewpoint) and an inability to talk things out creates environments ripe for runaway behavior. Teenagers are not robots who should always be expected to jump just because parents tell them to, nor are teenagers psychics who can determine if what their parents expect from them is the same as what their parents ask or demand of them. In families that produce runaways, there are often many mixed messages being sent back and forth where, just as in *Alice's Adventures in Wonderland,* nothing is exactly as it seems. A teen will try to please parents only so many times and — failing on every count — is likely to run if there is no room for negotiation and clarification of parental demands and teenage needs.

Some parents think their teenagers are insensitive, egotistical people who don't care about anyone but themselves and their friends, and who are unaware of any stresses their parents may be experiencing. This is rarely true, but it is a belief that causes parents to miss many of the signals of an impending runaway episode. The fact is that adolescents are exquisitely sensitive to everything around them but are often inept at expressing what they are feeling and seeing. The bread-and-butter issues of job security, where the income to pay one's bills will come from, how to keep up with inflation, how to guard against bankruptcy are problems that affect teens very much. Teenagers are sensitive barometers, measuring and reflecting the pressures that exist in their families. When they see that there is little they can do to help, or if they are left out of major family decisions because parents incorrectly assume their kids don't care, some teens react in the way they think will best solve their problems: they run. Often, the running is an altruistic gesture. Consider the motiviation of the teen who left so his family would have one less mouth to feed, and contrast it with the motiviation of the parent who threw his thirteen-year-old twins out of the house because they ate too much, and who told the emergency youth service worker helping his children,

> "What's the use of having kids if there's no one out there to take 'em off your hands and care for 'em when the going gets tough? I don't owe my kids nothing, they never did nothing for me and I won't keep 'em in my house."

To the parents who have forgotten what it was like to be in junior and senior high school, school problems may not seem a valid reason for triggering a runaway episode. But if you consider the teenage viewpoint, it becomes understandable. School is the adolescent's home away from home, one area of life where control is ostensibly in the teen's hands, not the parents'. When things go awry either socially or academically the teen's feelings of being the master of all he surveys may crumble, for to fail in school is to fail as a teenager and that can feel intolerable. Because adolescents are notorious actors and reactors, running may seem a more viable alternative than staying to face the music and solve the problems causing the school difficulties. Parents who put undue pressure on their teenagers regarding academic performance (for example, expecting Ph.D.-quality work from an average student), or who constantly pry into their child's day-to-day social activities, or parents who always assume the teachers are right and that nothing the teen relates about school (especially if unfavorable) is accurate may inadvertently create runaway situations.

Leaving home is rarely an instantaneous decision. It is usually a response to longstanding patterns of conflict that teens ultimately feel hopeless about. Generally, kids will try to resolve family problems themselves — by pleading with parents, adopting uncharacteristic behaviors to draw attention to themselves, thus defusing what they think is causing family dissension, sometimes even assuming adult roles to try to lighten parents' burdens. If these tactics don't work, if they have no other resources to turn to for help, teens are apt to run away as last-ditch efforts to bring about changes. The impulse to label such runaways as "deviant" is unfair since runaways (much like teenagers who contemplate and attempt suicide) are seeking solutions to problems but in socially unacceptable ways. Parents must try to remember this distinction: the methods are deviant; the children are not.

Some teenagers *need* to run from unsafe environments. In such cases the act of running can actually be a sign of health, for it serves as a safety valve to discharge tensions and prevent further harm to self or others. Interestingly, younger runaways and first-time runaways tend to trivialize their reasons for running because they are afraid or ashamed, or may want to protect their families' reputations. To face all the implications of their decisions is often too traumatic, so many of these teens show false bravado or coarse exteriors to mask their true pain. They should not be confused with another category of runaway teens who show this bravado — the casual runaway whose pattern is to be away from home for a day or two, often staying with friends but not informing family members. Such teens use casual running as a response to legitimate parental limit-setting or family blowups, disappearing with no intention of staying away forever. For them, running serves as a way of asserting independence, signaling their ability to function as adults in the "real" world. Ninety percent of these teens return home within a few days of their disappearances, and such episodes can happen even in close-knit, psychologically healthy families.

Clearly, the casual runaways come from home situations that are distinctly different from those of the teens who actually need to run for reasons of personal safety. Why, then, is there often such an element of surprise when a teen leaves home and doesn't return? Why is it that people interviewed by police or social workers involved in locating a missing teen may say, "This is such a shock, they are a lovely family?" It is because such families project a veneer of tranquility to outsiders — for example, the father is a good provider, the mother and kids are well dressed but quiet, the home is neat. Such tranquility is often a mask. It hides the conflict, tension, and discord that are really the prime movers of such a family's interactions. When the family's image and respectability remain intact a husband and wife can easily ignore any interpersonal problems because everyone sees that "nothing is wrong." Denial of conflict serves several purposes: by becoming strongly etched in a family's belief system it can allow miscommunication to flourish or can cover up heinous abuse of children (especially sexual exploitation or psychological abuse). How this works is illustrated by the case of fifteen-year-old runaway Carol:

> "My stepfather kept making passes at me and one night he
> snuck into my room after Mom had gone to sleep. He said he just
> wanted to teach me about sex, so I wouldn't get hurt by boys.
> After he raped me, he threatened to kill me if I told Mom."

When seen by a family therapist some months after Carol had run away and been returned home by court order, the parents said they had no marital problems. Carol's mother sided with her husband, refusing to believe her daughter's allegations. Such vigorous denial of wrongdoing and the pattern of spouses siding with each other against the teen's testimony are indications of just how resistant to change such families can be, and why they are so hard to treat — among the reasons why runaway statistics remain so high. The odds of teenagers like Carol running away repeatedly are predictably high if what they are trying to escape is not corrected.

Adolescents run for a number of different reasons, often a combination of reasons. Teens from every ethnic or socioeconomic group have the potential to be runaways. If we, as parents, are to stem the tide of teenage runaways we must never underestimate the depth and intensity of our children's feelings nor trivialize their problems. Only then will we be able to be alert enough to detect the warning signs.

Warning Signs

An impending runaway episode is usually preceded by obvious changes in the teenager. The girl who alters her image from prep to punk or the boy who switches his oxford-cloth button-down shirts for sleeveless leather motorcycle-gang vests is trying to communicate an unspoken message to their parents and all others in their lives. Sometimes teens are willing to discuss what that "something" is but at other times they may not even be clear about their motives except to say that "all the kids are doing it." Some teens go way beyond the change-of-image stage and may shift behavior gears completely: the studious teen may become a chronic truant, the responsible child who always followed directions may adopt sloppy work habits, conveniently "forgetting" to do things. Still others may change peer-group alliances and begin to hang out with kids they never had much in common with in the past.

"But," you may say, "all teens change like this over time; it's part of testing roles and trying to fit into the adult world." This is technically correct, in terms of the broad generalizations we make about the total spectrum of adolescent behavior. But the very things we might expect as normal for most adolescents may be warning signs of a runaway episode within certain families — the families in which any or all of the five major reasons for running exist. Some of the warning signs agreed upon by the professionals who counsel such teens are the very things that lead them to diagnose other teens as depressed or suicidal. The warning signs are not absolutes, then, but indicate the potential for a crisis in the teen's life, a crisis that may well play out as a runaway episode. Here is a compendium of the most reliable and obvious signs that someone is about to run:

(1) *Impulsive behavior* — the teen who begins to rebel, to "act out" and be unwilling to talk about just about anything with anybody. This is also a signal of suicidal tendencies. Parents must be aware of the ex

tent to which the impulsiveness of the teen deviates from the child's usual behavior patterns, which means they must first have a clear idea and understanding of the norm for their teen. Unfortunately, many do not have enough information to make an intelligent assessment.

(2) *Inability to tolerate frustrations.* In therapists' jargon this is called an inability to delay gratification; in reality, it translates into wanting everything here and now, this minute — instant answers, instant pleasures, instant results. An inability to tolerate frustrations translates into an inability to get along with others and may make the teen seem petulant, selfish, and sometimes even violent. It effectively undermines the possibility for problem-solving and often leads to alienation of adolescents from their family and peers.

(3) *Extreme changes in peer relationships.* The teen who in the past maintained pleasant relationships with a number of people — family, teachers, and peers — may suddenly reject both family and teachers, making negative statements about them, and may sever all significant ties with them to focus energies instead on a small group of friends. Conversely, the teen who withdraws completely from peers and remains virtually home-bound is signaling that something is wrong and is a candidate for a runaway episode.

(4) *Sudden mistrust of adults.* This may appear as resistance to adult-imposed regulations, as verbal statements that adults can't be counted on or trusted, or as unwillingness to confide in adults. Though these reactions may seem sudden to the parents, they have probably been brewing for some time but were discounted as typical adolescent behavior. The maxim "Don't trust anyone over thirty" doesn't really hold for the adolescents of the 1980s, so if you see behavior indicating your teen has this attitude it's time to pay attention to and confront the underlying issues.

(5) *Verbal statements about running away* are frequently made by teens who are seriously considering it. Parents may discount these messages, remembering younger childhood threats of a similar variety that were followed by packing a sack lunch, walking around the block, and returning when all the cookies were eaten. The teen who is hurting or in trouble, whose family is not providing the emotional or even physical essentials necessary to keep the family bonds strong and healthy is not being coy, is probably not making a joke, and should not be confused with the cute seven-year-old "runaway" of the past. The teenage candidate may make the statement many times and not act on it, but if attention isn't paid to the message there may be a breaking point when the message turns into reality.

There are other behaviors that are warning signs of running, but they also happen to be warning signs of adolescent depression and suicide. Sadly, many runaways are depressed kids, using the running as a kind of risk-taking, a suicidal gesture, and many end up dead. The signs of depression are:

(6) *Feeling and saying that one is hopeless, worthless, a zero.*

(7) *Drug or alcohol abuse.*

(8) *Academic problems* that had not existed before.

(9) *Magical thinking* — the idea that if you press the right buttons everything will be fine, and all problems will disappear. This clearly signals a break with reality, an inability to deal with pressures, and the need to believe in some power outside of the self to bring solutions. This is not to be equated with religious belief.

Not all runaways have been deprived or abused or had parents who didn't want them or who abandoned them. Some parents of runaways loved and tried to nurture their children, and knowledge of the warning signs will never guarantee the prevention of a runaway episode. Parents who care and want to help their teens must strive to do more than just be *aware.* They must understand the cumulative nature of stress and its impact on their teens, they must admit to the existence of problems when they do occur, confront them, explore options for solution, and get help if needed. The crux of the process is to include your teen in it, to listen and talk noncombatively, and not allow the problems that spark runaway episodes to multiply and get out of hand.

What to Do if It Happens to You

Just as it is possible to make generalizations about teenage runaways, it is possible to make generalizations about their parents. Most adults react to a child's disappearance with a predictable series of reactions: fear, anger, denial, shame, disbelief. Some are relieved that the major source of tension in their lives is gone, some feel intense guilt (especially if they have ever responded to their teen's statement "I'm going to leave home because you don't really care about me" with a "Go ahead, I dare you"). Some may feel completely rejected by a teen who has abandoned them personally as well as their family's values and beliefs. Almost all parents experience a sense of disorganization, of not knowing what to do first or whom to turn to for help.

It is possible to survive the impact of the immediate crisis and maximize the chances of locating your teen by implementing a cautious, clearly delineated plan of action. *The first thing parents must do is cope with their feelings of panic.* Admit how you are feeling, talk about your emotions, maybe even write them down if only to clarify them in your own mind. This may be difficult if your family is not used to communicating on anything but a superficial level. It is important to involve all family members remaining at home in this process, if only to demystify what you are experiencing at the moment.

You must determine whether your teen has really run away. Your instant reaction to a child's disappearance may temporarily blind you to the possibility that you may have forgotten a scheduled overnight hike or a class project requiring your teen's presence at a friend's home for the weekend. Call your teen's friends, friends' parents, teachers, clergy — anyone your child was in regular contact with — to try to locate his or her whereabouts. If nothing turns up or if someone has seen your teen hitching a ride on the nearest highway, you have cause to suspect the worst. You are not helpless, however, and the situation does not have to be hopeless.

Notify the authorities about your teen's disappearance. You will need to tell school officials (if your teen had been in school), any employers, and possibly the police. The reason we say "possibly" when referring to the police is that there is no guarantee that the police will be able to locate your runaway. Most police departments require a forty-eight hour wait before you can file a missing-person report — enough time for your teen to get far away from home and into an underground network of runaways who will likely shelter your teen and render him or her virtually invisible. Additionally, although most states are members of the Interstate Juvenile Compact, an agreement to search for missing children, unless a parent knows the city or state the teen is in, and unless there are solid leads about the teen's whereabouts, it's not likely the police will look for the runaway. It is an overwhelming task to look for all the runaways in this country, and available police manpower is insufficient. The New York City Police Department's Runaway Unit, for example, has four police officers, one detective, and one sergeant to cope with the runaway problem in a city considered the Mecca for runaway teens.

Sadly, until October 12, 1982, when President Reagan signed a law mandating the creation of a national clearinghouse of computerized information listing the names and descriptions of missing children and unidentified bodies so parents could determine from the F.B.I. whether their children were on such a list, there had been no single center parents could turn to for information. This clearinghouse will eliminate the frustrations of dealing with overlapping police jurisdictions, will enable parents to double-check that local police are cooperating in a search, and will allow the F.B.I. to take information directly from parents if a state or local police department refuses to enter the name of a particular missing teen on the computerized list.

If parents decide to file a missing-person report, they must also decide if they are willing to sign a warrant allowing the police to detain their teen if he or she is located. Detention situations may lead to court hearings that necessitate the presence of a lawyer. What happens is this: if you know the state your teen has run to, you can file a petition in juvenile court. Custody orders will be sent to that state, so that the runaway, if located, will be picked up by the police. A court hearing will follow, and the judge will decide whether to send the teen home, to a court in the home state for further hearings, or to a foster home. Running away is technically a "status offense," an act adults can do legally but forbidden to children. Some states put labels on runaways: PINS (persons in need of supervision), MINS (minors in need of supervision), JINS (juveniles in need of supervision), CHINS (children in need of supervision). Legally, states and localities have the option of deciding whether status offenders are entitled to the same protections as delinquents; state courts can put limitations such as curfews and reform-school sentences on a runaway's life if the teen is apprehended and sent to court. All of these consequences present a real Catch-22 for parents of runaways.

Call the various runaway hot lines that exist. A list of these telephone numbers is given in the Appendix. These national hot lines act as clearinghouses for local hot lines and also provide referral services pertaining to legal aid, free clinics, housing, Traveler's Aid, drop-in centers, local runaway shelters, and Salvation Army services. Some can arrange conference calls between parents and runaways, while all can serve as a neutral third party to negotiate between parents and runaways. Many of these hot lines are toll-free and operate twenty-four hours a day, seven days a week. Parents and runaways can leave messages on the hot lines that are kept completely confidential.

Be realistic about what might happen to your teenager, and be prepared to cope with the worst. Runaways are easy targets for criminal elements, especially drug dealers and pimps looking for prostitutes to add to their stables of salable male and female sex partners. Teens will do almost anything to feel as if they *belong,* and becoming a prostitute is one way of belonging to an identifiable group and of surviving. Unfortunately, many of these teens are victimized and brutalized by their customers as well as their pimps, and end up as statistics on the F.B.I.'s list of unidentified bodies.

The runaways who don't connect with pimps or drug dealers have to find other ways to survive and tend to learn what Anna Kosof calls "the skills of the urban nomad": how to shoplift, steal, mug people, and con credit from neighborhood stores. Most runaways have no working papers (which require parental consent) and cannot legally be hired if they are under eighteen. Over the past decade, the juvenile crime statistics have increased along with the increasing numbers of runaways; it is a fact that runaways commit much of the crime, not necessarily out of malicious intent, but to survive.

If you think your teenager isn't capable of any of these activities, think again. The streets harden a person quickly, and the need to eat and be sheltered are powerful motivators for taking action, no matter how horrendous the action may be.

Be willing to consider counseling for you and your family. You will need to sort out the reasons why your teen left home, and a therapist or an objective third party can help neutralize and defuse the emotionally explosive situation. Counseling can help you understand what changes might be made in the family system to prevent other children from running or to prevent the runaway from leaving home again. Getting counseling has nothing to do with admitting guilt or accepting responsibility for your teen's behavior. It should be thought of as a fact-finding mission from which you have everything to gain and little to lose, a positive step towards growth, and an insurance policy increasing the potential for family harmony and happiness.

Prepare yourself for the first phone call, the first contact with your runaway teen. If you take the time to anticipate your own reactions you will be less likely to respond angrily or with guilt-inducing statements. Write down a speech, if you must, and keep it near the phone — and make sure it includes the words "I love you." Try to imagine your teen's emotions in making such a call, and understand that a runaway often calls home on impulse. If a parent's response is negative, vindictive, or even too prying, the odds are your teen will hang up and won't call again. If, on the other hand, the parent and other family members are prepared for the first contact and can respond with love and understanding, the prognosis for getting the teen to return home is improved dramatically.

Accepting the Runaway Back Home (and Beyond)

The emotions you will feel when you are reunited with your runaway are likely to be as intense and confusing as those you experienced when you first discovered the teen gone or when you got the first phone call. You have a right to your feelings and should not try to deny or downplay them. But you should not let them overpower you or so dominate your reunion that you will be out of control.

The teenager returning to you may seem like a stranger — hardened, street-wise, cynical, emotionally and physically depleted. The extent to which any of these characteristics exist depends in large part on how long the teen has been gone and with whom he or she has associated. Your teen may perceive you as an adversary, a person whose main interest is to pull in the reins tightly and destroy his or her freedom. Or your teen may see you as an agent of the authorities, an enemy who mired him or her in the juvenile justice system. If you are lucky, your teen will be happy to see you and relieved to have someone making his or her decisions. Whatever the reactions, tension is practically guaranteed. No matter where or how you decide to meet, it is advisable to:

(1) *Arrange to have a neutral third party present at the first reunion.* This can be a counselor, a member of the clergy, a favorite teacher, a law-enforcement official — someone who can act as a moderator for the

initial communications between parents, the runaway, and other family members, a defuser of tension, someone who can point out if and when either party is sabotaging attempts at honest discussion as well as facilitating positive encounters.

(2) *Be prepared for a "honeymoon" when you all return home.* It may seem as if everyone is walking on eggshells, and all of you are on your best behavior. This can't last and won't.

(3) *Be prepared for an "explosion" to follow the "honeymoon."* It is not possible to suppress pent-up feelings forever and you may find yourselves locked into the old battle lines, arguing within comfortable but dysfunctional patterns. This is not healthy. Instead, you must try to avoid accusations, express your feelings honestly and listen for the truths inherent in your teen's assessment of you and the rest of the family.

(4) *Try to believe that some clouds really do have silver linings.* The runaway crisis may have been the catalyst your family needed to confront its problems and begin learning to deal with and solve them.

(5) *Arrange for counseling of some sort that involves all the family members.* You don't have to make a long-term commitment, but give yourself at least three months with a professional who can help you put your family back together. Remember, if there are no changes in the way your family system operates, you are practically ensuring a repetition of the runaway episode.

(6) *If family members seem unable to change their ways of interacting, it may be necessary to consider alternative living arrangements for the teen.* This can involve an informal agreement with relatives to let your child stay for a cooling-off period, or it could be a more drastic decision to put your teen in foster care or give up custody altogether. Any of these options would be preferable to maintaining a destructive, dysfunctional family environment.

Runaway shelters across the United States are filled with teens who have run away from their homes a second or third time, but this need not be the case. There is now a national commitment to help runaways and their families, counseling services are widely available and socially accepted, and preventive measures in the form of public education about all facets of the runaway experience are available to anyone seeking to learn about them. Motivation and communication are key factors in stemming the tide of young runaways and its devastating effects on families and individuals. The task at hand is not easy but it is workable. Surely our children and our society deserve the effort.

20

Cults

. . . religious evil is the worst form of evil, for it masquerades in a social form that we have come to associate with all that is good and decent and ennobling.
— Ronald Enroth, *The Lure of the Cults,* 1979

Cults in the United States are attracting tens of thousands of followers each year. It is generally agreed that they flourish during times of economic and social uncertainty and that teenagers turn to them when the gaps between idealistic goals of adolescence and life's realities are so great that teens cannot envision productive futures for themselves. People who join cults are looking for answers to the problems they encounter in society as well as in their personal lives. Their desire for acceptance and belonging is often so great they do not see the fallacies in cult teachings, and certainly do not admit that cult life is based on practical applications of the idea that the ends justify the means.

Here are a few eye-opening facts:

(1) *Cults are potentially dangerous.* On November 18, 1978, the Reverend Jim Jones of the People's Temple in Guyana convinced over 900 of his followers (most of whom came from the United States) to commit suicide by drinking Kool-Aid laced with poison. Members of The Way International are required to take weapons training as part of their cult membership. The Church of Scientology uses paramilitary methods of discipline; ISKCON (International Society for Krishna Consciousness) is said to stockpile M-14 semiautomatic rifles, ammunition, and handguns at at least one of its farms.

(2) *Cults are wealthy.* The Unification Church of the Reverend Sun Myung Moon takes in more than $100 million annually just from members' street solicitations. This constitutes only a fraction of Moon's economic empire, which also includes extensive real estate holdings and ownership of a fishing fleet in Massachusetts. ISKCON earns $20 million annually from street solicitations, restaurant operations, book and magazine sales.

(3) *Cults are undemocratic.* The Indian mystic Bhagwan Shree Rajneesh owned twenty-two Rolls Royce automobiles at last count — wealth not shared with followers. Resident members of The Way International have been known to live on diets of rice and potatoes, getting only three hours of sleep nightly — a regimen not adhered to by its leaders.

Despite these startling facts, teens are turning to cults in record numbers. Looking for reasons and trying to understand motivations, parents can become bitter, frustrated, and angry, and family communications can easily disintegrate. The best tactic against the lure of cults is knowledge and understanding. When parents are prepared, have clear concepts of what their teens are likely to be doing and learning in any given cult, then they will be able to make rational decisions about how to proceed — whether to try to convince their adolescents to come home, to deprogram them, or to accept the teens' decisions regarding cult membership.

What Are Cults and Why Are They Dangerous?

Cults are defined as groups that exist in a state of conflict or tension with society because they deviate from a culture's established "norm." The ones we are concerned with have never broken away nor evolved from existing religions and should not be confused with religious sects such as the Amish or the Quakers. Cults have proliferated so rapidly that since 1965 more than 2,500 have evolved in the United States alone. Obviously, not all of these have been as economically successful as the Moonies or the ISKCONS nor as notorious as the People's Temple, but they share several characteristics that have led them to be dubbed "high demand religious groups," referring to their spartan regimens and strict commitments required from members.

Historically, these cults are unique because they are wealthy. The leaders often reside in splendor while the cultists live in poverty. These leaders (often still living) are charismatic and omnipotent figureheads; they are always men, and are sole judges of the intensity, depth, and quality of members' faith.

Recruitment procedures are often deceptive. For example, a front group for the Moonies called CARP (College Association for the .Research of Principle) has been known to recruit members without mentioning any tie to the Reverend Mr. Moon. Instead, they invite people to dinners, followed by weekend retreats, seven-day workshops, twenty-one-day sessions, and finally six-week training periods, after which the people can be indoctrinated into the "family" and Moon is revealed as their leader. At this point in time, the recruits are likely to be psychologically trapped and primed for the experience of cult life.

At the core of the cults' appeal is a utopian, idealistic vision that provides an answer to every question about the imperfections of our world. Although each cult leader professes to have the key to save humanity from itself, which is inherently appealing to adolescent minds frightened by the threat of nuclear destruction, the truth is that few cults sponsor any community aid programs or spend their money on civic problems.

People who decide to join cults are offered elusive rewards of happiness, salvation, and inner peace if they renounce their ties with family, friends, school, or prior jobs. Cult members are taught to feel superior to the outside world, to perceive others' religious lives as shallow. Cults discourage rational thought: doubt is equated with guilt, and members' fears or feelings of guilt are skillfully manipulated to enhance group purposes. Cults frequently make their members believe that one's eternal destiny is jeopardized if the cult is abandoned.

To accomplish this, cult members are mentally and physically isolated from all prior ties. Many cults establish quarters in geographically isolated areas and have the premises heavily guarded to prevent ease of entry or exit. The mental isolation is subtler, but by encouraging members to abandon all prior ties in times of need or conflict and to rely only on the cult, they accomplish their goals of being truly closed social systems. Newly initiated cultists are subjected to very sophisticated techniques which are geared to manipulate their thought processes and even alter their behaviors. Repetition of doctrine, peer pressure, and sleep and food deprivation lead to a psychological "snapping" which is said to feel like a major inner revelation and makes the recruit very suggestible. This is often followed by the use of specialized, nonsensical language patterns, "love-bombing" in which initiates are literally surrounded by people who tell them how much they are loved, and finally, by peer approval. All of this contributes to the creation of psychic boundaries separating the cultists from the outside world and helps them to believe that the cult alone can give them emotional and physical sustenance, that only the group can solve their problems.

Surprisingly, most cults are antiwoman, antichild, and antifamily. Few women attain decision-making positions and some cults encourage women to use sex to recruit members. Child abuse has been reported in many cults and in some cases, sexual abuse is used as a form of punishment. Some use sexual repression as a controlling force: Moonies must remain celibate for varying amounts of time after marriage; married ISKCONS can have intercourse only on the woman's most fertile day of each month and only with the goal of conception.

Cult converts do daily work that is often demeaning, including non-stop activities such as fund-raising, witnessing, chanting, indoctrinating, and sometimes even forced labor. Women are generally found in the kitchens or on cleaning crews; rarely are cultists' education, intelligence, training, or interests taken into account when their work is assigned. There can be negative physical ramifications resulting from sleep deprivation, malnutrition, and overwork that seem to be central to many cultists' everyday life-style. The psychological milieu of cults has been compared to prisoner-of-war camps during World War II when brainwashing techniques were popular. The physical and psychological aspects of cult life are inextricably linked and necessary if members are to be bound to the cults' group norms and strive for group goals.

Cult memberships are drawn largely from the post-high-school-age group of teens and young adults. About 50 percent are between the ages of eighteen and twenty-two at the time of first cult contact; only 3 percent are seventeen years or younger. Ethnically, 98 percent are white and from middle- to upper-middle-class economic backgrounds. College-educated people are alleged to be most vulnerable to cult propaganda.

Why would such individuals, certainly not the most seriously economically or socially disadvantaged, turn to cults? Some authorities believe that the deteriorating state of the family is the major culprit. Other experts suggest that economic factors are causative: given today's underemployment and relatively tight money, teens are realizing that good academic performance is no guarantee of financial security and in fact can be a liability insofar as it might overqualify them for certain jobs. Others say that parents are too permissive and do not realize their teens want some limits set for them; and still others assert that poor family communication patterns are at fault.

Whatever the cause, it is apparent that in some ways cults offer a good life. They replenish what seems to be missing in the adolescent's experience — loving, caring, consistent discipline and expectations, psychological security — all of which in practice equal control but at first are experienced as positive emotional feedback. Also, cults alleviate teens' very difficult tasks of having to deal with the sometimes impossible expectations of families and peers. Commentators have noticed that those adolescents who need a moratorium on growing up will join cults because all their decisions about jobs, education, sexual behavior and family planning can be made *for* them rather than *by* them individually. Cults may be a viable alternative to life in family situations where tension and confrontation are customary, where caring and communication are lacking or absent. Cults may in fact provide a positive life-style for those teens who have really thought long and hard about the implications of joining, who have done some preliminary research or have even "shopped around" and who have discussed it with their families prior to joining. Though in the minority, these people can be emotionally and spiritually enriched by cult life since presumably they have made free and informed choices.

At the same time, cults are dangerous because they simplify issues that are not really simple, and provide one single set of answers to questions that have many answers. In so doing, cults encourage their members to change their ways of thinking about things, to start criticizing things they never really cared much about to begin with (for example, teens who never paid attention to their parents' religious affiliations begin to denounce their parents as spiritually deficient hypocrites), and to become unable to function rationally or effectively outside of the cult environment.

Cults are also dangerous because they can short-circuit the teenagers' natural curiosities and desires to learn. The educational methods of cults rely heavily on repetition of doctrine, censorship of any reading materials not provided by the cults, and the stifling of questions in favor of total acceptance of a leader's words. This has caused some initiates to report having experienced a kind of tunnel vision similar to that of suicidal teens. Ensnared by a web of easy answers, the members cannot see the whole picture and nothing outside the tunnel is acceptable to the cultists. It is as though a blackout has been imposed on whole segments of the individuals' intelligence.

Because cults aim to replace one's natural family and support networks, they are dangerous insofar as they alter and destroy members' previous relationships with the "outside world." They often wrench families apart — creating scenarios of guilt, recrimination, and hysteria. Indeed, in families where parent-teen relations have already been strained, losing a child to a cult may be the straw that breaks the camel's back. Since most cults discourage visits from family members, there is the added strain of second-guessing what cultists are really doing. Most of the time, cultists are not permitted to contact natural family members even if there is a health crisis. Thus, cults of this sort differ sharply from religious sects, which encourage a combination of family togetherness and religious support to solve major problems.

The dangers of cults are real. The threats posed by cults to any given individuals and their families depends, of course, on what circumstances predated and predisposed the choice of cult life, what cult is joined, the age and sex of the member, and the family's reaction to that teen once the break with the family has been made. No matter what, it is important to remember that parents have options too.

If Your Kid Gets Caught

Parents of teens who join cults are typically shocked and bewildered at first. They usually can't explain the reasons for such a decision, and they almost invariably see it as a slap in the face — rejection in its most profound form. Over time, some parents become resigned to the idea since they don't know what else to do. Others react with anger and bitterness, looking forward to the day their child will admit the error of his or her ways. Still others react by mobilizing themselves into action, planning ways of rescuing their child and restoring family equilibrium.

What options are open to you if your teen gets ensnared by a cult? First, you must recognize that your teen won't *feel* trapped and will hear your claims to the contrary as empty words, proof of your insensitivity and callousness. Second, you should realize that your adolescent's perception of the cult is entirely different from your own: if recruits didn't feel that a cult's beliefs were fair, insightful, and humane, they wouldn't be involved in the first place. With these facts in mind, how you should proceed depends on whether your teen is still being recruited or has actually gone off to join the cult.

If you've been fortunate enough to find what's going on in the "recruitment" stage, look carefully at the following possibilities:

(1) If your teen is still legally a minor (under eighteen in most jurisdictions), you may be able to get a court order to prohibit cult members from further contact. You will obviously have to consult a lawyer to explore this option, but do it quickly, before things get out of hand.

(2) Consider steps you can take to remove your teenager geographically from contact with the cult. This may mean an extended family trip, or taking your teen to Uncle Harry's farm in Idaho for a few months, or even sending your teen off to a boarding school far from the reaches of the cult — expensive choices, perhaps, but not in comparison to the alternative.

(3) Call on expert help to demystify the hypnotic draw of the cult. A trusted teacher, a coach, or a close family friend may be willing to act as a go-between to get your adolescent to sit down and listen to reason. Ex-cultists, some of whom now work as deprogrammers (discussed below), may also be quite helpful here.

If your teen has already been committed to a cult, there are still some options you'll be facing. These range from complete disapproval and rejection of the idea (often leading to parental attempts to remove the teens legally from cults or forcibly remove them and deprogram them), to conditional approval (attempting to be both objective and honest), to complete approval of the decision. In the conditional approval category, parents may say nothing at first but prepare themselves to debate the issue at a later time, may purposely choose to remain ignorant about the cult, hoping that their teens will change their minds and come home if the parents are patient, or they may set up a bargaining situation in which they ask the teens to wait a few weeks before leaving for the cults in order to help acclimate the family members to the idea and help them understand the reasons for the decisions and the issues involved.

Parents whose adolescents have joined cults do not accomplish much if they wallow in anger and guilt, or remain in catatonic states of shock or confusion. The family style of communicating has been found to influence profoundly the outcome of the teen's cult involvement. Specifically, those families in which people are able to confront one another and speak their minds openly and without vituperation seem to be more successful at staving off the impact of cults on their adolescents than are those who don't talk at all or who talk *at* one another.

When the issue of cult membership clouds a family's relationship with a teenager, it may be extremely difficult for the parents to express loving and caring feelings for the cultist. But ex-cultists, deprogrammers, parents who have suffered through the process, and professionals who write about the cult issue all suggest that it is critical that you do not reject that cult member outright. It is desirable to lay the groundwork for the teen to feel accepted by family in spite of the cult issue. Specifically:

(1) Do not sever communication out of anger, fear, frustration, or feelings of rejection.

(2) Encourage the teen to return home once in a while even if accompanied by another cult member.

(3) If the teen comes home to visit, don't rush into a debate about the cult. Try to relate to the teen as your child with whom you've shared good times and bad, *not* as a cultist.

(4) Don't try to offer alternative religious choices when you are together.

As parents you may want to ask yourselves whether your definitions of success, spirituality, and happiness coincide with those of your teens. If they don't, try to determine why and when they began to diverge. Discuss whether you really know what has been important to your teenage cult member in the years prior to the cult decision. If not, what prevented you from knowing and what can you do to change this situation from now on? Try to consider the options your teen will have for a productive and successful life within a cult. Are you really knowledgeable or are you basing your reactions on hearsay or myth? Does the teen realize there may be other options besides the cult? How can you share this information together?

If after these questions have been explored, your teenager remains adamant in his or her desire to be a cult member, and as parents you cannot in good faith grant either total or conditional approval, there are a number of ways to proceed.

Legal Concerns and Parents' Rights

Parents have various rights regarding their children's lives. These include custody rights (which take into account determining where the child will live), the right to discipline the child, the right to determine religious training and education, the right to receive the child's earnings, and the right to determine the child's overall life-style (including some control over what friends they may be involved with, the kinds of entertainment they pursue, even the manner in which they dress). Historically, however, the courts have usually abstained from intervening in disputes between parents and children. Even though the courts are very gradually moving in the direction of granting more liberal rights of self-determination to children under the age of majority, this tendency does not seem to apply to issues involving cults and cult membership.

The legal issues involving disputes between parents and cults are complicated for several reasons. The major one is that cults can claim the protection granted by the U.S. Constitution for religious freedom — a provision which has been expanded in recent years by the courts. As a result, law-enforcement agencies are very reluctant to take on cults since the freedom-of-religion provision is so strong.

The Federal Bureau of Investigation — which in the early years of cult expansion was active in undercover activities such as cult infiltration in order to obtain information — is now severely restricted in its operations regarding the cults. Basically, what the F.B.I. is now allowed to do is step in only if a cult or its members violate a federal law — for example, if a cult is charged with kidnapping (keeping members against their wills). Prosecution is another matter that is tricky, because as one assistant deputy attorney general points out, what is brainwashing or kidnapping to a parent or relative may be *belief* to the alleged victim.

If your teenager is under the age of majority when the cult issue emerges, and since parents have the legal right to influence their childrens' life-style decisions, it would seem parents would be able to confront the cults head-on. However, this is seldom the case. Courts do not like to entertain disputes between parents and children over life-style issues, and cult membership is sometimes considered such an issue; furthermore, it is often difficult to prove that a cult has done any harm to your teen — especially if the teen appears to give testimony saying that he or she is incredibly happy and well cared for.

What can parents do? Cult commentators almost unanimously agree that parents should consider nonlegal options before turning to the law to rescue their teens from cults. (Nonlegal does not mean illegal.) Here are some examples of steps that can be taken prior to contacting the courts, for courts should be the place of last resort to which parents turn for help.

(1) *Arrange for a reevaluation.* In this procedure, parents hire a third party who is knowledgeable about the cult to sit down with parents and cultist to discuss the cult member's current life-style. It is like a debate with the third party as moderator. The reevaluator defuses the emotional intensity of a situation and can ease the way for a cult member to begin to listen to something other than cult doctrine. Such reevaluations succeed only when all parties agree to the process and when they are carefully preplanned, when parents and third-party members are accurately informed, and when acrimony and recrimination are kept out of the proceedings. Reevaluations do not involve the courts.

(2) *Arrange for legal conservatorship.* A child over the age of majority can be removed from a cult by means of a court order. A judge must decide that the teenager's mental and physical well-being is jeopardized before issuing a ruling. Then a *conservatorship* is granted for a limited time period during which the parents agree to seek help from professionals such as counselors, psychologists, even deprogrammers. What the conservatorship accomplishes is the reinstatement of the parents' rights over the teen's life-style and welfare. Obtaining legal conservatorship can be a very expensive procedure and is infrequently pursued and rarely granted.

(3) *Arrange for deprogramming.* Deprogramming is the option of last resort. Pioneered in 1971 by Ted Patrick, it has been associated with the snatching or kidnapping of cult members from the cult and subjecting them to bombarding tactics similar to those utilized by cults to obtain mind-control. In deprogramming, the purpose is to reverse the cult's input and replace it with "reality."

Today's deprogrammers are said to use more sophisticated procedures, for they tend to be ex-cultists themselves and have first-hand knowledge of how frightening deprogramming can be. They often work in teams, and charge fees averaging one to two thousand dollars if no travel is involved. They attempt to get the cultists to think for themselves, to confront the contradictions inherent in cult doctrines, and they ask probing questions designed to shake the cultists' belief systems in order to penetrate their mental barriers and tunnel vision. Parents are not involved in deprogramming; they yield the responsibility and the outcome to the deprogrammers.

Deprogramming is not necessarily legal. Deprogrammers risk arrest on kidnapping charges. Since 1980, two bills have been submitted to state legislatures — one in New York and one in Connecticut, proposing to legalize deprogramming. The New York bill was an amendment to the state's mental hygiene law. Though the word *cult* never appeared in the amendment, it specified that the court could appoint a temporary guardian at the request of a close relative for anyone age sixteen or older who had undergone "substantial behavioral change" and lacked the capacity to make "informed decisions or to understand or control his conduct." The guardian would then have been able to hold the person for a minimum of forty-five days and provide a "proposed plan of treatment." In spite of the fact that the bill specifically stated that custody could *not* be "for the purpose of altering the political, religious or other beliefs of the relative," it was soundly defeated. The Connecticut bill, which was similar, also failed. This points to the power of freedom of religion in America and underscores the difficulties parents may face when trying to extricate their teens from cults.

Success or failure of any of these efforts also depends upon how long a teenager has been exposed to a cult. Teens who have belonged to cults for longer than a year are highly resistant to deprogramming or reevaluation efforts and are likely to return to their cults in spite of parental efforts to the contrary. The outcomes are more favorable for the parents if the teens have belonged to cults for periods of less than one year.

Where to Find Help

The cult experience and its aftermath do not have to lead to social or emotional isolation of either parents or teenagers. Regardless of whether the adolescent exits from the cult voluntarily or involuntarily, certain patterns of behavior will necessitate the support of others.

Ex-cultists almost always experience a condition called "floating," which refers to a vacillation between life-styles, complicated by the fact that shortly after leaving a cult, most ex-members go into a period of mourning for the former life of total dedication. Such people often say that nothing else seems as meaningful as what they left. Additionally, when they begin to acknowledge that there was deception involved in the cult experience they may suffer from self-esteem problems, wondering how they could have fallen for such propaganda.

Ex-cult members may have problems dealing with social and sexual issues. Many find themselves faced with the very sexual pressures they were struggling with prior to joining a cult, and others may have more problems than before they joined, especially if their cult was a sexually abusive or restrictive one. They may need help in learning how to socialize and date, and may feel guilty if they find themselves enjoying normal social interactions.

Self-help groups and community-action groups that help ex-cultists and their families anticipate and conquer these typical problems can be used in addition to professional counseling or in place of it. Your best resources will include most or all of the following features:

(1) peer counseling by people who are similar in age and who have successfully emerged from the cult experience;

(2) informal counseling and referrals to professional counselors who have successful track records in helping ex-cultists and their families;

(3) family therapy to explore why the cult association came about, what needs weren't being met at home then and now, and what the separation from family actually accomplished;

(4) suggestions of techniques to deal with the natural and predictable feelings of guilt teen and parents feel;

(5) discussion of how to cope with reentry into a life-style that is not group-oriented.

These features may be found in residential programs or in less formal settings associated with family service agencies, churches, schools, mental health clinics and so on. A list of many organizations and programs providing assistance is given in the appendix. Legal assistance can be obtained free of charge through a local Legal Aid Society. You need not be alone in your confrontation with a cult.

21

Suicide

... and if you have no past or future, which, after all, is all that the present is made of, why then you may as well dispose of the empty shell of present and commit suicide.
— *Sylvia Plath,* 1950, freshman, Smith College

SUICIDE. The word leaps off the page and challenges you to take notice. Teenagers who are suicidal are also challenging you to take notice. Unfortunately, the behaviors that signal potential suicide are often ignored by family members, friends, and others (such as teachers, employers), who may misconstrue these signals as typical examples of the mood swings or rebellion of adolescence. Suicide statistics for the past twenty-five years show an alarming trend: teenagers are killing themselves at an epidemic rate, using suicide as a way to escape pressures that they are ill prepared to cope with. During this time period, there has been an increase of over 250 percent in suicides for females aged fifteen to twenty-four and over 300 percent for males in that same age group. All socioeconomic groups have been affected. There are approximately 27,000 suicides in the United States annually; one-fifth of these involve teenagers.

Recognizing Depression in Adolescence

Fact: The risk of a depressed person committing suicide is fifty times greater than for a person who isn't depressed.

Fact: Forty percent of adolescent suicides are due to depression.

261

Although many of us use the term *depressed* as a catchall phrase to describe ourselves when we're feeling down, upset, annoyed, frustrated, angry, or exhausted, depression is actually an illness. This serious psychological disturbance, only recently recognized as common among teenagers, is one of the earliest signals of potential suicidal behavior in adolescents. But all too frequently even severe cases of depression are missed or written off as "just a passing phase." Why this occurs may be gleaned from looking at the case of Roger Harrington.

Roger was a seventeen-year-old high school senior who seemed to have the world by the tail. In addition to being popular, he was a dean's list student who had been accepted at Yale and was planning to go on to law school. He was captain of the varsity baseball team and vice-president of the student council. In the spring semester of his senior year, his demeanor suddenly seemed to change. He became tense and irritable with his parents, barricaded himself in his room for long stretches of time, and began complaining about how complicated life was for him. For the first time ever, he began to cut classes and got a D on an important history term paper. He broke up with his girlfriend, avoided his circle of close friends, and generally seemed to lose interest in things that ordinarily brought him pleasure.

When his father tried to talk with him about what was happening, Roger told him, "I feel washed out. There's too much to do, and I'm kind of depressed about life in general." Mr. Harrington was both puzzled and angry at this explanation, and told his son, "How the hell can you be depressed? You've got everything in the world going for you. Get yourself together and snap out of this foul mood you've been in." Mrs. Harrington suggested that it was all just a case of "senior blahs" that would pass by the summer. One week later, the day before his graduation, Roger took his life by shooting himself in the head. The note he left on his typewriter simply said, "I just don't want to go on any more. I'm sorry."

The cause of Roger's suicide is, in retrospect, blatantly apparent. He had fallen into a profound depression which was strong enough to wipe out his will to live and to make the act of suicide attractive — an appealing release from the psychic pain he was experiencing. While Roger's was certainly not the typical teenage suicide, it illustrates why parents must be alert to the onset of depression in their teens.

While there's no sure-fire way of recognizing adolescent depression, authorities agree that a combination of symptoms from the following list is highly suggestive of this disorder.

(1) *Mood disturbances.* Depression is typically marked by a prominent and persistent sense of sadness, dejection, listlessness, and hopeless-

ness. Even if these features aren't present, a teen's loss of pleasure or enthusiasm in all or almost all of his or her activities can be an indication that the teen is depressed.

(2) *Changes in biological functions.* Appetite disturbances, sudden changes in weight, frequent tiredness out of proportion to levels of physical action, and sleep disturbances are frequently seen either singly or in combination.

(3) *Changes in thinking patterns.* Inability to concentrate, memory lapses, loss of self-esteem, guilt, and unusual anxiety are common; hallucinations (hearing voices, seeing "visions") and paranoia (feeling "someone's out to get me") are relatively rare.

(4) *Changes in behavior.* Social isolation, abrupt changes in behavior, rebellious behavior, and constant fidgeting or other signs of hyperactivity are common symptoms of adolescent depression. If your teenager sits through meals without entering the conversation, suddenly stops using the telephone, or drastically alters his or her study habits, you might be dealing with depression.

(5) *School problems.* An abrupt change in school performance, frequent problems with teachers, or habitual truancy may be warning signs.

(6) *Suicidal talk or behavior.* Fascination or preoccupation with death, dying, or suicide is a common feature of depression in adolescence and is *not* to be taken lightly.

However, as Roger's case shows, these signs and symptoms are not infallible warnings; in fact, they are often written off as temporary, meaningless events in a teenager's life. This happens undoubtedly because it can be difficult to distinguish these patterns from the everyday vagaries of adolescence — in other words, the distinction between normal and abnormal is primarily a matter of degree. Thus, parents must consider these key factors — duration, intensity, and seriousness — in assessing the possibility of depression. As a general rule of thumb, if symptoms from three of the above categories are present and last for more than a few weeks, or if talk of suicide is combined with any of the other symptoms listed, it's time to get professional help.

Teens who become depressed may experience some or all of a number of "trigger" situations that tip the behavior scale's balance from the normal range into the depressed range. Poor communication between family members, family conflict or marital problems, unrealistic parental expectations about the teen's capabilities and goals, death or separation from loved ones, illness or injury, major changes in life-style or goals, and parental depression can have a detrimental effect on a vulnerable adolescent. Therefore, it is imperative that parents understand that when a teen exhibits the changes listed above in the context of such trigger situations, it is possible that he or she is experiencing a lot of emotional pain and is signaling for help, even giving out a suicide warning. All too often, these signals are misunderstood and the help is nowhere to be found.

Suicide Warnings and What to Do about Them

Many teenagers make suicide pacts and unfortunately many teenagers die as a result of them. A story of one such couple made national headlines when *People* magazine reported their plight in its June 30, 1980, issue. Because theirs is a classic example of the kinds of warnings teenagers give over extended periods of time, and what happens when these are misinterpreted or ignored, we will examine their case in detail.

> Jason was sixteen and Dawn was fifteen when they met during the tenth grade and "fell in love." Deciding they wanted to get an apartment and live together, they both dropped out of school and got jobs at a local fast-food restaurant in their affluent suburban community. Dawn's father (a well-paid professional) refused to let her move in with Jason and threatened to send her to live with a relative miles away. He was unaware that Jason had been living in the attic of Dawn's family home from time to time; Jason's parents were unaware of this, too. Both sets of parents were involved in personal traumas of their own: Jason's were having marital problems and Dawn's were separated. On the night of the confrontation about the living arrangements, the teenagers borrowed Dawn's sister's car, crashed it at 110 miles per hour through an eight-inch cinderblock wall, landing 26 feet inside their local junior high school. Jason was killed; Dawn survived.

Was this an impulsive, romantic suicide pact motivated by what psychiatrists term the "Romeo and Juliet factor" or were the underlying motivations far from impulsive? Close analysis of the details of this couple indicate that warning signals of impending suicide had been given out over a long period of time and were missed or ignored.

(1) Jason had school problems and was frequently truant prior to dropping out of tenth grade.

(2) Jason wore a strand of wire for a belt and frequently told Dawn this was so he could strangle himself. The wire was a *visible* cue that together with the verbal statement about self-strangulation may be considered a "cry for help." Dawn never told Jason's parents about them, however.

(3) Jason was said to have been upset by the situation of the American hostages being held at that time in Iran, and by the threat of nuclear war.

Some suicidologists refer to the "proven constants" that can affect the incidence of suicides in any country. One of these is "a single dramatic event that seems to threaten the individual's happiness or future of the nation." The hostage situation and very real threat of nuclear war as a result of American intervention gone awry obviously affected Jason.

(4) Jason and Dawn and some other high school friends had formed a clique to fantasize about suicide, and it met for two months prior to the crash. Such fantasy is a fairly common part of the suicidal teenager's thought patterns and can include what experts call "magical thinking" — when suicide is considered to be one way to be completely powerful, in total control, rendering the suicidal individual *omnipotent*. Friends in the clique later said they thought the suicide fantasies were a joke — a common reaction of people to suicidal teens — and rationalized the fact that they didn't try to stop Dawn and Jason by stating that had they done so Dawn and Jason would have felt betrayed.

(5) The affluent suburban area in which they lived was described as having a feeling of pointlessness, offering teens very little to do in their spare time. The Menninger Suicide Research Project has discovered that during the past twenty years teens who seem to have every economic and social advantage have, in fact, become the high-risk suicide group. Simply put, Dawn and Jason were bored and alienated. Their parents' own lives were in disarray. The messages Dawn and Jason were receiving were like the ones the American Association of Suicidology considers a major factor in adolescent suicides: "If you go to school, it doesn't mean you'll get a job; if you get a job, it may not be meaningful; if you get married, it may not last."

(6) Jason and Dawn wrote out wills prior to thè crash. Dawn later remarked that she had lots of fun leaving things to people. Making out wills is one of the most salient warning signs of possible suicide, especially obvious when done by a younger person. The adolescent's attempt to "make final arrangements" may be carried out as if it were a lark or it can be a totally serious way of manipulating friends and relatives to make them feel guilty or punish them. Sometimes, the very determined decision to surrender one's belongings to friends and family may be accompanied by an aura of serenity which health care professionals call *the ominous calm*. Though such behavior looks confident on the surface and is in marked contrast to the more usual rebellious behaviors of the depressed, presuicidal adolescent, it is a *critical* danger signal.

Warning signs of suicide must be recognized and acted upon. Symptoms of depression, overt signs such as suicidal talk, bizarre suicide fantasies, self-mutilation, giving away treasured possessions, preoccupation with the subject of death in music, art, poetry, or in the teen's own written journals, verbalizing feelings of worthlessness, saying their families would be better off without them — such are the suicidal clues that would seem hard to miss but are all too often ignored.

In addition, another sign rarely noticed by parents is critical to understand if suicide is to be prevented. This is the apparent disappearance or lifting of the teen's depression. It is at just such a time that many suicide attempts are likely to be made. Two theories are commonly offered to explain this paradox: (1) only when the teen is no longer depressed can he or she have the psychological strength to plot and/or implement a suicide; and (2) a decision to commit suicide is a decision to exert one's control over life. Since control (or the lack of it) is often an issue for suicidal teens, the decision is cause for renewed optimism and the concurrent alleviation of depressive symptoms.

It is not an easy task to be so keyed into your teen's life that you can accurately assess the meaning of every behavior, the nuance behind every statement. We are not suggesting you should; even health care professionals may miss such clues. But a little knowledge goes a long way, and awareness may enable you to intervene at a critical moment and save your child's life.

Once parents become aware of the suicidal impulses of their teenager they may panic, hiding their own fears by refusing to discuss their observations about their child's behavior. This is all wrong. It is crucial that you open the lines of communication with your teenager and let him or her know how you are feeling. Don't be combative, don't try to reassure your teen that there is nothing to worry about if there clearly is. Try to listen to your teen with an open mind; then reflect back and rephrase what you believe he or she is saying and thinking to ensure that your understanding is accurate. If you choose to speak openly about your teenager's suicide wish, your frankness may be embarrassing to your child, so you need to weigh the pros and cons of such a direct approach. Suicidal teens need to know they are loved by their parents, so say it even if you feel compelled to add that you don't necessarily like all the things that have been going on lately. It may help to let your teen know that there is such a thing as "positive failure" (a concept used by many psychotherapists, which asserts that the effort of doing something is positive in spite of the outcome) and that you really don't expect perfection all the time!

If you fear a suicidal act is imminent and your teenager lives at home, you should clear your house of all possible lethal weapons including razors, household cleaners, other household poisons (insecticides, gardening fertilizers, mouse or rat poisons, and so forth), ropes, pills, car keys, sharp kitchen utensils. Do not leave your teen alone in the house. Try to get in touch with his or her friends, teachers, school officials, coaches to get their views of the situation and to share information that might help you get a clearer picture of what is really going on. Most important of all, get professional help. Whether you first contact a suicide prevention center, a community mental health center, an emergency room, a family service agency, a student health service, or a private physician, don't panic — act. Suicidologists stress the importance of latching on to your child's will to live. Don't get into a debate or give direct advice but try to identify the "trigger," focus on it, be supportive, and suggest feasible options to replace the teen's suicidal impulses. When parents learn to recognize the warning signs of suicide and know, intellectually at least, what to do about them, the parents are modeling a very positive behavior: they are letting their teenager know that it is possible to talk about worries and problems and that it is not necessary to use suicidal threats or suicidal acts as a means of communication.

Dealing with Suicide Attempts

, Fact: More than 400,000 American teenagers attempt suicide each year; about one in 100 succeeds.

Once a teenager has made a suicide attempt it is no longer possible for parents and other family or friends to ignore the suicide warnings. When the threat of suicide has become an actual attempt, the teenager has reached a point where the pain is intolerable and (although the teen may not be able to articulate this) to live life, if it means continued suffering, is simply not desirable.

Teenagers who make suicide attempts are sending out signals that therapists call cries for help. Such children have usually failed in their efforts at communicating in so-called normal ways. Their warning signs have probably been ignored or missed by family and friends. This unfortunate fact is shown clearly in the following conversation between a mother and her sixteen-year-old daughter who had taken a massive overdose of aspirin (these remarks come from the first therapy session this family had):

MOTHER (*accusingly*): You never confided in me . . . you never let me help you.
DAUGHTER: Are you nuts? You were so busy worrying about my dating, you never saw the obvious.
MOTHER: Obvious? All you wanted me to do was make sure your clothes were ready for your weekends and give you your telephone messages.
DAUGHTER (*sadly*): Mom, do you know how many times I came up and started to talk to you and you'd tell me you were too busy cooking or ironing or something? (*Now switching to anger*) Oh, what's the point? I'm leaving this office — you won't ever listen to me!

As in this example, attempts at verbal communications may not work because the teens' acting-out, rebellious behaviors may have alienated the very people with whom they were trying to connect. By the time they decide on attempting suicide, such teens probably are feeling isolated, alone, and abandoned by the families they need for a base of love and support. In addition, the fairy-tale myths many teens believe in: that happiness equals possessions or things, that happiness comes from having no problems at all rather than from learning how to cope with and overcome problems, and that happiness comes from conformity to an "ideal" rather than from the ability to develop one's individual strengths and talents, all tend to handicap the presuicidal teenager because it is impossible to live up to a myth.

Parents of teens who have attempted suicide should try to understand that this behavior is not necessarily perverse. Many therapists believe that suicide is not "flight" but a very twisted form of "fight," a way to lash out at the world and to punish those you believe have hurt you. The suicidal attempt of an adolescent may even be compared to a small child holding his breath until he turns blue: he doesn't really want to kill himself but he certainly wants to get some attention and scare his parents into noticing him.

A suicide attempt, then, is not a crazy or insane act; it is, oddly enough, a defensive action and a problem-solving technique. It can even be therapeutic, since the attempt sometimes breaks the cycle of depression and pushes the teenager towards a clearer understanding of what is really going on in his or her life. Parents of suicidal teenagers must keep telling themselves that every person who supposedly wants to die also wants to live. This fact can help you help your teenager to deal with the aftereffect of shock that often results from a suicide attempt.

The person who attempts suicide is obviously very upset and possibly irrational. Yet, at the very moment of the attempt, he or she believes the act is a rational one. Frequently, after a suicide attempt the teenager may feel it wasn't worth it and may say it was all a mistake. A bit later, the teen may be unable to believe that he or she even tried to commit suicide. And sometimes there really is a silver lining in the cloud, for the attempt may be the catalyst that helps the teen to rebuild a life based on realistic goals rather than myths, and productive rather than destructive problem-solving methods. If this is to happen, the teenager must have support from others.

If the teenager denies he or she needs help it becomes the parent's responsibility to decide whether to hospitalize the teen to allow for a cooling-off period for everyone involved. Hospitalization can be a time for the teen to get through the very worst of the self-destructive feelings and impulses, and to start to pull the threads of a disintegrating life together into a stronger fabric with the help of professional therapists. A teenager may not believe that his or her parents really care what happens; but in a hospital setting it becomes more difficult to deny the fact that others really do care — simply stated, hospitalization inundates the patient with caring people!

If hospitalization is neither feasible nor desired, suicide prevention centers are excellent resources for dealing with suicide attempts. You can find your local center by looking up "Suicide" in the phone book. These centers function as first-aid stations and limit their services to emergencies, usually handling only immediate crises. Though they do not generally offer long-term care they maintain lists of reputable therapists and agencies that can provide long-term assistance.

Help for the suicidal teenager after the attempt has been made often includes three essential ingredients: psychotherapy, preferably involving the family; antidepressant medication to ease the teen through the bleakness of a postsuicidal crisis; and a plan for crisis intervention so that another attempt either will not be made and/or will not succeed. Professional therapists can help teenagers to discover what they had been doing that they didn't really want to do, what obstacles have made it difficult to achieve goals, what happened to trigger depression. Therapists can also help teens discover ways of escaping from these problems by refocusing on more productive ways of coping based on individual strengths and talents. Such a process may take many months, and parents should not expect a miraculous overnight transformation. It is not easy, after all, to externalize problems and look at them objectively. Parent and teenager alike must come to believe that if a person has the courage to die as he or she chooses, that person should also have the courage to live as he or she chooses. Your teenager needs the family's love and support in order to develop the courage necessary to make the choice of life.

If Suicide Succeeds

The loss of a child is one of the most traumatic events parents may experience during their lives. When that loss is due to suicide, a number of emotions surface that complicate the normal grief process. The survivors of a successful suicide are often ashamed and may believe their family has been disgraced or tainted by the act of suicide itself. The shame is usually accompanied by a sense of confusion and much self-recrimination. Parents almost always blame themselves and are, in turn, subject to the blame of others. In the United States there is a tendency for families of suicides to isolate themselves, thus making it even harder for them to cope with the reality and pain of the teen's suicide. Suicidologists explain that the reason for such isolation has to do with our culture: since the only culturally acceptable motive for suicide seems to be altruism (for example, fasting to death for a political cause) and since most suicides are not motivated by altruism, the surviving family members receive little or no support from others in coping with their grief. As a result, they become mired down in an incessant search for explanations for what has happened, attempting to get over their guilt.

The grief process of suicide survivors is first marked by shock, disbelief, and horror that the actual form of death was self-imposed. Then, parents and other relatives may begin to feel rage and resentment against the child who has chosen this way out. Guilt is the next feeling to take hold: guilt about the anger they are experiencing, and guilt about the suicide act. There are situations where in the heat of an argument a parent may have wished his or her child dead when teenage-parent confrontations were particularly troublesome. If this teen actually commits suicide, such a parent is likely to feel more guilt and remorse than one would expect, and may need therapy to overcome these feelings. Unfortunately, grief is not always resolved in families of suicidal teens. Because of society's basic disapproval of suicide and the lack of support from outside sources for the survivors, the grief may grow over time rather than dissipate.

When a teen commits suicide, his or her survivors move to the center stage and the suicide recedes into the background. Siblings can be as adversely affected by the tragedy as are the parents: the siblings may be torn between loyalties to their dead brother or sister and the desire to ease things for their parents, to make up somehow for their family's pain and suffering. If help is not available, if social isolation continues for the family, then it is a real possibility that the survivors will themselves become suicidal.

The question of whether "suicide begets suicide" is an interesting one. If it is true that suicide survivors have a statistically greater risk of themselves dying from a self-inflicted act, then perhaps there is something in the family dynamics to make this true. One group of researchers suggests there is a genetic connection, another suggests that suicide is a learned behavior, a kind of deathly habit that can be picked up from close relatives. Others suggest that it is the suicidal person's behavior patterns that somehow become imprinted in the minds of other family members, waiting for the right moment to take hold. Some people suggest that families use a kind of scapegoating mechanism, consciously or unconsciously, to replace the suicide with a new "victim" who will be blamed for the suicide's death and, likewise, become suicidal. Whatever it is that actually happens to cause a suicide, the family must be helped, be allowed access to what one therapist calls "postvention." This involves the opportunity to air one's feelings and come to terms with the tragedy, *openly* in a noncensuring environment. It is critical if the lives of other family members are to be preserved and the family is to remain intact. Parents must be helped to realize that they aren't necessarily the heavies in the suicide drama, yet they must also be helped to assess realistically the parts they played in that drama.

What kind of treatment is best to help one deal with the aftermath of suicide is a question with no single answer. Treatment can be complicated because the outpourings of grief may ebb and flow with time. In addition, many therapists have found that suicide survivors may be quite resistant to treatment for as long as a year after the loved one's death. In some cases, self-help groups have been most effective in helping people express their grief. Family therapy and individual therapy are other alternatives that some find useful. The point is that if a suicide has touched your life, you must remember that you do not have to hide your grief or be alone with it. Give yourself permission to feel — rage, fear, misery, relief. You must feel before you can heal. You may ask the questions "Why?" or "What if?" — just don't allow them to dominate your life. A suicidal teenager is a manipulative person; do not allow his or her death to continue to manipulate your life. Seek help from any of the sources suggested above. If no self-help group exists in your area and you feel this is the right vehicle for your healing, then start one. You can obtain assistance for such a task from social service agencies, even your clergyman. Learn as much as you can about suicide: knowledge is a powerful tool for prevention. You may find it comforting to go out into the community and share your experiences, thus teaching others about teenage suicide. You might want to start by talking at your child's school, painful though it might be at first.

What counts is that you are able to turn the suicide, the grief, and the guilt into something positive for yourself, for others, and for the memory of your child. That memory need not be tarnished because of the nature of his or her death. You were not ultimately responsible for it and you should not allow that suicide to be a cross borne by you for the rest of your life.

22

How to Find (and Coexist with) Competent Professional Help

There are times when parents must come to grips with the fact that a teen's problems are either so troublesome or so out of control that the parents are powerless to help. This is not a sign of parental failure, but instead a sign of the adolescent's need. Nevertheless, some parents feel ashamed to admit that there's a difficulty they haven't been able to resolve, and they avoid seeking professional help until the problem escalates to a full-blown crisis situation. Others steer away from finding help for their teens because they mistakenly worry that a counselor or therapist will usurp their authority and pry into their lives. Sometimes, though, parents are relieved to call on an outsider for help. As one mother put it, "As soon as we'd made the decision to find a therapist, I felt like a huge weight was lifted from my shoulders."

Once the decision has been made to get professional help for a teen or family dealing with adolescent problems, it's not easy to know how to proceed. This chapter is a guide to locating a professional counselor or therapist and evaluating that person's credentials and competence, as well as providing helpful pointers on what therapy can and cannot do. Finally, some suggestions are given for dealing with your teen while he or she is getting help.

Recognizing When Outside Help Is Needed

Fourteen-year-old Ellen was creating constant conflicts with her parents. She talked on the telephone for hours at a time. She got

272

C's in school. She was crazy about boys and showed little interest in anything except her collection of rock 'n' roll records. She recently admitted to her parents that she'd been smoking marihuana for almost a year, and said she had no intention of stopping.

Fifteen-year-old Harold was a model of obedient behavior. An A— student who was also a top tennis player on his school team, Harry rarely disobeyed his parents or talked back to them. His strangest quirk was that he preferred eating by himself, so every night he carried dinner up to his room to study as he ate.

Ellen's parents were confused and angry over her behavior and thought they needed help to "straighten her out." But when they consulted their family physician, they were reassured that her "problems," although distressing, were a very normal part of growing up. Harold's parents, on the other hand, were oblivious to the serious problem he had. For months he had used the ploy of "taking dinner to his room" to go on a self-starvation diet of only 200 calories a day. Caught in the throes of anorexia nervosa, Harold eventually required hospitalization and intensive therapy.

As those two examples show, it isn't always easy to tell when outside help is required or even when a serious problem exists. Things are not always what they seem to be, and the rebellious, emotional outbursts of adolescence can be normal developmental milestones *or* signs of trouble. However, there *are* some ways of determining when your teen has a serious problem that requires outside help. These can be summarized as follows:

(1) Persistently reclusive behavior
(2) Self-destructive behavior (e.g., suicide attempts, use of dangerous drugs, dieting excessively)
(3) Precipitous changes in personality
(4) Marked deterioration in academic performance
(5) Compulsive behavior that interferes with everyday functioning
(6) Incapacitating fears or anxieties
(7) Repeated outbursts of violence or sadistic behavior
(8) Lack of contact with reality
(9) Very low self-esteem

In addition to these primary signals, parents should also be aware of other signs that trouble may be brewing. Is your teen caught in a cycle of repeated failures? This can be a sign of the "giving up" syndrome, in which teens stop trying because they believe they're doomed to failure anyway, so why make an effort to improve. Is your teen characteristically impulsive to the point of continually disregarding the consequences

of his or her behavior? Unbridled impulsiveness can have dire consequences — from teenage pregnancy to law-breaking to self-destructive
acts — so it needs to be tamed. Does your teen's "limit testing" take on
malicious overtones? Rebellion and reaction against parental authority
should be allowed to go only so far before you decide to take action. But
sometimes your action is disregarded completely — your teen acts as
though you didn't exist. Tolerating this type of situation is good neither
for your sanity nor for your teen's welfare.

There is another set of circumstances that should be a tip-off to you for
the need for outside help: when you can no longer communicate with
your teen without becoming overly emotional and punitive. No matter
how justified you may feel in your anger — and teenagers' parents can be
quite justified in being angry at times — you won't be able to handle
things effectively in this condition. When things have deteriorated in
your relations with your teen to the point that you are unable to act objectively, you must turn to a third party to mediate and relieve the tension.

Parents are never completely objective about their families, but
there's no reason to be ashamed of this natural fact. If you're questioning
whether your adolescent needs some form of counseling, there are two
other steps you can take to assist you in reaching a decision. The first is so
obvious that it's often overlooked: talk with your teen to find out how he
or she feels and whether he or she would like some outside help. One father was startled to hear his son say, "Gee, Dad, I've wanted to see someone but I didn't think we could afford it." The second option that can
also be pursued is to get a consultation for purposes of evaluation. This
gives you the benefit of someone else's perception of your teen's situation
and helps take the burden of decision-making off your shoulders.

Choosing and Using a Referral Source

Once the decision has been made to seek professional help, you
need to do some exploration. It's not usually advisable simply to pick out
a therapist's name from the Yellow Pages; instead, you'll do best by
seeking a referral to a competent, caring professional with special expertise in the area of your teen's difficulty. Referrals can either be obtained
informally — from talking with friends, colleagues at work, or relatives — or can be arranged on a more formal basis. Possible referral
sources of the latter type include your family physician, your child's physician, a school guidance counselor (or school psychologist), your clergyman, or even your lawyer. In addition, community resources may be
available that provide a referral network. Depending on the nature of
your teen's problem, a suicide hot line, a drug education program, or various self-help groups may be useful to contact.

Whatever type of referral source you use, be prepared to describe the situation, as you see it, in reasonably detailed terms. Is the problem pervasive or in one isolated area of your teen's life? Is it of relatively recent duration or has it been present for a long while? What impact is it having on your family? Why do you think counseling or therapy is called for right now?

Furthermore, don't accept the referral you are given without doing some questioning on your own. Here are three things you may want to ask about specifically:

(1) Do you know the person you're recommending by reputation only or have you worked with him or her in the past?

(2) Have you made prior referrals to this person? If so, what happened?

(3) What special qualifications does this person have that makes him or her a good choice for working with my teen?

How to Evaluate Professional Credentials and Competence

Certificates and diplomas do not by themselves indicate good therapists, but finding out about a professional's background can help prevent you from sending your teen to see an unqualified person. If you are referred to someone who refuses to discuss his or her professional credentials with you, no matter what reason is given, make a hasty retreat and start over. If, on the other hand, the professional you are talking with gives you a synopsis of his or her credentials, here are a few things to keep in mind.

(1) *What graduate degrees has this person earned and what institution awarded them?* Graduate-level education is a decided plus for any counselor or therapist you're considering, but be certain that it was in a pertinent field. An M.B.A. or a Ph.D. in economics isn't very good preparation for counseling teens. Also, beware of degrees from schools you've never heard of. While these *might* be legitimate (you can check these out at the library, if you wish), there are many diploma mills that provide phony degrees for a price.

(2) *What postgraduate training has this person received?* Many academic centers provide an education based principally on theory. Practical training often comes after receiving a degree. In evaluating postgraduate credentials, be sure not to be fooled by fancy certificates that may indicate attendance at a two-day workshop. By itself, this is hardly the most rigorous training a person can get.

(3) *Is the person certified or licensed as a counselor or therapist?* While credentials of this sort don't guarantee competence, they are indications that at least minimal academic and training qualifications exist.

(4) *How much experience does this person have in working with adolescents and in dealing with the particular type of problem your teen has?* In general, it pays to be skeptical of someone who is either just out of training or who rarely works with teens unless you've got very good evidence of their competence (say, a rave review from your physician). Counselors or therapists who specialize in working with adolescents are usually much better choices than professionals who work primarily with adults.

(5) *Beware of counselors or therapists who offer guarantees that their approach will work.* No reputable professional would offer any sort of guarantee, since none can be given. There may be reason for an optimistic outlook — in fact, if a case seems hopeless most therapists would say so — but exaggerated claims of past success ("I've never had a failure in my practice") should alert your suspicions.

(6) *Pay attention to your intuitive judgment.* If you're not impressed by the counselor or therapist's demeanor, if he or she seems abrupt or uninterested, or if you don't feel confident about the person's approach, think hard before enlisting this person to help your teen. Such intuitive judgments often prove accurate.

There are a number of other considerations you may also wish to keep in mind that may not directly reflect on a counselor's or therapist's competence but have a lot to do with the type of help your teen will receive. For example, the value system the professional has may influence your teen's behavior — what kind of advice will be given about potentially troublesome areas like drugs or sex? In a more practical vein, what arrangements are there for availability of help to you or to your teen in emergencies? How often will counseling sessions be held? What policy is followed regarding confidentiality?

In the final analysis, there is no sure-fire way of picking a counselor or therapist who will mesh perfectly with your teen. There are talented, dedicated counselors who have no formal graduate degree, just as there are professionals with impeccable credentials who turn out to be duds. There are counselors and therapists whose personalities may suit you perfectly but are unacceptable to your teen, and others who rub you the wrong way but provide a perfect source of identification for your child. Remember, though, that in selecting a counselor or therapist for your adolescent there's nothing that prevents you from doing some comparison shopping before making up your mind.

One last word is in order. Since the whole purpose of selecting a competent professional is to benefit your teen, be sure to involve him or her in the search for a counselor or therapist. While teens may be resistant to the idea of seeking someone at first — especially if it's presented as a form of punishment or if they are frightened that they'll be told they're "crazy" — the chance to play a part in selecting their own therapist is hard to pass up.

A Layman's Guide to Sources of Help

Here's a brief rundown on the categories of professionals you're likely to encounter as you and your teen search for a counselor or therapist.

A *psychiatrist* has earned a medical degree and has taken specialized residency training for three or four years after medical school. Psychiatrists have two unique advantages over other types of therapists which may or may not be applicable to your teen. Because they are M.D.s, psychiatrists can prescribe drugs (which can be useful in treating depression or other severe emotional disorders) and can perform physical examinations and medical testing, which can detect underlying health problems that may not be readily apparent. In addition, psychiatrists can hospitalize adolescents when required, which most other therapists can't do.

A *psychologist* has earned a doctorate (either a Ph.D., Ed.D., or Psy.D.) and obtained postgraduate supervision as well. Some psychologists are specially trained in counseling or therapy; others have special capabilities in diagnostic (psychometric) testing, which can be helpful in evaluating your teenager's personality and mental health.

A *social worker* has completed a master's degree (M.S.W.) and usually received supervised clinical experience, as well. Social workers have been trained to analyze and work with emotional problems in a social context, so they're especially aware of family dynamics and peer group interactions.

Marriage and family therapists can have either doctorates or masters' degrees. They are specially trained to treat family problems and generally focus in their work on communications and the nature of relationships within the family.

In addition to these categories, there are several other types of helpers you might wish to consider. *Pastoral counselors* are members of the clergy with extra training in counseling techniques. *Alcohol and drug abuse counselors* may or may not have graduate degrees, but are specially trained to deal with substance abuse problems. Some of them — but not all — are ex-addicts or alcoholics themselves. *Psychiatric nurses* have masters' degrees and supervised experience in working with the emotionally disturbed.

In most instances, the category from which you choose a therapist or counselor is less important than the person's competence and ability to relate to your teen.

What to Expect from a Therapist

You have the right to expect the following things from your teen's counselor or therapist:

(1) An initial evaluation that is discussed with you;

(2) A general plan of treatment, including a tentative time-frame and the objectives being worked towards;

(3) Recommendations for you about handling problems with your teen while therapy is in progress;

(4) Periodic reports on your teen's progress or lack of progress;

(5) A clear description of fees and charges.

You should *not* expect these things, however:

(1) A magical, instantaneous cure;

(2) Discussions of the content of sessions with your teen that divulge confidential information;

(3) Having the therapist be a person who will listen to *your* problems and anxieties and suggest what you should do;

(4) Having therapy take the place of parental responsibility.

Ten Ways to Complicate Therapy (Plus Ten Ways to Help Out)

(1) Disagree with everything your teen's therapist says.

(2) Condemn your teen's therapist for being too lenient, too strict, or too wishy-washy.

(3) Accuse your teen of wasting your money in therapy.

(4) Be secretive about any communications you have with the therapist. Give your teen the sense that you and the therapist are in a conspiracy together.

(5) Compete with the therapist for your teen's loyalty and admiration.

(6) Delegate all parental responsibility to the therapist.

(7) Encourage your teen to become dependent on the therapist; quash any attempts at independent thinking.

(8) Find out exactly what was said in every therapy session — after all, you're paying for them.

(9) Constantly test your teen to see if he or she is emotionally stable.

(10) Threaten to stop therapy if you don't see faster results.

If these ways of complicating your teen's therapy sound unappealing, perhaps you'd rather choose from the following list instead. It's designed to facilitate things rather than cause interference.

(1) Respect the therapist's viewpoint even if it differs from your own.

(2) Instead of condemning the therapist, appreciate the fact that a responsible adult is trying to help your teen.

(3) Be open and honest in telling your teen about any discussions you've had with the therapist unless you've been specifically prohibited from doing so.

(4) Don't try to compete with the therapist for your teen's response; instead, realize that you occupy very different positions in your teen's life.

(5) Be a positive role model who demonstrates appropriate, responsible behavior for your teen — don't say one thing and do another.

(6) Realize that your role as parent isn't abdicated when your teen is in therapy.

(7) Promote responsible independence in your teen whenever possible.

(8) Don't pry into the content of therapy. If your teen wants you to know what was said, he or she will tell you.

(9) Don't provoke your teen into fights or rebelliousness. Try to maintain cordial, stable relations.

(10) Don't threaten termination of therapy as a kind of punishment Both you and your teen might wind up losers.

While counseling and therapy are no panaceas, they provide comfort, support, and guidance that can be critically important in straightening out an adolescent's woes. Parents should see the counselor or therapist as their ally, working towards the common goal of a stable, happier teen who can become a trouble-free adult.

23

Calling the Police

The standard image of police as callous law enforcers is not an accurate description of their relationship to parents who call for help with their teenagers. Police can be allies, providing the structure within which a problem can begin to be solved — as when a teen is missing and the police implement the initial steps needed to locate the child. Police can serve as counselors — as when they are called in the heat of a family argument and help defuse the immediate tension by serving as mediators in a debate. Police can be providers of emergency health care — as when a teenager who is threatening suicide cannot be dissuaded by parents and may already be suffering from self-inflicted wounds. Calling the police, then, does not always signal that a teenager has committed a crime. It does signal a crisis situation and the fact that parents may be powerless at that moment to deal rationally and effectively with it. Certainly, there is no shame in asking for help to try to prevent a more serious crisis developing from an existing one.

Analyzing a Difficult Decision (and Its Consequences)

Parents call the police about their teens in two different types of situations. In some cases, there is no other option, as when a life-threatening situation exists (a teen is high on angel dust, has stolen a shotgun, and is threatening to kill his sister, who he thinks is a witch). In other cases, parents who have been struggling with an adolescent's misbehaviors for some time finally reach a boiling point from which there seems no turning back, as in the following example. A teen has been warned repeatedly to stop harassing a former girlfriend but continues to do so, now adding physical intimidation to what had been a phone and letter campaign. Nothing his parents have done has succeeded in changing his behavior and they can't afford psychiatric help. Requesting the intervention of the police represents a difficult decision for the parents of any teenager regardless of whether the adolescent is an incorrigible who lacks good judgment and a reasonable sense of right and wrong, or whether the teen is actually committing criminal acts.

To help make the decision about the appropriateness of police intervention, and to anticipate the consequences if they do (or don't) call, parents should consider the following questions.

(1) *What is the nature of the offense?* There is a big difference between a verbal threat and actual physical abuse. One-time adolescent pranks are not the same as repeated, wanton destruction of property. Drinking a few bottles of beer is not as serious as taking a bottle of sleeping pills.

(2) *Is anyone or anything endangered as a result of this activity?* Your answer should include an assessment of degree of danger and whether the teen is endangering his or her own safety and well-being.

(3) *Are the standards I am using to judge the seriousness of the behavior reasonable or perhaps too strict?* Police will not step in if the adolescent's "crime" is violating the family curfew on two consecutive weekends. They might need to become involved if your teen has a pattern of nightly curfew violations accompanied by drunkenness and property destruction.

(4) *What are the worst things that could happen to my teen and my family if I called the police?* Some of the consequences might be: your teen could be arrested, sent to a juvenile correction facility, put on probation, or sent to an adult jail. Your family could be embarrassed by negative publicity. Your other family members and friends could make you feel guilty, disloyal to your own kin; you could be labeled stool pigeons. Your teen might come to hate you and refuse to speak to you. You might create a permanent rift in the family. People might judge you by your teen's actions and assume you were inadequate parents. You might be ostracized by people you thought were your friends. You might be investigated by the police.

(5) *Could anything positive happen if I called the police?* Some of the consequences might be: you would be admired by family and friends for your courage to face the problem and do something constructive to solve it. Your teen would respect you (perhaps begrudgingly) for standing up to him or her. Your teen will stop the objectionable activity because it is now clear you mean business — that is, by calling the police you have

shocked the teen into recognizing the need to change the behavior and the consequences if he or she doesn't. Your friends will rally around you to help get you through the crisis. The police will actually help you solve the crisis. Your teen may be placed under court custody but will benefit from contact with a court-appointed probation officer, or from a court-instituted rehabilitation program. You too will gain access to sources of assistance that you may not have known about. You might get involved with other parents of teenage offenders and find strength and support from discussing your experiences and sharing your solutions. You may actually save your teen's life or your own.

This kind of analysis should make it clear when the potential benefits of contacting the police will outweigh the negative ramifications of your action. If you have exhausted all other options and feel you are being realistic about what the police can do, as well as being cognizant of what they might do to your teen, go ahead and make the call.

Facing up to Reality

There comes a moment in every crisis situation when parents must face the reality that there is no more they can accomplish by themselves, that their teenager is impossible to control, is incorrigible, or worse, a criminal. That moment is painful because it in some ways defines the parent-child relationship and the direction it is about to take, much as the moment when your teen gets into the car to drive away to college marks a transition that is about to occur in how you will relate to your child. In a way, the police take over the parents' functions — much as a college does — by temporarily becoming the teen's primary source of direction and rules.

Facing up to reality may be different for different families. For some, to be able to finally admit that the problem requires police intervention may be cathartic — a release of previously unspoken fears and tensions, accompanied by a feeling of hope. For others, the reality may be much bleaker — accompanied by dread and shame, especially if the teen has committed a criminal act that practically guarantees incarceration of some kind should the police be called in. For still others, it represents just one more problem to be solved in their lives and doesn't have much of an emotional impact.

Parents must also face up to the reality that there are limits to what the police will be able to do for their teens. Law enforcement officers are not therapists or miracle workers. Police intervention — while it can bring back a runaway teen and arrange for family counseling — will not reverse the physical damage done to her body by the four self-induced abortions demanded by her pimp while she was a prostitute. Nor can police intervention magically erase the years of arguing and aggravation caused in a family by an incorrigible teen's malicious activities.

To try to ease the trauma to all family members — offending teen included — when that moment of reality hits and it is clear that the police are needed, parents should be aware that the following things may occur:

(1) *You may experience a sense of panic.* Since you don't routinely deal with the police, you may have fears of what they can do to you, temporarily forgetting your rights and forgetting that they are coming as a result of your request.

(2) *You may feel guilty and wish you hadn't called.* There is always the temptation to want to protect your child and give him or her one more chance. This feeling is especially strong right after you make that call to the police. You may feel as if you are the guilty party. Resist these temptations to blame yourself. If the police come and you have changed your mind, you can always say it was a mistake, tell them thank you, and continue on as you were. Just remember the boy who cried "Wolf" — you may find you need the police at some other time, and they may not be as likely to respond quickly should you repeat the calling-denying pattern too often.

(3) *Your teen may beg you not to call or try to convince you to change your mind.* You are the adult who is in control at the point of the call. It may be the first time you have shown your teen you are capable of making a decision and going ahead with it. If your adolescent is used to having weak parents who can be intimidated, your new strength may be frightening, and he or she may try desperately to regain the control. The call to the police may be the most important thing you can do to improve the reality of the situation. Don't back down just when you are exhibiting strength and the courage of your convictions.

(4) *You may experience an incredible sense of calm.* Knowing you are about to have an immediately recognizable source of authority on your side can be very reassuring.

Facing up to the realities of having an impossible teenager and a family situation that is miserable is very difficult. You should not expect to feel euphoric about your decision, but you should give yourself credit for taking action. By facing up to reality yourself, you provide a positive role model for your teen to do the same. The police are going to be there to help you do it.

Stealing

Many parents tolerate their children's pilfering of small items and may even encourage a pattern of stealing without realizing it. The dad who tells his son that it's OK to rip up a piece of the ball park's Astroturf following their team's World Series win, the mother who encourages her daughter to put a few of the beauty salon's hair clips into her purse since "we can't get them in the store and we've paid a bundle for the haircut anyway," the father who brings home typing paper and ribbons from the office "since the supply room is overstocked and no one will miss them," the parents who bring home souvenir towels from the plush hotel they stayed at in Boston are all partly responsible for their teen's behavior should stealing become a problem.

Like any other adolescent misbehavior, stealing has degrees of seriousness apart from any moral considerations of right or wrong. Sneaking into the movies or dropping a slug into the subway turnstile are examples of the most modest form of stealing. Isolated instances of shoplifting are also relatively low on the seriousness scale and may represent a form of teenage bravado more than criminal intent. Often, a group of teens hanging around a shopping center for an afternoon all decide to play a perverse version of the game of "chicken," attempting to see who can pilfer the most items in a given time without getting scared or getting caught. This doesn't necessarily mean your teen is a criminal, but it does mean he or she is vulnerable to peer pressure and has terribly poor judgment. It may also be the first step in a loosening of self-control that occurs in teens who are predisposed to stealing bigger things in more dangerous situations. Parents rarely call in the police when shoplifting is an issue — they often don't know about it, they don't think it serious if they do, or the store's security force takes the teen to task and the parents don't need to call the police since the kid is in trouble already.

If parents do feel the need to bring in the police — because the teen's shoplifting has increased in frequency, or it places the teen in dangerous situations, or by bringing stolen goods home the teen is endangering the welfare of other family members — then they must have evidence to prove their teen's guilt, and they should know exactly what they want to accomplish by notifying the police. Do they want to scare their kid or do they want the teen in a rehabilitation program? Are they afraid to get help from other sources such as psychological counselors because they are worried that the counselor might discover their part in the teen's behavior? Do they realize their teen might get a permanent police record and that it could negatively affect that kid's future? Or do they believe that unless the police step in at that moment, the teen will have no future? These issues must be thought through prior to calling the authorities.

More serious forms of stealing are those that are premeditated acts involving breaking and entering, violations of others' rights (e.g., muggings and armed robberies), and threats of or actual violence. Teenagers who commit such crimes often need money to support drug habits or pay off gambling debts, and couldn't care less about the goods they steal except as ways of getting quick cash through a fence.

Parents of such teenagers must proceed with caution if they are thinking of notifying the police. These kids are dangerous, and if they suspect what their parents are up to they might run, or worse, might turn on their parents. Once again, evidence is needed — absolute proof that the teen committed a crime. Sometimes notifying the police and providing them with information about your teen's habits, associates, and hangouts, will give the police enough leads to stake out your teen's probable next target. The reality of our court system is that it is so overloaded with juvenile offenders that unless the police can apprehend a teen during or immediately after a crime has been committed, the likelihood of prosecution is very poor. And if your purpose is to help your teen break the cycle of crime by calling in the police, you must realize it might not work unless you do your homework first.

What if your teenager steals from the family itself? A son charges $400 worth of clothes on his family's MasterCard and sells them to a friend for $100 so he can buy his girlfriend a necklace without his mother finding out. A daughter needs money for a trip to Washington, D.C., during spring break, and her parents say it is unnecessary and refuse to help her pay for it. She pawns her mother's favorite gold bracelet to get enough cash to reserve her place on the trip. These sorts of things go on all the time, and some parents consider them to be offenses serious enough to warrant police intervention. However, this is one area where calling the police may not work, since domestic arguments of this nature are considered by law enforcement officials to be family matters that are better resolved without police involvement.

Stealing is no joke. Your teenager should be held accountable for his or her actions regardless of whether the deed is low or high on the scale of seriousness. Sometimes calling the police can break the incipient cycle of crime, but it won't solve the problems underlying the child's need to steal.

The Battered Parent

Battered children have become the focus of an intense national awareness effort. Battered wives are finding help from courts that are increasingly sympathetic to their plight and shelters are springing up nationwide to provide temporary housing and counseling to such women and their children. We know of no such programs to aid battered parents, however. But the reality is that adolescents do abuse their own parents — sometimes frequently and savagely — yet this major problem is something still shrouded in silence and shame.

Who are the battered parents? What kinds of families produce children who would physically endanger their parents? According to Families Anonymous, a self-help group whose members are parents of troubled adolescents, children who abuse their parents typically come from families where there is much verbal abuse in addition to other forms of physical abuse, often between siblings or between parents. Psychotherapists are in general agreement that love is absent or severely restricted in the relationship of victimized parent and abusing teen, and the frustration that results from this emotional void can lead the teen to lash out physically.

Often, an attack against a parent may be provoked by a minor disagreement.

> Carolyn was going out on a date and asked if she could borrow her sister's loafers. When her sister refused, Carolyn started screaming at her. Their mother came in and asked them what was going on. When she suggested that Carolyn wear her own Docksiders, Carolyn threw the loafers at her mother from two feet away, hitting her in the eye and causing a gash that required stitches.

Sometimes an attack may be provoked by the parent's own aggression

> Jonathan came home from the barber with a streak of orange in the front of his hair. Proud of his punk look, and feeling very "with it," he interrupted his dad (who was talking on the phone) to find out what he thought. His father, infuriated at being interrupted in the first place, and horrified at his son's appearance, cursed and slapped him in the face. The son retaliated immediately by grabbing the phone receiver and smashing his father in the mouth, knocking out a front tooth.

And sometimes an act may seem unprovoked. Whatever the apparent reason, no teen should have so little self-control that he or she would abuse a parent. But then again, the same is true of parents. Family violence of this sort can ruin everyone's lives and set a precedent for future generations to repeat the pattern.

What recourse do parents have? They can meet violence with violence, if they are physically matched, but there are no winners in this sort of brutal competition. They can accept being battered — which lets their teens act irresponsibly, without control. Or they can set boundaries and enforce them — they will not allow the teen to remain at home, they will try to commit the teen to a mental institution, they will require the entire family to attend family therapy, they will call the police.

As with stealing, family violence is an area the police don't usually want to get involved in for purposes of prosecution. Of course, they will respond to an emergency call if your teen is beating you up and another family member calls. But generally, such things are classified as domestic matters. Families Anonymous members report that many shared the experience of filing assault and battery charges against their teens, only to have the police make them feel guilty for doing so. But if you really feel you are endangered by your teen, by all means file charges. The police can help if you are persistent and can convince them (and yourself) that you have no other options.

Dealing Drugs

Many parents turn their heads when they find out their teens are peripherally involved in the drug scene — a kid smokes pot on weekends, "borrows" some of Mom's Valiums to calm down after a hard exam, "investigates" what cocaine is like at a friend's party. It is not easy, however, to turn your head if you find out your teenager is a drug dealer. Parents can rationalize their child's taking drugs by saying the teen is merely bending to peer pressure and not harming anyone else; but dealing drugs clearly affects other people, potentially endangers lives, and can expose the teenage dealer to a world of crime and violence. That is hard to rationalize.

When an adolescent is dealing, parents may become so distraught that they decide to contact the police. Their reasons may vary: they don't want drugs in their home since they worry about their own reputations as well as about the welfare of their teen; they believe that since drugs are illegal only the police can be counted on to track down the teen's source and prevent further drug deals from occurring. They may fear for their own lives, expecting gangster types to show up demanding the money from their teen, and perhaps annihilating them all should the teen fail to sell all of the drug allotment. They may fear their teen, especially knowing the cumulative effects some drugs have on a person's ability to control impulses.

If parents call the police, they must be willing to tell them what they know. Police will not be able to come to a person's house and confiscate drugs unless they have obtained a search warrant and no evidence will be admissable in court without this search warrant.

In criminal matters such as drug dealing, the police aren't likely to be as supportive to the teen as they would be if they were asked to help locate a runaway. If your teen is dealing drugs and you report him or her, you are practically ensuring that an arrest will follow, and a criminal record be established. Parents must be willing to face these harsh realities if they choose to call the authorities, but sometimes there's no other choice.

When Your Teen Gets in Trouble with the Law

What do you do if you're sitting at home watching television on a Friday night and you get a call from the police saying your teen has been picked up and is being held at the station? First — don't panic. Find out what's happened and why your teen is being held. Was there an accident? A crime? Was your teen directly involved or is he or she being held as a witness or accomplice? Are formal charges being brought? Next, you must decide if an attorney is needed. Unless you are absolutely certain that your teen is not in trouble or in danger of being charged with a crime, hire a lawyer right away. A lawyer can advise you and your teen immediately and take direct action to protect your teen's rights. If necessary, a lawyer can arrange bail as soon as possible. This is no small matter, because there are dozens of instances each year where a teen who has had no previous problems with police commits suicide out of despair in the first few hours after being arrested. In addition, teens placed in prisons — even briefly — may be raped or beaten by other inmates. Lawyers can also facilitate communications with the police or the court and can help the family understand the complicated workings of the legal system.

Our American system of justice makes the assumption that a person is innocent until proven guilty, and you should be willing to adopt this stance too unless the evidence against your teen is overwhelming. As shocked or disappointed as you might be — or as frustrated, if you saw this coming — now is no time to desert your teen. Family solidarity is called for. Understandably, however, the circumstances of your teen's problems will color your reaction — stealing a car is one thing, murder is quite another. If the nature of the alleged crime is flabbergasting to you, it may be necessary to get help for yourself by seeing your doctor or a crisis counselor who's trained for handling emergency situations.

What happens next will depend in part on the criminal justice system, your teen's age, the seriousness of the offense, and your teen's prior record. Your attorney can help steer you through this complicated time in ways that space doesn't permit us to discuss. But after some form of resolution has been reached — charges get dropped, your teen is found innocent, your teen is found guilty but released to your care, your teen is put on probation, or your teen is incarcerated — you must still formulate a plan for what happens next. Fortunately, a brush with the law may frighten your teen into walking the straight and narrow. One amazed mother put it this way, "Now all I can say is that I wish he'd been arrested when he was younger. It turned him into a new person overnight." But all too often, improvement — if any — is only temporary, and the teen becomes a repeat offender. The following steps can minimize this possibility, however:

(1) Get professional help in analyzing why your teen has gotten in trouble with the law. This may entail legal advice, consultation with school personnel, and psychiatric or psychological evaluation.

(2) Get your adolescent involved in counseling or therapy. (It's amazing what a good therapist can accomplish in helping troubled teens change their lives around.)

(3) Be a forgiving parent, not a constantly condemning one. But set firm limits and enforce them strictly.

(5) If your teen is on probation, be sure he or she fulfills all necessary requirements. Talk frequently with the probation officer to see exactly what's going on.

(6) Insist that your teen break off with friends who have criminal records. This must be a nonnegotiable item, so you'll need to make the consequences of defying you on this one severe, such as taking away your teen's driver's license or confining your teen to your home on weekends.

(7) Help your teen decide on clear goals for his or her life and encourage working towards these.

(8) Provide a family atmosphere of love, acceptance, and cooperation rather than one of dissonance and rejection.

Even if you try to follow these pointers, you may not succeed in rehabilitating your teen. You can't feel too guilty about this if you've really made the effort, though. There comes a time when it's necessary to admit that your best efforts may not be enough — when your teen has chosen a way of living that is beyond your control and even beyond your understanding.

PART FOUR

Positive Parenting Revisited

24

Going to Bat for Your Kids

Going to bat for their kids is something all parents do in varying degrees throughout their children's lives. When you stop another toddler from throwing sand at your three-year-old in the playground, you are going to bat; when you step in to coach a Little League team whose real coach is ill so your child and others can compete in the championships, you are going to bat; when you agree to pay for music lessons for a teen who wants desperately to be a professional pianist (though you wish she'd become a doctor), you are going to bat.

Other situations arise during adolescence, however, that call for a different sort of parental involvement. These "going to bat" situations can be roughly divided into two categories — those that involve injustice victimizing your teen, and those that involve special types of opportunity. In either case, "going to bat" describes your willingness and ability to act on behalf of your child in situations largely beyond his or her control.

Parents as Advocates and Agents

Parents act as advocates for their teens by doing things that preserve and protect their teenagers' rights. This parental role is somewhat like a lawyer's in that it may involve defending the teen against unjust accusations or lodging protests when your teen is being discriminated against. Fortunately, active advocacy is not needed very often during the day-to-day life of most adolescents.

Acting as an agent for your teen is somewhat different. Here, parents try to act on their child's behalf to create a special opportunity that otherwise might not exist. For instance:

> Dr. Larsen knows that his eleventh-grade daughter is interested in science and calls the laboratory director at a local hospital to arrange an unpaid summer job in which his daughter will learn to do basic clinical chemistry analyses. Had she gone in to ask for such a job by herself, she would have been turned down right away.
>
> Mrs. Golden's son is trying to organize a fund-raising dinner to buy new equipment for the school gymnastics team. His mother contacts a friend at the local radio station, who arranges to have Tom Seaver as the guest speaker and provides free publicity for the event.
>
> Carol Webster is a seventeen-year-old aspiring writer whose short stories have been rejected everywhere they've been sent. Her mother asks a cousin who's a literary agent to look at the stories, and with his help Carol finds a small literary magazine that accepts her work and asks to see more.

As these examples show, parents acting as agents can help their teens in innumerable ways. The payoff is not just to the teen, either; such "agenting" gives parents a sense of satisfaction and the knowledge that they've contributed meaningfully to their child's success. Furthermore, teens are apt to have renewed respect for parental capabilities when the agent's role works out.

When and How to Help

Helping your teenagers by going to bat for them is a far more complicated process than lending them money, letting them borrow the family car, or offering good old-fashioned advice. You must involve yourself directly in your child's problem, and that's not always easy to do.

Deciding when to go to bat for your teen involves a number of different considerations. First, you need to assess the seriousness of the situation. There's no need to make a big fuss over a trivial matter, even if it seems unfair or unpleasant to your child. Second, you should be sure that you go to bat only with your teen's knowledge and consent. Otherwise, it may seem that you're being manipulative. Third, you should avoid going to bat to fulfill your own needs rather than your child's — your help of this sort may be unwanted. Finally, you need to be certain that in going to bat for your teens you're not depriving them of the chance to achieve something by themselves. Your purpose is to *assist* your teens, not take on their responsibilities.

Adolescents' requests for parental help with homework assignments provide a perfect example for discussion. There's nothing wrong with being a resource person for your teens. By all means, show them how to use the card catalogue in the library, or help them organize a bibliography for their history paper. But don't be so concerned with your teens' grades that you wind up doing their work. It may be interesting to learn about the use of humor in Mark Twain's novels as a reflection of nineteenth-century American social mores by writing your teen's term paper, but your enthusiasm and generosity gives your teen the message that it's OK to cheat. Beyond this, the teen also learns that it's easy to beat the system if you can get someone else to do your work for you. Even if it's not schoolwork that you're tampering with — whether it involves working on merit badges needed for Eagle Scout status, doing the science fair display your teen is too busy to complete, or writing a college application essay for your teen — it's both dishonest and counterproductive to do your teen's work and it's the wrong way to help.

What about situations where your teen has been unfairly treated and you must function as an advocate? Here are a few guidelines that can be useful:

1. Talk with your teen to learn as much as possible about the situation.

2. Find out what your teen wants to do — and why.

3. Decide if your teen's assessment of the problem is accurate and realistic.

4. When necessary, acquire additional factual information, researching relevant issues as though you were preparing a legal brief.

5. Consult with experts who can provide facts and viewpoints to enhance your case.

6. Develop strategies based on the previous steps to maximize the chances that your advocacy will be successful. Whom do you need to talk to? Will a letter be more persuasive than a phone call? What will you do if your first attempt at change doesn't produce the desired result?

7. If your choice of strategy involves personal contact, take time to rehearse what you're going to say and how you'll say it. If possible, have someone you respect role-play the situation with you to help you anticipate what might happen.

8. Be diplomatic. Advocacy conducted in anger is apt to be ineffective and can aggravate the situation until it's even worse than when you stepped in. If you're not in control of your emotions, you can't be of much help.

9. Never intervene in a way designed to embarrass or humiliate your teen.

With these points in mind, we'll turn to a consideration of several specific types of situations in which advocacy may be required.

Dealing with School Personnel

Teachers and administrators are professional people and don't like to be treated as though they were slaves or servants. School personnel feel as strongly about the ways they conduct their business as you feel about how they deal with your teens. Since they spend many more hours a day in direct contact with adolescents than you probably do, their perspective is not only different from yours but may actually be more accurate. School personnel are not uniformly patient, pleasant, competent, or fair, but they try to do their best and appreciate being treated as professionals.

When you have to go to bat for your teens by dealing with school personnel, it is very important that you have your facts straight. If your teen is complaining that Mrs. Rose assigns fifty pages of reading a night in English class and it's impossible to keep up, you need first to do your own homework. You may discover that the class is doing a unit on children's literature, and that the assignment is to read fifty pages (approximately two books) of Dr. Seuss each night for a week. On the other hand, if the fifty pages are in *The Rise and Fall of the Roman Empire,* your teen may have a legitimate gripe.

The two most common complaints teens voice about their teachers are "My teacher doesn't like me" and "My teacher is unfair." While these complaints are sometimes exaggerations or cover-ups for poor academic performance, there are times when the teen may be right. Useful questions to consider here include: Is your teen getting an uncharacteristically low mark? Do others in the class have the same complaint? Is there objective evidence of a conflict with one particular teacher?

> Kyle, an honor-roll student who was active on several varsity teams, unexpectedly got a C+ from his English teacher in the first semester of his junior year. When his parents called to discuss this, the teacher indicated that Kyle's grade was lowered because he had missed several classes as a result of the basketball team's traveling schedule (legitimate absences according to school policy). When the teacher refused to reconsider her position, the parents spoke to the principal of the school, who arranged a conference. The teacher was instructed to raise Kyle's grade and Kyle was transferred to a different English section for the second semester.

Unfortunately, there are various ways in which teachers treat students unfairly. In one classic example we learned about recently, a Catholic boy was ridiculed in front of his history class by a teacher who had seen him picketing outside an abortion clinic. Suddenly, the student began getting low grades on papers and essay exams in this class, prompting the parents to meet with the guidance counselor to seek a solution. At first confronted by denial of any prejudice on the part of the teacher, the parents made their case convincingly by having witnesses to the teacher's classroom harangue, showing that the drop in grades began immediately after this occurrence, and producing the actual papers to prove that they merited higher grades than they had received.

Dealing with school personnel can be tricky because parents rarely have the same insights into their teen's personality and academic capability as do teachers. You may think your son is brilliant but his teachers see him as a clown. You may write off your daughter's lack of interest in homework because you know she's not college-bound, while her teachers think she is gifted but not working up to her potential and are frustrated in their attempts to get her to produce. Therefore, when you decide to deal with teachers or administrators, be prepared to share your perceptions of your teen prior to solving any problems you have come to complain about.

When you deal with school personnel, be prepared for individual differences. Not all teachers or administrators appreciate parental involvement equally — some feel threatened and may be put on the defensive, while others will use your concern as permission to contact you with every little triumph or setback of the teen. Most school professionals fall somewhere in between. Don't be put off by an abrasive personality or seduced by an overly friendly one. Your goal is to help your teen solve some problem at school, and you must not let personality factors of others unduly impede or influence you.

Parents of exceptional children — whether they are physically or mentally handicapped, have behavior problems, or are extremely gifted or talented — are more likely to have to go to bat for their kids and remain actively involved with school personnel than are parents of teens who don't have exceptional needs. In such cases, involvement equals "monitoring" — making sure the kids are actually getting the special schooling they are entitled to (see Chapter 11) and being willing to be active advocates if they aren't. Under these circumstances, parents shouldn't worry that they are going to be perceived as adversaries or that school personnel will resent their demands, because too often special students cannot or will not speak up for themselves and parents must do it for them.

Whatever actions you take, cooperation and a realistic understanding of what teachers and administrators can and can't do for your teens are the keys to productive outcomes.

Dealing with Other Authority Figures

Teenagers come in contact with many different authority figures in their lives who are neither parents nor teachers. Among those included in this group are clergy, coaches, friends' parents, scout leaders, community leaders, politicians, employers, police, and volunteer workers. Obviously, some of these authority figures are in positions that demand a kind of protocol. Right or wrong, the reality is that a teen may be expected to be more sedate or circumspect in the presence of a priest than in the presence of his softball coach. Teens tend to get into difficulty when they don't know appropriate ways to behave or perform in different situations with different adults and, as a result, can get into trouble because their actions are misinterpreted.

> Gary was a french-fry cook at a fried chicken restaurant and was accused by the manager of making snide remarks about him. Gary denied the remarks were snide, and told the manager he was making a big deal out of nothing. He tried to come back to work the next two nights but was barred from entering the door. Gary finally told his parents about what happened and agreed to let them help.

Gary's parents contacted the franchise's district supervisor to obtain facts about employee rights and employment policies to prepare themselves for a meeting with the manager of the restaurant. By having a game plan and doing their homework, they were acting as responsible advocates determined to search for a reasonable and equitable solution. During their meeting, they were informed that Gary's behavior had negatively affected the morale of other workers. If he brought a written apology the next day, though, he could come back to work on a probationary basis until he could prove himself to be a reliable worker. Gary's parents were pleased with the outcome, and wrote letters to the manager and the supervisor thanking them for their assistance in clarifying and solving the problem.

Had this not resulted in problem resolution, Gary's parents might have chosen to be more aggressive advocates. They might have lodged a formal, written complaint with the district supervisor, taken the issue to a labor relations arbitration board, or hired a lawyer to present their son's case. If none of this had solved their problem, and they had proof that Gary had been denied due process and was treated unfairly, they might even have arranged a local boycott of the restaurant or contacted the media to draw attention to their plight. Usually, such extreme measures are suggested only if the problems your teens face involve serious breaches of ethics, or rights, or are clear-cut examples of bias or violence against the adolescents. Unfortunately, aggressive advocacy can be an emotionally draining way of helping your kids, and there are no guarantees you'll win.

Going to bat for your teen when you are dealing with other authority figures can be complicated by several factors. A coach or a volunteer worker is likely to be a lay person with no particular training or expertise in youth leadership other than a desire to work with kids. If they are put in charge of large groups that they can't control, or don't know how to implement their authority, they can become the teens' adversaries out of frustration at their own ineptitude rather than because the kids are really bad. Therefore, when you attempt to intervene on your teen's behalf, it may seem like the blind leading the blind. Frequently, adult authority figures assume that the teens they work with know what is expected of them when in fact, they don't. Carole, a fourteen-year-old candy-striper in a hospital, assumed she should go into the intensive care unit with her magazine cart because her trainer (also a volunteer) never told her not to. The uproar this caused among the nursing staff sent Carole running out of the building in tears. When her parents complained about their daughter's experience, they got nowhere since the trainer said all candy-stripers were expected to know enough to stay off the critical care floors.

You can help your teen deal with other adult authority figures by making them aware that such problems exist. Together you might choose to do some fact-finding. If you want to let your daughter go on an overnight scouting trip, make sure the leaders are fully trained according to scouting policies. If you have any doubts, talk to the leaders or volunteer yourself. If your child wants to get involved in youth group activities, make sure you all know how much time this will take from their school or work responsibilities, and what the policy is for missing meetings, or how much emphasis is placed on group participation rather than individual achievement. Prepare your teen to troubleshoot in advance rather than having to rely on you to act as a parental advocate after a problem has occurred.

Maximizing Your Teen's Opportunities

A Catch-22 lurks in the very concept of maximizing your teen's opportunities. By doing anything to enhance your teen's chances for success, you may inadvertently short-circuit his or her chances to learn and grow from doing things independently of you. Whenever you attempt to maximize your teen's opportunities, you must exercise restraint and good judgment. It is one of the most difficult tasks of parenting an adolescent.

Many parents try to help their teens by coaching them about etiquette, appearance, the "proper" ways to speak, and things they should speak about in order to impress people. For some families, providing this sort of training is all they do to help maximize their teens' opportunities. They assume that once the basic information is in place, it is up to the teens to do something with it.

Other parents try to use their connections to get preferential treatment for their children. Getting the teen a summer job at your office, doing a favor for someone in the hopes that someday you can collect on the favor and use it to your child's advantage, donating money to your alma mater year after year so your teen will be accepted even if less than an academic whiz kid are some of the ways parents try to maximize their children's opportunities.

Better ways, though, are those that enhance teens' self-confidence and self-esteem, and give them chances to develop many skills and polish some to near-perfection. Many parents make major financial sacrifices to give their teens skating or dancing lessons, hoping it will prepare them for unique and profitable careers like those of Dorothy Hamill and Gelsey Kirkland. Parents who allow their teens to get really involved in an all-consuming passion — whether horses, cooking, archeology, or weight-lifting — are helping their teens to see that it is possible to become the best they can at something, to see projects through to completion, and to make contacts and earn a reputation for excellence in the process. Teaching teens to write a résumé for a position they really want, and to have the confidence to sell themselves is more useful in the long run than getting that job for them and hoping it will work out.

Your Role in the College Admissions Process

Like many things in life, the college admissions process requires careful advance planning, so don't think you can start the summer before your adolescent's senior year. If your teen has taken a three-year curriculum that's heavy on basket-weaving and commercial art but deficient in English, math, and foreign language, you won't be able to remedy the situation easily. So during your child's sophomore year of high school begin familiarizing yourself with the requirements of colleges your teen might like to attend.

Next, recognize that while the better colleges want to see good grades, high school courses shouldn't be chosen just because they're easy. One Ivy League admissions officer told us, "We'd rather take a student with a B+ average who's taken several honors courses than a student with an A average in regular classes who's refused to challenge himself." While you shouldn't push teens into signing up for advanced courses that are too difficult for them, taking the easy route doesn't give students a competitive edge when college applications are sent in.

One useful strategy is to enroll your adolescent in a summer school course at a nearby college. This type of experience can serve several different purposes. It can allow a teen to focus on an academic area they haven't done particularly well in (without other courses to distract them, they may be able to demonstrate proficiency). Or a summer course at college can be an opportunity to pursue some special interest — computer programming, art history, archeology — that isn't available in your high school. If the teen gets a good grade, this can be sent to the colleges he or she applies to and provides them with notice that the teen is ready to handle college-level work. (If the grade isn't very good, you aren't under any obligation to report it.) Some colleges will even accept transfer credits from such summer courses.

Academic performance is not the only yardstick used by colleges in selecting incoming students. While you can't do much to improve your teen's college board scores (cram courses are only marginally helpful in this regard), special talents or unusual accomplishments are also taken into consideration. Although your teen may not be a concert pianist or an Olympic diver, you may be able to help create other credentials that will set your child's application apart from the crowd. These depend, of course, on your teen's interests and capabilities, but almost any college-bound student can organize a school or community project that will attract an admissions officer's attention. Whether it's a fund-raising drive for UNICEF, a congressional write-in campaign on a public affairs matter, or a hobby that turns into a small-business venture, energies devoted to these sorts of activities are likely to pay dividends at college application time.

There are appropriate and inappropriate ways of going to bat for your teen when the college admissions process is at stake. It is inappropriate to make your adolescent's choices. Even if you are sure he or she would do best at M.I.T. in mechanical engineering, don't force the issue if the teen's choice is U.C.L.A.'s film-making program. It is inappropriate to write your teen's college application essay, to encourage misrepresentation of facts, or to take the responsibility for completing such applications yourselves.

What is appropriate is to discuss your teen's strengths and weaknesses to help devise a marketing strategy that will make the applicant look attractive on paper and will help during an in-person interview. Make sure your teen answers the actual questions on the application form and doesn't write an answer to an essay question that isn't there. It is perfectly fine for parents to act as editors — correcting grammar and sentence structure, proofreading for errors — or even to type the application or pay to have it typed, as long as the parents don't change the content. Parents can and should encourage their teen to complete the application process promptly. The sooner an application is received, the more likely it is that it will be read by admissions officers without the pressures of time and overwhelming numbers of competing applications.

Parents can help their teens prepare for the college interview by reading through the catalogue together, devising questions the applicant might want to ask, arranging a trip to the campus, arranging for the teen to meet with alumni ahead of the interview — all of which make it clear that the teen has an honest interest in the school and is familiar with its strengths as well as curious about its weaknesses. Role-playing a college interview may also help to defuse a teen's tension. Topics usually covered are: why do you want to come here? what are you like as a student and as a person? have you had any meaningful experiences? what are your academic and cultural interests? what is your family like? Teens should also be prepared to talk about their plans for the future, their past work experiences, books they've read recently, and current events.

If parents are asked to speak with their teen's interviewer, they must be diplomatic, especially if the school is not the place they would like to see their child attend. They should avoid negative comments about their teen or the school and attempt to highlight their child's assets. You can admit that a teen has weak points — just temper the statement with some explanation of how he or she has attempted to resolve any problems. An interviewer is not a therapist, and parents should not try to unload their anxieties about whether or not their teen will be accepted.

Two other types of parental input can enhance an adolescent's chances of being admitted to a particular college, but they are both special situations that are not broadly applicable. First, most colleges give a degree of preferential treatment to the children of alumni. If your teen is interested in attending your alma mater, even if only as a last choice, be sure to capitalize on your status. Second, don't be ashamed to call on friends, relatives, or business acquaintances who might have some influence at your teen's top choice colleges for a little help. A recommendation from a source of this type — or, better still, a cluster of these recommendations — will usually weigh in your teen's favor. After all, this is what going to bat is all about.

Last, remember that nothing is final where college admissions are concerned. If teens don't get into their favorite college the first time around, they can reapply the following year and transfer. If a teen is rejected everywhere, a year off to work or get some life experience may make for a more attractive candidate the next. And, believe it or not, students have survived the ignominy of not attending an Ivy League school.

Preparing for college is a prolonged process in which parents do have an important role to play. The key here, as with everything else when dealing with an adolescent on the brink of adulthood, is perspective. It is advisable not to step over the line that separates parental and adolescent responsibilities. Otherwise, when you go to bat for your teen you may wind up striking out.

25

Sharing and Caring

As parents, we all recognize that we are responsible for the welfare of our children. This responsibility transcends our dual roles of protector and provider and encompasses an emotional bond that is one of the most important aspects of being a parent. In this chapter, we will examine two principal components of this interaction with our teens — how our sharing and caring get expressed and how, sometimes, they may be problematic.

The Joys of Sharing (and Its Risks)

To care deeply about another person involves wanting to share with them emotionally, spiritually, and materially — to give of ourselves to someone else. Although the pure altruist will claim it is the giving that makes us feel good inside, most of us prefer a little something in return. Sharing is thus a two-way process; otherwise it is simply a form of giving.

We get a special exhilaration from sharing with our children for many different reasons. Foremost, sharing brings us closer together. We reveal aspects of ourselves to our offspring that they might never have seen; in return we get a unique look at who they are and what they think and feel. This function of parent-child sharing is of particular importance during adolescence because teenagers' perceptions of who we are as parents become inevitably distorted in their struggle for independence. The objective here is not to present yourself as a perfect person (your teen won't buy it anyway), but to offset the natural tendency towards alienation by letting your teen see the real you, blemishes and all, at close range.

Parent-teen sharing also serves as a time for communication in a more sophisticated manner than has occurred before. Not only can you take genuine pleasure in shared celebrations — a sixteenth birthday, a wedding anniversary, a family dinner in honor of your teen's first-place finish in the cross-country meet — you can also share in times of agony, frustration, and pain. If something is troubling your adolescent, sharing can help relieve the burden and put his or her troubles in a more realistic perspective. While your consolation may not make the problem go away, your teenager may be surprised to learn that you've had similar experiences and survived them ("Gee, Dad, I never knew you were rejected at your first-choice college"). This can work in the reverse direction, too. If something is troubling you, talking about it with your teen may help you feel better and may occasionally point the way to a solution.

Another important but often overlooked function of sharing is the role model it provides for your teens. From your willingness to be open about yourself, you encourage your adolescent's openness with you. You can, in effect, help your teenager see where self-disclosure is appropriate and useful and also where soul-baring is unnecessary or even dangerous.

The skills of appropriate sharing will help you and your teen in all social areas. Communication with relatives, such as your spouse and your own parents, is likely to be enhanced. Sharing is not a self-contained skill but one that carries over into all human interactions. People, for the most part, respond with warmth and comfort to someone willing and able to appropriately share of themselves. If you become adept at sharing, you may even find your adolescents' friends coming to you for solace or advice. While this may seem to be both a compliment to your sensitivity and a nice way to help you keep in touch with your own teen's environment and status, proceed cautiously because it can also cause some jealousy and resentment on your teenager's part.

There are other risks involved with sharing. When we venture ourself for acceptance and understanding, we also open ourself to being hurt by the response or actions of the person with whom we shared. Inappropriate sharing especially (sharing at a bad time, or an improper place, or with a person not sufficiently close to you to feel comfortable with your revelations) can result in deceit, betrayal, and humiliation. Our words may be misinterpreted; the person may react with fear or distrust and feel forced to return the sharing before they are ready.

The best way to avoid these negative reactions — and there are never any guarantees — is to become adept at appropriate sharing. Be cautious about the person, time, and place. If the person seems hesitant to move your relationship to a more intimate level, your self-disclosure will be met with embarrassment on their part that might be communicated to you as coldness, brazenness, insult, or sarcasm.

In the book *The Women's Room* by Marilyn French, Mira decides she wants the relationship between herself and her fifteen- and sixteen-year-old sons to become closer and more intimate. They have been at private school for several months; she has been doing graduate work at Harvard. To rebuild the bonds she once felt between herself and her sons, she invites them to spend Thanksgiving weekend with her. She tries to force them to share their lives by asking questions to which they give perfunctory answers. Finally, in desperation, she reveals herself, talking about her divorce from their father, her unhappiness at Harvard. Her behavior mostly frightens the boys, who don't know what to make of her outburst and are not yet comfortable enough around her to return the sharing. Intimacy cannot be forced.

Inappropriate sharing is sometimes considered (especially by teens) as an invasion of privacy and, in the strictest sense, it is — an invasion of our inner, private sanctum. Here are some signs that may help you assess the appropriateness of self-disclosure and sharing:

(1) Are you in a private place? Without privacy, even if the other person did elect to share certain information with you, he or she may be afraid someone else would hear. A quiet, secluded spot (preferable to a noisy, crowded area where no one is likely to hear or notice you; few persons wish to shout their innermost thoughts and feelings) encourages concentrated thought and honest revelation.

(2) How long have you known the person and, more important, how long has your relationship been on an intimate, sharing level? Mira had certainly known her sons a long time — their entire lives — yet their relationship had always been one of caretaker to child rather than friend to friend. Her boys needed more encounters with their mother in this new role, and more time to understand the relationship in its new mode.

(3) It's safest to try a *little* sharing first, before exposing your heart and soul to someone. This way, if they aren't ready to hear what you're saying, you have less to regret and have supplied them with fewer weapons with which to hurt you.

Why Togetherness Is Not Enough

As Mira learned with her teenage boys, physical contact alone is not sufficient to understand or appreciate another person. She had bathed and fed them, chauffeured them to basketball games and Boy Scouts, swabbed iodine on their scrapes, and yet the day arrived when she realized she had no idea who they were. What did they think when they awoke in the morning? What was their favorite flower? How did they feel about the divorce?

Sitting in front of a television set four hours each night with your family will not provide answers to those questions. Physical contact is important (especially if it goes beyond mere presence) but minds and hearts must touch, too. Many adolescents speak of feeling closer to their parents while away at college than ever before, and much of this is attributable to the altered methods of communication between them. Because of the geographical distance, teens and parents must write to each other or make phone calls, talking on a one-to-one basis. Communication thus becomes more concentrated, personal, thoughtful, and revealing. A whole new side of teens and their parents emerges as they work harder at communicating and sharing — as if to make up for the lack of physical contact.

Some parents, to be sure, never spend time with their teenagers beyond the routine contacts of everyday living. If your personal interactions with your teen are mainly confined to a quick hello at breakfast and the weekly handing over of the allowance, something has already gone wrong. Despite the fact that adolescents need independence, to allow your child to become a virtual stranger is to risk falling out of touch and being perceived as uninterested or rejecting.

To prevent this sort of distancing you must be willing to interact with teenagers on their own terms, not just on yours. You need a certain willingness to do things they want to do, even if it's only for the sake of being together. While you're not expected to accompany your adolescents to the next punk rock concert in town or learn how to body-surf so you can spend time together, there are other, less painful, ways to accomplish the same objective.

Talking is the simplest, and least expensive, form of togetherness. Too frequently, parents talk with their teenagers only when there's a problem to solve, an assignment to give, or a lecture to be delivered. When was the last time you asked your adolescent's opinion of a front-page news story or the likely outcome of the pennant race? How long has it been since you've discussed a book together or talked about a movie you've both seen? For talking to become a truly effective opportunity for togetherness, of course, you shouldn't monopolize the conversation and you must be willing to listen to your teen's views with respect, not disregard them as childish notions.

Another neglected aspect of togetherness is the chance for parents to be occasional spectators at their teen's activities. If your daughter is on the school swim team, or your son is competing in the county golf championship, or you've got a budding musician in the family, you have some golden opportunities to watch them perform. While your teenager may protest, saying "You'll make me nervous" or "It's no big deal," your presence at these activities is an important way of showing you care and will be remembered by both of you with fondness. Don't make the mistake of one well-meaning father, though, who dutifully attended his seventeen-year-old son's last varsity basketball game (having missed all the others) only to sit in the stands poring over a briefcase full of office work. Teenagers correctly see this sort of behavior as hypocrisy, so if you're not going to be courteous enough to show interest, don't go.

Togetherness measured by the clock alone is not a sufficient way of judging your availability as a parent. Togetherness, to be truly meaningful, needs to be interactive and sharing. Adolescents won't always be ready for togetherness when it's convenient to you, but your willingness to be available upon request and your perspicacity in recognizing when your presence is needed, (even if not requested), will go a long way in cementing parent-teen relations. Most important of all is the quality of time you and your teen spend together, the key ingredient in the recipe for successful interaction.

Dealing with Bad Tidings

All of us face moments of sadness in our lives. As parents, we have special responsibilities in teaching our children how to cope with such occurrences. A grandparent dies, your teen's best friend comes down with leukemia, a favorite teacher commits suicide — what do you say and do? First, you should recognize that your adolescent probably needs your support and advice more in dealing with these events than with the positive aspects of growing up. Next, you should try to be honest and open about your own feelings instead of trying to pretend that everything's fine. Teenagers need to learn that grief and sadness are acceptable emotions, not just a sign of weakness, and your behavior provides an important role model for them. If they're unable or unwilling to talk about their grief at first (which is a very common occurrence) you might suggest that they put their thoughts down on paper as a way of coming to grips with their emotions. Don't rush them, though, because teenagers sometimes need a while to think about the most highly charged feelings churning in their minds in order to bring them under control. For this reason, it's also important to give your teens a good deal of privacy at such times. If they want or need your company they will let you know.

Adolescents sometimes respond to tragedies in their lives by temporarily becoming hostile, which can be their way of combating their sense of helplessness. Sometimes, in contrast, a somber event pushes teenagers into docile, passive dependency as though they have given up living. While both types of reactions are common and completely normal, if these patterns persist too long they're likely to be harmful. The parent's task here is to recognize the difference between the acute reaction phase — lasting a few days to a few weeks — versus a longer, more profound shock period.

Teenagers, like all of us, try to come up with rational explanations for the events they come in contact with and, like all of us, they eventually realize that life is logical only up to a point. Senseless accidents, harrowing illnesses, and other types of tribulations and setbacks are not always understandable, and this can be particularly vexing to the adolescent. Harold Kushner, author of *When Bad Things Happen to Good People,* wisely points out: "When we are stunned by some tragedy, we can only see and feel the tragedy. Only with time and distance can we see the tragedy in the context of a whole life and a whole world."

Caring Isn't Just a State of Mind

Caring is a state of being, not just an attitude. Often we must show in tangible ways that we care. How do we translate the love and concern we have for our teens into something tangible they can't overlook? One effective way is to show we listen by remembering what has been said to us. Gary, age sixteen, had a regular part-time job during the summer as a messenger boy in a stock brokerage house. He was careful to tell his parents what days he worked and what hours — they never changed from week to week. His parents, though, could never manage to remember his schedule and often planned family outings on days he could not attend. Regardless of their reasons for doing this, in Gary's mind they didn't care enough to make a note of his work schedule. They could have showed they cared about him simply by paying more attention to his commitments.

Your caring actions may not be applauded or even noticed, as far as you can tell, but teens are seldom vociferous in praising the kind intentions of their parents. If you think they don't notice, try stopping the bright note you leave them each morning before going to work, or stop cooking an alternative entrée to spinach soufflé because you know your daughter hates spinach. This may sound a lot like the television commercial where the mother is surprised her kids notice the switch in fabric softener — but its basic tenet holds a lot of truth. We don't notice the niceties until they're gone.

Showing your teen that you care, however, can also be taken too far. Parents, for instance, who do a million thoughtful things for their kids — not out of the joy of doing but to make their teens feel grateful, guilty, or trapped into being nice to them — often find their apparently good intentions backfire. Kids resent the suffocating nature of this sort of kindness. "Stop doing things for me," Cindy finally exploded to her father. "Stop caring so much. Leave me alone." The anger results from having the balance of sharing and caring shifted too far in the parents' direction. Cindy felt she was *supposed* to return all the niceties, and didn't think those expressions of her love ought to be forced out of feelings of ingratiation. It's unfair both to parents and teenagers to try to manipulate love and caring. You may get your teen to show a little more thoughtfulness temporarily, but his or her lack of sincerity will soon become apparent and taint those kind actions.

One other aspect of caring deserves discussion. Very often, parents who ardently love their children never manage to express this emotion in words. They believe, of course, that these feelings are automatically understood by their teens, but this isn't always true. Teenagers often see their parents primarily as critics and disciplinarians ("Did you leave your dishes on the table *again?*" "You could improve your chemistry average if you'd just spend less time on the phone") and without occasional words of affection, the teen may have only the most abstract sense of being loved or, worse yet, may feel totally unloved and unappreciated. To guard against falling into this trap, be sure you put your love and affection into words that your teenager hears on a regular basis.

Consistency Revisited

Parents need to share as consistently as possible. You can't be like a clam, opening and shutting without much understandable reason or warning. And it's not fair to keep jumping back and forth between being aloof from your teen's world and suddenly wanting instant closeness. This only confuses kids (and adults, too) as to where they stand in your hierarchy of intimacy.

Teens especially, whose whole lives seem in a state of flux, need something that's predictable and reliable. For this reason, if you listen empathetically to their romantic tribulations one day and then ignore the continuing saga the next, you do them no favor. No one expects you to be Super Parent, however, and times will arise when you are unable to pay as much attention to them as they need. This difficulty is often relieved by explaining why this isn't a good time for them to share these things with you, and then designating an alternative time (preferably the same day) when you can discuss it and devote your full concentration to them. As long as you're being honest, your teen will probably understand your dilemma and would rather postpone the discussion to a time when you can fully attend to it than relay the situation to a deaf ear.

A different problem arises as parents have to manage the juggling act between being supportive, sympathetic, sharing people and being critics and limit-setters for their teens. You can't really expect adolescents to jump with joy at a chance to be with you after you've just upbraided them for some shortcoming or act of malfeasance. Neither is it realistically possible to postpone all confrontations in the interest of fostering togetherness, since the most effective confrontations usually need some temporal relation to the problem. Thus, you've got to make decisions — sometimes on an hour by hour basis — balancing the benefits of sharing with the need for attending to a problem that may propel you into the mode of parent-as-authority-figure. Ideally, you will become skillful at discussing problems, rather than yelling about them, which may help keep things in some perspective. Nevertheless, often your teenager won't feel like being around you, much less sharing with you, which is simply a part of parenting an adolescent you'll have to learn to accept.

Dealing with Rejection

Sometimes, no matter what your good intentions, your attempts to share and to show you care will be rejected by your teenagers. They may be in a bad mood, they may be trying to hurt you simply to test their power over you, they may not even realize the effect on you of their rejection. Remember, they are still learning the finer points of socializing and communicating.

Try not to take their rejection too personally. This may seem like the hardest thing to do at the time ("How else should I take it?" you might think; "they have rejected *me* personally"), but it is sound advice. As a parent, you are obligated to give your teens the benefit of the doubt. Don't retaliate with verbal brutality or displace your hurt into anger or revenge.

Instead, learn to express your feelings of rejection as concisely and objectively as possible. Teens are also learning the consequences of their actions, and this sort of feedback can be parlayed into a good communication lesson. The point here is not to make your teen feel bad, but to show him or her that the action has been construed as rejection (regardless of what was really intended) and help them understand what rejection feels like.

Rejection is a possible plus at times, too, a necessary and healthy consequence of your teen's growing up. Kids must surrender their parents, at least temporarily, to form their own personalities and identities. This can mean rejecting their care and affection as well as their limits and discipline. Knowing that this is a natural phase of maturing can ease your hurt. Stay alert, though, to rejection meted out merely as sadistic game playing. Teens must understand that intimacy and emotion are not to be idly trifled with unless they intend to spend most of their lives as hermits.

Parents may inadvertently reject their teens, too. Adolescents tend to be overly sensitive, so a casual comment may trigger a deeper reaction than expected. An effective strategy for resolving an unintended slight is first to give the teens some time to come to terms with their own emotions and calm down a bit. Then try to explain the encounter from your own perspective, working out the miscommunication as you go. Not only is the rejection absolved, but another communication skill (negotiation) has been rehearsed to everyone's benefit.

26

Letting Go

Letting go is as hard for teens as it is for parents, although it's unlikely that either group will admit it to the other. Adolescents want to be let go of by their parents in their struggle to become adults in order to claim all the status they imagine the post-teenage years will bring. In the process, their needs to be nurtured and cared for don't disappear; they just change form, and the teens may be embarrassed to admit how much they still love and need their families. Parents don't want to let go, in part because their identities have been focused for so long on the job of raising children that it may be frightening to envision life without the clear-cut goal of turning out "good kids." They may not want to let go if this means they will be left alone.

Adolescent letting go means giving up some of the comforts of family life. It means teens must learn how to be separate individuals though they may still want to maintain close family ties. It means learning to assume responsibilities for self that were previously taken care of by their parents. Parental letting go basically means giving teens permission to be teenagers and do all the wacky things that our society allows and encourages them to do. It means altering the ways we relate to them and how we support them (both monetarily and emotionally). It means being available — but unobtrusively — and it means constantly revising our definitions of parenting as our teens mature and strive to become caring, competent, healthy adults.

Understanding the Dynamics of Individuation-Separation

The typical teenage complaint, "My parents treat me like a little kid," is at the heart of the process of separating from the family in order to become one's own person. Of course parents treat their children as children — an eighty-five-year-old mother consistently introduces her fifty-four-year-old son, a bank president, as "my baby" — this is human nature. The struggle for independence from the family is universal, and both parents and teens must contribute to its resolution.

One of the central tasks of adolescence is to extricate oneself from family ties, both psychologically and physically. To aid in this process, teens often develop affiliations with adults in their lives who become, in effect, substitute families. A favorite teacher, a coach, or a neighbor may assume the advisor/confessor/adult role model for the teen while parents become relatively ignored. Friends' parents are often admired and held up as paragons the teens would like their own parents to emulate — in part because the teen sees these parents on their best behavior, not in the trenches of family squabbles and bickering. The separation process is also assisted by teens' spending more time at other people's homes than at their own, and by nonfamily activities that provide an environment for becoming one's own person. Taking a job, for example, not only provides pocket money (an essential for feeling independent) but also creates a situation in which the teen is not subject to parental supervision.

Many parents have trouble letting go. In some cases, this is because they think of their teens as children who still need constant supervision and care. For other parents who have gotten past this barrier, it is difficult to let go due to anxieties over their teen's vulnerability to the world. One father of a seventeen-year-old girl who worked as a counselor at a camp for economically underprivileged children was convinced that one of the campers might physically assault his daughter. He couldn't bring himself to discuss this because he didn't want to admit he was racially prejudiced — a fact of which his daughter was well aware anyway. Finally, after two weeks of intense anxiety, he confronted her, and the two of them were able to talk about the fears he had and her own perceptions of her job.

Some parents become envious or even angry when other people seem to have better relations with their teens than they do. They fail to understand that these relationships are appealing to teens precisely because they are not governed by parent-child "rules." The teen is free to accept or reject advice on its face value without putting up with side messages like "Don't mumble when you talk to your mother," "Don't slouch so much, you'll get lousy posture," or "Can't you see I'm busy now?" In fact, it is precisely this atmosphere of acceptance that teens value most in these nonparental relationships. Feeling accepted, rather than judged, they feel freer to be themselves.

Parents who have trouble letting go may also be trying to shield their teens from the possibility of failure. This was the case with seventeen-year-old Joellen Rohan, who was hired by a large department store to sell budget women's sportswear. Her mother thought Joellen wouldn't do well since she had never cared much about fashion. Even before the job began, she told Joellen that she hoped she wouldn't be disappointed. The first few weeks her daughter worked, Mrs. Rohan came to the store every day and paced up and down the aisles of the budget sportswear department to see how she was doing. During coffee breaks, Mrs. Rohan would try to coach her to improve her sales techniques. This caused her daughter such embarrassment that she asked to be transferred to the hardware department because her mother had no knowledge of tools. As a result, Joellen had to be retrained, and lost some customers she naa begun to accumulate.

This is an example of a parent whose motives were admirable but whose methods were awful. It is important to let your teens succeed or fail by their own doing; parental interference, even if well-intentioned, can inadvertently undermine the individuation-separation process which, in the long run, just makes it harder for teens to assume adult roles.

Letting go doesn't mean relinquishing all ties with your teen. It doesn't require forgetting the past and it doesn't, or shouldn't, prevent you from having a future influence on your child's life. But parents should remember that sometimes adolescents need to say good-bye to their families before they can say hello. The teen's feelings of dependency and immaturity must be allowed to dissipate in order for a less dependent relationship with the family to begin. Try to relate to teens as they are now, not as they were a few years ago. Researchers have found that parents who constantly compare what their teens do or say today with past habits, achievements, and so on may cause the teens to feel their parents are pushing them back into childhood, infantilizing them, and making it harder for them to assume adult roles, because it appears their parents don't want them to assume them.

Teens must do a similar sort of mental gymnastics in altering their perception of adults. They must start to think of their parents as people and not just parents, and in so doing must try to recognize not only their parents' human weaknesses, but their strengths as individuals who are as multifaceted as the teens perceive themselves to be. Each teen is many people rolled into one, but so is each parent. Separation is a kind of pendulum that swings back and forth; when the arc between parent and teen becomes wide enough, individuation can occur. It's nice to know that the pendulum moves in two directions, though, because it creates the options of kids returning home and renewing old family ties but on a different basis. Families who can successfully negotiate the path towards individuation-separation lay a foundation for eventually developing an interdependence in which teens and parents share a realistic appreciation of one another.

Preparing Your Teenager for Independence and Growth

Sometimes it seems as if all that teenagers really want is to be free of adult domination and authority and be able to make their own decisions and act on them. And parents certainly seem to long for the magic moment when the daily hassles of coping with adolescence will be a thing of the past — when teenagers will miraculously become loving, respectful, productive people who not only can get along with their parents but can like them as well. The trick is, how do we get there?

Preparing your teenager for independence and growth means to first prepare yourself for that teen's departure (either physically or emotionally) from the family. Many parents are surprised, after wishing their teenagers would go away and give them some peace and quiet, to feel an incredible sadness and sense of regret when the kids actually do go. In some cases, this sadness becomes a kind of panic reaction, and the parents make it very difficult for the teens to make the separation work. The mother in the Wisk commercial who pays a surprise visit to her older teenage son's new apartment and tells him he has "ring around the collar" as he proudly points out his very own kitchen, is a metaphor for the dilemmas of allowing our teens to be independent.

How can parents prepare themselves gradually and intelligently? Reading this book is a first step. We suggest that the following topics be discussed with your family members:

(1) *What is our notion of the right age, or right time, for our children to grow up and move away from home?* It may be that your teens and you share the same time-frame or that your views are very different. Negotiation may be indicated.

(2) *How did our parents prepare themselves and us for our departure? Are we following the same patterns with our teens?* It may be that your ideas are based on what was appropriate for your generation and not for your teenager's. Looking at the past can yield important clues and insights, and may add a touch of humor to an otherwise emotionally draining time.

(3) *What will life be like when our teens are independent?* If you have a clear image of what you think may occur, and your teens have their own conceptions, compare and contrast them. You may think your kids

will never want to come home; your teens may be thinking they'll be home on weekends, or for dinner twice a week, or that you'll continue to do their laundry. Though imaginary scenarios rarely play out the same way in real life, you'll at least be able to acknowledge the image and adjust it to the reality as it occurs.

(4) *Make a list of your priorities now. Also, make a list of what you anticipate your priorities will be as the teens become increasingly independent.* Are there still any non-negotiable things you expect from your teen? Are you conscious of your own changing needs that may result from a teen becoming less dependent on you? Do you intend to allow your emotional ties to loosen? What sort of future relationship do you hope you and your teen will have? Keep these lists in an accessible place and check them from time to time. Seeing things in black and white sometimes makes it easier to make adjustments when they are indicated.

Having done this, parents should be more secure or comfortable allowing their teens to become independent people.

Preparing your teens for independence and growth obviously doesn't occur all at once. In reality, it's the by-product of how you have handled all the triumphs, traumas, and day-to-day events during your teen's adolescence. Some of the things that should be happening in your family to enhance the process of adolescent maturation are as follows:

(1) *Give your teens increasing responsibility for managing their own affairs.* Whether this means refusing to iron your daughter's blouses, or requiring that your son gets a part-time job to contribute to his college fund, or making it clear that if your teen drives the family car it is to be returned with a full tank of gas or no more driving privileges will be granted, these sorts of demands place responsibility for self squarely on the adolescent's shoulders. They also can be a source of tremendous self-confidence for the teen when the requirements are fulfilled, and they show the teen that adult life isn't all fun and games.

(2) *Give your teens increasing responsibility for managing their own money.* Giving kids an allowance, letting them work for other people, and letting them spend their own money is very important. Teens need to learn to budget for things and discover the limits of their purchasing power.

(3) *Give your teens increasing permission to think for themselves, even if it means questioning family values.* Teens should be encouraged to discuss family values, parents' political beliefs, and how decisions and judgments are made. But be sure to let them air their own opinions without being put down, because this is an important ingredient in developing self-confidence. Teens who form their own ideas rather than just mimicking parental views are better equipped for becoming tolerant adults who recognize that there can be more than one correct response to many questions or situations.

(4) *Help your teens see you as you really are so they can become the persons they really are.* As we have said so many times in this book, communication with your teens is crucial. Since younger teens may cling to the childish need to believe their parents are omnipotent or perfect, while older teens may think their parents are always wrong, it is very important that parents shatter both these illusions. By being honest about themselves, by admitting to imperfections or occasional failures and being willing to discuss their faults, parents provide concrete proof of an important truth — that adults aren't perfect, adulthood doesn't require perfection, and it is possible to lead happy and productive lives in spite of setbacks. This can alleviate a lot of your teens' performance pressures and give them permission to try doing things they might otherwise be afraid of failing at and disappointing you as a result.

(5) *Give your teens permission to make mistakes.* Everyone needs to realize that mistakes can happen — the important thing is to develop the capacity to learn from what's gone wrong. If you have been in the habit of undoing your teen's mistakes, you deprive your child of an important learning opportunity.

(6) *Let your teens know you understand their anxieties, that leaving home can be scary, and they have permission to take their feelings out on you temporarily.* Researchers have found that separation from the family can be most difficult just after graduation from high school and prior to college or job commitments that necessitate a physical move away from home. An interesting study done recently at the Yale Psychiatric Institute revealed that incoming college freshmen were very anxious about leaving home, expressing anger towards their parents. Apparently such anger helps the teens separate and make a psychological transition from home to college, as well as masking a fear of being unable to break the ties with parents. While the students who were most afraid of this were also the angriest, the same students, interviewed later in the freshman year, after having adjusted to college life, felt increased attachment towards their parents.

It is important that parents and teens both understand that angry, rejecting feelings may pop up but are a normal part of becoming independent from the family. They should not be taken as personal affronts or as invitations to fight. If such feelings persist long after the transition to college or job, however, they may indicate deeper problems.

Once teens are living away from home and are functioning independently, a new phase of parenting comes into play. Recognize this as a transitional time in their lives where your role is to keep a deliberately low profile. Let them know you're available for consultations or help when necessary, but not for providing constant supervision or management of their lives.

As teenagers mature, the consequences of the decisions they make for themselves become greater. "What course should I sign up for?" may become "What college should I choose?" and "Who should I go to the prom with?" may become "Who should I marry?" Ultimately, the decision-making belongs to the teens, who, at the conclusion of adolescence, have many of the legal rights of adults anyway. Therefore, parents should try to lay the groundwork for teenage independence and growth early in adolescence by rewarding their teens with increasing responsibility and self-determination each time the teens demonstrate the competence and capacity to live life responsibly.

Don't Misjudge Your Child's Capacities

The fantasies parents have about their children even before they are born persist in varying guises and to varying degrees throughout life. It seems we perpetually wonder what our children will become, and often in the process we let our imaginary plans for them cloud what they really can or want to do. We can make the adolescent's search for identity very difficult when our fantasies don't happen to match theirs.

Misjudging a child's capacities is more than expecting A's at school from teens who struggle to get C's. It really is a series of parental blunders that may involve negating your teen's interests, assuming things about him or her without discussing these things together, and even imposing unmanageable or impossible standards on your teens. Sometimes it involves underestimating the teen's capabilities; at other times, overestimating them.

Parents who misjudge their teens' capabilities often use academic performance in school as the gauge. However, this is not always an accurate barometer of competence. Academic excellence at one high school may translate into mediocre preparation for college and is certainly no guarantee of future academic or employment success. A teenager who almost fails all his math courses in high school may become a computer programmer later in life. The student who can't write a decent essay in English class and refuses to read Shakespeare ends up making a living writing advertising copy for TV commercials. You just never know.

Just because your teen is a social butterfly, don't assume he or she will want a career in the public eye even if you see a future TV news anchorperson. And just because your teen is quiet and shy or, conversely, is a troublemaker who has been thrown out of several schools, don't lower your expectations accordingly. Sylvester Stallone of *Rocky I, II,* and *III* fame was practically an incorrigible teenager but is now a writer, producer, director, actor, sex symbol, and millionaire.

To avoid misjudging your child's capabilities, try to do the following:

(1) Actually ask your teen where he or she thinks his or her strengths and weaknesses are. You may be surprised at your differences of opinion.

(2) Check your teen's school record. You may discover strengths you were unaware of, revealed in teachers' comments though not necessarily reflected in actual grade-point averages.

(3) Talk to people other than school personnel who know your teen and are more objective than you are. You may think you are talking about two different teenagers!

Remember, all teenagers have idiosyncrasies, many procrastinate to such an extent that they may actually seem less capable than they are, and few have even scratched the surface of their talents by the end of adolescence. To misjudge their capacities is to inhibit their emotional and intellectual development, and make it difficult for them to believe in themselves.

Parenting a College-Age Teen

Your daughter calls from Michigan State to say she's just given up her dorm room to move off-campus to her boyfriend's apartment. Or your son writes from U.C.L.A. to let you know he's decided to drop out of school for a year — he's going to Alaska to photograph Kodiak bears. Or you get a letter from the dean's office at Duke telling you that your eighteen-year-old is now on academic probation. Who said that life would get easier when the kids went to college?

Many parents seem to regard college acceptance as a great dividing line in their relations with their teens. Once a place in the freshman class has been obtained, a subtle change seems to overtake their style of parenting as they sense that the process of letting go is nearing its final act. They begin to view their college-bound students with a new respect and status, grateful perhaps that the teen has had enough on the ball to get this far. At the same time, parents are faced with a certain element of reality — their adolescents will be out of sight and out of range of parental admonitions . . . they'll finally be on their own.

Some parents give a sigh of relief at this stage, but for others the process of separation is painful or anxiety-provoking. As one father succinctly put it, "I know he's a smart kid, but I'm afraid he's in for a rude awakening. Now he's really going to see what life is all about." What do parents worry about most regarding their teens' being away at college? Intriguingly, academic performance is rather low on the list. Instead, parents rank social life, romance, exposure to drugs, and finances as the areas they're most concerned with.

When a teen first enters college, it's likely to be a painful experience in a number of ways. The high school newspaper editor gets C's on her English papers, the All-County halfback finds he's struggling to keep from being cut from the football team, and the senior class's "Most Popular Boy" has a hard time getting a date. Teens in these positions tend to be unsure of themselves both academically and socially, and until they have a chance to settle in and learn the system they may find the college experience disheartening rather than thrilling. Parents need to be supportive and understanding as this is occurring, taking particular pains to avoid placing even more pressures on the teens' shoulders. Here is a simple list of cautionary pointers you may want to keep in mind:

1. Accept the fact that your teen is on his or her own.
2. Don't interfere with your teen's life.
3. Don't pry — it isn't necessary to know everything they're doing.
4. Don't be alarmed if teens are out of touch with you for a while. (Chances are, if something is wrong they'll let you know.)
5. Don't be disappointed with mediocre grades the freshman year.

When Does an Adolescent Become an Adult? (Or, Is There Life after Adolescence?)

In the United States, there is no consensus as to when an adolescent becomes an adult. The federal government determines the age at which one can vote and enter military service. Different religions select certain birthdays as the time to mark the passage from childhood to adult status. States have varying ages at which a teen can drive or drink. Our legal system can declare a teen an "emancipated minor" when it is clear that the teen wants to be financially and psychologically independent of family, thus making the teen — rather than the parents — responsible for his or her behavior. Some people think marriage confers adult status, others think that giving birth or fathering children makes them adults. Some think it happens when they move out of a parent's home, others think that teens become adults when they enter the job market and obtain part-time or full-time employment, making it possible for them to be financially independent of their families regardless of their actual ages.

However, external factors such as age, place of abode, or financial independence really offer little insight about when an adolescent becomes an adult because they don't tell us whether psychological independence has been achieved.

Consider the following cases:

Kristen, a high school dropout, ran away from home at age seventeen and became a prostitute. She admitted to at least 800 sexual encounters in less than a year on the streets. When she became pregnant at eighteen, she returned home to have her baby and stayed. Her mother cares for the child and Kristen is back in school.

Carlos, nineteen, was given a minor-league baseball contract after high school. He moved 1,000 miles from his parents but calls them every night. They have final approval of all of his contract decisions.

Irene, eighteen, has been dancing in the touring company of a Broadway musical since she was sixteen. Her mother, a divorcée, travels with her as a companion, since they genuinely like each other's company. Irene pays all her own bills, takes care of her own wardrobe, and handles all business negotiations through her agent.

Which of these teens is an adult? In the eyes of the law, they all are. Clearly, in terms of their experience in the world, they all are. But psychologically, it would seem that only Irene has successfully made the break from dependence to interdependence. She is responsible for her own decisions and makes them without parental interference, while she relates to her mother both as a friend and a parent. This contrasts with Carlos, who seems tied to home in spite of geographical distance. Kristen has clearly not made the internal, psychological separation from her family that is a prerequisite of adult status. According to psychoanalyst Peter Blos, runaways substitute physical distance for emotional distance, since the latter may be harder to achieve. The fact that Kristen returned home and stayed may be considered proof that she wasn't ready to become an adult.

There is definitely life after adolescence, but not all of us choose to live it as adults. Some people shy away from the responsibilities and decision-making that adulthood implies by remaining perpetual students or dilettantes. These people have difficulty finding that elusive adult identity, and use schooling much as others would use therapy — as an outlet, a way of coping with their fears. Unlike those who choose therapy, however, such people rarely admit their problems. Many will take training in one field, complete the course requirements, but when it's time for the interviews and job hunting to begin, will decide they're not prepared enough to do a really good job. So they reenroll for more schooling, or may change gears completely, deciding that there's not enough money or challenge in what they thought they wanted to do. Starting their reeducation from scratch, they put off employment indefinitely, often being a terrible financial drain on their families.

Then there are the perpetual adolescents, adults whose lives seem to be spent in eternal search of adolescent bliss. They spend more time with their peer group than with their families, would rather bowl with the guys or gals than play with their kids, they hang out in bars or on street corners almost as though they are still in teenage gangs, and behave impulsively, generally avoiding responsibility.

Clearly, then, adolescent behavior isn't confined to the ages from thirteen to nineteen. Adulthood is a state of mind as well as a socially prescribed set of behaviors. Parents need to let go of their adolescents to free them to become adults. It is a separation that requires parents to understand their teens' unique qualities, that loosens control in order to allow the teens to take control

Appendix

The resources that are available to help parents and their teens negotiate crisis situations, learn to identify areas of need, and devise strategies to cope with and solve difficult problems vary widely. Sometimes it is hard to know where to look for help, especially when economic constraints make paying for private counseling, health care, or legal advice all but impossible. Currently in the United States there are ample resources: hot lines, hospitals, government agencies and information clearinghouses, public agencies, private agencies, advocacy groups, self-help groups that offer health care, counseling, crisis intervention, legal advice on a sliding fee scale according to one's ability to pay or free of charge regardless of one's economic status. This broad spectrum of resources shows that no one seeking assistance should have to go without.

Public service hot lines may be toll-free (those having 800 before the phone number) and may operate twenty-four hours a day. Other hot lines cost only the price of the phone call. All can be utilized as your first step in gathering information about how to solve a particular problem you and your teenager are facing. You may find it easy to talk to someone on a hot line because of the anonymity — this may give you the courage to say and admit things you wouldn't feel comfortable disclosing to a friend or family member. You may find the call to the hot line makes it possible for you to take positive action about confronting your dilemma. Making a call may be a way of defusing a tense, potentially explosive situation. Do not be embarrassed to call a hot line. The people who staff the phone lines are trained to help you with a particular kind of crisis and will not judge you. *Calling a hot line is a concrete way of taking control of the problem rather than letting it control you.*

Some agencies or special-interest groups provide references in the form of literature: pamphlets, bibliographies, lists of resources, descriptions of services that might be available in a particular geographical area, and so on. To obtain this kind of information you must write to them directly and wait for a reply, which may take weeks. If your situation does not demand immediate action, doing research of this sort can be very valuable to assure you that you are taking the right steps to solving the problem. If your aim is advocacy, we recommend this approach.

This appendix lists resources according to broad categories of problems. Where there are appropriate hot lines, they will be listed at the start of each section. The phone numbers and addresses are correct as of the time of publication; occasionally groups or organizations change these numbers or may switch to phone numbers that are no longer toll-free. We apologize in advance if this happens and causes inconvenience to our readers.

Locating Competent Professional Help

American Association for Marriage and Family Therapy (AAMFT)
924 West Ninth Street
Upland, CA 91786. (800) 854-9876; California: (714) 981-0888

American Association of Sex Educators, Counselors & Therapists
(AASECT)
11 Dupont Circle NW, Suite 220
Washington, DC 20036. (202) 462-1171

American Civil Liberties Union
22 East 40th Street
New York, NY 10016. (212) 725-1222; Night: (212) 725-0349
(They provide free legal assistance nationwide.)

American Medical Association (AMA)
535 North Dearborn Street
Chicago, IL 60610. (312) 751-6600

American Psychiatric Association
1700 18th Street NW
Washington, DC 20009. (202) 232-7878; Night: (202) 232-7879

American Psychological Association
1200 17th Street NW
Washington, DC 20036. (202) 833-7600; Night: (202) 966-1294

American Public Health Association
1015 187th Street NW
Washington, DC 20036. (202) 467-5000

Child Welfare League of America, Inc.
67 Irving Place
New York, NY 10003. (212) 254-7410

Coalition for Children and Youth
1910 K Street NW
Washington, DC 20006. (202) 785-4180

National Association of Social Workers (NASW)
Suite 600
1425 H Street NW
Washington, DC 20005. (202) 628-6800

National Self-Help Clearinghouse
33 West 42nd Street
New York, NY 10036. (212) 840-7606

National Self-Help Resource Center
2000 S Street NW
Washington, DC 20009. (202) 338-5704

Family Problems: Abuse, Lack of Control

(When things get tense at home, when parents feel as if they may abuse their teenager or cannot control potentially explosive or violent situations, the following resources may be utilized.)

Child Abuse Hotline: (800) 552-7096

Child Help USA: (800) 422-4453

Parents Anonymous: (800) 421-0353; California: (800) 352-0386

Child Abuse Prevention Effort (CAPE)
Northwood Towers
5245 Oxford Avenue
Philadelphia, PA 19124. (215) 831-8877

National Center on Child Abuse and Neglect
400 6th Street, SW
Washington, DC 20024. (202) 245-2856

Parents United (their focus is on incest and abuse)
P.O. Box 952
San Jose, CA 95108. (408) 280-5055

Adolescent Sexuality

(Abortion, contraception, unintended pregnancy, sexual information and misinformation, sexually transmitted diseases, homosexual or lesbian sexual preferences)

National Abortion Federation: (800) 772-9100; Washington, D.C.: (202) 546-9060

National Health Information Clearinghouse (Health and Human Services) (800) 336-4797
(They provide information on specific diseases, disorders or conditions, can give answers on the phone, make referrals to local organizations. They do not make diagnoses; they do deal with all health issues — not just those related to sexuality.)

V.D. Hotline (Operation Venus); (800) 227-8922; California (800) 982-5883

Department of Health and Human Services
200 Independence Avenue SW
Washington, DC 20201. (202) 245-6343
(This is a federal agency that you can contact for information on just about any health issue; they operate the National Health Information Clearinghouse listed above.)

National Institute of Health
Room 309, Building 1
9000 Rockville Pike
Bethesda, MD 20205. (301) 496-4461

National Right to Life Committee, Inc.
419 7th Street NW, Suite 402
Washington, DC 20004. (202) 626-8800
(They offer suggestions about alternatives to abortion when unintended pregnancy occurs.)

The Federation of Parents and Friends of Lesbians and Gays, Inc. (Parents FLAG)
P.O. Box 24565
Los Angeles, CA 90024. (213) 472-8952
(They will send you information about any groups in your area.)

Planned Parenthood Federation of America, Inc.
810 7th Avenue
New York, NY 10019. (212) 541-7800; Night: (212) 866-3032
(They can act as a resource for information on birth control, abortion, sex education, population growth; they provide low-cost reproductive

health care and focus on teenagers' taking responsibility for their own sexual activity.)

Sex Information and Education Council of the U.S. (SIECUS)
80 Fifth Avenue, Suite 801-2
New York, NY 10011. (212) 929-2300
(Provides reading lists on sex education, adolescent sexuality, and similar topics.)

Alcohol and Drug Abuse

Cocaine Hotline (800) COCAINE

Hazelden Foundation
Educational Materials
Box 176
Center City, MN 55012. (800) 328-9000

Alateen
P.O. Box 182
Madison Square Station
New York, NY 10159-0182. (212) 683-1771

Alcoholics Anonymous, World Services Inc.
P.O. Box 459, Grand Central Station
New York, NY 10016. (212) 686-1100

Drug Enforcement Administration (DEA)
1405 Eye Street NW
Washington, DC 20530. (202) 633-1249

Families Anonymous
P.O. Box 528
Van Nuys, CA 90508. (818) 989-7841
(It provides self-help peer counseling based on A.A.'s principles for relatives and friends of those with drug use or related behavior problems.)

Narcotics Education, Inc.
P.O. Box 439
6830 Laurel Street NW
Washington, DC 20912. (202) 722-6726; night: (301) 439-4590

National Clearinghouse for Alcohol Information (NCALI)
P.O. Box 2345
Rockville, MD 20852. (301) 468-2600

National Council on Alcoholism, Inc.
733 3rd Avenue
New York, NY 10017. (212) 986-4433

National Clearinghouse for Drug Abuse Information
Parklawn Building, Room 10A-43
5600 Fishers Lane
Rockville, MD 20857. (301) 443-6500

National Institute on Drug Abuse
Parklawn Building, Room 10-05
5600 Fishers Lane
Rockville, MD 20857. (301) 443-6245

Odyssey Institute, Inc.
24 West 12th Street
New York, NY 10011. (212) 741-5570
(Their focus is on youth problems, drug abuse, treatment programs, services, and advocacy.)

Education

(School problems, advocacy, positive parental involvement, special students)

National Committee for Citizens in Education (NCEE) (800) NETWORK
National Parent Teacher's Association Action Center
700 North Rush
Chicago, IL 60611. (312) 787-0977

Student Information Center (Department of Education)
Federal Student Aid Programs
P.O. Box 84
Washington, DC 20044. (301) 984-4070

Department of Education
400 Maryland Avenue SW
Washington, DC 20202. (202) 245-8564

Educational Clearinghouses

(They produce bibliographies about special areas of education.)

Clearinghouse on Handicapped and Gifted Children:
The Council for Exceptional Children
1920 Association Drive
Reston, VA 22091. (703) 620-3660

Clearinghouse on Reading and Communication Skills:
National Council of Teachers of English
1111 Kenyon Road
Urbana, IL 61801. (217) 328-3870

Clearinghouse for Science, Math, and Environmental Education:
Ohio State University
1200 Chambers Road
Columbus, OH 43212. (614) 422-6717

Clearinghouse for Social Studies/Social Sciences
ERIC
855 Broadway
Boulder, CO 80302. (303) 492-8434

Clearinghouse on Tests, Measurements and Evaluation:
Educational Testing Service
Rosedale Road
Princeton, NJ 08541. (609) 921-9000

Clearinghouse on Urban Education:
Columbia University Teachers College
P.O. (Box 40)
New York, NY 10027. (212) 678-3437

Educational Resources Information Center (ERIC)
19th and M Streets
Washington, DC 20208. (202) 254-6050
(ERIC provides copies of reports, curriculum guides and journal abstracts.)

Juvenile Delinquents, Antisocial Adolescents and Youth in Trouble for Committing Any Illegal Acts

(Legal rights, resources, advocacy groups, counseling, education)

Children's Defense Fund
122 C Street NW, 4th floor
Washington, DC 20001. (202) 628-8787

Department of Justice
Room 5114
10th Street and Constitution Avenue NW
Washington, DC 20530. (202) 633-2007

National Council on Crime and Delinquency
760 Market Street
Suite 433
San Francisco, CA 94012. (415) 956-5651

National Juvenile Law Center
3701 Lindell Boulevard
St. Louis, MO 63108. (314) 454-1722

Eating Disorders

American Anorexia Nervosa Association, Inc. (AANA)
133 Cedar Lane
Teaneck, NJ 07666. (201) 836-1800

Anorexia Nervosa and Associated Disorders, Inc. (ANAD)
P.O. Box 271
Highland Park, IL 60035. (312) 831-3438

BASH (Bulimia Anorexia Self Help) Inc.
522 North New Ballas Road
St. Louis, MO 63141. (314) 567-4080
(BASH publishes a very informative newsletter pertaining to eating disorders and has been a leader in the field of self-help.)

Runaways

National Runaway Hotline/Switchboard (Health and Human Services)
2210 North Halsted
Chicago, IL 60614. (800) 621-4000; Illinois: (800) 972-6004

Operation Peace of Mind
P.O. Box 52896
Houston, TX 77052. (800) 231-6946; Texas: (800) 392-3352
(Both of these hot lines can serve as neutral third parties to negotiate between parents and runaways. Messages can be left and are guaranteed complete confidentiality. The National Runaway Hotline/Switchboard can arrange conference calls between parents and runaways. The hot lines serve as clearinghouses for local hot lines and provide referral services pertaining to legal aid, free clinics, housing, Traveler's Aid, drop-in centers, local runaway shelters, Salvation Army services. The hot lines operate 24 hours a day, 7 days a week.)

Child Find: (800) 431-5005; New York: call collect (914) 255-1848
(This hot line deals with missing children and some runaways. The 800 toll-free number should be used if you have information on a missing child or want to find out about a certain child; Child Find will accept collect calls from New York State residents who have information about missing children.)

National Youth Work Alliance (NYWA)
1346 Connecticut Avenue NW
Washington, DC 20036. (202) 785-0764
(NYWA is an excellent resource for information on runaway centers, and other youth problems. They are the publisher of the *National Directory of Runaway Programs,* which gives the name, address, and description of every Runaway Center in the country, as well as several introductory articles on runaways and runaway centers [5th ed., 203 pp., paperback, $9.95 — includes postage and handling].)

Cults

American Family Foundation
P.O. Box 336
Weston, MA 02193. (617) 893-0930

Free Minds, Inc.
P.O. Box 4216
Minneapolis, MN 55414. (612) 378-2528

Spiritual Counterfeits Project
P.O. Box 4308
Berkeley, CA 94704. (415) 540-5767

Suicide

Center for Studies of Suicide Prevention
(National Institute of Mental Health Alcohol, Drug Abuse and Mental Health Administration)
Public Health Service
5600 Fishers Lane
Rockville, MD 20857.

(There are literally hundreds of suicide-crisis intervention centers nationwide and space does not allow us to list them here. They are generally listed in the Yellow Pages under "suicide" or "mental health services — suicide." If you cannot find such a listing in your locality, call any hospital emergency room or family service agency and proceed from there. If even that is not available, call the police.)

Suggested Readings

Part One: General Issues

Branden, Nathaniel. *"If You Could Hear What I Cannot Say": Learning to Communicate With the Ones You Love.* New York: Bantam Books, 1983.

Dragastein, Sigmund E., and Elder, Glen H., Jr. *Adolescence in the Life Cycle.* Washington, D.C.: Hemisphere Publishing Corp., 1981.

Fields, Suzanne. *Like Father, Like Daughter: How Father Shapes the Woman His Daughter Becomes.* Boston: Little, Brown and Company, 1983.

Friday, Nancy. *My Mother/My Self: The Daughter's Search for Identity.* New York: Delacorte Press, 1977.

Kohl, H. *Growing with Your Children.* Boston: Little, Brown and Company, 1978.

Nicholson, Luree, and Torbet, Laura. *How to Fight Fair With Your Kids . . . and Win!* New York: Harcourt Brace Jovanovich, 1980.

Pogrebin, Letty Cottin. *Family Politics: Love and Power on an Intimate Frontier.* New York: McGraw-Hill Book Co., 1983.

———. *Growing Up Free: Raising Your Child in the 80's.* New York: McGraw-Hill Book Co., 1980.

Schowalter, John E., and Anyan, Walter R. *The Family Handbook of Adolescence.* New York: Alfred Knopf, 1981.

Werner, Emmy E., and Smith, Ruth S. *Vulnerable but Invincible: A Longitudinal Study of Resilient Youth.* New York: McGraw-Hill Book Co., 1982.

Part Two: Problem Solving

Sexuality

Borhek, Mary V. *Coming out to Parents: A Two-Way Survival Guide for Lesbians and Gay Men and Their Parents.* New York: The Pilgrim Press, 1983.

Burkhart, Kathryn. *Growing into Love.* New York: G.P. Putnam's Sons, 1981.

Calderone, Mary, and Johnson, Eric. *The Family Book about Sexuality* (revised edition). New York: Harper and Row, 1981.

Carrera, Michael. *Sex: The Facts, the Acts, and Your Feelings.* New York: Crown Publishers, 1981.

Corsaro, Maria, and Korzeniowsky, Carole. *STD: A Commonsense Guide.* New York: St. Martin's. 1980.

Fairchild, Betty, and Hayward, Nancy. *Now That You Know: What Every Parent Should Know about Homosexuality.* New York: Harcourt Brace Jovanovich, 1979.

Gordon, Sol, and Gordon, Judith. *Raising a Child Conservatively in a Sexually Permissive World.* New York: Simon and Schuster, 1983.

Grossman, Rochel, and Sutherland, Joan (ed.). *Surviving Sexual Assault.* New York: Congdon and Weed, Inc., 1983.

Hass, Aaron. *Teenage Sexuality.* New York: Macmillan Publishing Co., 1979.

Herman, Judith. *Father-Daughter Incest.* Cambridge, Mass.: Harvard University Press, 1981.

Kaplan, Helen S. *Making Sense of Sex: The New Facts about Sex and Love for Young People.* New York: Simon and Schuster, 1979.

Lieberman, E. James, and Peck, Ellen. *Sex and Birth Control: A Guide for the Young* (revised ed.). New York: Harper and Row, 1981.

Rush, Florence. *The Best-Kept Secret: Sexual Abuse of Children.* Englewood Cliffs, N.J.: Prentice-Hall, 1980.

Silverstein, Charles. *A Family Matter: A Parent's Guide to Homosexuality.* New York: McGraw-Hill, 1977.

Drugs and Alcohol

Cohen, Sidney. *The Substance Abuse Problems.* New York: The Haworth Press, 1981.

Drug Abuse Council, The. *The Facts About "Drug Abuse."* New York: The Free Press, 1980.

Etons, V. *Angel Dusted: A Family's Nightmare.* New York: Macmillan Publishing Co., Inc., 1979.

Evans, W.O., and Cole, Jonathan, O. *Your Medicine Chest: A Consumer's Guide to Prescription and Non Prescription Drugs.* Boston: Little, Brown and Company, 1978.

Forrest, G. G. *How to Cope with a Teenage Drinker: New Alternatives and Hope for Parents and Families.* New York: Atheneum, 1983.

Krupski, Ann Marie. *Inside the Adolescent Alcoholic.* Center City, Minn.: Hazelden Foundation, 1982.

Levy, Stephen J. *Managing the "Drugs" in Your Life. A Personal and Family Guide to the Responsible Use of Drugs, Alcohol and Medicine.* New York: McGraw-Hill Book Co., 1983.

Linkletter, Art. *Drugs at My Door Step.* Waco, Texas: World Books, 1973.

Nale, S. *A Cry for Help.* Philadelphia: Fortress Press, 1982.

North, Robert, and Orange, Richard, Jr. *Teenage Drinking: The Number One Drug Threat to Young People Today.* New York: Macmillan Publishing Co., Inc., 1980.

Woodward, Nancy Hyden. *If Your Child Is Drinking.* New York: G.P. Putnam's Sons, 1981.

School Problems and Related Issues

Buskin, Martin. *Parent Power: A Candid Handbook for Dealing With Your Child's School.* New York: Walker & Co., 1975.

Cohen, M. *Helping Your Teen-Age Student: What Parents Can Do to Improve Reading and Studying Skills.* New York: E.P. Dutton, 1979.

Coleman, John, ed. *The School Years: Current Issues in the Socialization of Young People.* London: Methuen, 1979.

Jones, Phillip, and Jones, Susan. *Parents Unite! The Complete Guide for Shaking Up Your Children's School.* New York: Peter H. Wyden, 1976.

Kappelman, Murray M., and Ackerman, Paul R. *Between Parent and School.* New York: The Dial Press, 1977.

Lynn, R. *Learning Disabilities: An Overview of Theories, Approaches, and Politics.* New York: The Free Press, 1979.

Miller, Bernard S., and Price, Merle (eds.). *The Gifted Child, the Family and the Community.* New York: Walker and Co., 1981.

Miller, Mary Susan, and Baker, Samm Sinclair. *Straight Talk to Parents: How You Can Help Your Child Get the Best out of School.* New York: Stein and Day, 1979.

Mopsik, Stanley I., and Agard, Judith A. (eds.). *An Education Handbook for Parents of Handicapped Children.* Cambridge, Mass.: Abt Books, 1980.

Nielson, Linda. *How to Motivate Adolescents: A Guide for Parents, Teachers, and Counselors.* Englewood Cliffs, N.J.: Prentice-Hall, 1982.

Rioux, William, and Joyce, Nancy Cahill. *You Can Improve Your Child's School: Practical Answers to Questions Parents Ask Most about Their Public Schools.* New York: Simon and Schuster, 1980.

Velten, Emmett C., and Simpson, Carlene T. *Rx for Learning Disability.* Chicago: Nelson-Hall, 1978.

Zucker, R. F., and Hegener, K. C. *Peterson's Guide to College Admissions.* Edison, N.J.: Peterson's Guides, 1980.

Social Skills, Risk Taking, Self Esteem

Campbell, Ross. *How to Really Love Your Teenager.* Wheaton, Ill.: Victor Books, 1981.

Clark, Aminah, Clemes, Harris, and Bean, Reynold. *How to Raise Teenagers' Self-Esteem* (ed. Janet Gluckman). Sunnyvale, Cal.: Enrich, Div./OHAUS, 1978.

Eagan, Andrea Boroff. *Why Am I So Miserable If These Are the Best Years of My Life?* Philadelphia: J.B. Lippincott Company, 1976.

Fine, Louis L. *After All We've Done for Them: Understanding Adolescent Behavior.* Englewood Cliffs, N.J.: Prentice-Hall, Inc., 1977.

Kizziar, Janet, and Hagedorn, Judy. *Search for Acceptance: The Adolescent and Self Esteem.* Chicago: Nelson-Hall, 1979.

Moriarty, Alice. *Adolescent Coping.* New York: Grune and Stratton, 1976.

Norman, Jane, and Harris, Myron. *The Private Life of the American Teenager.* New York: Rawson, Wade, 1981.

Offer, Daniel, Ostrov, Eric, and Howard, Kenneth. *The Adolescent: A Psychological Self-Portrait.* New York: Basic Books, 1981.

The Antisocial Adolescent

Apter, Steven J. *Troubled Children/Troubled Systems.* New York: Pergamon Press, 1982.

Blos, Peter. *The Adolescent Passage: Developmental Issues.* New York: International Universities Press, Inc., 1979.

Bybee, Rodger W., and Gee, E. Gordon. *Violence, Values, and Justice in the Schools.* Boston: Allyn and Bacon, Inc., 1982.

Falkin, Gregory P. *Reducing Delinquency: A Strategic Planning Approach.* Lexington, Mass.: Lexington Books, 1979.

Feldman, Ronald A., Caplinger, Timothy E., and Wodarski, John S. *The St. Louis Conundrum: The Effective Treatment of Antisocial Youths.* Englewood Cliffs, N.J.: Prentice-Hall, Inc., 1983.

Goodwin, Blanche, and Craig, Eleanor. "Day Treatment: Rethinking School Phobia" in *Phobia: A Comprehensive Summary of Modern Treatments,* ed. Robert L. Du Pont. New York: Brunner/Mazel, Publishers, 1982.

Johnson, Grant, Bird, Tom, and Little, Judith Warren. *Delinquency Prevention: Theories and Strategies.* Washington, D.C.: U.S. Department of Justice, Office of Juvenile Justice and Delinquency Prevention, 1979.

Ross, Alan O. *Psychological Disorders of Children: A Behavioral Approach to Theory, Research and Therapy,* 2nd ed. New York: McGraw-Hill Book Co., 1980.

Ross, Patricia. *Trouble in School: A Portrait of Young Adolescents.* New York: Avon, 1979.

Seltzer, Vivian Center. *Adolescent Social Development: Dynamic Functional Interaction.* Lexington, Mass.: Lexington Books, 1982.

Woodson, Robert L. *A Summons to Life: Mediating Structures and the Prevention of Youth Crime.* Cambridge, Mass.: Ballinger Publishing Company, 1981.

Part Three: Crises

Divorce

Francke, Linda Bird. *Growing Up Divorced.* New York: Simon and Schuster, 1983.

Galper, Miriam. *Co(Sharing Your Child Equally)Parenting: A Source Book for the Separated or Divorced Family.* Philadelphia: Running Press, 1978.

Lamb, Michael E. *Nontraditional Families: Parenting and Child Development.* Hillsdale, N.J.: Lawrence Erlbaum Associates, 1982.

Ricci, Isolina. *Mom's House/Dad's House: Making Shared Custody Work.* New York: Macmillan Publishing Co., Inc., 1980.

Roman, Mel, and Haddad, William. *The Disposable Parent: The Case for Joint Custody.* New York: Holt, Rinehart and Winston, 1978.

Victor, Ira, and Winkler, Win Ann. *Fathers and Custody.* New York: Hawthorn Books, Inc. 1977.

Visher, Emily B., and Visher, John S. *How to Win as a Stepfamily.* New York: Dembner Books, 1982.

Wishard, Bill, and Wishard, Laurie. *Men's Rights: A Handbook for the 80's.* San Francisco, Calif.: Cragmont Publications, 1980.

Eating Problems: Obesity, Anorexia, and Binges

Bennett, William, and Gurin, Joel. *The Dieter's Dilemma: Eating Less and Weighing More.* New York: Basic Books, Inc., 1982.

Boskind-White, Marlene, and White, William C. *Bulimarexia: The Binge/Purge Cycle.* New York: W.W. Norton and Company, 1983.

Bruch, Hilde. *The Golden Cage: The Enigma of Anorexia Nervosa.* Cambridge, Mass.: Harvard University Press, 1978.

Chase, Chris. *The Great American Waistline: Putting It On and Taking It Off.* New York: Coward, McCann and Geoghegan, 1981.

Chernin, Kim. *The Obsession: Reflections on the Tyranny of Slenderness.* New York: Harper and Row, 1981.

Corliss, Richard. "The New Ideal of Beauty," *Time,* August 30, 1982, 120:9, 72–77.

Gross, Meier. *Anorexia Nervosa.* Lexington, Mass.: Collamore Press, 1982.

Levenkron, Steven. *Treating and Overcoming Anorexia Nervosa.* New York: Charles Scribners' Sons, 1982.

————. *The Best Little Girl in the World.* New York: Warner Books, 1978.

Mayer, Jean. *Overweight.* Englewood Cliffs, N.J.: Prentice-Hall, Inc., 1968.

Millman, Marcia. *Such a Pretty Face: Being Fat in America.* New York: W. W. Norton & Co., 1980.

O'Neill, Cherry Boone. *Starving for Attention.* New York: Continuum, 1982.

Palmer, Richard L. *Anorexia Nervosa: A Guide for Sufferers and Their Families.* New York: Penguin Books, 1980.

Polivy, Janet, and Herman, C. Peter. *Breaking the Diet Habit: The Natural Weight Alternative.* New York: Basic Books, Inc., 1983.

Vincent, L. M. *Competing with the Sylph: The Pursuit of the Ideal Body Form.* New York: Berkeley Books, 1981.

Unintended Teenage Pregnancy

Anastasiow, Nicholas J. "Adolescent Pregnancy and Special Education." *Exceptional Children,* 1983, 49:5, 396–401.

Bode, Janet. *Kids Having Kids: The Unwed Teenage Parent.* New York: Franklin Watts, 1980.

Byrne, Donn, and Fisher, William A. (eds.). *Adolescents, Sex, and Contraception.* Hillsdale, N.J.: Lawrence Erlbaum Associates, Publishers, 1983.

Calderone, Mary S. "Is Sex Education Preventative?" in *The Prevention of Sexual Disorders: Issues and Approaches,* ed. C. B. Qualls et al. New York: Plenum Press, 1978.

Chase, Janet. *Daughters of Change: Growing Up Female in America.* Boston: Little, Brown and Company, 1981.

Foster, Sallie. *The One Girl in Ten: A Self-Portrait of the Teen-Age Mother.* Claremont, Calif.: The Arbor Press, 1981.

Green, Cynthia P., and Potteiger, Kate. "Teenage Pregnancy: A Major Problem for Minors." Washington, D.C.: Zero Population Growth, 1977.

Lewis, Howard R., and Lewis, Martha E. *The Parent's Guide to Teenage Sex and Pregnancy.* New York: St. Martin's Press, 1983.

McGuire, Paula. *It Won't Happen to Me. Teenagers Talk about Pregnancy.* New York: Delacorte Press, 1983.

Oettinger, Katherine B. *Not My Daughter: Facing Up to Adolescent Pregnancy.* Englewood Cliffs, N.J.: Prentice-Hall, Inc., 1979.

Teenage Pregnancy: The Problem That Hasn't Gone Away. New York: The Alan Guttmacher Institute, 1979.

Zelnick, Melvin, Kantner, John F., and Ford, Kathleen. *Sex and Pregnancy in Adolescence.* Beverly Hills, Calif.: Sage Publications, 1981.

Runaways

Anson, R. S. "Bodies for Sale: End of the Road for Runaways." *Mademoiselle,* August, 1981, 87:216–218.

Barrett, Katherine, and Fincher, Jack. "Teenage Runaways: A Family Tragedy, A National Epidemic: Why Teenagers Run Away and How to Stop Them." *Ladies Home Journal,* August, 1982, 99:8, 81.

Blau, M. "Why Parents Kick Their Kids Out." *Parents' Magazine,* April, 1979, 54:64–69.

Brenton, Myron. *The Runaways: Children, Husbands, Wives and Parents.* Boston: Little, Brown and Company, 1978.

Kosof, Anna. *Runaways.* New York: Franklin Watts, 1977.

Madison, Arnold. *Runaway Teens: An American Tragedy.* New York: Elsevier/Nelson Books, 1979.

National Youth Alternatives Project. *National Directory of Runaway Programs.* Washington, D.C.: NYAP, 1976.

Raphael, Maryanne, and Wolf, Jenifer. *Runaways: America's Lost Youth.* New York: Drake Publishers, Inc., 1974.

Rubin, Arnold P. *The Youngest Outlaws: Runaways in America.* New York: Julian Messner, 1976.

Stierlin, Helm. *Separating Parents and Adolescents: A Perspective on Running Away, Schizophrenia, and Waywardness.* New York: Quadrangle/The New York Times Book Co., 1974.

Cults

Beckford, James A. "A Typology of Family Responses to a New Religious Movement." *Marriage and Family Review,* Fall/Winter, 1981, 4:3, 4, 41–55.

Behrens, David. "The Cult Crisis: The Power of Cults." *Glamour,* August, 1982, 80:8, 268.

———. "The Cult Crisis: One Who Is Now Free." *Glamour,* August, 1982, 80:8, 270–271.

Enroth, Ronald. *Youth, Brainwashing, and the Extremist Cults.* Grand Rapids, Mich.: Zondervan Publishing House, 1977.

————. *The Lure of the Cults*. Chappaqua, N.Y.: Christian Herald Books, 1979.

Hershell, Marie, and Hershell, Ben. "Our Involvement With a Cult." *Marriage and Family Review*, Fall/Winter, 1981, 4:3, 4, 131–140.

Jeffery, Jonathan B., and Jeffery, Patricia W. "Information Search Strategies: Cults and the Family." *Marriage and Family Review*, Fall/Winter, 1981, 4:3, 4, 175–180.

Marciano, Teresa Donati. "Families and Cults." *Marriage and Family Review*, Fall/Winter, 1981, 4:3, 4, 101–117.

Reif, Robin. "My Brother's Quest for Peace and Tranquility Ripped My Family Apart." *Glamour*, August, 1982, 80:8, 269+.

Rudin, James, and Rudin, Marcia. *Prison or Paradise? The New Religious Cults*. Philadelphia: Fortress Press, 1980.

Schwartz, Lita Linzer, and Kaslow, Florence W. "The Cult Phenomenon: Historical, Sociological, and Familial Factors Contributing to Their Development and Appeal." *Marriage and Family Review*, Fall/Winter, 1981, 4:3, 4, 3–30.

Singer, Margaret Thaler. "Coming Out of the Cults." *Psychology Today*, January, 1979, 12: 72–73.

Slade, M. "New Religious Groups: Membership and Legal Battles." *Psychology Today*, January, 1979, 12: 81.

Sparks, Jack. *The Mind Benders: A Look at Current Cults*. Nashville: Thomas Nelson Inc., Publishers, 1977.

Stoner, Carroll, and Parke, Jo Anne. *All God's Children: The Cult Experience — Salvation or Slavery?* Radnor, Pa.: Chilton Book Co., 1977.

Sussman, Alan. *The Rights of Young People: The Basic A.C.L.U. Guide to a Young Person's Rights*. New York: Avon Books, 1977.

Suicide

Bergson, Lisa. "Suicide's Other Victims. *The New York Times Magazine*, November 14, 1982, p. 100.

Giovacchini, Peter. *The Urge to Die — Why Young People Commit Suicide*. New York: Macmillan, 1981.

Griffin, Mary, and Felsenthal, Carol. *A Cry for Help: Exploring and Exploding the Myths about Teenage Suicide — A Guide for All Parents of Adolescents*. New York: Doubleday and Co., Inc., 1983.

Hendin, Herbert. *Suicide In America*. New York: W. W. Norton & Co., 1982.

Hyde, Margaret D., and Forsyth, Elizabeth Held. *Suicide*. New York: Franklin Watts, 1978.

Kiev, Ari. *The Courage to Live*. New York: Thomas Y. Crowell, Publishers, 1979.

Klagsburn, Francine. *Too Young to Die: Youth and Suicide*. Boston: Houghton Mifflin, 1976.

Madison, Arnold, *Suicide and Young People*. New York: The Seabury Press, 1978.

McCoy, Kathleen. *Coping with Teenage Depression: A Parent's Guide*. New York: The New American Library, Inc., 1982.

O'Roarke, Mary Ann. "The Alarming Rise in Teenage Suicide." *McCalls*, January, 1982, 109: 14+.

Plath, Syliva. *The Journals of Sylvia Plath,* ed. Ted Hughes and Frances McCullough. New York: The Dial Press, 1982.

Reynolds, David K., and Faberow, Norman L. *The Family Shadow: Sources of Suicide and Schizophrenia.* Berkeley: University of California Press, 1981.

Waggoner, Dianna. "A Teenage Suicide Pact Stuns A Quiet Seattle Suburb and Leaves Parents Asking Why?" *People,* June 30, 1980, 13: 20–23.

Competent Professional Help

Barkas, J. L. *The Help Book.* New York: Charles Scribner's Sons, 1979.

Evans, Glen. *The* Family Circle *Guide to Self-Help.* New York: Ballantine Books, 1979.

Gartner, Alan, and Riessman, Frank. *A Working Guide to Self-Help Groups.* New York: New Viewpoints, 1980.

Kovel, A. *A Complete Guide to Therapy: From Psychoanalysis to Behavior Modification.* New York: Pantheon Books, 1976.

Lieberman, Morton A., Borman, Leonard D., et al. *Self-Help Groups for Coping with Crisis.* San Francisco: Jossey-Bass Publishers, 1979.

Quinnett, Paul G. *The Troubled People Book: A Comprehensive Guide to Getting Help.* New York: Continuum, 1982.

Dealing with the Police

Dobelis, Inge N. (ed.). Reader's Digest *Family Legal Guide: A Complete Encyclopedia of Law for the Layman.* Pleasantville, N.Y.: The Reader's Digest Ass'n. Inc., 1981.

Sloan, Irving J., J.D. *Youth and the Law: Rights, Privileges and Obligations,* 3rd ed. Dobbs Ferry, N.Y.: Oceana Publications, Inc., 1978.

Zarr, Melvyn. *The Bill of Rights and the Police.* Dobbs Ferry, N.Y.: Oceana Publications, Inc., 1970.

Part Four: Positive Parenting

Going to Bat

deOliveira, P., and Cohen, S. *Getting In! The First Comprehensive Step-by-Step Strategy Guide to Acceptance at the College of Your Choice.* New York: Workman Publishing, 1983.

Gottesman, D. M. *The Powerful Parent: A Child Advocacy Handbook.* Norwalk, Ct.: Appleton-Century-Crofts, 1982.

Letting Go

Faber, A., and Mazlish, E. *Liberated Parents, Liberated Children: Letting Go. A Dialogue in Autonomy.* New York: Grosset and Dunlop, 1974.

Feuerstein, Phyllis, and Roberts, Carol. *The Not-So-Empty Nest. How to Live with Your Kids after They've Lived Someplace Else.* Chicago: Follett Publishing Co., 1981.

Index